COUNT MARCELLINUS AND HIS CHRONICLE

Count Marcellinus
and his Chronicle

Brian Croke

OXFORD
UNIVERSITY PRESS

OXFORD
UNIVERSITY PRESS
Great Clarendon Street, Oxford OX2 6DP

Oxford University Press is a department of the University of Oxford.
It furthers the University's objective of excellence in research, scholarship,
and education by publishing worldwide in

Oxford New York

Athens Auckland Bangkok Bogotá Buenos Aires Calcutta
Cape Town Chennai Dar es Salaam Delhi Florence Hong Kong Istanbul
Karachi Kuala Lumpur Madrid Melbourne Mexico City Mumbai
Nairobi Paris São Paulo Shanghai Singapore Taipei Tokyo Toronto Warsaw

with associated companies in Berlin Ibadan

Oxford is a registered trade mark of Oxford University Press
in the UK and in certain other countries

Published in the United States
by Oxford University Press Inc., New York

British Library Cataloguing in Publication Data
Data available

Library of Congress Cataloging in Publication Data
Data applied for
ISBN 0-19-815001-6

1 3 5 7 9 10 8 6 4 2

Typeset by Regent Typesetting, London
Printed in Great Britain by
Biddles Ltd., Guildford and King's Lynn

ACKNOWLEDGEMENTS

This book began life in the mid-1970s as an Oxford thesis, under the inspiration and guidance of John Matthews. The prolonged gestation from thesis to book has resulted in a broadening of perspective to incorporate the activity of chronicle writing in late antiquity and the use of the chronicle in later centuries. This interlude has also coincided with an upheaval in the way all historiographical texts are evaluated, analysed and interpreted, thereby necessitating a reconsideration of the nature and role of the chronicle genre as historical narrative. For late antique texts, especially histories and chronicles, the implications of this historiographical revolution remain largely unexplored.

Through the different phases of production in Oxford, Washington, DC, and Sydney over so many years I have thankfully benefited most from the expertise, counsel and encouragement of Elizabeth Jeffreys, Robert Markus, and John Matthews. I am also grateful to Richard Burgess, Averil Cameron, Mike Clover, Jill Harries, Ken Holum, Edwin Judge, Cyril Mango, Steven Muhlberger, Alanna Nobbs, Roger Scott, and Michael Whitby who read all, or part, of some version of this work and offered valuable comments and corrections. They do not necessarily agree with all that is contained in it, let the reader be warned. Finally, I wish to thank Massimo Gusso for making me aware of his work on the chronicle and providing me with relevant material.

Brian Croke

ACKNOWLEDGEMENTS

CONTENTS

MAPS

ABBREVIATIONS

References to Marcellinus' chronicle are by year and entry number (e.g. 381. 2) in Mommsen's edition (*MGH AA* 11. 37–104); translated quotations are from Croke (1995), as corrected where required by Whitby (1996).

AASS	*Acta Sanctorum*, 71 vols. (Paris 1863–1940).
ACO	*Acta Conciliorum Oecumenicarum* (ed. E. Schwartz, Berlin and Leipzig, 1922–84).
Agath.	Agathias, *Histories* (ed. R. Keydell, Berlin 1967: *CFHB*).
Ann. Rav.	*Annales Ravennatenses* (ed. W. Koehler), in *Medieval Studies in Memory of A. Kingsley Porter*, i (1939), 125–38, cited by section and page number.
Anon., *Strat.*	Anonymus, *Peri Strategias* (ed. and tr. G. Dennis, *Three Byzantine Military Treatises* (Washington, DC, 1985): *CFHB*), cited by section number.
Anon. Val.	*Anonymus Valesianus* (ed. Th. Mommsen, *MGH AA* 9. 249 ff.), cited by section and page number.
AClon.	*Annals of Clonmacnoise* (ed. D. Murphy, *The Annals of Clonmacnoise*, Dublin 1896), cited by year and page number.
AI	*Annals of Innisfallen* (ed. S. MacAirt, *The Annals of Innisfallen*, Dublin 1951), cited by year and page number.
AT	*Annals of Tigernach* (ed. W. Stokes, 'The Annals of Tigernach: Third Fragment. A.D. 489–766', *Revue Celtique* 17 (1896), 119–263), cited by year and page number.
AU	*Annals of Ulster* (ed. S. MacAirt and G. Macniocaill, *The Annals of Ulster. Part 1 Text and Translation*, Dublin 1983), cited by year and page number.

Auct. Havn.	*Auctarium Havniense Prosperi* (ed. Th. Mommsen, *MGH AA* 9. 304–39) cited by section and page number.
Barb. Scal.	*Barbarus Scaligeri* (ed. Th. Mommsen, *MGH AA* 9. 249ff.), cited by section and page number.
Bede, *DTR*	Bede, *De temporum ratione* (ed. C. Jones, Turnholt 1977: *CCL*) cited by section number.
Call., *V. Hyp.*	Callinicus, *Vita Hypatii* (ed. C. Bartelink, Paris 1971: SC).
Cand.	Candidus (ed. and tr. R. Blockley, *The Fragmentary Classicising Historians of the Later Roman Empire*, ii, Leeds 1983), cited by fragment and page number.
Cass., *Var.*	Cassiodorus, *Variae* (ed. Th. Mommsen and L. Traube, *MGH AA* 12).
CCL	*Corpus Christianorum. Series Latina* (Turnholt, 1953–)
Ced.	Cedrenus (ed. I. Bekker, Bonn 1838–9: *CSHB*), cited by volume and page number.
CFHB	*Corpus Fontium Historiae Byzantinae* (1967–)
Chron. ad 846	*Chronicon ad AD 846* (tr. J. Chabot, Paris 1903: *CSCO Scr. Syr.* 3. 4), cited by section and page number.
Chron. ad 724	*Chronicon ad AD 724* (tr. J. Chabot, Paris 1903: *CSCO Scr. Syr.* 3. 4), cited by section and page number.
Chron. Alex.	*Eine Alexandrinische Weltchronik* (ed. A. Bauer and J. Strzygowski), (Denkschrift der Kaiserlichen Akad. der. Wiss. zu Wien, Phil.-Hist. Kl. 51, Vienna 1905).
Chron. Edess.	*Chronicon Edessenum* (ed. and tr. I. Guidi, Paris 1903: *CSCO Scr. Syr.* 3. 4), cited by section and page number.
Chron. Gall. 452	*Chronica Gallica ad a.452* (ed. Th. Mommsen, *MGH AA* 9. 615ff.) cited by section and page number.
Chron. Gall. 511	*Chronica Gallica ad a.511* (ed. Th. Mommsen, *MGH AA* 9. 615ff.) cited by section and page number.
Chron. Pasch.	*Chronicon Paschale* (ed. L. Dindorf, Bonn 1832: *CSHB*), cited by page and line number.

CIG	*Corpus Inscriptionum Graecarum* (Berlin 1828–77).
CIL	*Corpus Inscriptionum Latinarum* (Berlin 1863–).
CJ	*Codex Justinianus* (ed. P. Krüger, *Corpus Iuris Civilis*, 2, Berlin 1928, repr. 1964).
CLA	*Codices Latini Antiquiores*, vol. 2, 2nd edn. (ed. E. A. Lowe, Oxford 1972).
CLRE	*Consuls of the Later Roman Empire* (ed. R. Bagnall, Alan Cameron, S. Schwartz, and K. Worp, Atlanta 1987).
Coll. Avell.	*Collectio Avellana*, 2 vols. (ed. O. Günther, Vienna 1895–8: *CSEL*).
Cons. Const	*Consularia Constantinopolitana* (ed. R. Burgess, *The Chronicle of Hydatius and the Chronica Constantinopolitana*, Oxford 1993), cited by year and page number.
Const. Porph. Caer.	Constantine Porphyrogenitus, *De Caerimoniis* (ed. J. Reiske, Bonn 1829–30: *CSHB*), cited by section and page number.
Cont.	Continuator of Marcellinus (ed. Th. Mommsen, *MGH AA* 11. 104 ff.) cited by year and entry number.
Cor. *Ioh.*	Corippus, *Iohannidos* (ed. J. Diggle and F. R. D. Goodyear, Cambridge 1970).
Cor. *Iust.*	Corippus, *In Iustinum* (ed. and tr. Averil Cameron, London 1976).
cos.	Year of consulship
CP	Constantinople
CS	*Chronicon Scotorum* (ed. W. Hennessy, London 1866), cited by year and page number.
CSEL	*Corpus Scriptorum Ecclesiasticorum Latinorum* (Vienna 1866–).
CSCO Scr. Syr.	*Corpus Scriptorum Christianorum Orientalium, Scriptores Syri* (Paris 1903–).
CSHB	*Corpus Scriptorum Historiae Byzantinae* (Bonn 1828–97).
CTh	*Codex Theodosianus* (ed. Th. Mommsen, Berlin 1904–5).
Cyr. Scyth.	Cyril of Scythopolis, *Lives* (ed. E. Schwartz, *Kyrillos von Scythopolis*, Leipzig 1939), cited by chapter and section number.

El. Nis.   Elias of Nisibis, *Chronicon* (ed. E. W. Brooks, Paris 1954: *CSCO. Scr. Syr.*), cited by page and line number.

Epit.   *Epitome de Caesaribus* (ed. F. Pichlmayr and R. Gruendel, Leipzig 1970).

Eun.   Eunapius of Sardis, *Histories* (ed. and tr. R. Blockley, *The Fragmentary Classicising Historians of the Later Roman Empire*, ii, Leeds 1983), cited by fragment and page number.

Evag. *HE*   Evagrius, *Historia Ecclesiastica* (ed. J. Bidez and L. Parmentier, London 1898).

Exc. Sangall. *Excerpta Sangallensia* (ed. Th. Mommsen, *MGH AA* 9. 249 ff.), cited by section and page number.

F. Vind. Pr. *Fasti Vindobonenses Priores* (ed. Th. Mommsen, *MGH AA* 9. 249 ff.), cited by section and page number.

FGrH   *Die Fragmente der griechischen Historiker* (ed. F. Jacoby, Berlin/Leiden 1923–).

FHG   *Fragmenta Historicorum Graecorum*, 4 vols. (ed. C. Müller, Paris 1848–51).

GCS   Die Griechischen Christlichen Schriftsteller der ersten drei Jahrhunderte (Leipzig 1897–).

Genn.   Gennadius, *de viris illustribus* (ed. C Bernoulli, Fribourg 1895).

Greg. Tur. *Hist.* Gregory of Tours, *Historia Francorum* (ed. W. Arndt and B. Krusch, MGH. Scriptores Rerum Merovingicarum I. 1, 2nd edn., Hanover 1951).

GS   Th. Mommsen, *Gesammelte Schriften*, vols. 1–8 (Berlin 1908–13).

HE   *Historia Ecclesiastica*.

Hyd.   Hydatius, *Chronica* (ed. R. Burgess, *The Chronicle of Hydatius and the Chronica Constantinopolitana*, Oxford 1993), cited by year and page number.

Inst.   Cassiodorus, *Institutiones* (ed. R. A. B. Mynors, Oxford 1937).

Jo. Bicl.   John of Biclaro, *Chronicon* (ed. Th. Mommsen, *MGH AA* 11. 211–20), cited by section and page number.

Jo. Ant.	John of Antioch, fragments in *FHG* 4. 54–662 and 5. 27–38 cited by fragment with volume and page number.
Jo. Lyd. *De mag.*	John the Lydian, *De magistratibus* (ed. R. Wuensch, Leipzig 1903).
Jo. Mal.	John Malalas, *Chronicle* cited both by book and paragraph number (from E. Jeffreys, M. Jeffreys, and R. Scott, *The Chronicle of John Malalas*, Melbourne 1986) and by page and line number from the edition of L. Dindorf, Bonn 1832: *CSHB*), with additional material from *De insidiis* (ed. C. de Boor (Berlin 1905), 151–76) cited by fragment and page number.
Jo. Nik.	John of Nikiu, Chronicle (tr. R. Charles, *The Chronicle of John Bishop of Nikiu*, Oxford 1916).
Jord. *Rom.*	Jordanes, *Romana* (ed. Th. Mommsen, *MGH AA* 5. 1. 1 ff.).
Jord. *Get.*	Jordanes, *Getica* (ed. Th. Mommsen, *MGH AA* 5. 1. 53 ff.).
Josh. Styl.	Joshua the Stylite (tr. W. Wright, *The Chronicle of Joshua the Stylite*, Cambridge 1882).
Lib. Pont.	*Liber Pontificalis*, 3 vols. (ed. L. Duchesne, Paris 1886–1957).
Malchus	Malchus, *Byzantiaka* (ed. and tr. R. Blockley, *The Fragmentary Classicising Historians of the Later Roman Empire*, ii, Leeds 1983), cited by fragment and page number.
Mar. Av.	Marius of Avenches, *Chronica* (ed. Th. Mommsen *MGH AA* 11. 227 ff.) cited by section and page number.
Men.	Menander, *History* (ed. and tr. R. Blockley, *The History of Menander the Guardsman*, Liverpool 1985).
MGH AA	*Monumenta Germaniae Historica. Auctores Antiquissimi*
Mich. Syr.	Michael the Syrian, *Chronicle* (ed. and tr. J.-B. Chabot, Paris 1899–1924).
ND	*Notitia Dignitatum* (ed. O. Seeck, Berlin 1876).
Nic. Call.	Nicephorus Callistus Xanthopoulos *HE* (*PG* 145–7).

Notitia CP	*Notitia Urbis Constantinopolitanae* (ed. O. Seeck, Berlin 1876).
Nov. Theod.	*Novellae Theodosii* (ed. P. Meyer, Berlin 1904–5).
Nov. Just.	*Novellae Justiniani* (ed. R. Schoell and W. Kroll, Berlin 1928, repr. 1954).
Olymp.	Olympiodorus (ed. and tr. R. Blockley, *The Fragmentary Classicising Historians of the Later Roman Empire*, ii, Leeds 1983) cited by fragment and page number.
Oros.	Orosius, *Historia Contra Paganos* (ed. C. Zangemeister, Leipzig 1889: *CSEL*).
Pac.	Pacatus, *Panegyric on Theodosius* (ed. R. A. B. Mynors, Oxford 1964).
Pall. *Dial.*	Palladius, *Dialogus* (ed. P. R. Coleman-Norton, Cambridge 1928).
Paras.	*Parastaseis Syntomoi Chronikai*, in Averil Cameron and J. Herrin (eds.), *Constantinople in the Early Eighth Century* (Leiden 1984).
Pasch. Camp.	*Paschale Campanum* (ed. Th. Mommsen, *MGH AA* 9) cited by section and page number.
Patria CP	*Patria Constantinopoleos* (ed. Th. Preger, Leipzig 1901).
Phil.	Philostorgius, *Historia Ecclesiastica* (ed. J. Bidez and F. Winkelmann, Berlin 1981: GCS).
PG	*Patrologia Graeca* (ed. J. P. Migne, Paris 1857–86).
PL	*Patrologia Latina* (ed. J. P. Migne, Paris 1844–64).
PLRE 1	*The Prosopography of the Later Roman Empire*, i (ed. A. H. M. Jones, J. Morris, and J. R. Martindale, Cambridge 1970).
PLRE 2	*The Prosopography of the Later Roman Empire*, ii (ed. J. R. Martindale, Cambridge 1980).
PLRE 3	*The Prosopography of the Later Roman Empire*, iii (ed. J. R. Martindale, Cambridge 1992).
PO	*Patrologia Orientalis* (Paris 1907–)
Priscus	Priscus of Panion (ed. and tr. R. Blockley, *The Fragmentary Classicising Historians of the Later Roman Empire*, ii, Leeds 1983), cited by fragment and page number.
Proc. *Wars*	Procopius of Caesarea, *Wars* (ed. J. Haury and G. Wirth, Leipzig 1962–4).

Proc. *Aed.*	Procopius of Caesarea, *De Aedificiis* (ed. J. Haury and G. Wirth, Leipzig 1962–4).
Proc. *Anek.*	Procopius of Caesarea, *Anekdota* (ed. J. Haury and G. Wirth, Leipzig 1962–4).
Prosp.	Prosper of Aquitaine, *Chronicon* (ed. Th. Mommsen, *MGH AA* 9) cited by section and page number.
RE	*Paulys Realencyclopädie der klassischen Altertumswissenschaft* (ed. G. Wissowa *et al.*, Stuttgart 1893–).
s.a.	sub anno
SC	Sources Chrétiennes (Paris 1941–).
SEC	*Synaxarium Ecclesiae Constantinopolitanae* (ed. H. Delehaye, Brussels 1902).
Soc.	Socrates, *Historia Ecclesiastica* (ed. G. C. Hansen, Berlin 1995: GCS).
Soz.	Sozomen, *Historia Ecclesiastica* (ed. J. Bidez and G. C. Hansen, Berlin 1960: GCS).
Them. *Or.*	Themistius, *Orationes* (ed. G. Downey and A. Norman, Leipzig 1965–74).
Theod.	Theodoret, *Historia Ecclesiastica* (ed. L. Parmentier and F. Scheidweiler, Berlin 1954: GCS).
Theod. Anag.	Theodore Anagnostes, *Historia Ecclesiastica* (ed. G. C. Hansen, Berlin 1971: GCS), cited by section and page number.
Theoph.	Theophanes, *Chronographia* (ed. C. de Boor, Leipzig 1883–5), cited by *annus mundi*, page and line number.
ThLL	*Thesaurus Linguae Latinae* (Leipzig 1900–).
Typ.	*Typicon de la grande église*, 2 vols. (ed. J. Mateos, Rome 1962–3), cited by page and line number.
Vict. Tonn.	Victor Tonnenensis, *Chronica* (ed. Th. Mommsen, *MGH AA* 11) cited by section and page number.
Vict. Vit. *Hist. Pers.*	Victor of Vita, *Historia Persecutionis* (ed. C. Halm, *MGH AA* 3. 1).
V. Dan. Styl.	*Vita Danielis Stylites* (ed. H. Delehaye, Brussels and Paris 1923).
V. Marcell.	*Vita Marcelli* (ed. G. Dagron, Louvain 1968).

V. Mel.	*Vita Melaniae* (ed. D. Gorce, Paris 1962: SC).
Zach. Mit. *HE*	Zachariah of Mitylene, *Historia Ecclesiastica* (ed. and tr. E. J. Hamilton and E. W. Brooks, London 1899).
Zon.	Zonaras (ed. L. Dindorf, Leipzig 1868–75).
Zos.	Zosimus, *Nea Historia* (ed. F. Paschoud, Paris 1971–89).

Introduction: Analysing Chronicles

In the early 520s, before Justinian began his long tenure of the
Roman throne, one of his officials was a fellow-Illyrian named
Marcellinus. He has become better known as Count Marcellinus
or Marcellinus *comes*. Resident in the imperial capital of
Constantinople, Marcellinus wrote a number of works on historical and topographical subjects. All that survives, however, is his
chronicle. It was produced as a continuation of the chronicle of
Jerome from AD 379 to the death of the emperor Anastasius in
518, was later updated to 534 in the reign of Justinian and was
subsequently continued by others. The chronicle has always been
considered a significant historical record for the period it covers,
especially the late fifth and early sixth centuries. Yet this study is
the first extensive treatment of Marcellinus and his chronicle.
As such, it aims to set the chronicler and his work in their full
contemporary and historiographical context.[1] At the same time,
this study both offers a model for investigating and evaluating
the late antique chronicles in general, and also provides the basis
for a more wide-ranging analysis of the nature and function of
chronicles as a mode of both interpreting and presenting the past.

THE NEED FOR THIS STUDY

A rather long book devoted to a rather short book may well
provoke suspicion; all the more so in the case of the chronicle
of Marcellinus for its importance and influence are simply not
comparable with that of other more famous short works. The
justification for this study stems, however, from the relative
neglect and distorted understanding of Marcellinus' chronicle and
works like it. It has long been customary for students of late
antiquity in particular to complain about the chronicles. They
frequently voice irritation at the content and brevity of the many
extant chronicles; sometimes they even express contempt for the
ability and integrity of the chroniclers themselves. There is a

---

[1] This study underpins and complements the translation and commentary on the
chronicle published in Croke (1995) with corrections in Whitby (1996), 222–5.

widespread attitude that the chronicle material we have to work with for the period is inherently inferior, its authors second-rate and mediocre, its audience ill-educated and undemanding. The emergence of the chronicle as a stylized historiographical genre in the late Roman empire is viewed as symptomatic of an age of decadence and decline in society and literature, particularly in the writing of history. The chronicle itself is regarded as a mere embryo of classical narrative historiography exhausting the talents and resources of those incapable of more disciplined, penetrating and grandiose writing. Bury, for example, spoke of 'bald notices in chronicles written by men who selected their facts without much discrimination', while Jones saw the modern historian of the fifth-century west as 'reduced to bare annalists who give lists of the consuls with occasional notes of battles and church councils', and to 'crude and meagre annalistic chronicles'.[2] Summing up Byzantine chronicles in particular, Browning claimed that 'their view of history, so far as they could be said to have had one, was naïvely theological . . . they were uncritical and undiscriminating in the choice of events which they narrated, and included much that was trivial or sensational'.[3]

Such views are deeply rooted in an outdated association of late antiquity (and Byzantium) with decadence and decline. They are even more fundamentally rooted in a traditional historiographical dichotomy, originating in the Renaissance and canonized in the nineteenth century, between 'history' (a product of 'high' culture) and 'chronicle' (a product of 'low' culture). The former is regarded as embodying readability, truth, and a sense of what is important about the past, while the latter represents shallow content combined with simplicity of style and judgement. Even if such a distinction were real in some cases, it is based on what are essentially modern notions of historical truth and the nature of historical research and writing as an intellectual activity. On this view,

---

[2] Bury (1923*a*), 251; Jones, A. H. M. (1966), 3; cf. Jones, A. H. M. (1964), 200, 217, 1010; Dill (1899), 441; Lot (1961), 161; Gransden (1974), 31 and Molè (1980), 198. Such views remain in even the most recent, and otherwise subtle, overviews : 'Between the time of Ammianus Marcellinus (late fourth century) and Jordanes (mid-sixth century) historical inquiry was, if not dormant, then conspicuously derivative' (Kelley (1998), 104).

[3] Browning (1980), 34. On the Byzantine side, the same negative attitudes and rigid chronicle/history division are evident (cf. Afinogenov (1992), 13–33): Hunger (1978), 237 (note the chapter 'Chroniken als Trivialliteratur'); Browning (1980), 34–5; Kelley (1998), 71–4, and the pervasive historiographical judgment in Treadgold (1997).

history and chronicle are linked as different degrees of objectively representing a knowable and meaningful past. In the ancient world history was not seen this way,[4] however, nor was history linked with chronicle as such. Further, as a distinctly Christian form of representing the past, the chronicle has been encased in what is seen now as another false dichotomy, that between 'classical' and 'Christian' culture. The Christian chronicle of late antiquity had an altogether different purpose from a classical narrative history. It constitutes a relatively sophisticated mode of presenting the past. A prejudiced view of the genre will only distort an appreciation of any individual chronicler and his chronicle. What opinion would modern scholarship hold (one wonders) of the literary culture and ability of Eusebius, Jerome, Prosper, Cassiodorus, Bede, and Isidore if only their chronicles had survived?

There is one further component of this negative attitude towards the chroniclers and chronicles of late antiquity which needs recalling at the outset, and that is the way they are utilized. Too often the chronicles have been regarded by scholars as some sort of mine, or storehouse, of facts from which one can extract and ransack as desired. Furthermore, this inclination is perpetuated by the collective labels under which the chronicles frequently appear (e.g. 'Chronica Minora', 'Chronica Italica', 'Chronica Gallica'); so too, it is reflected in the anonymous way they are often cited (e.g. 'Chron. Min. 2, p. 91'), which is the practice throughout two of the main standard books for the period, a quarter-century apart: A. H. M. Jones's *Later Roman Empire* (1964) and Alexander Demandt's *Die Spätantike* (1989). Yet such a habit creates a false sense of uniformity and serves only to obscure, or even negate, the fact that each of the late Roman chronicles is a distinct and separate work, written by a particular individual from a particular point of view, the product of a specific and definable cultural and intellectual context. Each of the late antique chronicles is unique and independent and that is how they must be analysed, not as a monolith.

An even more serious shortcoming in the study of chronicles is that, like histories, they are usually evaluated, more or less exclusively, by criteria related to the historicity of their data as established by modern historians, that is, by their reliability as

---

[4] Press (1982), 121 ff.

3

'evidence' or as a 'primary source'.[5] In these terms they may even be measured and ranked by using what one scholar has labelled 'a sort of correctness quotient'.[6] Yet the chronicles must be understood first of all on their own terms, that is, by examining their purpose, structure and audience, as well as by criteria of truth and style appropriate to the chronicler's own time—not ours. In fact, it is one of the more ambitious aims of this book to identify and probe some of the presuppositions and prejudices which have traditionally afflicted serious study of the late Roman and Byzantine chronicles. It is hoped that such analysis, by highlighting the distinctive historiographical purpose and nature of chronicles such as that of Marcellinus, will contribute something constructive to current debates on the nature and development of Christian discourse (especially its definition as a component of 'popular' culture),[7] as well as to other current debates on genre and narrative in the domain of history writing.

Unfortunately, recent discussions of narrativity in historiography, profoundly important as they are, continue to operate within the paradigm of late antiquity as a period of 'decline and fall', and within the obsolete frameworks of 'classical'/'Christian' and of 'history'/'chronicle'. While discounting the notion of a complete and objectively describable past they still tend to see chronicle and history as different degrees of representing reality, or to see one (chronicle) as being just the bones of the other (history). This mode of distinguishing historical narratives was first developed by Croce and Collingwood earlier this century,[8] and has been incorporated, more or less uncritically, into all subsequent work including that of Hayden White.[9] White's influence, in turn, has ensured its frequent endorsement and repetition so that chronicles can continue to be characterized as 'not works of history proper'.[10] More constructive for understanding

---

[5] Spiegel (1997), 98. Note the introductory and other editorial sections in Cameron, Averil (1989). [6] Partner (1977), 4.

[7] As exemplified in Cameron, Averil (1991), 36–9, 107–8, and (1993), 137 ff.

[8] Croce (1921), 11–26; Collingwood (1939), 202–3.

[9] White (1973), 5–7. Yet White, originally trained as a student of medieval history and whose earliest research and publications were devoted to the medieval church, is acutely aware of the limitations of formal distinctions between history and chronicle as evidenced by his later discussion ((1987), 6 ff.) of the St Gall annals and other medieval texts.

[10] Stanford (1998), 218. Similar sentiments can be found in Carr (1986), 59; Cook (1988), 21; Kellner (1989), 331; Callinicos (1995), 73–5; Jenkins (1995), 150; Berkhofer (1995), 117; Evans, R. J. (1997), 153, and McCullagh (1998), 300.

Marcellinus, however, is the realization that all modes of historical narrative are significant,[11] and that what is reported in a chronicle such as that of Marcellinus is no less 'event-worthy' than what
is recounted in more elaborate narrative forms.[12]

Further, as it is usually presented, the history of historiography
itself reinforces the negative characterisation of chronicles. This is
because it is presented as the story of the incremental development of history writing from what are seen to be primitive outline
forms (including chronicles) to the positivist scientific historiography of the nineteenth century onwards, or 'from poorer past
histories to better present ones'.[13] Such a model is based on
entrenched assumptions about an historian's objectivity, judged
by research in archival records, and the capacity of the past to be
fully and definitively represented in the historian's narrative. This
idealist model of the history of writing about the past also involves
spurious assumptions about the conceptual and technical inferiority of chronicles because they belong to an earlier, undeveloped
phase of the story of history writing. Further still, histories of
historiography tend to follow a standard pattern of describing a
succession of the 'great historians' of each era, thereby necessarily relegating chronicles to a marginal and inferior place. The
nature and function of chronicle writing as a serious and substantial historiographical enterprise needs to be reclaimed in the
history of historiography.

WHAT PROMPTED THIS STUDY

Following the political unification of the German states in 1871
control of the *Monumenta Germaniae Historica* (*MGH*), the collection
of sources for German history first planned out in 1819, fell to the
Berlin Academy. Thereupon, the then president of the Academy's
Historical-Philological Section, Theodor Mommsen (1817–1903),
seized the opportunity to turn the resources of the *MGH* to his
own ends. Somehow or other, he managed to persuade his
colleagues that the works of the fourth-century Roman senator
Symmachus and the African Victor of Vita, among others, were

[11] As explained by Danto (1965), 112–42 in response to the distinction made originally by
Croce.   [12] Cf. Veyne (1984), 65.
[13] Berkhofer (1995), 126. In the most recent example the story moves forward from
'protohistoriographical forms of writing' which include chronicle and local history-type
records before Herodotus (Kelley (1998), 15).

5

as significant for understanding German history as tenth-century Ottonian capitularies. In 1875, in presenting the reorganized 'Zentraldirektion' of the *MGH* with a programme of texts for a new section to be entitled *Auctores Antiquissimi*, Mommsen availed himself of the opportunity to provide editions of works he felt were urgently required. Since at least 1857 he had been stressing the need to study the late Roman chronicles in proper scholarly editions and he now proposed the editing of the Latin chronicles as his own special task.[14]

It is quite remarkable that at this point in his career Mommsen journeyed all over Europe (including two trips to England where he had never ventured previously) collating manuscripts for this purpose, and in the end produced the exactly 2,000 pages contained in the three volumes of the *Chronica Minora* (1892, 1894, 1898).[15] It was in the course of this enterprise, on 18 March 1889 in the Bodleian Library at Oxford, that Mommsen first confronted the most important manuscript of Marcellinus' chronicle which had long been hidden from view.[16] Indeed, Mommsen's introduction to the manuscript was important enough to be reported the following week in the London *Times*.[17] On the completion of the *Auctores Antiquissimi* Mommsen remarked to the Berlin Academy on the importance of his editions of the chronicles and of how only the resources of the *MGH* had made them possible.[18] They were a truly collaborative creation utilizing the efforts of Mommsen's vast network of scholarly contacts, and thereby epitomizing his approach to scholarly work as a co-operative venture.[19] With all this in mind, it puzzled me that, although Mommsen went to such lengths to provide proper editions of what he considered important historical documents, they have hardly been worked on since. What Mommsen considered urgent in 1857 is now of paramount importance because, as observed not long ago, these 'tantalizing but often important texts stand in urgent need of comprehensive research'.[20]

[14] Mommsen (1857), 626 (= *GS* 7. 754).

[15] Redlich (1916), 873; Fritz (1968), 242; Croke (1990c), 159–89, esp. 165ff.; Rebenich (1993), 133ff.

[16] *Bodleian Library Records* b. 593, unfoliated (for this, and other details of Mommsen's work in the Bodleian in 1885 and 1889, I am grateful to Bruce Barker-Benfield).

[17] *The Times*, Sat. 3 Mar. 1889, p. 6.

[18] Mommsen (1898), 288–9 (= *GS* 7. 693–4).

[19] Croke (1990c), 172.

[20] *CLRE* 47.

Mommsen always argued that in order to understand the late Roman world it is necessary to see it in the light not only of the Roman society and culture which preceded it, but also of the various societies and cultures which grew out of it.[21] This approach certainly holds true for the chronicles he edited, although they have not always been tackled that way. In recent years, at last, scholars have begun to approach the chroniclers of the western Middle Ages more as individuals and to analyse their chronicles as manifestations of a particular culture and outlook, rather than simply factual quarries.[22] Scholars are now being encouraged to read medieval historical texts as cultural phenomena 'by returning them to the social context in which they originated and from which they drew both form and meaning'.[23] Investigating medieval chronicles in terms of genre, function, literary intention, narrative technique, and audience has, in turn, thrown considerable light on the information contained in works we have come to catalogue as 'chronicles', and very often has helped clarify what otherwise seemed obscure or erroneous. It is now recognized that despite the chronicle's evidently simple literary form the chronicler's capacity to interpret is strongly evidenced by what material is included and what not, and by how events are grouped.[24] In particular, it has become clearer that the modern dichotomy history/chronicle was understood quite differently in ancient and medieval times, and that this has important implications for interpreting the chronicles as texts and the literary culture of their authors.[25] The late Roman and Byzantine chronicles have also recently begun to receive the attention they have long deserved.[26]

[21] Mommsen (1893), 43 (= *GS* 3. 177); (1891), 51 (= *GS* 6. 343). This approach is also evident in his recently published lectures on the Roman empire (Mommsen (1996), 405, 501).

[22] Schnith (1983), 1957; Partner (1977), 1–8 and 183–230; Spiegel (1997), xii, 84, 98, 110, 177. Much the same situation applies to the early medieval historians too (Goffart (1988), 14–15).

[23] Spiegel (1997), 110.   [24] Wood (1992), 14.

[25] For this dimension see various studies of Guenée: (1973), 997–1016; (1977), 1–17; (1980), *passim*; (1984), 3–12. There has hardly been any comparable work on the Byzantine chronicles. The directions were set out in Beck (1965*b*), 188–97 but they have been largely ignored (Lubarskij (1993), 133).

[26] The main studies are principally, on the Latin side: Muhlberger (1990), Salzman (1990), Wolf (1990), Burgess (1993*a*), Favrod (1993), Croke (1995) and Placanica (1997); and on the Greek/Syriac side: Mosshammer (1979), Jeffreys, Jeffreys, and Scott (1986), Witakowski (1987), Mango (1988/9), Whitby and Whitby (1989), Jeffreys (1990), Conrad (1990), Conrad (1992), Palmer (1993), and Mango and Scott (1997). There are also valuable observations in Burgess (1990*b*), 116–24, and Whitby (1992), 59–66.

7

They have come to be understood as expressions of contemporary ideology and thinking about the nature and meaning of time.[27] Accordingly, it should be possible (so it seemed to me) to analyse any of the late antique chronicles with a view to delineating and understanding the viewpoint and background of its author, and how this directs the author's selection and interpretation of the facts he records. It was these two factors—Mommsen's editorial efforts and the new approach to medieval chronicles—which originally prompted me to undertake this analysis of one particular late Roman or, more accurately in this case, early Byzantine chronicler.

PUTTING AN ANNALISTIC CHRONICLE TOGETHER

There are two distinct stages in the shaping of an annalistic chronicle such as that of Marcellinus: (1) its construction, and (2) its copying. First, in order to make an annalistic chronicle you need a chronological framework, usually a consular list (or lists), either to copy as the framework for your own chronicle or else to insert annotations within the spaces between the consuls (if there is room). Having acquired your list (or lists) you then commence by recording entries under each consulship. These entries may simply be selected from a previous chronicle or variety of chronicles, and copied under the same date. Where the dating system of the source is different, however, the chronicler may easily make a mistake. For instance, when only names of consuls are available (e.g. 'coss. Syagrius et Eucherius') you can readily omit a consulship without realizing it, since there is no numerical succession to enable you to identify the omission. Your chronicle then progresses, as you continue to copy entries from a previous annalistic record and/or as you create your own entries from other documents of whatever kind (histories, theological tracts, letters, laws, inscriptions, etc.). When constructing entries from another document you will need to have the correct year and sometimes this will need to be discovered by some investigation. If your source allows you to pinpoint the exact consulship of the event you wish to include, there is no problem. Otherwise, you might be led astray, as was Prosper in recording the demise of the emperor Gratian.[28] Further, within your own lifetime you may use oral

[27] Cameron, Averil (1998), 17–18.   [28] Humphries (1996), 155–75.

8

accounts or memory alone but even that is no guarantee of chronological accuracy. If, however, you have only, say, an indiction date to go on, then you may easily put the event in the wrong consulship (as happened occasionally in Marcellinus' chronicle), or even in the wrong month when using different systems of months (as happened in the fragmentary chronicle preserved in the fifth-century Golenischev papyrus). Likewise, when using imperial years (as did the fifth-century Spanish bishop, Hydatius, or the so-called 'Chronicler of 452') the problems of maintaining an unambiguous chronology become even more difficult.[29] Such are the problems of composition which pervade the extant chronicles.

Second, having constructed and circulated your chronicle you are then exposed to the vagaries of copying. In the case of copying chronicles, all the usual pitfalls of copying texts apply; in addition, there are often far more numbers in a chronicle (that is, taking account of its format of reckoning successive years) and therefore a greater potential for corruption. Certainly there will be confusion when eponyms such as consuls are misreported or (worse still) left out, as happened in the case of the solitary manuscript of the chronicle of Marius, the sixth-century bishop of Avenches.[30] On top of that, you may not want a complete verbatim copy of the chronicle but you may wish to supplement what you are copying with extra items from here and there. Or you may decide to summarize the chronicle's longer entries, or leave particular ones out altogether (as the fifth-century Gallic scholar Prosper did to the fourth-century chronicle of Jerome, or as the scribe of manuscript B and a later reader did to Hydatius, and as occurred in some manuscripts of Marcellinus). There was always the opportunity, too, to tamper with the text immediately as an early scribe of Jerome's chronicle did in shifting the blame for unpopular and harsh exactions in Illyricum (s.a. 372) from Probus (cos. 371) to Equitius (cos. 374).[31] Finally, you may want to simplify the format by employing, say, just one dating system instead of the chronicle's two or three, or indeed you may wish to incorporate a

---

[29] Hydatius: Thompson (1982), 137–229; Muhlberger (1990), 279–307; Burgess (1993*a*), 27–46. 'Chronicler of 452': Muhlberger (1983), 23–33; Jones and Casey (1988), 368–98 and Burgess (1990*a*), 185–95.

[30] Morton (1982), 107–36, esp. 110–15 (with photograph of manuscript facing p. 109), cf. *CLRE* 51.

[31] Explained in Mommsen (1889*a*), 604 and Hardy (1890), 284.

9

dating system absent from the original chronicle (as the Frankish writer known as Fredegar did to Hydatius and the 'Chronicler of 452' did to Jerome). Then, having completed the chronicle you are copying you may choose to continue it on (using the same or a different dating system) to a fixed point such as the current year; or you may decide to add a pre-existing continuation, and perhaps even continue that continuation. John of Biclaro, for instance, continued the chronicle of Victor of Tunnuna, who continued Prosper, who in turn had continued Jerome, and he ended with a chronological summary—just as Jerome, Prosper, and Victor before him. Later on, someone may decide to correct or supplement your manuscript (as AD dates were added to the later 'Chronicler of 452') or else continue your manuscript from whatever point you finished, or simply incorporate another chronicle into it. The bewildering manuscript traditions of the late Roman annalistic chronicles exhibit all these features. The special problems thereby presented to editors of the chronicles may be gauged from the numerous attempts to produce an edition of the chronicle of Eusebius, or rather of the Armenian and Latin versions of Eusebius.[32]

So, when editing and discussing a chronicle such as that of Marcellinus all the scribal and editorial habits just noted have to be taken into account. To some extent we are very fortunate in the case of Marcellinus in having a manuscript (Bodleian, *Auct.* T 2.26) produced within about half a century of the autograph original. Even then, however, there are problems with entries omitted. Likewise, this same manuscript provides the oldest complete copy of Jerome's chronicle, yet even then it does not include some genuine entries of Jerome which are preserved only in later manuscripts. The shape and tradition of chronicle manuscripts are therefore important, doubly so when the manuscripts are acephalous and anonymous. In the case of these particular manuscripts the natural tendency has been to systematize and simplify, that is to delineate a fully-formed original chronicle (such as the so-called 'Ravenna Annals') from the variegated manuscript tradition; whereas what we have is a situation where every single manuscript is itself a unique chronicle, and where over time commonality of material emerges as one chronicle copies an earlier one (Chapter 5).

[32] Mosshammer (1979), 37–83 and Grafton (1993), 514–36.

ANALYSING MARCELLINUS' CHRONICLE

Trying to extricate a chronicler's point of view and background from his chronicle (Chapters 1–4) can be a frustrating business, for the scale of the chronicle's content imposes a real limitation. There is little scope for the personal digression and grandiloquent moralizing characteristic of Herodotus or Ammianus, for instance, and one is generally left with little more than apparently miscellaneous facts listed under a particular year. Nevertheless, the very process of the selection and omission of facts, and the way they are configured within the author's narrative, often tells us much about an author. Inevitably, however, an analytical approach of this kind has to be, for the most part, indirect and allusive, which brings in its wake the danger of overstatement. So too, the usually limited geographical and chronological range of the chronicle's content forces one to scrutinize a chronicler's material from a variety of disparate vantage points and to tackle every problem to which the chronicle gives rise. Consequently, in blending these different perspectives into a unified interpretative picture it is not always easy to keep the central object, the chronicle, in the forefront of the reader's notice. In addition, a chronicle always presents special problems of literary construction and textual transmission which need to be properly understood and addressed—hence the considerable attention they receive in this book (Chapters 6–8).

Despite these limitations, an attempt at reconstructing the textual tradition and background of the chronicle of Marcellinus *comes*, for example, has considerable value. It illustrates how a deeper understanding of the author's career, together with his cultural and social background, as well as his audience, can provide a clearer and fuller guide to interpreting the information recorded and to understanding the historiographical perspective of the author. Such an analysis is also valuable for the light it scatters more widely on late antique society and literary culture. Yet Marcellinus is in several respects atypical of most late Latin chroniclers. At least we know more about his life and work, relatively speaking, than we do, say, of Hydatius and the African bishop Victor of Tunnuna. Then there is the fact that, although Marcellinus wrote in Latin, he lived in a predominantly Greek-speaking city.

The most substantial study of the chronicle until now (Holder-Egger, 1877) was primarily concerned with identifying the chronicle's sources of information, but it predates the rediscovery of the Oxford manuscript of Marcellinus (1889) and Mommsen's subsequent edition (1894). Except for the recent philologically focused research of Gusso (1991, 1995, 1996, 1997), the little scholarly attention otherwise devoted to Marcellinus has tended to concentrate on his relationship with the historians of the Goths, Cassiodorus and Jordanes—a relationship explained in terms of Italian politics and Italian cultural circles, particularly his relation to the prestigious and powerful Anician family—and has been dominated by dubious source criticism.[33] Yet Marcellinus lived, and wrote his chronicle, in Constantinople; the city itself and the eastern empire as a whole, particularly the Balkans, provide the central focus of his narrative. In terms of outlook and emphasis he therefore stands in closer proximity to his contemporary John Malalas than to Hydatius, Prosper or any other Latin chronicler. Both Marcellinus and the Byzantine chronicle tradition exemplified by Malalas share a common fount and exemplar in the chronicle of Eusebius. They also show the essential similarity and commonality between the variety of chronicle forms which followed Eusebius. Although Marcellinus does not appear in histories of Byzantine literature (he is even absent from most histories of Latin literature),[34] he is essentially an early Byzantine chronicler and this fundamental perspective is emphasized throughout this book.[35] It cannot be presumed that a Latin writer in sixth-century Constantinople must be an émigré embedded in the culture and society of the west, and an alien to the mainstream of life in the imperial capital. Like Corippus in his poem on Justin II, Marcellinus must be understood and explained as a Latin speaker reflecting both the attitudes and viewpoints of contemporary

---

[33] This line of argument is exemplified by Momigliano (1956), 271ff. and Wes (1967), *passim*. It has been continued more recently by Zecchini (1983), 48–52, 90–1 and (1993), 65–90, but subjected to critical review in Croke (1983a), 81–119 and Gusso (1995), 587ff.

[34] A notable exception is Dihle (1994), 485. That the chronicle is more often quoted second-hand, rather than actually consulted directly, is indicated by its inclusion in a catalogue of Greek (!) authors in Grant (1976), 329.

[35] To my knowledge, the only explicit acknowledgments of Marcellinus as a Byzantine chronicler, besides his inclusion in the *Oxford Dictionary of Byzantium* in an article by B. Baldwin (1991), are to be found in Newton (1972), 525 and Karayannopulos/ Weiss (1982), 283–4.

Constantinople with its increasingly Greek intellectual and literary culture.[36]

Above all, this book is intended as a contribution to our understanding of the Roman culture of the author's lifetime in the late fifth and early sixth centuries. In the chronicle of Marcellinus we see how an educated official of the imperial court viewed and construed the world around him and the course of historical change, especially events in the reigns of Anastasius, Justin I and Justinian through which he lived. His reactions to contemporary events in his native Illyricum and in Constantinople, as well as his frequent eyewitness descriptions of them, present interesting testimony to what one person close to the imperial court considered important for his audience. More generally, Marcellinus' chronicle enriches our understanding of society and politics in the imperial capital, and raises broader questions about Christian life, liturgy and culture in the sixth century. In particular, the chronicle underlines the central role of imperial and religious ceremonial in Byzantine public life. The chronicle's frequent reference to processions and liturgical commemorations reflects the significant extent to which the ritualized ceremony of Byzantine urban life had already been established by the early sixth century.

Finally, Marcellinus' configuration and presentation of the past arise from the contemporary historiographical discourse in which they are embedded. The distinctive views and outlook of Marcellinus, mainly elicited from scattered entries in the chronicle, complement those of other contemporaries such as John Lydus, Jordanes, John Malalas, and Procopius. It is only by defining the commonality of attitudes and understanding between all these different writers, in the light of the culture and expectations of their audiences, that we can measure their individuality and thus comprehend better the dynamic complexity of political and social change during the reign of Justin and the early part of that of Justinian. The chronicle of Marcellinus and its representation of the period from the late fourth to the early sixth centuries provides an illuminating perspective on the wider issues underlying the transition to Byzantine habits, values, and attitudes.

[36] Cameron, Averil (1976), 4–5.

PART I

THE WORLD OF MARCELLINUS

1

Marcellinus *Comes*: The Man and his Work

Any historical work is inevitably permeated and shaped by the viewpoint and culture of its author. To understand the viewpoint and culture which permeated and shaped the chronicle of Marcellinus it is therefore necessary to begin with the chronicler himself. Yet, the search for the mind and milieu behind Marcellinus' chronicle, his only extant work, is singularly difficult. One has to collate and analyse the chronicle's entries in order to sketch in its background, as well as the author's attitudes and pre-occupations. Accordingly, it is the purpose of this initial chapter to lay the foundations for this whole study by presenting and interpreting the records which bear on the career and work of Marcellinus—who he was and what he did.

TESTIMONIA

As with most minor literary figures of antiquity, very little is known directly of Marcellinus and hardly anything has ever been written about him.[1] What is known is derived, in the first instance, from what he tells us about himself in the *Chronicle*. Then there are the notices by his contemporary, the scholar and former secretary to the Ostrogothic kings of Italy, Cassiodorus, recorded in his *Institutiones* written in the 550s following his return to Italy from Constantinople.[2]

In the preface to his chronicle Marcellinus begins by pointing out that Jerome translated into Latin the chronicle of Eusebius of Caesarea (first composed in Greek in the early fourth century and subsequently updated to AD 325) and then continued this chronicle to the time of the emperor Valens so that the total time

---

[1] The main guides are: Schanz, Hosius, and Krüger (1920), 110–12 and Baldwin (1991), 1296. There is, for example, no article on Marcellinus in *RE*, nor even in the latest edition (1996) of the *Oxford Classical Dictionary*.

[2] For the date, as well as the nature and purpose, of Cassiodorus' handbook: Jones, L. W. (1946), esp. 32; O'Donnell (1979), 202–14.

covered (Creation to AD 378) amounted to 5579 years in all, at least by Jerome's reckoning:

After the marvellous work from the creation of the world down to the emperor Constantine, which Eusebius of Caesarea composed in Greek—recording the beginnings of this present era, its timespan, years, kingdoms and the good qualities of men as well as the inventors of the various arts and also the monuments from almost all regions—our Jerome translated the whole work into Latin and continued it in the Roman language down to Valens Caesar. Consequently, both authors of this work calculated with astonishing ingenuity that this world would at that time have been five thousand five hundred and seventy-nine years old.

Then Marcellinus states that he, a *comes* and *vir clarissimus*, added to Jerome's work another 140 years from the consulship of Ausonius and Olybrius (379) to that of Magnus (518), and that he later added a further sixteen years (reckoning inclusively) from the first consulship of Justin I (519) to the fourth consulship of Justinian (534) before laying aside his work:

So I, Marcellinus, a count and man with the rank 'Most Distinguished', have continued the work of these same authors (following only the Eastern empire) with simple straightforward calculation, counting by means of the indictions and consuls written below, for one hundred and forty years—namely from the seventh indiction and the consulship of Ausonius and Olybrius during which Theodosius the Great was also appointed emperor, summarising down to the consulship of Magnus in the eleventh indiction. Further, I have added another sixteen years from the first consulship of Justin Augustus to the fourth of Justinian Augustus (there being one hundred and fifty-six years altogether), and have attached this to my own unpretentious work.

From this brief statement by Marcellinus himself, we turn to the fuller information of Cassiodorus contained in the *Institutiones*. This work was designed as a practical handbook for the new monks at Cassiodorus' monastery at Vivarium near Squillace in Southern Italy. It is a sort of bibliographical introduction to both religious literature (Book 1) and secular literature (Book 2). The first book begins by explaining, in order, which scholars have interpreted the individual books of the Old and New Testaments (1. 1–10), then follow chapters on the various divisions and combinations of all these books (1. 11–14) and how to approach the comprehension and emendation of Biblical manuscripts (1.15–16). Next Cassiodorus turns to what he calls 'Christian Historians' (*historici*), writers who 'narrate ecclesiastical matters and describe changes which occur at various times' and who are potentially instructive for the reader because they see the Creator as the moving force behind all that happens on earth. So Cassiodorus' understanding of history is that it embraces all man's activities while history writing takes many different forms. Within this broad definition he is able to locate not only the ecclesiastical historians (Eusebius, Socrates, Sozomen, Theodoret) but also Josephus, whose history of the Jewish nation was a model for histories of the early Christian nation. Cassiodorus next moves on to the fifth-century Spanish writer Orosius who wrote a history of the follies and disasters experienced in man's past, then turns to Marcellinus:

Marcellinus too has traversed his journey's path in laudable fashion, completing four books on the nature of events and the locations of places with most decorous propriety; I have likewise left this work for you.[3]

In Cassiodorus' view all these books, including those of Marcellinus on the nature of events and the locations of places, are related to history.[4] Presumably too they all served the same audience. Also under the label of 'historians' Cassiodorus next passes to the authors of chronicles; first Eusebius, then Jerome, and then Prosper and Marcellinus:

[Jerome] has been followed in turn by the aforesaid Marcellinus the Illyrian who is said to have acted first as *cancellarius* of the patrician Justinian, but who later, with the Lord's help upon the improvement of his employer's civil status, faithfully guided his work from the time of the emperor (Justin) to the beginning of the triumphant rule of the emperor Justinian.[5]

From this passage we learn that Marcellinus was an Illyrian who, so Cassiodorus was told (probably when in Constantinople himself in the early 550s), had once been a *cancellarius* to Justinian before the latter became emperor, and who afterwards continued his chronicle to the early years of Justinian's reign.

---

[3] *Inst.* 1. 17. 1.

[4] The usual understanding of *historicus* included writers of geographical and topographical works such as those of Marcellinus (*ThLL* 6. 3. 2842 s.v. *historicus*).

[5] *Inst.* 1. 17. 2, as interpreted in Croke (1982*b*), 225–6.

Next, Cassiodorus provides a brief overview of the great Latin theologians and exegetes—Hilary, Cyprian, Ambrose, Jerome, and Augustine (1. 18–22), as well as his own contemporaries Eugippius and Dionysius Exiguus (1. 23), followed by a chapter on the enthusiasm needed for reading the scriptures and their commentators (1. 23), and then a chapter on 'Cosmographers to be read by the monks' (1. 25) by which Cassiodorus intended that 'you may clearly know in what part of the world the individual places about which you read in the sacred books are located'. To acquire this knowledge he recommends reading the fifth-century cosmographer Julius Honorius, followed by Marcellinus:

> Marcellinus too, concerning whom I have already spoken, should be read with equal care; he has described the city of Constantinople and the city of Jerusalem in four short books in considerable detail (*Inst.* 1. 25. 1).

This completes the testimony we have for the life and work of Marcellinus and the picture must now be filled out from here. In order to elucidate Marcellinus' preface and these notices in the *Institutiones* of Cassiodorus we need to know exactly when Marcellinus was *cancellarius* to Justinian, and precisely what his position involved; and then we need to explain, as far as possible, what he was doing before and after leaving the service of Justinian; and finally what was the nature and structure of his other works cited by Cassiodorus and which are both now lost— one on Constantinople and Jerusalem, the other on times and places (assuming, as proposed below, that Cassiodorus is describing two separate works).

CAREER AND CHRONICLE

It is not known when or where Marcellinus was born, what education he had or how he was occupied before writing his chronicle in 518. If, for the sake of a working hypothesis, Marcellinus was in his forties when he wrote the chronicle and subsequently entered the service of Justinian, then he will have been born in the 470s. He could, however, have been born either much earlier (460s) or much later (490s). In any event, on the reckoning of our hypothesis, he could have been involved as a young soldier in the campaigns of the 490s, or (like the *notarius* Jordanes) he may have been involved in the administrative support for the army. At the cost of anticipating conclusions argued more fully in the following chapters, the internal evidence of the chronicle suggests that he had strong military connections and that he came originally from somewhere in the centre of the Prefecture of Illyricum, perhaps in the vicinity of modern Skopje. The area of Illyricum he knows best is that included by the late Roman provinces of Dardania, Dacia Ripensis, and Upper Moesia. There he would have been brought up in an area constantly under threat from the incursions of different tribal groups: Huns, Goths, and Bulgars. Yet he managed to survive it, securing at the same time a solid enough education in both Latin and Greek.

Marcellinus exhibits many of the features characteristic of late Latin,[6] and it is evident that he also knew Greek which is unsurprising for someone from the linguistic border-zone straddling Illyricum and Thrace. There are traces of Greek orthography in the chronicle, and it is clear that he made direct use of documents in Greek (see Chapter 6). The claim that he enjoyed the fullest rhetorical education which befitted his rank is hard to justify, at least on the basis of the chronicle.[7] Admittedly some of Marcellinus' description is vivid, but it should not be thought that such expression can only represent the imprint of rhetorical training, especially since it seems that he actually witnessed the disturbances in Constantinople he so clearly describes in 501, 512, and 532. Nor is it certain that he had an extensive theological education;[8] again one must be wary of assessing the extent of his theological reading and knowledge purely on the evidence of the chronicle. The quotation from Jeremiah (s.a. 517) may, or may not, be based on a familiarity with the Old Testament as a whole. Furthermore, his brief biographies of ecclesiastical writers are taken arbitrarily from Gennadius (see Chapter 6) and he had not necessarily read the theological works to which he refers.

Marcellinus' accusative absolutes and other less 'classical' constructions would hardly recommend him to the admirers of his own contemporary, the African grammarian Priscian. Nor does a line from one of the panegyrics of Claudian and an etymological

---

[6] For a complete list see Mommsen (1894), 57. It is not easy to localize Marcellinus' Latin although certain features of oral and Balkan Latin can be detected (cf. Mihaescu (1978), 9–10).

[7] Holder-Egger (1877), 55 suggests that the style of Marcellinus shows the influence of contemporary schools of rhetoric and that this is especially evident when he is not relying on written sources.   [8] Ibid. 56.

point from the republican comic playwright Plautus entitle him to be counted among the highly educated and literary-minded aristocracy of his day.[9] Nonetheless, the chronicle is not a very extensive document and there is danger in assessing any writer's culture purely by his chronicle; it would, for instance, be grossly misleading to judge Eusebius, Jerome, and Prosper by their chronicles alone. Marcellinus' literary culture must not therefore be underrated, nor should the chronicle be held up as necessarily the product of limited literary culture and style.

Of Marcellinus' family absolutely nothing is known despite the attempt of some to link him with Marcellinus the *magister militum* who established himself in Dalmatia in the 460s and with the nephew of this Marcellinus, namely the emperor Nepos.[10] In the chronicle Marcellinus neither gives any hint of relationship nor singles out for special mention either the *magister militum* Marcellinus (s.a. 468. 2) or Nepos (s.a. 474. 2, 475. 2 and 480. 2). Moreover, the name 'Marcellinus' was itself quite common in the fifth and sixth centuries.[11] Marcellinus, as we shall see, first appeared in Constantinople around the turn of the sixth century and spent the remainder of his life there, although at some stage (probably before his career with Justinian in the early 520s) he made a journey of unspecified itinerary which provided material for his detailed books 'On the Locations of Places'.[12] This journey, as argued below, was primarily to the Holy Land but may also have taken him as far afield as Dara, the great fortress on the Persian frontier recently constructed (*c.*507/8) by the emperor Anastasius.

When, then, did Marcellinus come to Constantinople from his Balkan homeland? It is sensible to take as a lower limit the period 498–501 in which he begins to describe events in sufficient detail to suggest personal experience or direct access to eyewitnesses.

---

[9] These are the only two references to non-Christian Latin literature in the chronicle: 399. 1: *omnia cesserunt eunucho consule monstra* (Claudian, *In Eutropium*, 1. 8); 496. 2: . . . *elephantum, quem Plautus noster* [*Casina*, 846] *lucabum nomine dicit.*

[10] As suggested, though only speculatively, by Holder-Egger (1877), 49–50 and Sundwall (1915), 100–1, cf. *PLRE* 2. 708–10 s.v. 'Marcellinus 6', and 777–8 s.v. 'Iulius Nepos'.

[11] Mommsen (1894), 41. *PLRE* 2 records ten Marcellini, while *PLRE* 1 has twenty-three and *PLRE* 3 has four.

[12] This appears to be how we should interpret Cassiodorus' phrase *itineris sui tramitem laudabiliter percurrit* (*Inst.* 1. 17. 1); that is literally rather than figuratively which is evidently the understanding of L. W. Jones (1946, 117: 'has traversed his journey's path in laudible fashion').

Direct personal observation of, or involvement in, local events may explain Marcellinus' account of the parading in the hippodrome in 498 of the captured Isaurian rebel Longinus (s.a. 498. 2). More detailed still is his record of the expedition of the *magister militum* Aristus which in 499 set out against the Bulgars who had been devastating the Balkans. He enumerates the total troops and wagons, the total losses, and the names of individual counts or military officers (s.a. 499. 1). Perhaps he himself had seen the 15,000 troops (not many less than on Belisarius' more famous expedition to Africa in 533) and 520 wagons moving through Thrace, and perhaps he wondered with the other onlookers about how many would return. Even if not, he certainly had access to detailed information on the expeditionary force. Perhaps he was even involved himself as part of the Illyrian army on this campaign. Then in 501 there is a riot in the theatre between the rival groups of supporters, the Blues and Greens, whose mutual antipathy was sharpened during the reign of Anastasius (s.a. 501. 1–3). By any standard of disasters this was a shattering experience and one which could therefore have profoundly affected Marcellinus as an observer or local witness. In any case it led the emperor Anastasius to abolish the 500-year-old Brytai festival.[13]

If the theatre disaster in 501 suggests a *terminus post quem* of about 500 for Marcellinus' arrival in Constantinople from his native Illyricum, the date is not contradicted by the only specific first-person indication Marcellinus gives of his residence in Constantinople and his witness to events there: under the year 484 he records the persecutions instigated by the Arian Vandal king, Huneric, against his catholic subjects in North Africa.[14] Many of the catholics suffered mutilation before being exiled and found their way as refugees to Constantinople. The deacon Reparatus whose tongue had been cut out gained fame through his miraculous preaching at Constantinople and was honoured by the emperor of the time, the Isaurian Zeno, and his wife Ariadne.[15] Marcellinus says he actually saw (*ego conspexi*) such people walking around the city with their tongues excised and their hands lopped off but who were evidently able to speak normally (s.a. 484. 2).

---

[13] For details on the 501 riot see Cameron, Alan (1973), 231, 234 and Croke (1995), 111.

[14] The cruelty of Huneric made a deep impact on the church, both east and west: Coll. Avell. *Ep.* 95. 63 (*CSEL* 35. 391); Greg. Tur. *Hist.* 2. 2; Zach. Mit. *HE* 8. 1.

[15] Vict. Vit. *Hist. Pers.* 3. 6. 30.

Although these victims would have come to Constantinople as early as 484 they could obviously still be seen at the time Marcellinus might have arrived (*c.*500) and well beyond. The historian Procopius (*Wars* 2. 8. 4) and the exiled African bishop Victor of Tunnuna, both resident in Constantinople, refer to the presence in the city of these victims even further into the sixth century; at least by the 560s Victor could see their graves.[16] Furthermore, since the original persecution continued to be commemorated liturgically at Constantinople each year on 8 December (probably the date of their arrival in the city in 484) it was familiar enough to the chronicler's audience.[17] In this instance, as with so much of the chronicle we can identify the public liturgical context of the chronicle's information. Marcellinus' precise date—'This Arian cruelty began to be inflicted on the devoted worshippers of Christ in the month of February'—suggests that his description of Huneric's edict is taken from some written document to which he added his own observations.[18] In other words, Marcellinus' own comment cannot be taken as necessarily suggesting that he was in Constantinople himself as early as the mid-480s.

If Marcellinus came to Constantinople around 500, what was he engaged in during the period of thirty years or so before we can last trace him in 534 when the updated version of his chronicle was written? Between 500 and 518 we have no clue to his position and can only speculate. Perhaps he took part in Anastasius' Persian War in 503 and 504, if that is why the Persian war is the only event described in these two years; possibly too it was during this period that he undertook his *iter* to the Holy Land (*Inst.* 1. 17) and perhaps further afield. Besides these possible excursions we have to assume that until 518 he was, for the most part, resident in Constantinople for he refers to local happenings more frequently than earlier in the chronicle: the Brytai riots in 501, the erection of a statue of Anastasius in the Forum Tauri in 506, a faction riot in 507, a fire and the excavation of the harbour of Julian in 509, another fire in 510, the monophysite sedition in 512, the rebellion of Vitalian (514/15) and the visit of the Illyrian bishops in 516. Although we can only guess at Marcellinus' activities and

---

[16] Vict. Tonn. 479. 1 (II. 189) cf. 567. 2 (II. 206) also *CJ* 1. 27. 1, 4 (April 534)—noted by the lawyer Evagrius (*HE* 4. 14).

[17] *SEC* 287. 28–289. 36 and for further comment: Lackner (1970), 182–202.

[18] For the date: Laterculus A 10 (*MGH AA* 13. 459); *Pasch. Camp.* s.a. 484 (9. 746) with Courtois (1955), 297–9.

official position before he wrote his chronicle to 518, we are on more certain ground for the years covered by the updated section of the chronicle to 534, thanks to Cassiodorus who tells us that Marcellinus was *cancellarius* to Justinian while the latter was still a 'patrician'.

Most magistrates with judicial functions, including provincial governors, had *cancellarii* among their *officium*.[19] As a *cancellarius*, Marcellinus would have been responsible to Justinian 'the patrician' for regulating audiences and controlling the presentation of petitions. Such a position would normally have involved him in all his employer's confidential business.[20] He may also have played some part in the paperwork of troop organization and distribution. Certainly that is the very sort of activity we find *cancellarii* to generals engaged in during the time of Justinian where the commander Narses is seen arriving back in Ravenna in 552 after subjugating Lucca and splitting up his army. He entered Ravenna along with his bodyguards, household slaves and those responsible for the administrative archives and for regulating access to the general. These men were the *cancellarii* (Agath. 1. 19. 4). Along with this expansion of function, an increase in status is observed also by the sixth century. *Cancellarii* had become men of senatorial status and were known as *comites*, and some had acquired the rank of *vir clarissimus*.[21] Hence—*ego vero vir clarissimus Marcellinus comes* (Marcellin. *praef.*).

On the elevation of his uncle Justin to the imperial throne in July 518 Justinian was about forty years of age and a *candidatus* in the palace guard.[22] By 520 he was *comes domesticorum*, that is in charge of the imperial household.[23] Since neither of these offices entitled the holder to the services of a *cancellarius* then it must be taken that Marcellinus was not as yet in the employ of Justinian, although (as argued above) he had already been in the city some twenty years. As already noted, we have no idea what position he held before that of *cancellarius* and probably no likelihood of ever

---

[19] Jones, A. H. M. (1964), 603. On *cancellarii*, especially the particular officials to which they became attached: Mommsen (1889*b*), 478–80 (= *GS* 3. 417–19); Seeck (1889*a*), 1456–9 and Morosi (1978), 127–58; for *cancellarii* to *magistri officiorum*: Clauss (1980), 59.

[20] Morosi (1978), 133.

[21] Seeck (1889*a*), 1459; Morosi (1978), 143. There is therefore no need to suppose that the title of *comes* reflects a position such as *comes commerciorum* or *comes metallum per Illyricum* as did Hodgkin (1892*a*), 708 n. 1.

[22] Vict. Tonn. 518. 2 (II. 96) cf. 520. 1 (II. 96): *ex candidato*. Peter the Patrician quoted in Const. Porph. *Caer.* 93 (*CSHB* 428. 3). [23] Vasiliev (1950), 94 n. 70.

finding out. Perhaps, as a Latin speaker, he was employed in some *officium* or other for at that time that is where *cancellarii* normally originated.[24] By the year 520 Marcellinus either knew Justin and Justinian already or, as a fellow Illyrian, had been recommended to them. Moreover, it is likely that he was much the same age as Justinian. Indeed, Mommsen went so far as to suggest that Marcellinus' detailed description of the consulship of Justinian in 521 actually implied his close involvement with Justinian by that stage:[25]

The consul Justinian made this consulship the most famous of all eastern ones by being considerably more generous in his largesses. For two hundred and eighty eight thousand solidi were distributed to the people or spent on spectacles or on their properties. He exhibited simultaneously in the amphitheatre twenty lions and thirty panthers, not counting other wild beasts. Above all, after already donating the chariots, he provided caparisoned horses in the hippodrome, one final race being the only thing denied the clamouring populace (521).

Mommsen's interpretation is enticing but perhaps unnecessary. There is nothing in the detail to suggest the chronicler's official participation in the consular celebrations although it may indicate that he witnessed them personally.

At precisely this point, that is (according to the timetable proposed here), before Marcellinus entered the service of Justinian, the first edition of the chronicle to 518 had been completed. That the chronicle was written soon after the death of Anastasius, rather than much later, seems a reasonable enough assumption given the obvious comparison with the updated edition of the chronicle which was patently written soon after the last event it describes—the African triumph celebrated in Constantinople in 534.[26] As will become apparent later, it is the triumph that provides the very occasion for the updated edition and gives meaning to its enthusiastic account of Justinian's early years and the expectations to which they gave rise.

By 518 there were western continuations of Jerome's chronicle from 378 (Prosper, Hydatius) but apparently nothing for the past

---

[24] Jones, A. H. M. (1964), 603.

[25] Mommsen (1894), 42; cf. Holder-Egger (1877), 54.

[26] Holder-Egger (1877) 53 regarded the death of Anastasius not only as a convenient terminating point but made the unlikely and unnecessary suggestion that it was chosen because Marcellinus had nothing worthwhile to say about Justin if he were to continue to the actual time of writing.

half century (after the end of Hydatius), although there were probably manuscripts of Prosper and Hydatius in which their chronicles were continued on by later scribes. Certainly there was no
known continuation of Jerome in the East. An eastern continuation of Jerome would obviously be useful, so Marcellinus obliged.
If he knew the work of Prosper then he may consciously have seen
himself as providing an eastern counterpart to Prosper, at least for
the part which extends beyond Jerome. Whatever the motivation,
Marcellinus' chronicle apparently filled a gap and its popularity,
or at least its usefulness, led to its subsequent recommendation by
Cassiodorus as well as its updating by Marcellinus himself in 534
and its further continuation by an unknown author many years
later.

Now, the first edition of the chronicle to 518, in so far as it is
incorporated in the second, ends in a rather prosaic way with the
death of the monophysite emperor Anastasius. Had the orthodox
Marcellinus been writing much later in the reign of Justin we
might reasonably have expected him to have made more of the
return to orthodoxy under Justin who actively persecuted dis-
senters from the Chalcedonian orthodoxy on Christ's nature.
Indeed, that the chronicle ends with the death of Anastasius is in
itself yet another hint that it was written soon after that event
rather than later. This, after all, was the usual practice of the
late Roman chroniclers who were not normally bound by any
traditional classical obligation to avoid the reign of the current
emperor. Instead it was the chronicler's purpose to continue his
account to the very time of writing. This is the case with Hydatius,
Victor of Tunnuna, John of Biclaro, Cassiodorus, and Isidore. In
addition, it was for this same reason that individual chroniclers
kept their work up-to-date in subsequent years as Eusebius himself had done. Prosper, for example, updated his on more than
one occasion.[27]

We can feel reasonably confident, therefore, in presuming that
Marcellinus too completed the original edition of his chronicle
soon after the last event he describes (the death of Anastasius
on 9 July 518), that is, in or just after July 518, or perhaps early in
519 but no later.[28] Given this date, it follows that the opinions

[27] Muhlberger (1990), 55 ff.
[28] Since the chronicle includes the recall from exile of bishop John of Paltos (s.a. 512. 9:
Iohannem Iustinus Augustus, mox imperator factus est, revocavit) it may have been written after his

expressed therein belong to a relatively undistinguished Illyrian and not someone closely involved with the imperial court. It remains possible, however, that Marcellinus wrote his chronicle while in Justinian's service in the mid-520s but Cassiodorus seems to imply not, and there is nothing otherwise to support the idea. The original edition of the chronicle was most likely composed in the wake of Anastasius' death in July 518 and gives a fairly hostile picture of that emperor. It was very much pro-Illyrian and ortho-dox. Its production coincided with the accession of Justin and his immediate reassertion of an anti-monophysite policy at Constan-tinople, followed quickly by the re-establishment of relations with the Pope which revived the sense of ecclesiastical unity between East and West. The settlement also provided a new platform for the subsequent purposeful pursuit of heretics by the regime of Justin and his nephew Justinian.[29]

It was not until the chronicle was written and circulating that Marcellinus was drawn into the household of Justinian, maybe as early as 520 when, as *magister militum*, Justinian first became entitled to a *cancellarius*.[30] Cassiodorus says that Marcellinus was *cancellarius* when Justinian was 'still patrician' (*Inst.* I. 17), that is before being proclaimed emperor on I April 527 or *Caesar* in 525.[31] Patrician (*patricius*) was an exceptionally elevated title at this stage, giving its holder a higher status than a Praetorian Prefect. Yet Cassiodorus does not necessarily imply that Marcellinus was not *cancellarius* to Justinian before he became patrician, that is before 523.[32] It is therefore between the years 520 and 525, or 527 at the

recall. However, we do not know when John's recall took place. It is possible that it was immediate, if that is the import of Marcellinus' *mox*, so that it could be noted at Constantinople in July/August 518 and could therefore be included in the original edition of the chronicle. On the other hand, it may have been a year or so later. In that case, it means either that the chronicle was written somewhat later (519), or it was included in the updated version in 534. On balance, a date of composition around July/August 518 seems most likely.

[29] Vasiliev (1950), 136 ff.; Amory (1997), 216–17.

[30] Vict. Tonn. 520. 2 (II. 196). Justinian is designated on his consular diptych as *mag.eqq. et p.praes.* (*CIL* 5. 8210. 3). This was the opinion of Bury (1898), 524.

[31] Marcellin. s.a. 527; Evag. *HE* 4. 9. See also Vasiliev (1950), 96 n. 73.

[32] Vict. Tonn. 523. 3 (II. 197); Cyr. Scyth. *vita Sabae* 68; Jo. Nik. 90.16–18. Justinian was also *patricius* at the time of the devastating flood in Edessa in 525 (*Chron. Edess.* s.a. 836 (10)) and while still *magister militum* (John of Ephesus, *Lives of the Eastern Saints* 13 PO 17. 2. 189)—neither reference cited in 'Justinian 7' *PLRE* 2. 647. Victor of Tunnuna says that in 525 Justin was forced, against his will, by the senate to proclaim Justinian as *Caesar* (II. 197) which would further narrow the period of Marcellinus' service. Although this is normally dismissed as inaccurate (or ignored altogether as in *PLRE* 2. 647) it may well be correct (cf.

outside, that Marcellinus can be located, along with a certain Marcianus,[33] in the service of Justinian as *magister militum praesentalis* and (as we have seen) we can deduce from other evidence the nature of the employment.

An Illyrian familiar with Latin and Greek, as well as how an army worked, would appear to be the ideal candidate for a *cancellarius* to Justinian. The *cancellarius* did not need to be a man of bureaucratic experience and reputation. Even though the trend was setting in, *cancellarii* were not professional civil servants and it was quite possible for someone like Marcellinus to be appointed in an ad hoc fashion, that is, by invitation rather than seniority or proven efficiency in the ways of bureaucracy. If Justinian was attached to Marcellinus as a fellow Illyrian, as suggested by Mommsen (1894, 41), then it may have been the success of Marcellinus' recently published pro-Illyrian chronicle which confirmed the choice of Justinian, that is to say, it was a special honour bestowed on him by Justinian rather than the automatic result of a more conventional bureaucratic career such as that of John the Lydian.

This pattern of recruitment in the early Byzantine civil and imperial service and the function of national and family ties in securing appointment and advancement is well established,[34] and can be illustrated by the contemporary examples of Peter the Patrician and John the Lydian. Peter, born in Thessalonike, caught the attention of Justinian as a result of his historical abilities (Proc. *Wars* 5. 3. 30) and subsequently enjoyed a long diplomatic career culminating in the settlement with the Persian king in 563.[35] Regional affiliation and family ties also explain the career of John the Lydian. He secured a position soon after 511 in the office of the Praetorian Prefect through the agency of his fellow-Lydian Zoticus, and then advanced through a relative, Ammianus (*De mag.* 3. 26-7). In addition, at the very time Marcellinus was *cancellarius* to Justinian, Lydus was in the prefecture which eventually brought him to the emperor's attention, and resulted in his panegyric in 530 on the imperial victory at Dara.[36] Together, the

---

Vasiliev (1950), 95), for Victor otherwise records Justinian's positions very carefully (Vict. Tonn. 518. 2 (11. 196) ; 520. 2 (11. 196)).

[33] 'Marcianus', *PLRE* 2. 716-17.
[34] Pedersen (1976), 26, 33, 40.
[35] Men. fr. 6.1 (54-5), with Antonopoulos (1985), 49-53.
[36] Maas (1992), 33-4.

early stages of the careers of both Peter and John throw some force behind the probability that Marcellinus became *cancellarius* to Justinian in about 520 because of the popularity of his chronicle, and especially because he was a fellow Illyrian. Approaching the appointment of *cancellarius* from this angle makes it easier to explain why there is no other mention of this *vir clarissimus* in the extant documentation of the time.[37]

Marcellinus, then, came rather abruptly into the service of Justinian about 520, was closely involved with court business over the next few years and disappeared from his position equally abruptly. The assumption that Marcellinus continued in the employ of Justinian after he became emperor in 527[38] is contradicted by Cassiodorus' statement that he was *cancellarius* to Justinian the 'patrician'. This statement which only makes sense in so far as it implies that when Justinian became Augustus in 527 (or possibly *Caesar* in 525) Marcellinus' appointment lapsed. Nor is there any reason for assuming Marcellinus was a 'favourite' of Justinian.[39]

Precisely what occupied Marcellinus between 527 (or 525) and 534 is not known although it may have been at this time that he produced the other works to which Cassiodorus refers (*Inst.* 1.17, 25). What is possible, however, is that as a former *cancellarius* he took his place among the senate of Constantinople as a new *vir clarissimus*, even though at this stage the clarissimate conferred senatorial status but not necessarily membership of the senate. If so, then (as plausibly suggested by Mommsen)[40] his experience may be protruding in what he regarded as the event most worth recording for the year 528:

In the one hundred and ninety-eighth year from the foundation of the royal city the emperor Justinian the Victor rebuilt the imperial box and its ancient throne designed for viewing and acclaiming the contests in the hippodrome, making it more elevated and brighter than it had been. With customary generosity he also reconstructed each portico where the senators sat as spectators (528).

It has also been asserted that the 'Marcellinus' sent by Justinian to Chalcedon in 552, along with other dignitaries, to pacify Pope Vigilius is the same person as the chronicler.[41] It is unlikely, how-

---

[37] A fact which puzzled Holder-Egger (1877), 49.   [38] Ibid. 49.
[39] As did Ebert (1889), 445-6.   [40] Mommsen (1894), 41 n. 4.
[41] Hodgkin (1896), 597; cf. 'Marcellinus quaestor', *PLRE* 3. 812.

ever, that a *cancellarius* to Justinian in the 520s should suddenly turn up thirty years later, at an advanced age, in such a specialist position as *quaestor*. It might be expected too that if Marcellinus was in such an important post as *quaestor* in 551 Cassiodorus would have mentioned the fact when writing his *Institutiones* not long after. In any event, Marcellinus was not an uncommon name. Further, it has been repeated frequently that Marcellinus became a monk after leaving the service of Justinian.[42] It is true that imperial officials sometimes retired to a religious mode of life and indeed that some *cancellarii* did become monks,[43] but in the case of Marcellinus the evidence adduced to support the claim dissolves on close inspection.[44]

The only concrete fact we have concerning Marcellinus after 527 is that he continued his chronicle from 518/19 to 534. Cassiodorus tells us that after Justinian became emperor Marcellinus continued his chronicle *domino iuvante* to the early part of the reign of Justinian (*Inst.* 1. 17. 2). In this way Marcellinus was able to display his gratitude to Justinian for previously inviting him into his service and in the updated section of the chronicle Justinian is certainly a central figure. Marcellinus describes in detail his consulship in 521 (quoted above), his elevation as Augustus in 527, his remodelling in 528 of the imperial box and the senatorial enclosure in the hippodrome at Constantinople (also quoted above), the promulgation of the *Codex Justinianus* (wrongly dated to 531), a pro-Justinian summary of the Nika riot of 532 and the reconquest of Roman North Africa and Carthage in 533/4:

The province of Africa, which is placed by most people in the third part of the world's division was liberated by God's will. The city of Carthage as well, in the ninety-sixth year since its destruction was restored after the Vandals had been driven out and subjugated and their king Gelimer captured and sent to Constantinople in the fourth consulship of the emperor Justinian, who received him in moderation since his country was stronger than it had been for some time. (534).

As a result Marcellinus displayed his 'fulsome appreciation' (Cassiodorus) for the regime of Justinian. To continue his by now renowned chronicle to the greater glory of Justinian was the most

---

[42] e.g. Mommsen (1894), 42; Bury (1923*b*), 39 n. 2; more recently O'Donnell (1982), 225 who assumes that Marcellinus was still alive in Constantinople in 551, which is possible.

[43] John of Ephesus, *Lives of the Eastern Saints* 56 (*PO* 9. 2. 197).

[44] Croke (1982*b*), 225–6.

effective means Marcellinus had at his disposal for demonstrating the gratitude and respect he felt for his former employer. Indeed, the fact that the chronicle ends on such a triumphant note suggests that the reconquest of Africa provided Marcellinus with a perfect occasion for continuing his chronicle, as suggested by the evident haste in which it was compiled. Haste is implied by the fact that in the updated section (519–34) there is (except for 519) only a single entry under each year as well as the only year left blank in the whole chronicle (522). Haste may also explain the surprising (because it is so recent) dating error: 531 instead of 529 for the Code of Justinian. It would seem that Marcellinus did not have time to locate and verify facts not readily available to him.

The reconquest of Roman Africa was a great achievement for Justinian whose grip on the throne had seriously slipped just two years previously during the Nika riots as a result of which 35,000 corpses (far more than Belisarius' African force) were strewn around the palace and hippodrome complex of the imperial capital. The Vandal victory was a proud and memorable moment for Belisarius too as he processed in triumph from his house to the hippodrome at Constantinople where were displayed the spoils of Africa and the Vandal king in chains, and it was equally memorable for those who witnessed the spectacle. This momentous event was publicized by the imperial court as the restoration of Africa's liberty and as the restoration of the province to the empire by the will of Almighty God. This is stated specifically in the preface to Justinian's textbook of Roman law, the *Institutes*, dated 21 November 533 (*Const. imp. maiest.*, p. xii), and in a law of 13 April 534 (*CJ* 1. 27. 1). Nearly twenty years later John the Lydian could point to the reconquest of Africa as a step towards the increase in the empire's greatness under Justinian (*De mag.* 3. 1. 2), and could remind his readers of the day Justinian wore the gold shoulder strap of triumph, the day 'God made Gelimer a prisoner for our empire' (*De mag.* 2. 2. 5). Jordanes too in 551 repeated the Justinianic line that it was a God-given victory (*Get.* 172) and the triumph was portrayed in mosaic in the Chalke of the imperial palace with Justinian and his empress surrounded by the senate (Proc. *Aed.* 1. 10. 16–18)—perhaps with Marcellinus among the depicted senators—and at Justinian's death the scene was embroidered on his funeral vestment.[45] Obviously it remained one of the

---

[45] The vestment is described by Corippus, *In Iustinum* 1. 276–93, part of which depicted

two high-points of the reign, as noted by Menander looking back from his vantage point in the 580s.[46]

On any reckoning the defeat of Gelimer was a significant achievement. The heady days of the late republic and early empire, when all manner of conquered nations trailed along the Sacred Way at Rome behind the victorious general, were long since gone. In the decades prior to Justinian Roman generals rarely smelt the scent of victory at all, preoccupied as they were with holding the line against usurpers and invading tribes. The increasing imperial monopoly of victory and the way an emperor's victoriousness was expressed merely reflected broader developments in public and ceremonial life, especially at Constantinople.[47] Like so much else, the triumph itself took on more the shape of a liturgy, a religious ceremonial in which the whole population could be seen as participating. The triumph was now a telling reflection of continuity and stability in the life of the empire.[48] At Constantinople triumphs had been few and far between: Theodosius I celebrated a victory in 386, Theodosius II was proclaimed victor for defeats over both the Persians and Huns in 422,[49] while Justinian himself revelled in a similar twofold triumph over the Persians and the Bulgars in 530.[50] All these occasions gave rise to spectacles of triumph in the hippodrome. Indeed one observer in the reign of Justinian regarded triumphs as the most splendid manifestation of imperial ceremonial.[51] They were also characterized by statues and dedications and by other forms of enthusiasm and gratitude.

The triumph of Justinian in 534 must also have given rise to many imperial encomia, both literary and iconographic, even though Belisarius was permitted to share in it—a unique honour.[52] We know of the Chalke mosaic, not to mention the famous gold medallion whose electrotype is in the British Museum[53] but no contemporary panegyric survives. One man's response to this magnificent occasion is to be seen, however, in Marcellinus'

the restoration of Africa to Justinian's empire (1. 285–7) for which see Cameron, Averil (1976), 140–2. Note also the depiction of the triumph on gold vessels: Cor. *Iust.* 3. 121f. with Cameron, Averil (1976), 184.

[46] Men. fr. 5.1 (48–9).
[47] McCormick (1986), 125–9.
[48] MacCormack (1981), 73–8 and Cameron, Averil (1979), 8–9.
[49] Holum (1977), 153–72 and Croke (1977), 347–67.
[50] Croke (1980), 188–95.
[51] Anon. *Strat.* 3. 15
[52] Proc. *Wars* 4. 9. 1–16; Anon. *Strat.* 32. 8.
[53] Toynbee (1944), 183.

continuation of his chronicle which was probably inspired by this very event. The chronicler may not have possessed the grandeur of style and the flourish of the panegyrist; or rather the format of the work scarcely gave an opportunity to display it. His contribution to the triumph and the euphoria which it generated was more modest. The continuation of the chronicle is best construed as the personal response of Marcellinus to the reconquest of Africa, although it should not necessarily be construed as a piece of Justinianic propaganda specifically engineered for the senatorial aristocracy of the capital.[54] There is, nonetheless, an element of propaganda in Marcellinus' notice for he does not mention Belisarius at all; rather he ascribes the victory exclusively to Justinian.

Since Marcellinus' primary aim in continuing his chronicle was to include the triumph of Justinian there is no need to assume that the period to 518 was revised extensively. A few minor alterations were necessary: Pope Hormisdas was now dead (in 523) so the length of his reign could be added (515); the bishop John of Paltos in Syria had been recalled from exile by the emperor Justin (512.9), although this entry may have been included in the original edition of the chronicle in 518; possibly too Marcellinus was able to add the death of Laurence the octogenarian bishop of Lychnidus who came to Constantinople in 516 (516.3), that is, if he died after 518. Certainly, he could now add to his preface the titles he presumably did not possess at the time of the original edition of the chronicle—*comes* and *vir clarissimus*. We can be fairly confident that these few necessary changes comprised the only revisions made in 534 to the first edition, although it has been surmised that Marcellinus' entry on the end of the Roman empire in 476 was only added to the 534 edition after he had discovered it in Cassiodorus' recently compiled *Gothic History*.[55] This is an extremely fragile (and unlikely) hypothesis.

Nevertheless, it has been proposed that the first and second editions are clearly discernible in the manuscript tradition of the chronicle by suggesting that the St Omer MS (S) represents the original edition because the entry on the life of Jerome is not as full as that in the archetypal manuscript (T) in the Bodleian Library, Oxford.[56] This is not, in fact, the case. The shorter ver-

---

[54] As suggested by Irmscher (1964), 471, 474
[55] Gusso (1995), 606–19.
[56] Vaccari (1953), 34.

sion of the life of Jerome in S is actually a summary of the longer version in the other MSS,[57] and one made by the scribe of S or someone in that tradition. The summary version was necessitated by the fact that the preceding entry in S (s.a. 392. 1) had been lengthened because the scribe had added extra details from Orosius to Marcellinus' notice on the death of Valentinian II. The only other abbreviated entries in S occur at the very beginning of the updated edition (s.a. 519), made necessary again by the insertion immediately before of an extra entry (concerning the Anastasian fortress of Dara) and included in the chronicle itself. These abbreviations and interpolations are the work of a later scribe and do not indicate revisions undertaken by Marcellinus himself.[58]

OTHER LITERARY WORKS

We know nothing of Marcellinus' status and whereabouts after 527 except that he continued his chronicle in Constantinople in 534. It was probably after 527 too that he brought to completion the other works credited to him by Cassiodorus: (1) a four-volume work under the title *De temporum qualitatibus et positionibus locorum* (*Inst.* 1. 17. 1); and (2) a detailed work, also in four books, being a description of Constantinople and Jerusalem (*Inst.* 1. 25. 1). It has sometimes been thought that Cassiodorus is here referring to one and the same work by two different descriptions,[59] but this is not necessarily so. Not only are the contents denoted by the titles perfectly distinct, but Cassiodorus who knew all Marcellinus' works at first hand positioned the two works in question here in entirely different categories in his *Institutiones*—one under 'historians', the other under 'cosmographers'. Consequently, although it is not impossible that Cassiodorus is providing two distinct descriptions of the same work, the following discussion proceeds on the assumption of two separate works. When they were written by Marcellinus—whether the 520s (or earlier), 530s or 540s—is simply not known.

[57] Based on the original *de viris illustribus* since S includes the additional comment that the *De viris illustribus* was written *contra Porphyrium et Iulianum Augustum* which comes from the preface to Jerome's work.

[58] Argued in detail in Croke (1984*b*), 77–88.

[59] e.g. Mommsen (1894), 42; Schanz, Hosius, and Krüger (1920), 112; Moricca (1943), 1363; *PLRE* 2. 711 s.v. 'Marcellinus 9'.

De temporum qualitatibus et positionibus locorum

This work does not survive and there is no direct indication of its use or even its existence in the period after Marcellinus and Cassiodorus, which makes it even more difficult to define its scope and contents. However the title is interpreted, it looks like a work which combines two quite different topics. Perhaps therefore there were two books devoted to each topic. If so, then the first two books probably dealt with *qualitates temporum*.

Although this vague title has been rendered by the equally vague 'on the nature of events', the context of the passage in which it occurs (combined with Cassiodorus' use of *tempora*) leads to the conclusion that what Marcellinus was writing about here was literally the 'qualities of times'.[60] This would appear to signify detailed discussion of Christian chronology, that is the chronological subdivision of history and the characterization of individual eras, the age of the world, projected date of the second coming and other similar problems constantly being worked over by Christian scholars in subsequent times. Bede's various chronographical works, for instance, may have stood in the same tradition as these books of Marcellinus. A consideration of such questions would at least account for Cassiodorus' inclusion of this work in the section on 'Christian Historians'.

The other two books 'on the locations of places' must have had a similar purpose in order for both books to be closely coupled as a work of 'Christian History'. Yet again, the precise content of these books has to be surmised. They may have provided some sort of guide to Christian topography and onomastics, biblical and ecclesiastical. In any event, Cassiodorus certainly gives the impression that the 'locations of places' were determined not just from books but also from Marcellinus' own travels (*Inst.* 1. 17. 2: *itineris sui*), and the very title suggests that what characterized each place in these books was its precise location (*De positionibus locorum*).

A perfect example of what such a description may have looked like is the entry on the foundation of Dara to be found in editions of Marcellinus' chronicle and which begins 'Dara a city of this kind was founded in Mesopotamia. Dara, a certain estate located 60 miles south from Amida and fifteen miles west from the city of

---

[60] Croke (1984*b*), 77–88.

Nisibis . . .' (s.a. 518). Although normally taken to be an integral part of the chronicle itself this Dara entry clearly does not belong to that work. Moreover, it occurs in only a single manuscript of the chronicle (S) and is located between the end of the original edition of the chronicle (518) and the first year of the updated version (519). It is curious that such an important account of Dara should be one of the only two additions made to the chronicle in the S tradition. All in all, it is compelling to think that the main reason for its inclusion in the chronicle is because it was written by the same person—Marcellinus. This, together with the locational nature of its introductory sentence, suggests that the description of Dara in S almost certainly represents the only extant fragment of Marcellinus' work *De temporum qualitatibus et positionibus locorum*. The scribe who originally added this entry to his copy of the chronicle may have taken it from Marcellinus' original work or maybe from some later collection of extracts in which it was included. In any case it is not necessary to suppose that there must have been a copy of the work at St Omer in the eleventh century, although that is possible. Finally, bearing in mind Cassiodorus' contention that this work was based on Marcellinus' own travels, one may well conclude that what we have here is an eyewitness account of the Anastasian fortress.[61] Indeed, as explained below, a case can be made in favour of Marcellinus having toured Roman Mesopotamia.

On the Cities of Constantinople and Jerusalem

Like the work on times and places, the four volumes of the detailed work on Constantinople and Jerusalem do not survive and we have no indication of their use by any subsequent writer. Cassiodorus had a copy in his Vivarium monastery catalogued under the heading of 'cosmographers' (*Inst.* 1. 25). It is possible that Bede had access to Marcellinus' work at Jarrow in the eighth century since it was almost certainly among the numerous manuscripts there. Moreover, it was probably contained in the magnificently worked *Codex cosmographorum* which had originally been brought to Northumbria from Rome and which was exchanged for a large piece of King Aldfrid's land.[62] Apart from Bede, there

---

[61] Croke (1984*b*), 82 ff.

[62] Bede, *Vita Abbatum* 15. This particular *codex* may well have belonged originally to Cassiodorus and held in his Vivarium library (argued by Courcelle (1969), 395).

is one definite trace of the work. In a letter written in the twelfth century to the abbot of the monastery of Tegernsee (south of Munich) a request was made to send their copy of this particular work of Marcellinus.[63] When the monastery was dissolved in 1803 its library passed to the Hofsbibliothek in Munich but no trace of the manuscript containing the work of Marcellinus can now be found. So, once again the contents and structure of the work have to be inferred.

Cassiodorus does not say how the four books on Constantinople and Jerusalem were divided up but it is reasonable to suppose that there were two books devoted to each city. The books were not perhaps lengthy—Cassiodorus calls them *libelli*—though scrupulously detailed (*minutissima ratione*). Marcellinus was no doubt capable of compiling a detailed first-hand account of Constantinople and its regions. He lived there for a long time and knew the city well. From the chronicle itself a considerable body of important information about the physical appearance of the city in the early sixth century can be extracted (discussed in detail in Chapter 4).

Despite the loss of Marcellinus' description of Constantinople it may be possible to gain some impression of its general character from similar works which do survive. For example, there is the *Notitia Urbis Constantinopolitanae* which dates from the time of Theodosius II,[64] but which in at least one reference work is thought to be part of Marcellinus' lost books on Constantinople.[65] It begins with a short preface and then describes each of the fourteen regions of the city in turn: their extent and contents including the number of baths, streets, and private residences. Marcellinus' work may have been similar in scope but perhaps more detailed on the topography of the different regions. Above all, if it was anything like his other works, it may have been constructed with a particular religious or ecclesiastical slant, that is to say a concentration on churches and monasteries, and/or the function of specific areas and buildings in the well-developed religious cere-

---

[63] *Epistulae ad Tegernseenses* 83 in *Codex Diplomatico-Historico Epistolaris* [*Thesaurus Anecdotorum*, vi] (ed. B. Pez), Augsburg 1729, 53: 'E. to B. [the names are omitted] *Rogo benivolentiam tuam, dilectissime, ut aliquos ex subiectis mihi transmittere dignetis . . . Marcellinum de situ Hierosolymorum et Constantinopolitanorum*'.

[64] Ed. O. Seeck (Berlin 1876).

[65] Dekkers (1961), 507 n. 1270 ff., cf., Riese (1878), xxxiii.

monial of the city and its Christian shrines.[66] If it was not like the *Notitia* then perhaps Marcellinus' account of Constantinople was similar in character and detail to the works of some of the later 'patriographers' whose descriptions of the monuments and topography of Constantinople still survive.[67] Such works, that of Hesychius for example,[68] already existed in the age of Marcellinus.

The lost books on Jerusalem are less difficult to characterize for there still exists a substantial body of descriptions of Jerusalem and other holy places which are largely the work of early Christian pilgrims, so that Marcellinus' description may have resembled, for example, pseudo-Eucherius' letter to Faustus *de situ Hierosolimae*.[69] The geographical and historical setting of the Old and New Testaments, the *terra sancta* or Holy Land, became of increasing interest as the teaching and knowledge of Christian scriptures spread throughout the Roman world. Journeys of devoted pilgrims to this area prior to the fourth century are recorded but the real impulse for the establishment of systematic pilgrimages came with the first alliance of church and state in the early fourth century.[70]

The Palestinian Eusebius of Caesarea knew the Holy Land well and had long been interested in it before he came to know Constantine, and it was under his influence that Constantine undertook his building programme in Jerusalem and nearby. Experts and materials, not to mention funds, were sent by the emperor to Jerusalem for building churches at Bethlehem and the Mount of Olives.[71] At the same time Constantine's mother Helena established a new model of piety in the form of the elaborate imperial pilgrimage to the Holy Land.[72] Thereafter, the pace of pilgrimage picked up as more and more pilgrims began to arrive from both east and west, by sea as well as overland to Constantinople, thence across the harsh region of Anatolia into Syria and on to Palestine. This was precisely the route followed by a pilgrim

---

[66] Maraval (1985), 92–101 and 401–11.
[67] Ed. Preger (1901).
[68] Cf. Cameron, Averil and Herrin (1984), 3.
[69] Ed. I. Fraipont, *Itineraria et alia geographica* (*CCL* 175A), 237–43.
[70] Maraval (1985), *passim*.
[71] Eusebius, *Vita Constantini* 33. 25–41. For Constantine's building activities in the Holy Land: Armstrong (1976), 3–17.
[72] Hunt (1982), 31 ff.; Holum (1990), 66–81.

from Bordeaux in 333 just a few years after Helena first arrived in the Holy Land.[73]

By the late fourth century the Holy Land had come to support a large number of pious persons; some itinerant, others permanent. Naturally enough it was only the well endowed who could sustain themselves and their retinue on such a long and costly journey so it is no surprise to find that it was Roman aristocratic households that were represented in Jerusalem and elsewhere at this time.[74] Nonetheless, it gradually became easier for others to participate in the prized experience of having stood where Jesus stood, and having prayed where he prayed, thereby enabling yet others on the pilgrim's return to share vicariously in the pilgrim's spiritual rewards.[75] Gradually there arose special patterns of hospitality and sustenance provided mainly by clergy and monks. Indeed in the life of the church pilgrimage became an important institution with profound and widespread effects observable in the rapidly evolving church calendar, as well as in the increasingly biblical framework of the liturgy.[76] Pilgrimage had a striking effect on Palestine too especially as an increasing source of wealth.[77] The lavish spending of rich and noble patrons like Melania and the empress Eudocia, wife of Theodosius II, gave rise to a flourishing building activity in the Holy Land in the mid-fifth century.[78] This in turn probably made pilgrimage even more attractive and popular.

Most of the pilgrims who set out on the journey to Palestine in the fourth and fifth centuries were tracing a well-worn circuit, and they already set out with a fair idea of the topography of the Holy Land, taking with them a guide, a written account of the area and its shrines together with a map.[79] Amongst these might be included the conveniently entitled *Onomasticon* of Eusebius and its map, either in the original or in Jerome's translation.[80] The most instructive and interesting of the extant guides, however, are those

---

[73] *Itinerarium Burdigalense* (ed. P. Geyer and O. Curtz) in *Itineraria et alia geographica* (*CCL* 175), 1–26.

[74] Hunt (1982), 155ff.; Walker (1989).   [75] MacCormack (1990), 7–40.

[76] Hunt (1982), 107–24.   [77] Ibid. (1982), 137ff.

[78] *V. Mel.* 40 (monastery on Mount of Olives), 57 (martyrium of St Stephen). For Melania in Jerusalem: Gorce, (1962), 43–4, 72–4. For Eudocia's building activities in the Holy Land and the sources: Armstrong (1969), 17–30. More generally but still relevant: Cameron, Alan (1982), 212–91; Holum (1982), 183–6.

[79] Wilkinson (1976), 95 and (1977), 16–20.

[80] Ed. E. Klostermann, *Eusebius Werke*, iii (GCS 11, 1904).

of Egeria (written in the early 380s for her community in Spain) which describes in detail her journeys through the Holy Land itself, plus her visits to Egypt and Edessa,[81] and of the pilgrim Antoninus from Piacenza (written *c*.570) which covers much the same range.

These types of handbooks for future travellers could be compiled from the accounts narrated by previous pilgrims, such as the Gallic bishop Arculf who came to the Irish foundation of Iona and narrated his account to the abbot Adomnán (d. 704) who, in turn, composed it as the *de locis sanctis*;[82] or else compiled entirely from written sources (including maps) like that of the sedentary Bede.[83] There were many such accounts in circulation. Adomnán, for example, knew of several which he chose not to consider in his own work,[84] and it is conceivable that among the treatises on Jerusalem known to him was that of Marcellinus. After all, the chronicle of Marcellinus and other Latin works written in Constantinople in the early sixth century, such as Priscian's Grammar, were being copied in Irish monasteries at the time of Adomnán.[85]

As the pattern of pilgrimage developed yet further in the fifth century, travellers to the Holy Land came in search not only of biblical sites but also to see and gain the blessings of the increasing number of holy men scattered throughout the region. It was in these solitaries that spiritual life was concentrated, and after the Council of Chalcedon (451) they adopted firm stances on fundamental theological questions. The inevitable consequence of this situation was that the local churches at Jerusalem, Bethlehem and elsewhere became entangled in the disputes of the monks, as did the pilgrims themselves. Nonetheless, following the death of Eudocia in 460 until the earlier part of the sixth century, it appears that there was a decline in patronage and in the numbers of pilgrims to Palestine, although the later fifth century seems to have been a busy period for the expansion and construction of

---

[81] Ed. R. Franceschini and R. Weber, in *Itineraria et alia geographica*, i (*CCL* 175), 37–90 which should be read in conjunction with the annotated translation and introduction by Wilkinson (1971).

[82] Ed. L. Bieler, *Itineraria et alia geographica*, i (*CCL* 175), 183–4.

[83] Ed. P. Geyer, *Itineraria et alia geographica*, i (*CCL* 175), 251–80.

[84] I. I (*Itineraria et alia geographica*, i. 185).

[85] Bieler (1963), 43, 94, 124; Smyth (1984), 124 ff. For the general context of direct contacts between Constantinople and Ireland: Hillgarth (1966), 444–5, and Ch. 8, below.

monasteries.[86] Monks also provided a vital link in the process of identifying and promoting biblical sites.[87]

This situation then seems to have changed in the time of Marcellinus when we again catch a glimpse of the frequent traffic between Constantinople and Jerusalem, and for this we are mainly dependent on the saints lives of Cyril of Scythopolis.[88] John the Hesychast, for example, arrived in Constantinople at the end of the reign of Zeno (474–91) and proceeded from there to Jerusalem (Cyr. Scyth. *Vita Johannis Hesychasti* 4). Some time later Basilina, a deaconess of Hagia Sophia, brought her nephew to John in Jerusalem (ibid.), while the monk Theodosius received a visit in the early sixth century from Acacius, an *illustris* who had travelled from Constantinople to meet the holy man (Cyr. Scyth. *Vita Theodosii* 3). Even in the post-Chalcedonian period of theological difficulty emperors continued the tradition of building in the Holy Land: hospices, monasteries, and churches, the most startling of which is perhaps the Church of the Virgin which Justinian built in Jerusalem and portions of which have recently been discovered.[89] As the numbers of pilgrims began to increase again so did the number who fell ill, like Antoninus of Piacenza.[90] In 531, therefore, Sabas journeyed to Constantinople to petition Justinian to build a new hospital for them in Jerusalem and in return the holy man promised the emperor the reconquest of Africa and Rome (Cyr. Scyth. *Vita Sabae* 70–1).

It is against this background that we should view the two extant pilgrim descriptions which date from the time of Marcellinus: the *De situ terrae sanctae* of a certain Theodosius written in the reign of Anastasius,[91] and the *Breviarius de Hierosolyma*. The latter is anonymous and could conceivably be part of Marcellinus' lost work. It survives in two separate versions stemming from a common

[86] Among the identifiable remains collected in Murphy-O'Connor (1980) note those at Khirbet Mird (221), Khan el-Ahmar (216–17), Mar Saba (242–3), Har Hordos (205–6), the monastery of George of Koziba (254–5) and the monasteries of the desert. Background in Chitty (1966), 65–100.

[87] Sivan (1990), 54–65.

[88] Chitty (1966), 101–42 for details.

[89] Avigad (1977), 145–51.

[90] Antoninus Placentinus, *Itinerarium* 46 (*CCL* 175).

[91] Ed. P. Geyer, *Itineraria et alia geographica*, i (*CCL* 175), 115–25; the author is normally thought to have been an African (e.g. Geyer, 114) because he speaks of Arianism as 'the religion of the Vandals' (c.14). This may be so, but in any case his details on Urbicius (c.28), the construction of Dara (c.29) and the deacon Eudoxius (c.30) suggest that Theodosius wrote in Constantinople.

original and may have been designed for public display as a means of actually attracting pilgrims.[92] The *De situ terrae sanctae*, on the other hand seems to have been more of a working notebook based on a mixture of written sources and detailed local maps.[93] At the very least, both these compilations testify to an interest among the Latin-speaking community of Constantinople in the time of Marcellinus in undertaking pilgrimages to the Bible lands, exemplified by the general Hypatius who was a fellow-Illyrian and nephew of the emperor Anastasius.[94] The popularity of pilgrimage was maintained by a steady flow of pilgrims from the west who, like Egeria in the late fourth century, used Constantinople as their base. Indeed, as the account of Adomnán makes clear, Constantinople itself had become an integral part of the pilgrimage.[95] Marcellinus' two books on Constantinople would doubtless have been beneficial to the pilgrim's time in the imperial capital.

There is every likelihood that Marcellinus' pilgrimage (for that is what it must have been) took him all over the eastern provinces of the empire, as it did for other pilgrims.[96] In the late fourth century Egeria journeyed out to Carrhae, the city of Abraham, where she discovered that monks had been attracted to the city from far and wide in order to celebrate a special local feast.[97] In Marcellinus' own day, if not his own work, the author of the *De situ terrae sanctae* reached up to Melitene and evidently to Dara. His account records precisely the distances from Edessa to Dara and from Dara to Amida 'which is on the Persian border'.[98] The inclusion of this data would only appear to make sense if it was used by pilgrims in their journeys. Later in the sixth century the itinerary of Antoninus of Piacenza was much clearer: from Damascus to Heliopolis and from there to Emesa where the head of John the Baptist was discovered (as explained by Marcellinus, s.a. 453), then from Epiphaneia to Apamea and then Antioch. From Antioch Antoninus went to Chalcis and from there to Carrhae; from Carrhae he took in Barbalissus and Sura, the site of much

---

[92] Ed. R. Weber, *Itineraria et alia geographica*, i (*CCL* 175), 109–12; there is no direct indication of where this work was written.

[93] Sources: Wilkinson (1977), 184–92; maps: Tsafrir (1986), 129–45.

[94] Cyr. Scyth. *Vita Sabae* 56, with Greatrex (1996), 123.

[95] Adomnán, *De locis sanctis* 3. 1–5 (*CCL* 175A. 227–34). For the role of Constantinople in the pilgrimages of late antiquity: Matthews (1975), 137–9; Maraval (1985), 92–102.

[96] Maraval (1985), 84–8 and 329 ff.

[97] Egeria 20. 5–6 (cf. 48. 1, 49. 1–3) with Hunt (1982), 60–1.

[98] *De situ terrae sanctae*, 32.

suffering by Sergius and Bacchus. In this context it would not be at all unusual if a pilgrimage undertaken by Marcellinus extended along the traditional and busy trade routes of the empire and introduced him to the key cities of Syria and Mesopotamia.

Cassiodorus informs us (*Inst.* 1. 17. 2) that Marcellinus' books on the locations of places were based on his own travels (*itineris sui tramitem*) and we have seen that this may have taken him as far as Dara, especially since other pilgrims appear to have been there. It seems reasonable to presume that his detailed books on Jerusalem were also largely the product of his own observation.[99] He will of course have had access to written documents as well: not only earlier pilgrim accounts and the *Onomasticon* of Eusebius but also maps of the city such as that copied in mosaic at Madeba,[100] as well as that of Julius Honorius, a cosmographer recommended, in conjunction with Marcellinus, by Cassiodorus.[101]

Although Marcellinus' books on Jerusalem do not survive there is some indication in the chronicle of his interest in and knowledge of the area which, if he had not already completed the journey by the time the chronicle was written, he probably acquired from others who had. Of all the relic translations from Jerusalem to Constantinople in the fifth century Marcellinus seems particularly interested in those of Stephen. Although he does not mention the transfer of relics to Pulcheria's new church of St Stephen in 421 he does record (copying Gennadius) how Lucianus discovered them first in 415 and then how Orosius brought them back to the west. In 439 he mentions the return of the empress Eudocia from Jerusalem with other relics of Stephen and goes on to say that they are currently venerated in the church of St Laurence. Marcellinus must be alluding here to the liturgy held in the church on 16 September each year, which commemorated the original translation of the relics to Constantinople in 439.[102]

Following a mysterious turn of events in 443 the empress Eudocia was banished by Theodosius from Constantinople and retired to Jerusalem once more. This is the background to the story which Marcellinus, alone of the extant accounts, tells: her

[99] *PLRE* 2. 711 but not necessarily a journey from Constantinople to Jerusalem.
[100] Gold (1958), 50–71.
[101] *Inst.* 25. 1 with the text in Riese (1878), 21 ff.
[102] *SEC* 52. 4–6. The church of St Laurence was completed by Pulcheria in 453 (Marcell. s.a. 453. 5) and the relics of Stephen brought there only then. For the church itself: Janin (1969), 300–4.

ministers, the priest Severus and the deacon John were put to death on the orders of the emperor by the *comes domesticorum* Saturninus. Then, continues Marcellinus:

Eudocia, spurred on by some grief or other, murdered Saturninus forthwith. On the command of her husband the emperor she was immediately stripped of her royal attendants and remained in the city of Jerusalem until her death. (444. 4)

Under the year 419 Marcellinus notes the appearance of Christ on the Mount of Olives:

Our Lord Jesus Christ, who is always and everywhere present, appeared from a cloud above the Mount of the Olives near Jerusalem. At that time both male and female of many tribes of the neighbouring races were awe-struck, not so much by what they saw as what they heard, and believed. They were cleansed in the sacred fountain of Christ and there shone out the Saviour's cross which, through divine command, was immediately impressed on the tunics of all those baptized. (419. 3)

This epiphany and subsequent appearance of the shining crosses on the tunics of the baptized is not otherwise recorded. Nor is its exact relevance to the chronicle clear. However, it must have had some interest and significance for the chronicler's audience. In this respect, it best fits into the category of events whose importance in the chronicle derives from the fact that they were commemorated annually at Constantinople in the time of Marcellinus. We have seen how this accounts for the entry on the Vandal persecution in 484 and Eudocia's return to Constantinople in 439 with some relics of St Stephen. Others will be discussed later. The appearance of Christ on the Mount of Olives in 419 may also have been celebrated liturgically each year at Constantinople in the time of Marcellinus. At least we know that on 7 May each year the Byzantines celebrated a remarkably similar occurrence in the reign of Constantius II.[103] It could even be that Marcellinus was somehow mistaken in assigning this event to 419, that is, about a century too late. In any case, it seems most likely that some such liturgical function explains Marcellinus' mention of the apparition which itself illustrates the role of the Holy Land in the religious life of the sixth century Byzantines.

---

[103] *SEC* 661. 28–662. 27. For the original event: *Cons. Const.* 351. 4 (237) with Hunt (1982), 155–6.

The discovery and veneration of relics along with divine apparitions—Marcellinus mentions (from Orosius) Ambrose's appearance to Mascezel the brother of the rebel Gildo (398. 4)—were an important component of the spiritual culture of a man like Marcellinus. This explains why the longest entry in the chronicle is the discovery and transmission of the head of John the Baptist in 453. Although this is traceable to a written source, it reflects originally the oral traditions circulating in the world of the Holy Land pilgrim. Furthermore, as with Christ's appearance on the Mount of Olives in 419, this discovery of John's head had an established role in the religious life of the Byzantines (including Marcellinus) because it was remembered each year with a liturgy on 24 February, the date given in the chronicle for the original reception of the head in 453 (*SEC* 485. 29–487. 7).

Specific and detailed information relating to Jerusalem and the Holy Land is otherwise rare in the chronicle and it is not safe to assume that it could only have been acquired from a first-hand knowledge of the topography and history of Palestine. There is Marcellinus' confused (or textually corrupt) reference to a rebellion in 418 and under 516 he is able to locate precisely the spot where Helias the orthodox bishop of Jerusalem died—'a village called Haila'. Marcellinus, therefore, at some stage (probably before 518) made a journey to the east which took in Jerusalem. On his return to Constantinople (probably some years after) he would have written a detailed description of the city which does not survive. Despite its loss his interest in Palestine is clearly evident in some of the chronicle's entries, as is his familiarity with Constantinople. What gave unity to a four-volume work on Constantinople and Jerusalem would appear to be its focus on the cities as centres of religious life and religious ceremonial. Jerusalem and its environs had long been a sacred city and as the location of Christ's last days provided a natural locus for the development of liturgy, especially stational liturgy, and pilgrimage. From the late fourth century Constantinople too became a holy city for the Christians with its collection of relics and shrines incorporated into a rapidly developing liturgical and ceremonial life.

To recapitulate: Marcellinus came to Constantinople, possibly with local army experience behind him, around the turn of the sixth century from his native Illyricum and spent the remainder of his life in the imperial capital. His precise occupation throughout this lengthy period is not known, except that within the period 520 to 527 or so he held a position as *cancellarius* to his fellow-Illyrian Justinian. This post may have been earned by the popularity of his chronicle, which first appeared in 518/19 and which covered the period from 379 to the death of Anastasius. In 534, in the buoyant atmosphere of Justinian's reconquest of Africa, he continued his chronicle to that year. We also know of two other detailed works (each in four books) from the pen of Marcellinus but they do not survive, their date is unknown and their contents can only be inferred. Furthermore, for the volumes on the locations of places and the topography of Jerusalem Marcellinus drew on material collected, it seems, from his own travels. While these were probably concentrated in the Holy Land there is reason to believe that his pilgrim journey took him all the way out to Dara. All we are left with, then, is the chronicle.

2

Marcellinus and Illyricum

According to Cassiodorus (*Inst.* 1.17.2), Marcellinus was an Illyrian (*Illyricianus*) and this information must be considered accurate. After all, Cassiodorus was familiar with the full corpus of Marcellinus' work; more importantly, he was in close contact with the Latin-speaking community of Constantinople amongst whom the chronicle found its first readers. Nor is it impossible that in Constantinople in the late 540s/early 550s Cassiodorus had actually met Marcellinus, or people who had known him (if the chronicler was now deceased). Yet, even without Cassiodorus' statement we would be compelled to think Marcellinus an Illyrian simply because he has so much to say about Illyricum in the chronicle; and what he does say is generally of a precise and relatively full nature, suggesting knowledge of local personalities, geography and affairs. Henceforward, the task is to set out the Illyrian background and context of the chronicle; first, by defining exactly what area Marcellinus and Cassiodorus understood to be encompassed by 'Illyricum', and then by amplifying and explaining the information in the chronicle in order to discover what Marcellinus' native region meant to him. His Illyrian background and identity governed the selection of material for his chronicle, shaped the story he told, and reflected his own personal perspective on events in that region.

DEFINING ILLYRICUM

To understand late Roman Illyricum, and to evaluate its importance to Marcellinus, it is essential to begin by defining the geographical scope of the area. Illyricum was, however, of different size and shape at different times in the Roman empire. Even in the period under detailed inspection here—from Theodosius I to Justinian—'Illyricum' denoted both a diocese (of the western prefecture of Italy) and a prefecture.[1] Two questions, therefore, arise

[1] The various complex shifts of hegemony in Illyricum are traceable through Burns (1994), 46–52 (with reference to earlier literature).

at the outset: what does Cassiodorus mean by *Illyricianus?* How can the 'Illyricum' of Marcellinus, as evident in the chronicle, be defined? *Illyricianus* is not a Cassiodoran fabrication. A later contemporary of Marcellinus, the chronicler Victor, an exiled bishop from Tunnuna near Carthage but who wrote in Constantinople, dubs as *Illyricianus* both the emperor Anastasius from Dyrrachium (Durres) in the province of Epirus Nova and Justin from Bederiana near Scupi (Skopje) in Dardania.[2] Both Epirus Nova and Dardania were provinces in the prefecture of Illyricum. That *Illyricianus* signifies the prefecture is confirmed by the usage of both Marcellinus himself (s.a. 479. 1; 499. 1; 516. 1; 530) and Jordanes (*Get.* 300) in Latin, as well as by that of their contemporary John Malalas (18. 26 (442. 15)) in Greek; that is to say, it is a conventional and precise administrative designation for the whole area of the prefecture, just as we find it in the official usage of public documents.[3] Consequently, Cassiodorus' view of Marcellinus as *Illyricianus* is someone belonging by birth or residence to the prefecture of Illyricum, the territory extending southwards from the Danube to Crete with its civil and ecclesiastical capital at Thessalonike in the province of Macedonia Prima. It has nothing to do with Illyrian language or ethnicity.

Illyricum was a diverse area geographically and linguistically (and therefore culturally), with no apparent unity except for administrative purposes. This prefecture which comprised the dioceses of Dacia (containing the provinces of Moesia I, Praevalitana, Dardania, Dacia Ripensis and Dacia Mediterranea) and Macedonia (containing the provinces of Epirus Nova, Epirus Vetus, Achaea, Thessaly, Macedonia and Crete) was 'Illyricum' in sixth-century Constantinople.[4] Bordering Illyricum on the east was the diocese of Thrace, part of the Prefecture of the East under the jurisdiction of its Praetorian Prefect who was based at Constantinople. This diocese consisted of the provinces of Scythia, Moesia II, Thracia, Haemimontus, Rhodope and

---

[2] Anastasius: Vict. Tonn. 491. 1 (II. 191); Justin: Vict. Tonn. 518. 1 (II. 196).

[3] e.g. *CTh* 10. 10. 25 (10 Dec. 408) and throughout the *Notitia Dignitatum.* where *Illyricianus* denotes army units originally formed in the prefecture of Illyricum (e.g. *Or.* 32–7). The designation of this broad section of the Balkans occupied by several different tribes as 'Illyricum' has a long tradition (cf. App. *Illyrike* 1. 1–6).

[4] *ND Or.* 3. 5–19. According to the *Notitia* both Dacia and Macedonia included 'pars Macedoniae Salutaris'. What this means has not been resolved. We can do no better than the solution of Jones, A. H. M. (1964, 1420) that the province had recently been suppressed when the *Notitia* was drawn up.

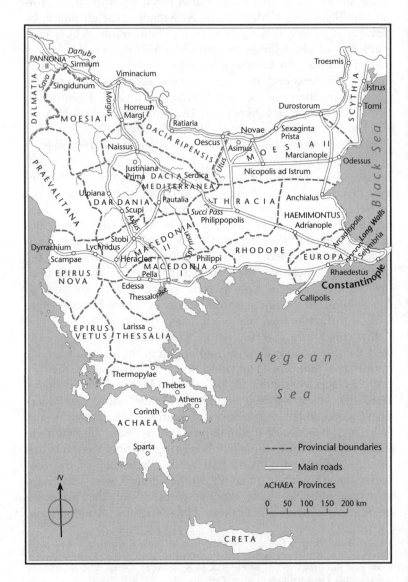

Map 1. The Illyricum of Marcellinus

Europa. In the later Roman period the distinction between Latin-speaking Illyricum and Greek-speaking Thrace was not always clear, especially in the overlapping area between them. Adjacent to the prefecture of Illyricum in the west was the diocese of Pannonia which formed part of the prefecture of Italy. Thessalonike was, after 441, the prefectural capital of Illyricum and it had been the episcopal capital of the so-called 'papal vicariate' of Illyricum since the formation of the new prefecture.[5] This is the administrative situation in the time of Marcellinus, and as we find it set down in the exactly contemporary *Synekdemos* of Hierocles.[6]

Precisely where within this area lay the *patria* of Marcellinus is beyond discovery, although a reasonable conjecture is possible. Marcellinus denotes by 'Illyricum' the general area of the prefecture (e.g. 441. 3, 442. 2, 481. 1, 516. 3, 517, 530) and he does refer to the individual provinces by name: Dacia Ripensis (447. 5, 483); Macedonia I and II (482. 2, 517); Thessaly (482. 2, 517), Dardania (518. 1), Epirus Vetus (517) and Pannonia I and II (427. 1). Besides the provinces, Marcellinus mentions many of the cities of Illyricum: Serdica (516. 3), Naissus (441. 3, 516. 3), Pautalia (516. 3), Singidunum (441. 3), Lychnidus (516. 3) and Larissa (482. 2). The distribution of these places mentioned is relatively scattered. There is no particular locational cluster to suggest any special interest in a given area. Furthermore, it is not possible to narrow down Marcellinus' Balkan Latin,[7] nor is there evident in the chronicle any first-hand geographical description which might provide a clue to the precise location of Marcellinus' origin. A close approximation may be deduced, however, from his rather detailed account of the earthquake which destroyed Scupi in 518. This is one of the lengthiest entries in the chronicle, a fact which by itself suggests that the event was of special interest to Marcellinus. He tells us that twenty-four *castella* were overturned in the quake—two lost all inhabitants, four lost half their inhabitants and buildings, eleven lost a third of each, seven lost a quarter of their structures and all their occupants. Scupi was utterly ruined although most of its citizens had already fled in the face of

[5] For the complexities surrounding the establishment of the papal vicariate see Greenslade (1945), 17–30.

[6] Ed. E. Honigmann (1939). The *Synekdemos* is basically a document of the time of Theodosius II with later revisions (Jones, A. H. M. (1971), 502–3) and written about 527/8.

[7] Mihaescu (1978), 9–10.

the invading Bulgars and Slavs. Mountains were levelled, trees uprooted and—so Marcellinus continues—a cleavage opened up in the earth thirty miles long and twelve feet deep. He concludes with a description of what happened at an obscure *castellum* called Sarnunto.

As in modern times, earthquakes in antiquity were events of special significance. Not only were they interpreted as clear and codified manifestations of divine displeasure, invariably giving rise to widespread penitential propitiation, but they also provided the imperial court with a customary opportunity to display *philanthropia* and imperial largess. Special envoys would be sent, and a detailed report (*relatio*) received on the disaster and its impact.[8] Usually the report would be publicly 'announced', in all its detail, at Constantinople.[9] Marcellinus' account would appear to resemble what we might expect from such an earthquake report. The precise detail of this description is striking. It has no counterpart in the late Latin chronicles but it is not unlike John Malalas' account of the quake at Antioch in 526 (17. 16 (419. 5–421. 1)) and other earthquake notices in Byzantine chronicles. The reason for its inclusion in the chronicle of Marcellinus was probably its special interest to him because it concerned the region of Illyricum he knew best, that is to say, he probably came from this very region himself. It may well be that Marcellinus made personal enquiries of the office of the governor of Dardania, or acquired this information from some fellow-Illyrian in the vicinity at the time, or simply utilized the official report announced in Constantinople. In any case, his account reads very like an official damage report of some sort. It may even be that he was himself involved in an imperial mission to Dardania in the aftermath of the earthquake in 518.

If Marcellinus did not come from the area around Scupi then there is insufficient information to propose alternative locations. If, as suggested in the previous chapter, there were some local affinities between Marcellinus and his employer Justinian then he may have come from the emperor's home-town of Tauresium (near the emperor's new metropolis of Justiniana Prima (Carichin Grad)) south of Naissus. Be that as it may, on several occasions Marcellinus makes detailed reference to rivers and towns in

---

[8] Leopold (1986), 816–36.
[9] *CTh* 8. 11. 4 (2 Feb. 383), with McCormick (1986), 190–6.

Illyricum and Thrace. There is the Margus (Morava) which flows down past Naissus to the east and on to the Danube. In 505 it was along this river, at Horreum Margi (Cuprija) to be precise, that a battle was fought between the Gepid, Mundo, and one of Marcellinus' heroes, the Roman general Sabinianus, with disastrous results from the Illyrian point of view. Marcellinus adds that Sabinianus fled to the *castellum* called Nato (505). There is no other trace of this fort and the place cannot be otherwise identified. Likewise, two other rivers provide a fair indication of the precise local information Marcellinus had at his disposal, either from personal knowledge or from written sources. Arnigisclus, Marcellinus reports, was killed in 447 near the river Utus (Vit) in Dacia Ripensis (447.5). This river flows into the Danube from the Haemus range and after the reconstitution of Dacia by the emperor Aurelian in the 270s it provided the eastern boundary of the new Dacia Ripensis. Finally, there is the river 'Tzurta' in Thrace.

Marcellinus' entry describes how in 499 the *magister militum* for Illyricum, Aristus, set out on campaign with a large army and was defeated in battle by the Bulgars 'beside the river Tzurta' (499. 1). This is one of the chronicle's more interesting entries, for reasons which will emerge later. The reading 'Tzurta' must be taken as accurate; yet, except for Jordanes' 'Tzortam' (*Rom.* 356)—probably copied directly from Marcellinus or his source—there is no other recorded reference to this river and it cannot be located at all. Perhaps it was one of the tributaries of the Hebrus (Maritza) which ran more or less parallel with the Balkan highway, at least that part from Serdica (Sofia) to Adrianople (Edirne). That must certainly have been the route taken by Aristus in 499, whether he departed from Naissus, the headquarters of the *magister militum per Illyricum,* or from Constantinople.

Marcellinus claims in his preface that he will devote most attention to the eastern empire. In analysing his information on Illyricum, however, much would be lost if attention was confined solely to Illyricum, strictly speaking. Marcellinus also provides some detailed information on events in the diocese of Thrace, and we will consider these too in discussing Illyricum. There is a prescription of time as well. To make full sense of the Illyrian background to Marcellinus' chronicle, attention needs to be directed briefly towards characterizing Illyricum (and the diocese of

Thrace) before focusing on the period covered by the chronicle of
Marcellinus, when a rapid change in the character and fortunes
of the area took place.

ECONOMY AND SOCIETY

In the Roman world Illyricum was never a precisely defined
region and its area was immense. The Illyricum of Marcellinus
extended from modern-day Hungary to the Aegean and within it
could be observed a variety of topography, resources, and settlement patterns. To characterize it as uniform in any of these
respects would be misleading. Progressing eastwards, the fertile
valleys of the Sava and Drava give way to the thick forest of
Moesia and Dacia Mediterranea as the road from Sirmium via
Singidunum on the Danube threads through the narrow passes
where the rough ridges of the Haemus and Rhodope begin to co-
alesce. Then it opens out suddenly into the plain land of Thrace
running on down to the shores of the Propontis and the Black Sea;
while slightly to the north the Balkan mountain ridge divides
Thrace from the expansive grainlands of the lower Danube, wind-
ing its way through the Wallachian plain to its delta. To the south
and west lay the rugged and less accessible uplands of Macedonia
and Epirus and the fertile littoral around the mouth of the
Strymon and Axius rivers.[10]

This diverse region was always of crucial strategic importance
which explains why it was the continual focal point of the struggle
for the empire, both internal and external. While the Goths and
Huns were being challenged along the Danube in the fourth century, up and down the great Balkan highway successive emperors
beat down one usurpation after another. It was also the empire's
main recruiting ground and this was one of the key factors in
the strategic importance of Illyricum; for whoever held sway
in Illyricum held the army and the vital potential to increase
it.[11] Throughout Illyricum the army was ever-present. The
commander-in-chief of the Illyrian army, the *magister militum per
Illyricum*, was based with his immediate troops in Naissus. Under
his command was a series of regional generals or *duces* stationed at

[10] A geographical overview of most of this area can be found in Obolensky (1971), 19–63;
for the Macedonian provinces in particular: Hammond (1967), ch. 1 and (1972), Part I.

[11] Exemplified for the late Roman period in Wozniak (1981), 351–82.

Singidunum (Moesia I) and Ratiaria (Dacia Ripensis). These troops were concentrated along the frontier provinces, as were the *duces* at Novae (Moesia II) and Troesmis (Scythia) under the *magister militum per Thracias*, instituted in the time of Theodosius II and stationed at Marcianople.

Emperors too frequented Illyricum. Throughout the fourth century we frequently catch sight of the imperial retinue en route back and forth from east to west: Constantinople to Trier, Milan and Rome. Generally speaking, the cities along the Danube and the Balkan highway and the Egnatian way were lively and civilized places well laid out and well plumbed. They had paved streets, large churches, theatres, granaries, and many fine houses richly decorated. The same is true of the cities from Thessaly to the Danube on the transverse routes of these two major arteries. In describing these cities we are dependent to a large extent on the literary accounts. Although the archaeological data is accumulating at a rapid rate, at this stage it provides an imbalanced picture.[12]

The strategic and fortified cities along the Danube and the Balkan highway were the key to Illyricum. Sirmium, for example, was the base for all campaigns on the northern frontier; hence emperors frequently wintered there. We are less well informed about the cities on the Danube frontier, although Ratiaria was large and populous.[13] We do not know much about the urban life of Macedonia either, except for Thessalonike where the late Roman walls still stand in a rebuilt form. Thessalonike was an important commercial centre. It boasted an imperial palace and hippodrome as well as a stadium.[14] Philippi too, to judge from the excavated basilicas, was a grand town.[15]

By the late fourth century, when Marcellinus' chronicle begins, this flourishing picture of Illyricum had begun to lose some of its gloss. The Danubian provinces which had been responsible for providing a safe defence were no longer so effective in protecting the empire from attack by tribes across the river. In general, Roman relations with the Marcomanni, Sarmatians, Quadi,

[12] General surveys: Jones, A. H. M. (1971), 1–27 (Thrace); Velkov (1977), Poulter (1992), 99–135. There are no comparable surveys of Macedonia in late antiquity, cf. Whitby (1988), 58.

[13] Velkov (1966), 155–75; (1977), 86; Poulter (1992), 131.

[14] Spieser (1984); Croke (1978a), 251–8; (1981c), 475–83.

[15] For which: Lemerle (1945), 75–84.

Goths, and the various other clans who appeared along the Danube in the period to the end of the fourth century met with mixed success. Treaties were made and broken, attacks occurred—some sporadic, some sustained, some successful, others disastrous. From the second decade of the fifth century the wealthy and elegant cities which thrived in the fourth century were already being required to defend themselves; and the burning of crops and villas brought new hardship to the proprietors of the estates which served the cities. In short, the economy and the landscape were being disrupted and the population itself forced to move into more defensible areas, all of which led the imperial government to devise measures for the security and rehabilitation of the threatened and ravaged area of Illyricum. Their efforts had little enduring success, as we shall see on proceeding to explain Marcellinus' account of his native region written from the security of the eastern capital.

HUNS IN THE CHRONICLE

From Marcellinus' perspective in sixth-century Constantinople, the late-fourth century encounters with the Goths and other tribal groups were relatively remote but still significant because they affected his own fatherland so directly. From 379, where the chronicle begins, frequent mention is made of conflicts in Illyricum and Thrace: Theodosius' victory over the combined forces of Alans, Goths, and Huns in 379, and its victory announcement at Constantinople;[16] the arrival of the Gothic chieftain Athanaric in Constantinople in 381, and his death not long after; the Gothic surrender in 382, and its pronouncement in the capital (*Cons. Const.* 382. 2 (241)); the defeat of the Greuthungi of Odotheus in Thrace in 386, and the celebration of the victory on 12 October; the invasion of Radagaisus and his Goths in 406 and their defeat near Fiesole (406. 2–3); and the sack of Rome by Alaric and his Goths in 410. For all these episodes Marcellinus relies on the history of Orosius but depends on his local Constantinopolitan chronicle source for precise dates.[17] The Goths, meanwhile, had been settled in Moesia, and the Huns

---

[16] Perhaps from Orosius 7. 34. 5 but more likely from a local chronicle, cf. *Cons. Const.* 379. 3 (241).

[17] More detailed analysis and annotation in Croke (1995), 55–70 and Burns (1994), 80–2.

were in both Pannonia and what is now eastern Romania from where Uldin launched his raid in 408. Marcellinus' chronicle provides only a select summary of the Goths' incursions into Illyricum and Thrace in the late fourth/early fifth century, and their encounters with the Romans. Still, these encounters had become important points of interest in the historical memory. They played a role in explaining how the Goths and others had been repulsed by imperial might before becoming settled in the Roman realm.

The Huns are first mentioned by Marcellinus only as part of a larger confederation of tribes defeated by Theodosius I in 379. Their movements in and around Pannonia and the Balkans in the earlier fifth century pass unnoticed in the chronicle. In 421, with the regular troops removed to the eastern frontier, Theodosius II invited some of the Goths in Dacia to settle in Thrace in order to bolster defences there. Shortly after this, in late 421/early 422 the Huns and their Sarmatian allies, by now settled close to the Danube, launched an invasion of Illyricum through the Succi pass and into Thrace. Marcellinus provides our only direct information for this: 'The Huns devastated Thrace' (422. 3).[18] Soon after, a truce was worked out and the Huns and their Sarmatian allies under king Rua returned to Pannonia, whence they were expelled (as we are informed by Marcellinus) in 427.[19] The Goths appear to have remained in Thrace and their progeny were later absorbed into the larger Gothic groups in Thrace.[20]

It was the Hun incursions of the 440s which caused most damage to the Balkan provinces and which Marcellinus, decades later, recorded with some sensibility. In fact his information on the invasions of Illyricum in 441 and of Illyricum and Thrace in 442 remains important in reconstructing the course of events in those years.[21] In particular, Marcellinus enables us to understand that in 441 the incursion of the Huns was confined to Illyricum (as far as Sirmium in one direction and Naissus in another) before a one-year treaty was negotiated with Aspar, while the invasion of

[18] Croke (1977), 347–67 and for events on the eastern frontier: Holum (1977), 153–72 and Croke (1984*a*), 59–74.

[19] Details in Croke (1995), 77.

[20] Heather (1991), 262–3 and (1996), 112, 127.

[21] In general Maenchen-Helfen (1973), 108 ff. and Seeck (1920), 290 ff. are to be preferred to Thompson (1948), who is over-reliant for his chronology on the demonstrably confused account of Theophanes (AM 5942 (102. 13–103. 8)).

the following year followed the Danube road from Ratiaria to Novae before moving onto Nicopolis where the Huns appear to have been halted. Thereupon a peace was negotiated with the *magister officiorum* Nomus.[22] Marcellinus' entry on the invasion of 447, however, highlights the enduring impact of the Huns on the minds of Byzantines:

A mighty war, greater than the previous one, was brought upon us by King Attila. It devastated almost the whole of Europe and cities and forts were invaded and pillaged (447. 2).

From this we gain some sense of the significance and scale of this violent intrusion: it was greater than the previous war and was focused primarily on the province of Europa, that is the province which included the Chersonnese and Constantinople. Moreover, in the phrase 'brought upon us' (*nostris inflictum*) Marcellinus offers a note of personal identification with those who suffered, while in recording the heroic death of the *magister militum* Arnigisclus, he pays tribute to the general's bravery: 'Arnigisclus the Master of the Soldiery, fought bravely in Dacia Ripensis alongside the Utum river and was killed by King Attila, when most of the enemy had been destroyed' (447. 5).

The terms of the peace were agreed on by Anatolius the new *magister militum praesentalis*: the Romans were to pay the Huns 2,100 lbs. of gold annually and 6,000 lbs. in arrears.[23] In addition, the Romans were required to ratify Attila's seizure of a stretch of land from Naissus to the Danube, which was later revoked. In 448 the Hun Edeco, along with Orestes the father of the last west Roman emperor Romulus, journeyed to Constantinople to complete the terms of the truce.[24] This is surely the occasion for Marcellinus' information (following Mommsen's punctuation) that the burnt out Troadesian porticoes of the city were restored by Antiochus at the same time as Attila's ambassadors were haggling over the tribute money (*legatis Attilae a Theodosio depectas olim pecunias flagitantibus*, (448.3)).

Attila's dealings with the emperor Theodosius II and his successor Marcian were increasingly distracted by his intention to ravage the western provinces if the empress Honoria were not

---

[22] Details in Croke (1981*a*), 159–70 and (1995), 85–6.
[23] Croke (1981*a*), 160–3; (1983*d*), 297–308; (1995), 88–9.
[24] Priscus, fr. 11. 1 (242–3).

duly espoused to him.[25] By this stage the Huns had turned westwards but were routed in 451 in the overrated battle of the Catalaunian Fields.[26] Marcellinus' interest is in the east, so he completely ignores Attila's campaign in the west (except for the misdated Honoria affair) until the Hun siege of Aquileia in 452 (452. 3), and then he does not follow up the fortunes of Attila in Italy and his later retreat. Two years later he records the death of Attila at the hands of a woman:

Attila king of the Huns, ravager of the province of Europe (*Europae orbator provinciae*), was stabbed at night with a knife brandished by his wife. Some people in fact relate that he was killed by coughing up blood (454. 1).

Attila is singled out as the 'ravager of the province of Europe' and it is interesting that Marcellinus records the differing opinions about his death. In sixth-century Constantinople Attila is remembered not as the legendary 'scourge of God' but as the devastator of the very province in which the eastern capital was located; and he indicates the Byzantine preference for the verdict of murder, rather than that of natural causes, to explain Attila's death. Finally, the Huns disappear from Marcellinus' account with the defeat and death of Attila's son Dengizich, and the victorious parading of his head at Constantinople towards the end of 468[27]— 'the head of Denzic, son of Attila, king of the Huns, was brought to Constantinople' (469).

Although the Huns could not be defeated by the army of Theodosius II they were eventually put to flight by Aetius and his allies in Gaul. This seems to be the reason for the high opinion held of the Illyrian, Aetius, in the east. Jordanes describes him as the 'man on whom the whole empire of the west depended' (*Rom.* 191, cf. *Get.* 176) and John of Antioch (probably echoing Priscus) remarks on his brave deeds against both internal and external enemies (fr. 201. 2 (*FHG* 4. 614–5)). Marcellinus reflects this same positive attitude to Aetius, only more so:

Aetius, the main salvation of the Western empire and a scourge to king Attila, was cut down in the palace together with his friend Boethius by the emperor Valentinian, and with him fell the Western Kingdom and it has not as yet been able to be restored (454. 2).

[25] For Attila in the West: Thompson (1948), 125–148; Maenchen-Helfen (1973), 131–2; and for the Honoria episode: Croke (1995), 80–1.   [26] Thompson (1948), 130–43.
[27] For the date: Croke (1995), 98.

For Marcellinus the death of Aetius marks the end of the western empire which, he adds, has not since been revived. That would seem a very significant statement to be making in 518, but from which point of view? The conventional period marker is, of course, 476 and Marcellinus records that as well—in fact he provides the earliest extant record of its use. Yet he also insists that the empire fell in 454. According to one scholar who seriously tried to explain this statement, it is related to the 476 date in that it signifies the 'beginning of the end'.[28] Marcellinus is blunter, however—the death of Aetius was *the* end. This should probably be seen as a hard-headed eastern view where, looking back from the early sixth century, Aetius' death marked the effective end of the west because after that there was no Roman general strong enough to restore political unity and authority in Italy. To Procopius, for example, Aetius was the 'last of the Romans' (*Wars* 3. 3. 15). The death of Aetius, coinciding with the defeat of the Huns, facilitated the final settlement of the Goths and Vandals on imperial territory which came to be seen by Marcellinus' time as marking the point of irreversible decline of Roman imperial authority.[29] At a later time it seemed that the empire had ended with Ricimer because he was the last man to wield effective independent power in the west.[30] Both these views reflect the purely pragmatic Byzantine perspective which, after all, was quite accurate in hindsight. As it turned out, Aetius was the last military hope for the west. Once again—as with Theodosius I, Marcian, and Justinian—Marcellinus' preference is for the strong military leader, a reflection of the ideology and expectations of the imperial capital and echoed by other near contemporary writers such as Procopius and Jordanes.

The Hun invasions of the 440s were a shattering occurrence with irreversible consequences. Cutting the main Balkan route from Sirmium through Singidunum and Margum to the Illyrian military headquarters at Naissus, thence to Constantinople and Thessalonike, punctured an enormous hole in Roman defences and one they could not hope to easily patch up again. At the same time it considerably reduced the empire's capacity to equip and feed the Roman army in the field or on station throughout

---

[28] Wes (1967), 126.
[29] Explained in Heather (1995), 29 ff.
[30] Theoph. AM. 5947 (109. 12).

Illyricum and Thrace. Precisely how destructive the invasions
were is a matter of debate. The financial burdens resulting from
the invasions may have been exaggerated,[31] but they certainly had
a great impact on morale. Attila may not have been a military or
diplomatic genius but he did weld together a large confederation
and give it direction.[32] In short, Marcellinus' entries on the Huns
tell the story of their invasion of Illyricum, first east then west, and
behind them we can see how the impact of their devastation
affected an Illyrian writing from the safety of the eastern capital a
couple of generations after his predecessors had actually experienced these grim events. They highlight how in sixth-century
Constantinople the decisive role of the Huns in the breakdown of
the Roman empire was recognized.[33]

GOTHS IN THE CHRONICLE

While confrontations with the Huns may have been a distant
memory in Marcellinus' day, those with the Goths and Bulgars
were occurring within his lifetime and within the borders of his
homeland. As one might expect, the chronicle records them in
some detail and includes several strong reactions to them. His
information therefore requires close attention. In the 470s and
early 480s the Pannonian Goths of Theodoric the Amal and the
Thracian Goths under Theodoric Strabo were engaged in a pro-
tracted, at times dangerous, competition for influence and sub-
sidies with three successive emperors—Leo, Basiliscus, and Zeno.
Both leaders of the Goths were, at different stages, drawn into the
vortex of imperial political intrigue at Constantinople. The stakes
were high and the balance of power was always delicate. The
Pannonian Goths, now led by Theoderic, had fought against the
overlordship of the Huns and, over a period of time in the 450s,
established their independence. Having shaken off the Hun yoke,
they sought what the Thracian Goths, led by Strabo, had already
achieved by the 470s—a treaty-based military status and role as
foederati, land in the fertile Thracian plain and close ties of family
and patronage with the imperial government.[34] The Pannonian

---

[31] Thompson (1948), 192–3; Maenchen-Helfen (1973), 180–1.
[32] Thompson (1948), 208–9.
[33] Heather (1995), 4–41.
[34] Heather (1991), 240ff.

Goths had moved into Illyricum and been settled north and west of Thessalonike. In 475/6 Theodoric Strabo was *magister militum* supporting the usurper Basiliscus but by late 476 Zeno had been restored to the throne and Theodoric's position was under threat. Theodoric the Amal was now in favour and was supporting Zeno from his base in Novae on the Danube. Both Gothic military leaders had about the same size army of 10,000 men. The conflict between them came to a climax in 477-8 when they found themselves tricked by Zeno into a head-on confrontation in Thrace, which resulted in embassies to Zeno and an uneasy outcome.[35] Next we find the Amal Goths in Macedonia, having apparently marched from Thrace via Stobi and Heraclea, before Theodoric decided to move into Epirus and settle his people in Dyrrachium.[36]

At this stage the testimony of Marcellinus becomes fuller. Under 479 he mentions Theodoric's ravaging of Greece which had been precipitated by the complex series of manoeuvres between Theodoric, Zeno, and Theodoric Strabo: 'Sabinianus warded off king Theoderic, who was ranting madly in Greece, by shrewdness rather than manliness' (479. 2). Theodoric seized Dyrrachium after going on ahead with his cavalry to capture it. Meanwhile the Roman envoy, the patrician Adamantius, opened negotiations with Theodoric and looked like securing an agreement for the Goths to settle near Pautalia just when news reached Dyrrachium that the Illyrian *magister militum* Sabinianus had captured the Goths' baggage train. Marcellinus evidently thought it smart rather than valorous (*ingenio magis quam virtute*) for the Illyrian general to have threatened the Goths by cutting off their supply lines. Sabinianus' direct action certainly found favour with the emperor who sensed the pressure on the Goths and recalled Adamantius.[37] As we shall see later, Marcellinus' support for Sabinianus may be taken as a subtle touch of Illyrian bias.

In his quest for land on which to settle and a Roman military post for himself, Theodoric had grown impatient with the emperor, Zeno. This prompted an expedition from his base at Heraclea Lyncestis (Vitola) to attack the relatively unscathed area of New Epirus. Theodoric subsequently brought considerable destruction in Macedonia and Dardania, especially the area of

---

[35] Ibid. 283-4.
[36] Wolfram (1988), 268-74 and Burns (1984), 52-63 (not always reliable on chronology).
[37] Heather (1991), 293.

Heraclea itself and Scampae. In the meantime, Zeno was attempting to dissuade him from continuing his pillaging of Epirus by offering him a suitable area for settlement (Malchus, fr. 20 (446–7)). Sabinianus favoured a policy of no compromise with Theodoric, but following the arrangements between them in 479 Theodoric's clan removed themselves peaceably to settle down in part of Lower Moesia around the provincial capital at Novae.

Meanwhile, Strabo and his Thracian Goths had evidently supported the attempted coup of Marcian and marched right up to Constantinople, but when the coup failed the Goths claimed to have moved to protect the emperor Zeno. When Strabo's support was repudiated by the emperor in 480 he marched on the capital (to Anaplus).[38] From Anaplus he turned away, possibly seeking to form a united front with the Amal Goths,[39] and headed west along the Egnatian Way. At Stabulum Diomedis, near Philippi, he was accidentally thrust onto a fixed spear and died, an event described by Marcellinus thus:

Theoderic, son of Triarius king of the Goths, together with his recruits, advanced in arms to Anaplous four miles from the city. However, he returned immediately without harming any of the Romans. Next while hastening into Illyricum, as he proceeded among his own moving wagons he was run through and transfixed by the point of a weapon set above his carriage and by the weight of his fearstruck horse, and died. (481. 1)

Following the accidental death of Theodoric Strabo, Theodoric the Amal was in a position to absorb the Thracian Goths into his own group to form the clan we know as 'Ostrogoths' but who remained just 'Goths' to Marcellinus and his contemporaries. He first moved into Macedonia and Thessaly and, as we learn from Marcellinus, destroyed the city of Larissa (482.2).

In favour once more with the court, in 483 Theodoric appears in Marcellinus' chronicle as consul designate and *magister militum* entrusted for the time being (*pro tempore*) with the care of part of Dacia Ripensis and Lower Moesia (483). Circumstances surrounding the appointment of Theodoric were the cause of much controversy, and in the entry of Marcellinus we can see traces of the anti-Theodoric faction at Constantinople who regarded him as insatiable such that he was 'almost pacified' (*paene pacatus*) by

---

[38] Malchus, fr. 22 (450–1) with Heather (1991), 294–6.   [39] Heather (1991), 298–9.

these new honours and positions from the emperor. By now Zeno was more lenient and needed support against the powerful Isaurian Illus.[40]

Theodoric next appears in Marcellinus' chronicle in 487 when his destructive outburst in Moesia is recorded :

Theodoric, king of the Goths, was never satisfied by the favours of Zeno Augustus and made a hostile advance with a large force of his own as far as the royal city and the town of Melantias. When most places had been engulfed by fire he went back to Novae, the city in Moesia whence he had come. (487)

Marcellinus provides our only extant record of this incursion and once again the distinctly anti-Gothic viewpoint is evident— 'never satisfied by the favours of Zeno Augustus'. Since 484 Theodoric had been settled in Novae once more. It was at this stage that Zeno decided to deflect Theodoric by encouraging him to attack the kingdom of Odoacer in Italy.[41] Under 488 and 489 Marcellinus briefly summarizes the Gothic expedition to Italy (488. 2), and the capture and death at Ravenna of Odoacer— 'misled by the lies of Theodoric' (489). Yet again Marcellinus' anti-Theodoric stance is evident. This hard-headed characteriza-tion of Theodoric as untrustworthy and insatiable must be taken as that shared by Marcellinus himself, that is, it reflects the view-point of someone who experienced the process of disestablishment and tension caused by the raids of Theodoric in Illyricum and Thrace. Marcellinus was also making clear to his audience that Theodoric, still in power in the west, had a dubious claim to his authority there and could presumably be challenged by the emperor.

With the death of Odoacer, Marcellinus' attention to events in the western half of the empire ceases (except for the imperial raid on southern Italy in 508). In the chronicle we hear nothing further of Theodoric and the Ostrogothic kingdom in Italy, nor is there mention of the Franks, Visigoths, or Burgundians. Marcellinus is now in the period of his own living memory, and his attention is riveted exclusively, as he foreshadows in his preface, on the east. Whether this reflects lack of interest or information cannot be fair-ly determined although it is only natural to expect that, writing for

---

[40] Ibid. 296–7, 300–1.
[41] Ibid. 305–6.

a local audience in Constantinople, his chronicle would reflect the interests and composition of his audience.

For the decade from 496 to 505 in Illyricum Marcellinus concentrates his attention mainly on military activities. First, under 496, he mentions a donative to the soldiery from the emperor Anastasius and another donative under 500, this time to the Illyrian soldiery only, through his tribune Paul. Imperial donatives were not exactly rare, usually coinciding with an imperial anniversary every five years. They were in many ways the ultimate reward for a soldier, the sort of thing a professional fighting man had come to expect and would not easily forget. Of all the donatives which Marcellinus could theoretically have mentioned between 379 and 534 he singles out these two from the same emperor and within five years of each other, one being to the Illyrian soldiery only. If it struck Marcellinus that the donatives of 496 and 500 were important events worth recording in a chronicle of this kind, then it is plausible to think that they were important to him because he, or his family, was on the receiving end as part of the Illyrian army. The record of the imperial donatives is a clear indication of the Illyrian bias of the Illyrian chronicler and this is more clearly reflected in his attitudes to the *magistri militum* in Illyricum under some of whom he may himself have served.

It was noted earlier how Marcellinus presents a partisan view in attributing to the Illyrian *magister militum* Sabinianus the credit for stopping Theodoric in 479. In fact his whole treatment of Sabinianus displays a distinctly positive personal reaction to the general. For example, the death of Sabinianus elicits from the chronicler the uncharacteristic comment on the transience of earthly life:

Death, which deservedly threatens this sinful world (*huic peccanti mundo merito imminet*), carried off Sabinianus Magnus before he could bring fresh help to the exhausted empire. (481. 2)[42]

In the opinion of Marcellinus Sabinianus' death cut short his potential to bring an effective force to bear in the defence of the worn out empire (*defatigatae rei publicae*). It was, by implication, a jibe at Zeno who had been held responsible for Sabinianus' death. Further, it suggests that Marcellinus saw the state of the empire in

---

[42] Following *PLRE* 2. 967 'Sabinianus Magnus' was taken as a full name in Croke (1995), 27. Here, as elsewhere (479.1, 505) 'Magnus' may denote 'elder' (cf. Salamon (1981), 116).

481, with two massed and menacing armies in Illyricum and Thrace, as being one of exhaustion and despair. Sabinianus, however, provided some hope of confronting this situation by his direct and forceful approach to Theodoric. Precisely what qualities constituted the basis of Sabinianus' reputation are outlined by Marcellinus:

Sabinianus Magnus was appointed commander of both the Illyrian services; he either bolstered the frail senate when panic-stricken and the just imperial census that had collapsed, or supported them when vulnerable. He was so much the best establisher and enforcer of military discipline that he can be compared to the Romans' former commanders. (479. 1)

There is no other trace of Sabinianus' rehabilitation of curial functions. Evidently he helped arrest the breakdown of city government and restored the apparatus of a census in Illyricum, perhaps during his tenure as *magister militum*. After the dislocation of the previous thirty years, one can easily imagine the necessity and value of a new census, which formed the basis of calculating tax liability. At the same time, the city councils in Illyricum were revamped and their tax-gathering functions were brought up-to-date. Marcellinus approved of these sensible economic measures and was possibly pointing critically to Anastasius' establishment of imperial officials (*vindices*) in each city to supervise the local revenue collection and expenditure.[43] Perhaps Sabinianus belonged to a curial family himself. Otherwise, we find that nothing is known of Sabinianus except for his brief (two year) tenure of the Illyrian generalship which led to a rather dubious posterity in the east. Sabinianus had originally failed to ensure the safety of the Roman ambassador Adamantius by swearing an oath to Theodoric. Later he succeeded in sabotaging the peace terms agreed on by Theodoric and Adamantius by exaggerating his own exploits against Theodoric to the emperor, thus encouraging him to continue the war. This is what Marcellinus calls Sabinianus' *ingenium* (479. 2). Although Sabinianus kept Theodoric's army at bay for a further eighteen months, Zeno was not convinced of the wisdom of Sabinianus' actions and had him executed.[44] Marcellinus' account presents a striking contrast to these facts so that we can legitimately conclude that he had some special interest in Sabinianus. Nowhere else do we find similar adulation for this

---

[43] Jones, A. H. M. (1964), 457.   [44] Jo. Ant. fr. 213 (*FHG* 4. 620).

general who, in Marcellinus' estimation, deserves comparison with former Roman generals (*priscis Romanorum ductoribus*). This judgement could be explained by a personal or family tie or because Marcellinus had himself served under Sabinianus and could speak from experience of his discipline.

It could also be that here Marcellinus is echoing the general opinion held of Sabinianus among the Illyrian community of veterans and refugees in Constantinople. In any case, the entries on Sabinianus display a clear Illyrian bias. If he did, in fact, know (or had served under) Sabinianus then he may well have known Sabinianus' son whose campaign against Mundo the Gepid in 505 is described in detail:

Sabinianus, the son of Sabinianus Magnus, was appointed Master of the Soldiery and gathered arms against Mundo the Goth. He set out to fight taking with him ten thousand armed recruits and wagons of arms and provisions. When battle had begun at Horreum Margi and many thousands of his men were lost in this conflict and drowned in the Margus river, and especially as the wagons had been lost at the fort called Nato, Sabinianus fled with a few men. (505)

The younger Sabinianus, who was married to the emperor's niece[45] and who was consul in that very year, had been sent with a large band of auxiliary Bulgars to unseat from Sirmium the Goths who were supported by the Gepid Mundo, but he was defeated and killed. The Gepids had been settled in Sirmium since the 450s and had clashed with Theodoric on his way through to Italy in 488. Now they had seized the strategic city and this is what provoked the hostile response of the emperor.[46] It is interesting that Marcellinus makes no mention of the Bulgars associated with Sabinianus. Perhaps he did not approve of this emergency alliance. In any case, the detail of this entry suggests that Marcellinus is describing something about which he had first-hand knowledge. He bothers, for example, to note the number of soldiers and to add the existence of the wagons for their maintenance, as well as naming the unlocatable fort (Nato) where they were eventually defeated. This is all unique extant information. More significant, though, is that it is again in treating Sabinianus that Marcellinus makes one of his rare personal comments: 'So

---

[45] Cameron, Alan (1978), 261.
[46] Details in Wozniak (1981), 351–82 esp. 363–73.

much of the soldiers' hope was destroyed in this unfortunate war that mortal men could never hope to make it up' (505).

In commenting on the defeat of Sabinianus as marking a point of no return in the military advantage of the empire over the barbarians Marcellinus gives the impression, especially when this is considered in conjunction with the record of the donatives (496, 500) and the judgement of the elder Sabinianus as a disciplinarian, that he understood the military. He may well have been a soldier himself and could have served under both Sabiniani.

Besides the Sabiniani Marcellinus has information on other Illyrian *magistri militum*. There is Mundo in 530 and Aristus whom we see in 499 on his campaign to check the Bulgars who were infiltrating Thrace:

The Master of the Illyrian Soldiery, Aristus, with fifteen thousand armed men and five hundred and twenty wagons, weighed down with the arms necessary for fighting, set out against the Bulgars who were invading Thrace. They engaged in battle beside the river Tzurta where more than four thousand of our men were killed, either in flight or in the collapse of the river's bank. There perished the soldiery's Illyrian gallantry with the deaths of counts Nicostratus, Innocent, Tancus and Aquilinus. (499. 1)

From the relative detail presented here it is tempting to infer that Marcellinus may have actually seen this immense army and its equipment trailing along the Balkan road into Thrace, or even to risk suggesting that he was part of it himself. The latter possibility is bolstered by the subsequent detail. First of all, he locates the confrontation by an obscure river not yet identified. He adds too that the Romans lost 4,000 men that day, that is, a quarter of all their troops, some the victims of their own flight and others of a collapsed riverbank. If Marcellinus had not actually seen this he may well have heard about it at first-hand. He concludes his brief account of Aristus' campaign registering the deaths of the military counts serving under him. These are only divisional commanders but he names them all. Normally Marcellinus does not bother to seek out the names of minor military officers. That he does here suggests that the task was effortless: that is, he knew them himself or of them at close-hand.

Of course, one might expect the Illyrian Marcellinus to reflect more concern for and more detail in describing his native Illyricum without actually knowing the persons singled out for commendation. Yet it remains a strong possibility that Marcellinus' interest in, and personal comments on, the Illyrian soldiery reflect the fact that he was himself a soldier. This would provide a neat context for the meaningful verdict on the campaign of Aristus—'there perished the soldiery's Illyrian gallantry' (*ibique Illyriciana virtus militum periit*); as well as those on the death of Sabinianus in 481 and his son's defeat in 505. Marcellinus implies that the emperor's enemies now have the upper hand since the 'Illyrian gallantry' has passed away. The appeasement policy of Zeno has won the day, unfortunately.

BULGARS IN THE CHRONICLE

If Marcellinus was in the battlefields of Thrace with Aristus in 499 then he was back in Constantinople in 501 assuming, as proposed previously, he was already settled there when he records the disastrous Brytai riots. Under 502 he mentions another Bulgar incursion, referring to them as 'familiar'(*consueta*): 'The familiar race of the Bulgars again devastated the oft-ravaged Thrace as there was no Roman soldiery to resist them' (502). One might well ask: to whom were the Bulgars 'familiar' in 502 if not Illyrians? In addition, one detects in the comment on the lack of imperial opposition the vindication of his reaction to the campaign of 499—the deterioration of the soldiery.

Bulgars first appear in *c*.480 when they were invited by Zeno to support him against the two Theodorics, but when the Amal Theodoric left for Italy in 489 the way was now open for the Bulgars themselves to devastate Illyricum and Thrace in order to extract concessions from the emperor.[47] They next appear in 493, referred to by a much later writer Zonaras (but utilising earlier documents) as 'hitherto unknown'.[48] In that year, so Marcellinus records, they defeated and killed the *magister militum* Julian, in Thrace, exactly where is unknown: 'Julian, the Master of the Soldiery, was struck by a Scythian sword while fighting in a night battle in Thrace, and died' (493).

In 499 the Bulgars defeated Aristus and killed a great many Roman troops.[49] As a morale booster, Anastasius sent a donative

---

[47] Jo. Ant. fr. 211. 4 (*FHG* 4. 619) with Browning (1974), 28ff. Note also Bury (1923*a*), 434–5 and Stein (1949), 61–4.
[48] Zon. 3. 137.   [49] Marcell. s.a. 499; Zon. 3. 140–1 with Croke (1980), 188–95.

to the Illyrian soldiery the following year although shortly after (502) the Bulgars once again devastated Thrace and met no opposition.[50] The Bulgars were feared and hated in Illyricum and Thrace, and Marcellinus reflects this. Moreover, if (as suggested) it was at precisely this time that Marcellinus himself came to Constantinople then this is probably associated with the Bulgars; that is, he either fled to the city at that time to escape them, or else retired there after the campaign of Aristus in 499 which met with such disaster.

The Bulgars disappear from view in the chronicle until 530 where we find Marcellinus recounting the campaign of Mundo, the same Mundo who had defeated Sabinianus in 505.[51] Mundo was now *magister militum* himself and his successful attacks on the Slavs and Bulgars caused Marcellinus to see him now as a valiant and successful general. This was a striking event to be recalled in 534 when there was great celebration of the achievements of Belisarius, whom Marcellinus never mentions. In 529 the Bulgars had invaded Thrace and defeated the Roman generals sent against then, one of whom, Constantiolus, Justinian was forced to ransom for 10,000 lbs. of gold.[52] Thereupon Justinian accepted Mundo's offer to help.[53] He first of all defeated the Slavs and, later in the year, the Bulgars. Marcellinus reports:

However, later in this consulship this same leader, fortunate in his bold-ness, hastened into Thrace and also killed, by fighting bravely, the Bulgars who were plundering it; five hundred of them were slain in the battle. (530)

Five hundred Bulgars were killed in the battle (Marcellinus) and many of their chieftains were captured and paraded in the hippo-drome at Constantinople.[54] It was a pleasing occasion for the emperor now that Thrace had been finally 'reconquered' and the impact of the triumphal emperor can be seen in the erection of the equestrian statue of Justinian in the hippodrome in this same year in which the victory over the 'Scythians' is noted.[55] By the time Marcellinus wrote the updated version of his chronicle the

---

[50] The donative: Marcell s.a. 500.2; the 502 invasion: Marcell s.a. 502.1.
[51] Explained in Croke (1982a), 125–35.
[52] Jo. Mal. 18. 46 (451. 3–16); Theoph. AM 6032 (219. 9–14).
[53] Jo. Mal. 18. 46 (450. 19–451. 9); Theoph. AM 6032 (218. 1–219. 8) with Croke (1982a).
[54] Theoph. AM 6032 (219. 10–14); Jo. Mal. 18. 46 (451. 14), not mentioning the triumph.
[55] *Anth. Plan.* 62 with Croke (1980), 193.

impact of Mundo's victory, consolidated by the activity of Chilbudius (Proc. *Wars* 7. 14. 1–6), was better appreciated as the Bulgars and Slavs had been forced back across the Danube. It is precisely because of Mundo's protection of Illyricum that he earns such an accolade from Marcellinus. Moreover, since Mundo had remained in the service of Justinian in Constantinople it is quite possible that this reaction of Marcellinus reflects his personal acquaintance with Mundo as well.

Besides defeating the Bulgars so decisively Mundo is also recorded by Marcellinus as the vanquisher of the Getae (either Slavs or Antae[56]) who had been recently invading Illyricum too:

Mundo, the Master of the Illyrian Soldiery, was the first Roman general to set upon the Goths who had previously been traversing Illyricum and put them to flight, after quite a few of them had been killed. (530)

We have no other evidence for Mundo's campaign against the Getae but it probably dates to the late 520s. The 'Getae' had first invaded Illyricum in 517 as we learn only from Marcellinus who introduces his entry with a reminder of the prophecy of Jeremiah 6: 22—'Behold a people cometh from the north country and a great nation shall be stirred up from the uttermost parts of the earth':

That famous woman who in the prophet Jeremiah is often enkindled by the north wind against us and our sins, forged weapons of fire and with the same weapons damaged a very great part of Illyricum. (517)

He then goes on to describe the devastation of Macedonia and Thessaly as far as Thermopylae and the deaths of those captives whom the ransom money (sent by Anastasius to the Illyrian Prefect) did not cover:

At that time both Macedonias and Thessaly were ravaged and the Gothic cavalry plundered as far as Thermopylae and Epirus Vetus. Through Paul the emperor Anastasius sent one thousand pounds of gold denarii to John, the Prefect of Illyricum, to ransom the Roman prisoners. Because that was not enough the Roman prisoners were either burnt while shut in their dwellings or killed in front of the walls of the enclosed cities. (517)

[56] The Getae are considered Slavs by Vasiliev (1950), 308 and Bury (1923a), 436 n. 2, Antae by Stein (1949), 105–6.

These brief notices (and many of them are sole surviving testimony for the events they describe) of the earliest Bulgar and Slav raids into the Balkans reflect the same Illyrian point of view as those describing the Hun and Gothic raids—that of a man whose native land was being ravaged and depopulated, and who was repulsed by the loss, particularly the defeat and death of Roman generals, but admired those whose efforts prolonged its life under Roman rule.

In Constantinople there was a large community of veterans and refugees from Latin-speaking Illyricum, especially surrounding the court of the Illyrian emperors Anastasius, Justin, and Justinian. Marcellinus lived among this community and wrote his chronicle primarily for them. This is indicated by his continuing interest in, and attention to, events in Illyricum while resident in the capital. Those entries describing events in Illyricum are all precisely detailed (numbers of troops, names of small places) like the revolt of Vitalian (514. 1, 515. 2), the visit of the Illyrian bishops to Constantinople in 516 and the earthquake in Dardania in 518. They are also much the longest of Marcellinus' entries and are very frequent to the end of the chronicle's first edition (s.a. 512, 515, 516, 517, 518) and for these notices of Illyrian affairs Marcellinus is often our only surviving testimony. It is therefore not unreasonable to assume not only that he knew the *magister militum* Mundo in Constantinople, but that he saw or met in 516 the bishops from Serdica, Nicopolis, Naissus, and Pautalia. He certainly seems to be well informed about them. So too, if not actually involved himself in some administrative capacity in the ransom by the Illyrian tribune Paul in 517, of those captured by the Slavs, he was still well informed about it. Indeed, since Paul was the functionary of the Illyrian *magister militum* in 500 and the Illyrian Prefect in 517 Marcellinus may have known him and took the information he records directly from Paul. Likewise, he may have known the long-serving Illyrian *magister officiorum* Celer who may be the source of the chronicle's entries on the Persian war in 503–5. Behind all these entries can be observed an interested and proud Illyrian absorbed in the life of cosmopolitan Constantinople but living with his compatriots and taking a keen interest in the fortunes of his homeland which he may well have once helped defend and had been forced to leave.

ILLYRICUM IN MARCELLINUS' TIME

In the lifetime of Marcellinus the provinces of Illyricum and Thrace were ravaged, partly deserted, and partly occupied by invading tribal groups; yet they were emerging into recovery as towns and cities were being progressively repaired and rebuilt. This general situation is neatly evoked in *Novel* 50 of Justinian (537) which provides for the transferral of the appellate jurisdiction of the *quaestor exercitus* from Moesia to Constantinople. Petitioners from Caria, Cyprus and the Cyclades had constantly complained of having to travel through regions 'disturbed by barbarians' (*a barbaris inquietatas*), probably overland from Thessalonike to Constantinople. During the Gothic raids in 479 Heraclea and Scampae were already deserted before the arrival of Theodoric, and in his negotiations with Adamantius he was encouraged to forego his claims on Epirus, since it was intolerable that the inhabitants of its large cities should be turned out to make room for the Gothic host. Adamantius told Theodoric to turn instead to Dardania where there was plenty of fertile land uninhabited at the time (Malchus, fr. 20 (446)), while Marcellinus himself tells us that the reason why the shattering earthquake in Dardania in 518 affected so few people was because most of the citizens had fled in fear of the barbarians—'it lost none of its citizens who had been fleeing from their enemy' (518. 1) he says of Scupi.

The invaders had disrupted not only land tenure and yield but trade as well. At Rhaedestus west of Thracian Heraclea merchant vessels no longer put in because of the nearby barbarians (Proc. *Aed.* 4. 9. 17). In this region local defences also needed to be kept strong. The citizens of Asimus (between Novae and Oescus) on the river of the same name had successfully resisted the Huns and now Justin I granted them exemption from serving in the army (Theophylact Simocatta, *Hist.* 7. 3. 4), while an undated law of Anastasius implies that ill-considered troop movements were leaving parts of Illyricum vulnerable (*CJ* 1. 29. 4). There was always a danger too that the dispossessed peasantry might make common cause with the invaders or rebel generals like Vitalian,[57] for whose revolt Marcellinus provides a detailed contemporary account.

The social and economic effects of the invasions of Illyricum in terms of population shifts are extremely important though little

---

[57] The interpretation of Velkov (1977), 58–9.

studied. We know, for example, that the citizens of Sexaginta Prista (Rousse) on the Danube retreated up the valley of the Chervi Lom river to the safety of higher ground, the more easily defensible Cherven whose early Byzantine walls have been discovered.[58] Similarly, the inhabitants of Nicopolis-ad-Istrum deserted the city after the Visigothic invasions for the rugged hill-top area of Veliko Turnovo, 18 km. away. Remains of several early Byzantine churches have been found there, and it seems that the new settlement was regarded as the official successor of the original Nicopolis and maintained not only its name but also its administrative role.[59] In the Gothic raid on Thrace the citizens of Heraclea simply retreated to a nearby fortress (whose remains have been located) thus leaving their deserted city to be put to the torch by Theodoric (Malchus, fr. 20 (440)). In attempting to cope with improving the defensive capability of these increasingly deserted provinces, Anastasius undertook a massive program of resettlement. Communities of Isaurians and other easterners were settled in Illyricum in large numbers as the many unearthed Byzantine churches of mainly eastern design make clear;[60] bar-barians were also settled in depopulated areas, as Marcellinus explains in the case of the Heruli (s.a. 512. 11).

Along with resettlement, Anastasius executed an extensive pro-gramme of rebuilding in the region which is increasingly being brought to light.[61] Stobi and Heraclea, for example, witnessed much rebuilding at this time.[62] It was presumably as part of this program, around the turn of the sixth century and in response to the decisive Bulgar victories in Thrace in the 490s, that Anastasius undertook the massive construction project of the Long Wall which stretched for 40 km. across the neck of the Thracian penin-sula.[63] These processes of reconstruction produced, however, a very different settlement pattern. New and rebuilt cities and towns were generally smaller and stronger than before, and the civic space which had contracted was taken over for ecclesiastical pur-

---

[58] Hoddinott (1975), 241.

[59] Ibid. 250; Poulter (1983a), 96–7.

[60] Hoddinott (1975), 240; Isaurians in Thrace: Procopius of Gaza, *Panegyricus Anastasii* 10.

[61] Poulter (1992), 131.

[62] Biernacka-Lubanska (1982), 217.

[63] Croke (1982d), 59–78 and Whitby (1985), 560–83, with Crow (1995), 109–24 and Crow and Ricci (1997), 236–62 (surveying the remains of the wall and noting its likely Anastasian construction).

poses. Churches were now becoming the dominant buildings and the focal points of civic life, a process to be seen in more detail for Constantinople. While the cities were less populated themselves, a larger population was settled throughout the local area and dependent on the city.[64]

Throughout the fifth century and the lifetime of Marcellinus Illyricum and Thrace remained the empire's most reliable recruiting ground, a strong factor contributing to the relative durability of the eastern empire. It provided the emperor Constantius III (Olymp. fr. 37 (200–1)), Marcian (Evagr. *HE* 2. 1), Leo (Cand. fr. 1 (464–5)), Anthemius (Sidonius Apollinaris, *panegyricus Anthemii*, 34ff.) and later, Justin II (Evagr. *HE* 4. 1) and Tiberius Constantine (ibid. 5. 11). In the time of Marcellinus we find that the emperors Justin and Justinian (Proc. *Anek.* 6. 1–3), as well as the general Belisarius (Proc. *Wars* 3. 11. 21), were all Illyrian. In fact, the soldiery were so prominent in Illyricum that other professions suffered an inferiority complex as a result. In 469 it took an imperial constitution to remind Illyrians that advocates were just as important to the state as soldiers (*CJ* 2. 7. 14). By the late fifth century there was little future for the peasant farmers of Illyricum. Many, like the future emperor Justin I 'who at home had to struggle incessantly against condition of poverty and all its attendant ills', headed off for the capital in search of a niche in the imperial army (Proc. *Anek.* 6. 1–3). Justin's 'rags to riches' story was particularly well known, it seems, in Constantinople. Procopius' description in fact, may owe something to a mural in one of the public baths of Constantinople. It was painted by a certain Marius of Apamea and depicted Justin's whole career, including his original migration to Constantinople, until he became emperor. As it happened, it was objected that the subject of the mural was in poor taste. The painter replied, however, that it was important to be reminded of the Illyrian Justin's career because it illustrated 'how God raises the poor man over the rich' (Zach. Mit. *HE* 8. 1).

The ambitious 'poor men' of Illyricum naturally drifted to the capital but many more put safety before ambition in gravitating to Constantinople. This process of migration (forced by insecurity) which is suggested by Procopius for the late fifth century,

---

[64] Poulter (1992), 123ff.

continued into the sixth. By 539 it was a serious problem, as Justinian recognized:

We have found that the provinces are gradually being deprived of their inhabitants and that, on the other hand, this our great city is becoming much more populous on account of the arrival of various men, and above all farmers, who abandon their homes and crops. (*Nov. Just.* 80 *praef.*)

It is in the context of this stream of refugees that we should interpret the appearance of Marcellinus in Constantinople at the turn of the sixth century. He may have come simply as a civilian refugee or, as suggested earlier, as a veteran. Illyricum continued to be a source of manpower for the army. Even when Illyricum was already so underpopulated during the war in Italy, late in the winter of 545, Belisarius could still find a few recruits there but they were low in quality; at least that is what Belisarius advised Justinian when requesting reinforcements (Proc. *Wars* 7. 12. 4). In 549 when Justinian appointed his nephew Germanus, commander-in-chief against the Goths he instructed him to begin recruiting in Thrace and Illyricum (Proc. *Wars* 7. 39. 9) and Narses was sent on a similar mission in 552 (Proc. *Wars* 8. 26. 10). The master of the cavalry Constantianus is also found in Illyricum gathering an army (Proc. *Wars* 1. 7. 26–7) and Illyrians can be seen at other times in the army of the Illyrian emperor Justinian.[65] In addressing his troops in Africa in 537 Germanus reminded them that it was Justinian 'who took you from the fields with your wallets and one short tunic each and brought you together in Byzantium and has caused you to be so powerful that the Roman state now depends on you'.[66] Procopius' idealized description of Justin's origin, as well as the pronouncements of the Illyrians Justinian and Germanus, illustrate the penury and hardship that beset the Illyrians in particular in the fifth and sixth centuries. It also shows how the Illyrians employed their traditional military reputation as a means of improving their social and economic status. This process consists of a long series of migrations illustrated in the person of Marcellinus.

A consideration of the chronicler's Illyrian context evokes a picture of a proud Illyrian who had apparently become caught up in

[65] Proc. *Wars* 7. 30. 6, 7. 39. 9 with Vasiliev (1950), 64–5.
[66] Proc. *Wars* 4. 16. 12–13; cf. the preamble to *Nov. Just.* 27 (535) establishing the office of the Praetor of Thrace.

the movement to Constantinople in the late fifth/early sixth centuries. From there he kept in touch with events in his own land. Certainly, the momentous defeats that followed these expeditions caused him much anxiety and reflection. One senses in these entries concerning Illyricum the voice of a participant; if not, then at least a close observer. Indeed he may himself have been part of the Roman army in Illyricum in the 480s and 490s, either as a soldier or as part of the military support structure. He strongly endorsed effective military action, to judge from his enthusiasm for the Sabiniani and Mundo. For Marcellinus, force rather than appeasement or subsidy was the way to deal with the empire's military threats—hence his preference for Aetius (454).

Writing his chronicle after the death of Anastasius in 518 Marcellinus took the view that Illyricum suffered because of vacillation and weak military leadership, evidently an implicit criticism of Anastasius and his predecessors. Particularly lamentable were the defeat and battle-field deaths of senior Roman generals such as Sabinianus (s.a. 481. 2) and Julian (s.a. 493. 2), not to mention the disastrous losses incurred by Aristus (s.a. 499. 1) and the younger Sabinianus (s.a. 505). Further, his support for Sabinianus' curial policy (s.a. 479. 1) may perhaps be construed as a critique of Anastasius and his establishment of *vindices* to assume responsibility for the local collection of taxes. In any event, when Marcellinus produced his chronicle in 518 Roman Illyricum was at the crossroads. He looked to the new regime of his fellow-Illyrian Justin, aided by his nephew Justinian, for more effective action in restoring and promoting strong government not only in Illyricum but throughout the empire. The emphatic victories of Justinian's armies in 530 and 534 which are highlighted in the updated edition of the chronicle perhaps reflect Marcellinus' ultimate satisfaction that the empire was again heading down the road of stability, security and strength.

3

Illyrians at Constantinople

In the preface to his chronicle Marcellinus makes clear to his audience that his preoccupation is chiefly with the eastern empire—*Orientale tantum imperium*. So we might reasonably expect to find little in the chronicle pertaining to affairs in the western empire, and then only in so far as such affairs affected Constantinople and the East. For Marcellinus the perspective and nomenclature of the *Chronicle* clearly divide East and West. There is a geographical east (*Oriens*: 418. 3, 420. 2, 484. 1, 529) and west (*Occidens*: 416. 1, 468), as well as an imperial east (*Orientale imperium*: Praef.; *Orientale respublica*: 379. 1) and west (*Occidentalis respublica*: 434, 454. 2; *Occidentalie imperium*: 392. 1; *Occidentale regnum*: 424. 3; *Hesperium regnum*: 454. 2; *Hesperium imperium*: 476. 2; *principatum Occidentis*: 465. 2). There are also designated eastern emperors (*Orientalibus principibus*: 379. 1) and consuls (*Orientalium consulum*: 521).

Not once after 395 does he refer to the Roman empire as a whole but only to its separate halves. However, on the occasions when he identifies himself as specifically Roman it is clearly as a citizen of the Roman empire as a whole, not just the eastern part of it. In speaking of 'us' (447. 2), 'our generals' (503), 'this expedition of ours' (529) and 'our emperor' (532, 533) he identifies himself as a citizen of the Roman world as distinguished from its foes, the Huns (447) and Persians (503, 529).[1]

The chronicle of Marcellinus is very much the product of his own experience and aligned to the background and expectations of his audience. Consequently, it is concerned primarily with places, events, and personalities in Illyricum and Constantinople. Little attention is paid to the rest of the Roman world. The western empire, for example, is only sketchily treated and that from a strictly eastern point-of-view. Further, after Theodoric's conquest of Odoacer in Italy in 493 there is no mention of the west except for the raid on Tarentum in 508. Likewise, Africa is scarcely noticed:

[1] *nostris* (447. 2); *nostri ductores* (503); *haec expeditio nostrorum* (529); *principis nostri* (532); *principe nostro* (533).

78

only Gaiseric's entry into Carthage (439. 3), the outbreak of persecution by Huneric against the catholics (484) and then the victory of Justinian (534). Clearly, Africa and the west were of lesser interest to Illyrians in Constantinople. More important, and this probably reflects the attitude of the imperial court and city as a whole, were wars in Isauria and against the Persians both of which are covered in the chronicle. This relative inattention to the west (and concentration on the east) merely highlights the centrality of Constantinople, the city where Marcellinus lived and wrote his chronicle, in the identity and perspective of the author and his immediate audience. In particular, it focusses attention on the nature of the audience for a chronicle written in Latin by an Illyrian at Constantinople, in the immediate aftermath of Anastasius' reign.

COMMUNITY AND COMMUNITIES IN CONSTANTINOPLE

The very location of Constantinople meant that it was always a busy entrepot, but after 330 when Constantine established it as his 'New Rome' the city acquired a new status and attraction. The population of the city increased gradually throughout the fourth century, reaching an initial peak around 360 and growing rapidly again from the 380s to its next peak in the early fifth century. This increase led eventually to the expansion of the city's harbours, the development of new docks, granaries, and cisterns, as well as the creation of a substantial and reliable water supply from 373.[2] By the turn of the fifth century the demands of physical security, especially the need to secure the city's water supply, had become more urgent. Refugees from the Gothic invasions of the Balkans, coupled with the permanent establishment of the enormous imperial court in the city, accentuated the demand.[3] It was not until 413, however, that the physical size of the city was considerably increased to take in an area within the new land walls completed in that year and this remained the outer limit of the city thereafter. The newly walled area not only helped protect the city's water but it also opened up necessary land both for cultivation of supplies for the city population and for burying its dead; it stimulated too the rapid growth in building of churches and monasteries at Constantinople from the time of Theodosius II onwards.[4]

---

[2] Mango (1985), 37V.; (1986), 119–24. [3] In general: Beck (1965a), 33–5.
[4] Mango (1985), 46–50; (1986), 125.

Precisely how many people lived in Constantinople in Marcellinus' day is unknown. Attempts to calculate it have produced widely divergent results, reflecting both the inevitable shortcomings of each approach and the unsatisfactory nature of the available information. Assumptions are required about the definition of 'house' (*domus*), relative density, figures for distribution of free bread, and so forth.[5] Still, it is useful to have at least a working figure: it seems to be commonly supposed that the population of Constantinople in the early fifth century was 200,000 to 300,000 and double that, roughly 500,000 to 600,000, by the time of Marcellinus a century later.[6]

A more meaningful question than the total population of Constantinople when Marcellinus lived there is who made up that number, how they were distributed and settled throughout the city, and how they interacted. Again, there is no information to work with for the sixth century but it is instructive to observe, and thereby extrapolate, the picture which emerges from the *Notitia* of Constantinople in the era of Theodosius II. This provides some quantifiable corroboration for what might otherwise be merely assumed; the area around the imperial palace (see Map 2) and in the western part of the city was more open (and partly cultivated) and populated more by the city's aristocracy; while closer in, around the ports and fora and along the Mese, lodged the city's labourers, craftsmen and unemployed. The lower ratio of *domus* per street in Region I (4:1) and Region II (3:1) together with the disproportionately few baths and bakeries in each region suggests that they were not so densely inhabited. This is easily accounted for since those regions took in the area of the imperial palace and related domains (*domus Placidiae, domus Marinae*) plus the churches of St Sophia and St Irene, the senate house, theatre and amphitheatre. It was a public part of the city with fewer permanent residents.

On the other hand, Regions IV to VIII might be expected to contain the most number of citizens. These regions comprised most of the areas of the craftsmen surrounding the porticoes of the Mese and the maritime districts, both around the harbour of Julian and along the Golden Horn. The most heavily populated region in terms of *domus* per street is Region XI (63:1), an elegant area sur-

---

[5] Jacoby (1961), 81–109.
[6] Charanis (1966), 445–63, cf. Stein (1959), 128 and 480 n. 194, but note the reservations of Mango (1985), 53–4.

rounding the church of the Holy Apostles and which included the *palatium Flacillianum* and the *domus Augustae Pulcheriae*; the least populated is Region V (*domus* per street 8:1) which took in the Forum of Theodosius (Strategion), the baths of Eudocia and Honorius, the cistern of Theodosius, the Troad, Valentinianic and Constantinian granaries as well as oil stores. On the Golden Horn the region included the Chalcedon steps which served traffic to and from the Asian suburbs. This region had the highest proportion of free bread outlets and the highest number of public bakeries. There was only one bakery in the more fashionable Region XI. Likewise, the disproportionate number of private baths in Regions IX (15), X (23), and XI (14) confirms the expectation that these neighbourhoods were mainly the preserve of the better-off.[7]

Despite the open space between the walls of Constantine and those of Theodosius most of the city, particularly on and around its ceremonial spine—the 'Middle Street' or Mese, the hippodrome and Augusteon—was noisy and crowded. For the early sixth century (around the time Marcellinus arrived there), Zosimus (2. 35) presents a lively glimpse of Constantinople: buildings are stacked close together with very little room for those both inside and outside while the citizens fight their way through compact hordes of people and animals. This crowded scene is confirmed for later in the sixth century by Agathias (5. 3. 6) describing the panic an earthquake would cause in such an overcrowded city. He mentions in passing that Constantinople was so built-up that there was no nearby space for people to congregate in safety during an earthquake. It has been observed that this density was a significant factor in the constant unrest at Constantinople in the fifth and sixth century, that is, it ignited general social, racial, sporting, and religious antagonisms.[8] Physical proximity could also have irritating personal effects, as Anthemius (the master-builder of Justinian's Hagia Sophia) discovered. Exasperated by his rhetorician neighbour Zeno, he devised an elaborate simulation of an earthquake which shook his neighbour's floor, as well as thunder and lightning which terrified Zeno (Agath. 5. 6. 8–8. 6).

Anthemius' experiences indicate that in Justinian's time a respectable rhetorician and an illustrious engineer lived in

---

[7] It confirms too that the high ratio of *domus* per street in these regions is based on the fact that *domus* in the *Notitia* includes noble households only and not all dwellings which is the usual interpretation (cf. e.g. Strube (1973), 127–8).

[8] In Beck (1973*a*), 17 and (1966), 25–6.

adjacent, undetached quarters and that this proximity fostered, if not generated, mutual tension and hostility. A law of 538 refers to the proverbial 'evil neighbour' who devises ways of getting around the law forbidding anyone from building closer than 100 feet from the sea in certain areas.[9] The problems of overcrowding (sanitation, light, etc.) in Constantinople are evident from the earliest when laws needed to be introduced regulating the distance between buildings.[10] Building regulations, however, did little to contain the overcrowding problem. Consequently, just after Marcellinus' updated chronicle, Justinian decided in 535 to re-introduce the office of *praetor* thus replacing the *praefectus vigilum*. John Lydus comments on how this was necessary due to the increasing frequency of violence and looting in the city (*De mag.* 2. 30. 5–6, cf. 1. 50. 9), and Justinian's law is a broadly based attempt to stem arson, looting, and theft in particular (*Nov. Just.* 13).

Apparently the law of 535 did not meet with immediate success and in 539 Justinian decided to strike more forcefully at the root of the trouble: first, by reducing the arms available to private citizens—henceforth only officially registered arms manufacturers can make arms and they may not sell them to any private person for any reason whatsoever (*Nov. Just.* 85); second, since one of the reasons for the escalation of violence and tension in the city was evidently the large number of 'unregistered aliens' who freely passed into it, in future the *quaestor* and his assistants shall ascertain from all foreigners entering the city their identity, origin, and purpose in coming to Constantinople. Their motives must be carefully scrutinized and, if litigious, then they must return home once their case has been heard. 'Thus', concludes the law, 'our outside cities will be inhabited too and this great city will be freed from confusion.'[11]

Certainly in the fifth and sixth centuries it was the constant flow of refugees attracted by the safety and opportunity of Constantinople which contributed the greatest increase to the city's population. Indeed, we have seen how Marcellinus himself fits into this context. The incursions of the Huns, Goths, and Bulgars in the Danubian and Balkan provinces turned thousands of small farmers and townsfolk towards the capital in search of a different fortune as illustrated in the person of Justin and his friends (Proc. *Anek.* 6.

---

[9] *Nov. Just.* 63, cf. *Nov. Just.* 165 (no date).
[10] Dagron (1974), 529–30 (including references).
[11] *Nov. Just.* 80. See further Beck (1973*a*), 17–18.

1–3) and as Germanus later reminded his troops.[12] Some came to Constantinople as refugees, as Justinian explained in the preamble to his *Novel* 80 establishing the quaestor's new controls, escaping invasions and other ordeals but also deserting their homes and farms. A famine in Phrygia, for example, caused one such influx (Soc. *HE* 4. 16) and the Vandal persecution in Africa another, as noted previously (Chapter 1). There was yet another powerful reason (although in *Novel* 80 Justinian seems to imply that this was too often a pretext for the growth of the city)—the presence of the court which attracted ambitious young litterateurs, like John the Lydian, eager to advance their careers. In addition, a host of other provincials were continually coming to appeal unto Caesar. Too often those who were only expected to pass through the imperial capital settled there. Justinian and Theodora were forced to build a hospice to shelter such people until they had a place to lodge (Proc. *Aed.* 1. 11. 26–7). Justinian's establishment of this 'transit camp' and the powers entrusted in 539 to the quaestorial office to control the city's immigration suggests that the resultant confusion (*Nov. Just.* 80) was a problem of considerable magnitude.

By the time of Marcellinus' arrival in Constantinople he was confronted with a society that was not only crowded and volatile but extremely cosmopolitan as well. The city was not a homogeneous entity but a patchwork of different communities. One way of describing it was that contained in the 'Oracle of Baalbek' which makes the (post-eventum) forecast that Constantinople will gather unto itself 'all the tribes of the 72 tongues'.[13] A brief glance at the Constantinople of Marcellinus is sufficient to illustrate the power and function of the capital in attracting the young and ambitious from a diversity of linguistic, cultural and geographical backgrounds, although for many of them a common Hellenic heritage served to blur their differences. Anastasius, Justin, and Justinian were Latin-speaking Illyrians, Peter the Patrician a Greek-speaking Illyrian. There were Africans like the celebrated rhetorician and grammarian Priscian; Johns from Lydia and Cappadocia, Narses from Armenia and so on. We get the impression from John Lydus, who secured his post through a fellow-Lydian and who hints at a Cappadocian preponderance in the office of the Praetorian Prefect of the East, that provincial and ethnic identities were an operative factor in early Constantinopolitan society. Moreover, I have also

---

[12] Cf. Beck (1965*a*), 33.   [13] 1. 93 (ed. Alexander).

suggested (Chapter 1) that this explains the appointment of the Illyrian Marcellinus to be *cancellarius* to the Illyrian Justinian.

There are many examples of a provincial dominance in the city: Lycians under Valens, Spaniards under Theodosius I, and Isaurians under Zeno. Furthermore, national feeling remained strong in the very cosmopolitan society of Constantinople. Valens' Lycians were not popular and the Praetorian Prefect of Theodosius, Rufinus, took measures to avenge their dominance,[14] while the Goths of Gainas were equally detested;[15] so too were the Isaurians courted by Zeno,[16] and John the Lydian quotes a couple of verses harsh to Cappadocians. Such ditties were evidently part of office gossip and they illustrate the problem of ethnic and national rivalries being generated and sustained in the crowded city (*De mag.* 3. 57. 2). A Lydian had no time for Cappadocians while no-one took to Isaurians, Goths, or Alans, the purge of Aspar's family where reasons of race were mixed in with those of religion bearing witness to the latter.[17] The very presence of different national cultures rubbing shoulders with each other in the imperial city was sufficient to touch off an occasional riot. Marcellinus records one such in 473—'a sedition arose in the hippodrome at Constantinople and many Isaurians were killed by the people' (473. 2).

In tenth-century Constantinople there were definable communities of Muslims, Jews, and Armenians centred around their respective houses of worship. In later times there were distinct quarters of Pisans, Genoese, and Venetians as well. Sixth-century Constantinople was no less cosmopolitan, and no less divided into ethnic enclaves; that is, the Goths and Cappadocians, for example, naturally tended to congregate together and probably had their own shops and churches. Constantinople in the time of Marcellinus was a series of such communities: self-contained and self-supporting to a certain extent, preserving their strong identity even in the public life of the capital. Specific evidence for this generalization is limited, however. The Chalkoprateia was a Jewish neighbourhood with its own synagogue;[18] similarly, in 400 during the reaction against the Goths a large Gothic community lived in the eighth region. This community was centred around a specifically Gothic (and Arian) church which was set ablaze at the time (*Chron. Pasch.* 567. 12–16). The regional cluster *ta Ioulianes–ta*

---

[14] Cameron, Alan (1970), 81–2.   [15] Stein (1959), 235–7.   [16] Brooks (1893), 209–38.
[17] Stein (1959), 360–1.   [18] Janin (1964), 44.

Areobindou–ta Olybriou around the church of St Polyeuktos in the eleventh region looks like a predominantly Latin-speaking aristocratic neighbourhood, dominated by the Anician family, and a focus for Latin culture.[19]

Origin and culture aside, it used to be thought that the Blue and Green factions were congregated in particular neighbourhoods, but that notion has been superseded.[20] Yet the church frequently mirrored the religious make-up of a particular area of the city. Not only did the Arian Goths have their own church but the 'Macedonians' had theirs outside the walls of Constantine, at least until 429 when it was confiscated, as Marcellinus notes (429. 2). In the later sixth century, when the emperor Tiberius enrolled the Goths as allies in the war against Persia, they asked for a church for their families while they were away.[21] So too the rival Alexandrian factions of 'Gaianitae' and 'Theodosianitae' built their own separate monasteries and churches at Constantinople.[22] In the fifth century the Alexandrian community in Constantinople was mobilized by Timothy 'the Cat' to have him reinstated as patriarch of Alexandria,[23] just as the archdeacon Thomas was elected as bishop of Amida in 505 by the citizens of Amida resident in the imperial capital.[24]

Although the sixth-century Constantinople of Marcellinus was an ethnically fluid society, the city subdivided into different communities with the prime and most pervasive unifying factors being geography, language and religion. In such a cosmopolitan society affiliations were more regional than purely ethnic and descriptors tended to reflect that. Marcellinus, for example, was described as someone from Illyricum (*Illyricianus*) rather than of a certain ethnic heritage. The chronicle of Marcellinus was written for a local audience of Latin speakers in the city who must have been quite numerous, and divided into three broad geographical groups: Italians, Africans, and Illyrians. In the end, however, they were all 'Romans', that is, citizens of the Roman empire and subjects of its emperor.

---

[19] Momigliano (1956), 249–90.
[20] Cameron, Alan (1976), ch. 4.
[21] John of Ephesus, *HE* 3. 26.
[22] Vict. Tonn. 540. 2 (II. 199). Monastic communities were frequently established on regional/religious lines (cf. Mango (1986), 125).
[23] Theoph. AM 5967 (121. 8–9).
[24] John of Ephesus, *HE* 2 (Nau, *ROC* (1897), 464).

LATIN-SPEAKERS: ITALIAN AND AFRICAN

The extensive communities of Italians, Africans, and Illyrians had at least one thing in common—Latin. So, first a word about the status of Latin in Constantinople at the time of Marcellinus. When the new university (to use an anachronistic, but convenient, term) was set up in the capital in 425 it had fifteen professors of Latin (ten grammar, five rhetoric) and sixteen professors of Greek. This was at a time when Latin was still the 'language of state', the language of law and administration. A century later, when Marcellinus lived in Constantinople, the situation had changed considerably as indicated by John the Lydian who was indignant that his diligently learnt Latin was not being put to good use in the prefectural office (*De mag.* 3. 42, 68). In 535 Justinian decided, although a Latin-speaker himself, that Greek should thereafter be the 'language of state'. This was the culmination of a trend which had received its first strong impetus from Cyrus of Panopolis nearly a century ago in the early 440s.[25] Yet Latin had never been merely the 'language of state', and even now that it had lost its predominance in the administrative bureaucracy (an indication of both the declining proportion of Latin-speakers in the city as a whole, and the reduced significance of the western provinces to the imperial government) the Latin-speaking community of Constantinople was still large.

In the first instance there was the traditional western senatorial aristocracy, highlighted by the pre-eminent family of the Anicii in whose milieu Latin studies flourished in the early sixth century.[26] The imperial dynasty of Theodosius with branches in both east and west survived at Constantinople in the family of Anicia Juliana, the daughter of the former western emperor Olybrius. She had long been resident in Constantinople where she acted as patron of litterateurs and holy men, as well as being responsible for the construction of the grand church of St Polyeuktos. She was also involved in supporting papal embassies in Constantinople seeking a solution to the Acacian schism.[27] She was not their agent, however, nor, strictly speaking, their 'patron' as they were not lodged in her mansion.[28] There were doubtless other old aristocratic western families who lived on in Constantinople. Likewise, some

[25] Dagron (1969), 29–76.   [26] Momigliano (1956), *passim.*   [27] Ibid. 212.
[28] In 518 Pope Hormisdas' legates were domiciled in a *mansio* set aside by the emperor (*Coll. Avell.* 158 (*CSEL* 35. 605)).

western families had their own households in the east as well. During the Nika riots in 532 the house of Symmachus, consul in the west in 485, who was well known in Constantinople, was burnt (*Chron. Pasch.* 623. 7). There was certainly a steady flow of aristocrats from west to east, and during the Italian war of Justinian the number of noble refugees from Italy rose considerably.

Another large group of Latin speakers in Constantinople was from Africa. Many disenchanted or proscribed during the Vandal overlordship, but who escaped or were exiled, ended up there.[29] Marcellinus himself saw (*ego conspexi*, 484. 2) the unfortunate victims of Huneric's persecutions while another contemporary chronicler, Victor of Tunnuna, was a victim of ecclesiastical persecution. However, two other eminent North African literati in Constantinople, Priscian (from Caesarea in Mauretania) and Corippus (from Carthage), left no explanation for their arrival in the city. Like the other national groups, it appears that the Africans tended to live together and be buried together in their own cemetery or section of a cemetery. This can be deduced from the fact that in 565 when bishop Theodorus died he was buried alongside other victims of Huneric's persecution who had passed away long ago.[30] Little is known of the Africans in Constantinople as a group except that it was due to the pressure of dispossessed African nobles in Constantinople that Justinian launched his expedition in 533 (Zach. Mit. *HE* 9. 17). Priscian and his literary activities indicate that Latin culture was strong and flourishing in Constantinople in the time of Marcellinus, especially within the circle of Anicia Juliana.

Priscian dedicated works to the distinguished senior senator and literary figure Symmachus (cos. 485) while he was in Constantinople in *c.*520,[31] and to a certain *consul et patricius* named Julian (*Institutio Grammatica* 2. 2), who has, in turn, been identified with the Julian of the *Codex Puteanus* of Statius' *Thebaid*.[32] Priscian was himself a teacher of Latin and we hear of some of his pupils. In Constantinople in 526/7 Flavius Theodorus, a *quaestor sacri palatii*, copied the *Grammar* of Priscian and the *de praedicamentis* of Boethius from the copy of a certain Flavianus, another pupil of Priscian.[33] There was obviously a good number of Latin works being copied

---

[29] Vict. Vit. *Hist.* 2. 2. 4; 3. 6. 30.

[30] Vict. Tonn. 567.3 (ii. 206).

[31] Details in Kaster (1988), 346–8.

[32] Symmachus: *PLRE* 2. 1045 ('Q Aurelius Memmius Symmachus iunior 9'); Julian: *PLRE* 2. 641 ('Iulianus 26'). [33] *PLRE* 2. 1098 ('Fl. Theodorus 63').

in Constantinople at the time of Marcellinus, including the chronicle of Jerome which Marcellinus himself continued.[34] So too Constantinople was a good place to learn Latin. When the Praetorian Prefect Phocas expressed a desire to learn Latin, John the Lydian arranged for a certain Speciosus to teach him for a fee of 100 pieces of gold, and he had a choice available to him in Constantinople. He could have been taught by an Italian but preferred to learn his Latin from an African because Africans spoke the language more agreeably (*De mag.* 3. 73. 1–7).

Marcellinus has traditionally been associated with this aristocratic literary coterie of Anicia Juliana; while his chronicle has been interpreted as being consciously supportive of the apparently pro-papal, pro-catholic, and pro-barbarian policy and historical perspective of the aristocratic Anician circle.[35] Certainly he was educated enough in Latin literature including poetry for which the chronicle preserves traces of Claudian (399. 1), and drama in the shape of Plautus (496. 2) whom Marcellinus calls 'our poet' (*poeta noster*). But although he may have been acquainted with some of the Latin scholars around Priscian there is no evidence for any such connections. Instead, as an Illyrian himself, he belonged to another sector of the Latin-speaking population of New Rome—the Illyrians.

LATIN SPEAKERS: ILLYRIAN

The Illyrian refugees and veterans from the Latin-speaking Balkan provinces probably constituted a large segment of the city's total population in the early sixth century. At the same time they should be clearly differentiated from the society of Priscian, Symmachus, and Anicia Juliana. Not all Byzantium's Latin-speakers shared the same enthusiasm for grammar, philology, and literature, and simply because Marcellinus wrote in Latin it does not follow that he belonged to a monolithic and closely circumscribed literary circle. Marcellinus and his chronicle are best understood as representing the Illyrian community of Constantinople which lay outside the orbit of the ubiquitous Anicii.[36]

[34] A copy prepared for the instruction of the sons of the prefect Marinus lies behind a Leiden manuscript of Jerome (*Cod. Scal.* 14).

[35] Beginning with Holder-Egger (1877), 55 but elaborated by Momigliano (1956), 276; Wes (1967), *passim*; Zecchini (1983), 48–52, 91 ('la tradizione anicia allo stato puro') and (1993), 76–7. [36] Cf. Momigliano (1956), 262 *contra* Holder-Egger (1877), 55.

In attempting to define more closely the size and style of the
Illyrian community the family of Justinian provides a good starting
point. Justin I left his home town of Bederiana and came to Constantinople to find a worthwhile career in the army. There was
little future for a small farmer in Dardania. It is a reasonable
presumption that Justin and his friends soon, if not immediately,
gravitated towards those from their home region who were already
settled in Constantinople. Later, the family of his sister, including
her son Justinian, also arrived in the imperial capital. They had a
contact and will naturally have sought out the company of their
Latin-speaking countrymen. So too, the process continued into
the next generation with Justinian's nephew Germanus, now an
experienced general, reminding his troops of how Justinian had
brought so many of them to Constantinople to enrol in the army
(Proc. *Wars* 4. 16. 12–13). The emperor Anastasius and his family
illustrate the same phenomenon. Anastasius, like Justinian and
Marcellinus was an 'Illyrian' (*Illyricianus*),[37] and secured his
advancement through a position in the court administration.
With Anastasius there rose to high civil and military office his
brother Paulus (cos. 496), brother-in-law Secundinus (cos. 511)
and his three nephews Hypatius (cos. 500), Pompeius (cos. 501),
and Probus (cos. 502) each of whom became senior *magistri militum*.
His own imperial status was doubtless enhanced when his niece
Irene, daughter of Paulus, married into the Theodosian imperial
family as the spouse of Olybrius (cos. 491), son of Anicia Juliana.[38]
Perhaps the betrothal of Anastasius' niece to the boy consul in the
very year of his accession was a deliberate attempt to shore up
his imperial credentials. Marrying into the current imperial
family also assisted the careers of Sabinianus (cos. 505), whom
Marcellinus greatly admired and lamented (505), and Moschianus
(cos. 512) who were both sons of Illyrian generals, married to a
niece of the emperor.[39] They were also fathers of the polyonymous
consuls Flavius Anastasius Paulus Probus Sabinianus Pompeius
Anastasius (cos. 517) and Flavius Anastasius Paulus Probus
Moschianus Probus Magnus (cos. 518).[40] Marcellinus, as an Illyrian
in the imperial administration, may well have known them all.

[37] References in *PLRE* 2. 78 ('Anastasius 4').　　　　[38] *PLRE* 2: 626 ('Irene').

[39] *PLRE* 2. 967–8 ('Sabinianus Magnus 4') and 766 ('Fl. Moschianus 2') with Cameron,
Alan (1978), 261 (plus stemma, 274).

[40] *PLRE* 2. 82–3 ('Flavius Anastasius Paulus Probus Sabinianus Pompeius Anastasius 17')
and 701 ('Flavius Anastasius Paulus Probus Moschianus Probus Magnus 5').

By the late fifth or early sixth century, the military high command was dominated not only by the nephews of Anastasius, and the husbands of his nieces, but by other Illyrian generals. Almost all the senior Roman generals hailed from Illyricum or Thrace, and Marcellinus may well have known many of them: Sabinianus Magnus,[41] whom Marcellinus strongly supported (cf. 479. 1–2; 481. 2) and under whose leadership he may have served himself; Aristus[42] whose expedition Marcellinus describes in detail (499. 1) and in which he may have participated; Celer (cos. 508),[43] possibly Marcellinus' direct informant for Roman movements during the war with Persia (503, 504); Cyril,[44] whom Marcellinus regarded with some contempt as lacking the hard self-discipline required for a proper general (514. 3); Vitalian (cos. 520),[45] whose rebellion against Anastasius was supported by Marcellinus (514. 1–3, 515. 2–4, 516. 1). To these, the military aristocracy in the period leading up to Marcellinus' chronicle in 518, might be added Gunthigis[46] whom Jordanes served as secretary (*Get.* 266), and Mundo[47] whom Marcellinus probably knew at Justinian's court and whom he came to find praiseworthy for his success in defeating the Goths and Bulgars who had threatened parts of Illyricum and Thrace (s.a. 530). All of these generals were Illyrians, and most spent a good deal of their working life in and around the imperial court in Constantinople, took part in the civic life of the capital, and were actively involved in religious policy and theological disputation.

The following generation of generals—for instance Germanus, as noted above, and Belisarius—followed a similar pattern. They were merely the next stage in a well-established career pattern for Illyrians at Constantinople. Moreover, they led armies which comprised a majority of Illyrians covering a wide variety of ethnic and linguistic backgrounds but united by their regional and imperial identity—Illyrians fighting for the Roman empire. Indeed, the contemporary nomenclature makes it difficult to distinguish between someone's ethnicity and their regional identity, let alone who was 'Roman' and who 'barbarian', and the extent to which such distinctions carried any political and social significance.[48]

---

[41] *PLRE* 2. 967–8 ('Sabinianus Magnus 4').   [42] *PLRE* 2. 147 ('Aristus 2').

[43] *PLRE* 2. 275–7 ('Celer 2').   [44] *PLRE* 2. 335 ('Cyrillus 3').

[45] *PLRE* 2. 1171–6 ('Fl. Vitalianus 2').   [46] *PLRE* 2. 526 ('Gunthigus qui et Baza').

[47] *PLRE* 2. 767–8 with Croke (1982*a*), 125–35.

[48] Details in Amory (1997), 278 ff.

Behind these glimpses of the families of Anastasius, Justin, and Justinian, along with the other Illyrian military leaders they promoted and depended on, may be inferred the existence of a large community of higher and lower-ranking military officers and functionaries, bureaucrats such as Marcellinus, Jordanes, and the *tribunus* Paul (s.a. 517), as well as veterans and refugees from Illyricum. They all lived together in a supportive community in the imperial city, and could maintain contact with their native land only a few days travel away and where so many still had families and friends. This is the natural explanation for the large number of visitors from Thrace and Illyricum which Procopius noticed (*Aed.* 4. 4. 2) in Constantinople. Doubtless many of them stayed for an extended period, some permanently. All in all, the existence of tightly knit neighbourhoods (based mainly on language, geography and religion) provided a quick introduction in the ways of the city and protected the new arrival against the shocks of transition.[49]

To what extent the Illyrian generals, other military officers, soldiers, imperial officials, and veterans pursued literary interests and inclinations is unknown. Of course, as generals they required a fair level of functional literacy since the army was underpinned by a vast amount of technical paper-work in the form of manuals, reports and logistical and other records. Moreover, to carry out much of this work they had literate officials such as Jordanes, *notarius* to a Roman general and later in Constantinople a writer of both Roman and Gothic history. It is clear from the best-known generals—Celer, Hypatius, Pompeius, Probus, Vitalian, and Justinian—that they were well-enough educated to be an obvious audience for Marcellinus' chronicle. Here they could be reminded of exploits familiar to them, how the Roman domain had been defended and especially of the times when the military had failed. Marcellinus' preference for strong military action by a well-led army presumably resonated with these generals in particular. Other aspects of the chronicle, such as civic life at Constantinople and the struggle to maintain a religiously orthodox state, would also have struck a chord since so many of the Illyrian generals were themselves involved in theological politics, as we shall see.

It is as an Illyrian that Marcellinus' presence in the capital parallels that of Justin. Unlike Justin, however, Marcellinus had

---

[49] Miller (1969), 122–3.

literary aspirations and capacities, although it is unfair to judge his Latinity entirely on the basis of the chronicle alone. Yet of all the chronicles written in the fifth and early sixth century Cassiodorus singles it out (together with that of Prosper) as the best of the continuations of Jerome. We have seen already (Chapter 2) the scale and bias of Marcellinus' treatment of Illyrian affairs in the chronicle and suggested that this would make most impact on an Illyrian audience. This predilection can now be reinforced by considering the attention accorded Illyrian matters after the time of Marcellinus' arrival in the capital (*c*.500). There is, first, the defeat of the younger Sabinianus at the hands of Mundo in 505—'so much of the soldiers' hope was destroyed in this unfortunate war that mortal men could never hope to make it up' (s.a. 505); and the horrible invasion of the 'Getae' (Slavs) in 517 for which Marcellinus provides detailed information on the ransom provided for those taken captive (517), and he may have been involved in the process of freeing the hostages. However, the most significant entries in this respect are those pertaining to the visit of the Illyrian bishops to Constantinople in 516 and the Dardanian earthquake in 518.

Comment has been made (Chapter 2) on the length and detail of our chronicler's account of the earthquake in Dardania. In fact it is the sort of detail that could only come from an official damage report of some kind. What is interesting is that Marcellinus should have access to such information and that he should consider it important to elaborate on it in his chronicle. This may be taken as a strong hint at the nature of his audience. He may well have sought out the information because he was concerned to know precisely what happened, which in turn suggests that he came from the region himself or at least had access to official local reports. Still more instructive is the visit of the Illyrian bishops in 516. The previous year forty pro-Chalcedonian bishops of Illyricum and Greece (probably inspired by Vitalian's success)[50] withdrew their allegiance to the bishop of Thessalonike, Dorotheus, and appealed to the Pope to admit them to direct communion with him. Having thrown their weight behind Vitalian, they were left insecure on his defeat by the emperor's forces. It is at this point that Marcellinus takes up the story: the emperor Anastasius invited to his presence the leaders of the Chalcedonian bishops of Illyricum—Laurence of Lychnidus in particular, as

[50] Charanis (1974), 103.

well as Domnio of Serdica, Alcissus of Nicopolis, Gaianus of
Naissus, and Evangelus of Pautalia. Alcissus and Gaianus died in
Constantinople and were buried together, Domnio and Evangelus
suddenly returned home 'through fear of the catholic Illyrian
soldiery' (*ob metu Illyriciani catholici militis*) which perhaps means that
attempts were being made in Illyricum to secure the support of
the army against the emperor if he continued to detain these particular bishops. Laurence, however, remained in Constantinople
'and was retained as if he had been exiled' (*ac si in exilio relegatus*)
and often argued the orthodox cause with Anastasius in the
palace. When Laurence originally came to Constantinople he had
been suffering for seven years from some foot affliction which
apparently restricted his movements. Later he was 'by his faith
and by the grace of Christ' miraculously healed in the church of
Cosmas and Damian and, being able to walk properly once again,
soon returned home where he died aged more than eighty. All this
detail comes from Marcellinus (516. 3).

This informative account, like that on the Dardanian quake,
implies the interest of both the chronicler and his audience.
Bishops and holy men visited Constantinople all the time and
there were countless examples for the period *c*.500–34. The visit
of the Illyrian bishops in 516 was not of paramount significance in
the broader context of Anastasius' religious policy but what makes
it worth recounting in the chronicle is its importance for the Latin
Illyrians in Constantinople. The presence of the Illyrian bishops
to argue the orthodox cause against the emperor will have given
rise to hospitality and meetings among the Illyrian community.
Moreover, it is not unlikely that they looked on the bishops as
representing them at court. Nor is it unlikely that all these bishops
were known personally to Marcellinus. It is the strong links of
family and information between the Illyrians of Constantinople
and those still in the provinces which are illustrated by Marcellinus' description of both the quake in Dardania and the visit
of the Illyrian bishops—evidence for the continuing interest of
Marcellinus and his fellow-Illyrians in their *patria* and evidence
too for the notion that Marcellinus intended his chronicle for a
mainly Illyrian audience. It is only a small step from this to the
hypothesis proposed earlier (Chapter 1) that the popularity of the
chronicle soon led to the appointment of Marcellinus as *cancellarius*
to the Illyrian Justinian.

ILLYRIAN CULTURE AT CONSTANTINOPLE

Since the chronicle was directed to the Illyrian community of Constantinople, it offers a clearer idea of the different elements which constitute the political and mental horizons of this community. It provides a summary guide to events in Illyricum itself in the fifth and sixth century but also highlights another distinctive feature of the chronicle—its emphatically orthodox viewpoint. Illyricum had always been an orthodox land (in the same sense that Syria and Egypt were soon to be monophysite). At Thessalonike in 380 Theodosius I was informed by bishop Acholius that Arianism had not yet gained a foothold in Illyricum and this evidently pleased the emperor;[51] while by the lifetime of Marcellinus a rigid orthodoxy still prevailed in his own land, as is evident from both a letter of Pope Gelasius to the bishops of Dardania[52] and their reply, promising to obey the Pope's commands and preserve their catholic viewpoint against all aberration.[53] In a letter of the following year (494) Gelasius repeats his praise for the orthodoxy of the Dardanian bishops.[54]

Being Illyrian implied not only orthodoxy but also a traditional acknowledgment of the jurisdiction of the bishop of Rome throughout the region. The so-called 'papal vicariate' based on Thessalonike remained a disputed issue in ecclesiastical relations between Rome and Constantinople. Yet in the predominantly Latin-speaking provinces of Illyricum, from where Marcellinus came, the Roman view held sway. It was, for instance, the open attempt of the Illyrian bishops to ally themselves with the papacy against the bishop of Constantinople in 515 which led to their being summoned to the capital by the emperor Anastasius in 516, as described by Marcellinus (516. 3). It is not surprising therefore for an Illyrian chronicler to record the succession of popes in his chronicle, while scarcely mentioning the patriarchs of Constantinople. In addition, he mentions the arrival of Pope John in Constantinople in 525 and describes the occasion he will have witnessed himself: the emperor's reception of the pope 'with magnificent honour' and the papal

---

[51] Soc. *HE* 5. 6; Soz. *HE* 7. 4.
[52] *Coll. Avell.* 79 (*CSEL* 35. 218–33).
[53] Ibid. 80 (223–5).
[54] Ibid. 101 (404–8).

celebration of the Easter Sunday mass 'in full voice . . . in the Roman ritual' (525).[55]

For those disinclined or unable to follow the theological subtleties and the ecclesiastical politics which form such a large part of the church histories written in Constantinople (and not translated into Latin by the time of Marcellinus) the chronicle provided a sort of potted history of the main events and personalities in the rise of orthodoxy. That such an outline was necessary and would be welcome is made most clear by the fact that this is precisely the task, at least in relation to the doctrines of Nestorius and Eutyches, which Liberatus set himself in his *Breviarium*.[56]

Marcellinus closely identifies himself and, by implication, his audience with those of orthodox belief and practice. 'We orthodox' (429. 1) is one way of avowing his standpoint, 'us catholics' (380) another. The language of being 'orthodox' and 'catholic' permeates the *Chronicle*. There are the 'orthodox' (512. 2) and the 'orthodox people' (403. 3), the 'faith of the orthodox' (494. 1, 513, 514. 1), the 'orthodox church' (380), an 'orthodox emperor' (380) and orthodox bishops (458, 484. 2, 512. 8). Likewise, there are 'we catholics' (484. 2), 'catholics' (512. 3) and the 'catholic people' (380), as well as the 'catholic faith' (470. 1, 516. 3), the 'catholic church' (379. 1, 392. 2) and the 'catholic custom' (512. 6). There are also 'catholic readers' (392. 2), the 'catholic fathers' assembled at Chalcedon (451) a 'catholic orator' in Ambrose (398. 2), a 'catholic bishop' (429. 1) and a 'catholic patriarch' (512. 9) in Flavianus. For Marcellinus and his community Jesus Christ is 'Our Lord' (419. 2, 525), and the prolific writer and student of the Christian sacred texts is 'Our Jerome' (*Praef.* 380, 392). When he cites the prophet Jeremiah as explaining the perpetual threat to 'us' (517) he means the people of God or all those with whom he could identify. When he speaks, however, of the 'catholic priests of Illyricum' (516. 3) and the 'catholic Illyrian soldiery' (516. 3) he is highlighting the close connection of identity and culture between the Illyrian army and the demands of orthodox belief and ritual. This is a window on the world of Marcellinus and his audience, and it is further exemplified by the campaign of Vitalian.

---

[55] Croke (1995), 123 but ignoring (p. 42) the problem presented by the evident omission of one or more words in the received text (Gusso (1997), 280).

[56] *Breviarium* 1 (*ACO* 2. 5, 99).

Marcellinus' heroes are the orthodox emperors, his villains the heretical ones. In fact the chronicle begins by elevating Theodosius I and Marcian to a distinct plane because of their active support of the right belief: 'Theodosius . . . was a singularly religious man and propagator of the catholic church surpassing all the Eastern emperors except for his emulator, Marcian, the third emperor after him' (379. 1). Theodosius was an example for orthodox tradition because he outlawed Arianism (at least officially), and Marcian was responsible for convoking the Council of Chalcedon. Marcellinus simply reflects the Byzantine tradition on Marcian epitomized by the hippodrome crowd at the coronation of Anastasius shouting the slogan 'Reign like Marcian'.[57] The death of Marcian elicits from the chronicler the evaluative comment that he was to be compared to the 'good emperors' (457. 1). On the other hand, Basiliscus is completely vilified—his despicable usurpation was aborted because he tried to promote the teaching of Nestorius (476. 1); and Anastasius' heretical tendencies completely colour Marcellinus' treatment of him, as we shall see.

Theodosius I is praised for his expulsion of the Arians from Constantinople in 380 and the restoration of the episcopal church—'our church'—to 'us catholics' (380), and there is mention of the council of Constantinople in 381 'against Macedonius who was blaspheming against the Holy Spirit' (381. 1). Here we see Marcellinus, and implicitly his audience, identifying with an incident 140 years ago which had become part of their living orthodox tradition. The Macedonians appear once again in 429 when Marcellinus says that 'we orthodox' confiscated the Macedonians' church 'without the walls' and seems to imply that even this is too light a punishment for their murder of the catholic bishop of Germae (429. 1). The anti-Arianism of the chronicler appears again in the murder of the family of Aspar by the emperor Leo in 471—'an Arian, together with his Arian family' (471); with reference to the persecution of Huneric in Africa (484. 2); and in the visit of Pope John to Constantinople in 525 which had been designed to take pressure off the Arian king Theodoric in Italy.[58]

Besides the emperors Marcian and Theodosius, the other outsize figure in the religious world of early Byzantine orthodoxy was

---

[57] Const. Porph. *Caer.* 1. 92 (425).
[58] Croke (1995), 123.

John Chrysostom, the resolute and resilient bishop of Constantinople in the time of Arcadius. The chronicle provides the basic facts, beginning with a brief summary (from Palladius' life of Chrysostom) of John's background and elevation to the patriarchate of the imperial city (398. 3). Then follows a notice relating back to the previous one, describing his exile to Armenia in 403, the miraculous fire which destroyed the 'great church' in the following year (404. 1), the first celebration of his annual feast at the imperial court (428. 2) and, finally, the return of his relics to Constantinople and their ceremonial deposition (438. 2). Even for the Latin-speaking Illyrians in Constantinople, John was the foremost figure and the city's annual liturgical commemorations in John's memory will only have reinforced and amplified his status. Also significant in their world-view was Jerome ('our Jerome') whose chronicle, written in Constantinople, Marcellinus was continuing and to whom he devotes a full and strongly supportive entry (392. 2) and Gregory of Nazianzen 'the most eloquent priest of Christ and teacher of our Jerome' (380). By contrast, the other key figures in the western church namely Augustine (429. 2) and Ambrose (398. 2) are scarcely noted, except for their deaths.

Still, what was most important for the orthodox of Marcellinus' time to grasp were the key events in the Christological controversies of the fifth century. Marcellinus begins by noting the appointment to the see of Constantinople of Nestorius (428. 1) and then the rejection of Pope Celestine's ultimatum which led to the council of Ephesus in 431. Nestorius is simply dismissed as that 'faithless bishop from whom the Nestorian heresy sprang' (430. 3). Next we come to the second council of Ephesus in 449 and the statement of Flavian's exile (449. 2) followed by the council of Chalcedon 'against Eutyches, leader of the most impious monks' (451) and a brief account of the so-called 'Tome' of Pope Leo (458). There is no mention of the Henotikon of Zeno nor of the episcopal wrangling and rivalries which surrounded and followed Chalcedon. Marcellinus, or at least his audience, was manifestly less interested in the history of dogma and the changing fortunes of individual patriarchates. Thus this sort of material is largely absent from the chronicle, an absence highlighted when it is compared to the chronicle of Victor of Tunnuna, also written in Latin in Constantinople but by a bishop with a different audience in mind. Victor's chronicle contains almost nothing but ecclesiastical politics and the development of episcopal rivalries.[59]

There is a contrast, however, between Marcellinus' treatment of the past and his treatment of the present, for considerable attention is paid to the fortunes of the patriarchates of Constantinople and Antioch in contemporary times. Whereas it would be tedious to explain previous rivalries and their impact, Marcellinus' orthodox audience was quite aware of (and doubtless held strong opinions about) the legitimacy of contemporary patriarchs. Hence we find Marcellinus condemning Anastasius' exile of the Constantinopolitan patriarchs Euphemius (494. 1, 495) and Macedonius (511), his sanctioning of the deposition of Flavian of Antioch and John of Paltos (512. 9) and of the appointment to the see of Antioch of Severus 'an adherent of the Eutychian heresy' (513). So too, it is Marcellinus' antagonism to the monophysite leanings of the emperor which causes him to dwell at length on the riots of 512 and to interpret the revolt of Vitalian in strictly religious terms—to secure the restoration of orthodoxy. Finally, Marcellinus mentions the death in exile of the aged patriarch of Jerusalem, Elias (516. 2).

Although strongly and consistently orthodox, Marcellinus reflects a view of this orthodoxy which may be taken as characteristic of Constantinople, or at least the Illyrians therein. There is a great deal of attention paid to the impact of Anastasius' policies in Constantinople but at the same time there is never a mention of the so-called 'Acacian schism' between the Pope at Rome (insisting on the condemnation of the former patriarch Acacius) and the court and patriarch of Constantinople which so completely absorbed the energies of the papacy throughout this period. This is all the more remarkable given the chronicler's Illyrian and pro-papal sympathy; but perhaps it simply was not important enough to mention in the context of the religious life of the eastern capital especially since it had been more or less settled by the time Marcellinus was writing his chronicle in the early months of Justin's reign. Nor does the chronicler, in introducing Nestorius and Eutyches for example, elaborate on their Christological beliefs. These were well known and readily assumed by the writer. One also gets the impression that his audience did not care much for the finer theological points. We see them in action in the

[59] Placanica (1997), XIV–XVII.

record of their encounter with the patriarch John in Hagia Sophia on Sunday 15 July 518 when, through persistent shouting of acclamations and slogans, they secured the condemnation of Severus and a liturgical commemoration of the Council of Chalcedon for the following day.[60] Marcellinus may well have been in the congregation that day. His chronicle certainly reflects this kind of approach to doctrinal issues, although his occasional entries on ecclesiastical writers, compounded with the assumption that he was a monk, have been taken as an indication of a sound theological education.[61] In this respect, Marcellinus' chronicle is similar to that of John Malalas which also evinces little interest in theological discourse and disputation. John, like Marcellinus, is more concerned with public religious practice and ceremonial than doctrine and belief.[62]

Marcellinus was not a monk, at least such an assumption is not required to explain his theological literacy. Certainly he used Orosius, Palladius, and the so-called *inventio* of the head of John the Baptist. However, his biographical entries in writers from Gennadius do not allow us to presume that he actually read the works referred to. In fact, it can be shown that he only uses Gennadius selectively and arbitrarily to plug up gaps in his chronicle (Chapter 6). Nonetheless, it is worth observing that in abbreviating the Gennadian entries relating to Isaac (459), Prosper (463), Theodulus (465), and John (486) he selects from among their several works the treatises of each against Nestorius and/or Eutyches. Perhaps he wanted to suggest to his audience that these were the chief theological writers of the orthodox tradition, as it had developed since Chalcedon. Marcellinus emerges from the chronicle as a pious layman strongly attached to the orthodox cause, who presents his like-minded audience with a summary account of the basic historical facts which gave rise to current theological positions. In fact, this is precisely the set of attributes we might expect to find among the community of Latin-speaking Illyrians at Constantinople and appears to be confirmed by the religious culture and activities of the Illyrian generals.

The Illyrian military aristocracy exhibited a strong level of support for the Council of Chalcedon. Hypatius, Celer, Pompeius,

---

[60] Vasiliev (1950), 136ff.
[61] e.g. by Holder-Egger (1877), 55.
[62] Croke (1990e), 14–15, 23.

and Vitalian (not to mention Justinian when he could still be described as an Illyrian general in the early 520s) were each engaged at different times on behalf of the orthodox cause.[63] By contrast, Probus stands out because he was a monophysite. He knew Severus of Antioch personally, in fact he introduced him to his uncle Anastasius in 508, and later (from 540–542) the leading monophysite John of Ephesus stayed at his house in Constantinople.[64] On the other hand, Severus was shunned by Hypatius and hated by Vitalian. The exiled patriarch of Constantinople, Macedonius, was actively supported by Pompeius.[65] It was the settlement in 518/19 of the Acacian schism which highlighted the role of the Illyrian generals in imperial religious policy. The settlement initiated by the new emperor Justin was supported strongly by the Illyrians, most of whom were actively involved in the meetings and correspondence leading to the settlement. When the papal envoys approached Constantinople they were met by Vitalian, Pompeius and Justinian. Each of these, along with Celer, was subsequently involved in discussions. Moreover, Vitalian, Pompeius, Justinian, and Celer were all in a position to write directly to the pope and receive a response.[66] On the other hand, Vitalian appears to have sponsored a relative of his who had come to Constantinople in 519 as part of a delegation of monks from Scythia Minor seeking resolution of their doctrinal conflict with the local bishop of Tomi. These so called 'Scythian monks', lead by John Maxentius and accommodated by Vitalian, found much interest but little support there and moved on to Rome before returning to Constantinople once more.[67] In the end, their doctrinal solution was taken up by Justinian.[68]

So, the Illyrian generals not only led armies but were informed and involved in theological and religious policy at the highest level. They reflected the Illyrian disposition to orthodoxy and support for the authority of Rome. Further, it may be supposed that their support for religious unity was allied to a belief that doctrinal unity was fundamental to political unity and strength. In pur-

[63] Cf. Greatrex (1996), 120 ff. on the shifting religious allegiances of Hypatius and Celer in particular.

[64] *PLRE* 2. 913 ('Fl. Probus 9').

[65] *PLRE* 2. 898 ('Pompeius 2').

[66] Details in Vasiliev (1950), 161 ff.

[67] ibid. 190–7.

[68] Bury (1923*b*), 376.

suing this agenda so relentlessly Justinian as emperor was really just following a tradition established by the previous generation of fellow-Illyrian military men. Promoting and defending doctrinal orthodoxy was an integral part of the cultural and political life of the court and the imperial city. Marcellinus, as an Illyrian associated with the army and as a functionary of the Illyrian general Justinian in the early 520s, must have been a witness to and perhaps directly involved in many of these discussions and transactions.

Here, then, we have the full Illyrian context of Marcellinus and his audience. The chronicle was written by an orthodox Illyrian who had come to live in Constantinople in the wake of the invasions of his homeland in the late fifth century. Arriving in the imperial capital, a crowded and cosmopolitan community, he naturally fitted most comfortably among the large number of mainly Latin-speaking Illyrians there. His chronicle was written primarily for them and it reflects events in which they would be most interested and attitudes with which they could identify. What emerges is the picture of a thriving community bringing to the volatile city its regional adherence and its particular stamp of Christianity—unwavering orthodoxy and a traditional allegiance to the church of Rome. Marcellinus and his Illyrian confreres fitted smoothly into the political and social life of the capital. They were primarily citizens of the catholic Roman Empire, a fact amply reflected in the chronicle of Marcellinus. Any Latin work would also be of interest to the other Latin communities in Constantinople and presumably would soon come to the notice of Anicia Juliana and those with Italian connections. A generation later Cassiodorus encountered the chronicle in his circle at Constantinople.

The Illyrians of Constantinople were not just in the city but of the city as well, and by the 520s no doubt a great many Illyrians had been longer inside the walls of Theodosius than in their own *patria*. What bound together the Illyrians and the other Constantinopolitan communities—Italians, Africans, Syrians, Armenians, and various Greek-speaking communities—was the public life and civic ceremonial of the city. To Marcellinus they were collectively 'Byzantines' (s.a. 472. 1, 480. 1, 491. 2, 512. 3). The chronicle in fact provides a distinctive picture of Constantinople itself and its public life in the early sixth century, as we shall now see.

4

Marcellinus and Constantinople

Marcellinus came to Constantinople from his native Illyricum around the turn of the sixth century and spent the rest of his life in the capital and wrote his chronicle originally for the Illyrian community there. Constantinople was the city and the society he knew best. Indeed, he was sufficiently familiar with the imperial capital to write a detailed description of the city (*Inst.* 1. 25. 1). Although his two volumes on Constantinople do not survive there is an abundance of material in his chronicle to bear witness to his observation of, and reaction to, the physical, social, and mental environment of the capital. The world of Marcellinus is essentially that of the Byzantine chronicle tradition as we see it the latter part of the chronicle of his contemporary John Malalas, for example; that is to say, the city and life of Constantinople itself largely circumscribe the focus of the chronicler, who devotes a disproportionate amount of space to the imperial capital.

This chapter, like that on Illyricum (Chapter 2), is based on the conviction that Marcellinus' information on Constantinople (and its role in the story which the chronicle unfolds) can only be properly understood in its broader contemporary context. The general approach is therefore to take a cross-section view of the city in the time of Marcellinus. Unfortunately, most extant accounts describe Constantinople as it was seen at a particular later time. For the fifth and early sixth century no first-hand account of the 'patriographer' type survives, except for Hesychius' description of the foundation of the city.[1] Instead, there is only the *Notitia Urbis Constantinopolitanae* which reflects the city of the 430s although it was once thought to be the work of Marcellinus himself.[2] Therefore, our picture of Constantinople in the time of Marcellinus has to be reconstructed from references scattered here and there in various contemporary and other records. In

---

[1] Hesychius, *Patria Constantinopoleos* (ed. Preger (1901), 1–18).
[2] *Notitia CP.* For its date (424–7) see Speck (1973), 135 ff.; for its association with Marcellinus see Riese (1878), xxxiii.

addition, in the period we are examining here (AD 379–534) the city underwent frequent and major changes in its appearance, not only because of periods of rapid growth (precipitated by the establishment of the imperial court there) and the needs of defence, but also because of frequent and damaging earthquakes and fires which assume a prominent place in Marcellinus' record.[3]

A city of late antiquity, built close together and with so much timber, always lived precariously in the face of fire. God's ire could easily strike in the shape of a conflagration at any time. In 433, for example, Marcellinus reports that most of the northern part of the city was razed to the ground in a blaze which raged for three days. The 'great church', the later Hagia Sophia, was twice gutted by fire before the Nika riots in January 532—in 404 and again in 446.[4] The Troadesian porticoes, which ran along the main artery of the city between the main gates of both the Constantinian and Theodosian walls, and the towers of the gates of the Constantinian walls were destroyed by fire in 448, as mentioned by Marcellinus.[5] The great fire of September 464 was the most devastating of all early Byzantine infernos. It began in the docks along the Golden Horn and spread right across the city to the Harbour of Julian, burning eight of the city's fourteen regions (465. 2).[6] Its impact on the city's economic and civic life cannot be overestimated.[7] The later fire in 491 destroyed, according to Marcellinus, 'part of the city and most of the hippodrome' (491. 2). He also records another fire in the hippodrome in 507 when the northern stairway and its arches collapsed, while in 509 a fierce blaze reduced to ashes both porticoes extending from the Forum of Constantine to the statue of Perdix (509). Marcellinus also notes, as an eyewitness, the Nika riots in 532 when so much of the city was left rubble. In addition to those described by Marcellinus there were fires at Constantinople in 388, 400, 406, 428, 476, 498, and 512.[8] They ensured a regular rebuilding of extensive parts of the city.[9]

[3] For earthquakes: Downey (1955), 596–600; for fires: Schneider (1941), 382–403.

[4] Schneider (1941), 383 n. 2 is mistaken to think that Marcellinus under 446 describes the fire of 404.

[5] Janin (1964), 93, followed by Dagron (1974), 272, wrongly attributes this damage to a quake.

[6] Detailed references in Schneider (1941), 383 and Croke (1995), 97 (explaining the date of September 464, and not 465, as usually stated). [7] Mango (1985), 51.

[8] Janin (1964), 35 (ignoring Schneider) also lists a fire in 469 which is actually a doublet of the 464 fire in the Chronicon Paschale (Whitby/Whitby (1989), 91 n. 296).

[9] Mango (1986), 124–5.

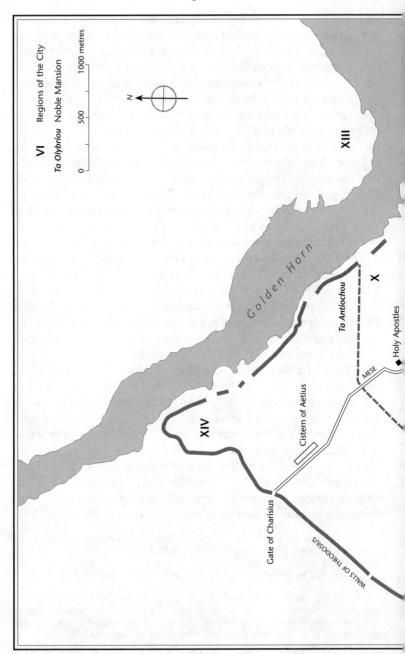

Regions of the City

VI

Ta Olybriou Noble Mansion

N

0   500   1000 metres

XIII

Golden Horn

Ta Antiochou

X

MESE

Holy Apostles

XIV

Cistern of Aetius

Gate of Charisius

WALLS OF THEODOSIUS

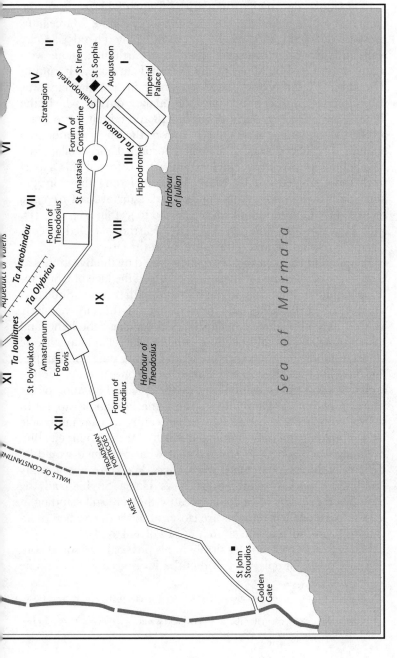

Map 2. The Constantinople of Marcellinus

Even more destructive than these frequent blazes were the recurrent earthquakes the city experienced. Again, Marcellinus provides detailed testimony. In 447 most of the Theodosian city walls and fifty-seven towers collapsed in an earthquake along with many statues and buildings in the Forum Tauri (a.k.a. Forum of Theodosius).[10] According to Marcellinus, in 479 the city was subjected to 40 successive days of quakes during which the Troadesian porticoes, burnt down in 448 and rebuilt, were again levelled along with several churches; even the mighty statue and column of Theodosius I in the Forum Tauri collapsed.[11] Marcellinus remains our chief extant witness for all this. Apart from those singled out by Marcellinus, including those in 396 and 400,[12] there were several other quakes (or at least tremors) recorded for Constantinople in the period to 534: in 403, 407, 417, 438, 442, 467, 487, and 525. Like fires, earthquakes led to considerable rebuilding and refurbishment in the city.

Frequent fire and earthquakes, interpreted by the Byzantines as God's sign of warning for their sins, changed the face of Constantinople quite dramatically in the fifth and sixth century. Similarly, subsequent earthquakes and fires disfigured the city regularly as well and necessitated extensive and regular rebuilding and refurbishing. So it will not do to project Marcellinus' picture of Constantinople onto a composite tenth-century one, for example, for the city was often being forced to reconstruct. As for the archaeological traces, symbolized by the splendid isolation of the 'Burnt Column' of Constantine, the same limitations apply. In such a compact and continuous urban centre as Constantinople later rebuilding not only eliminated much of the previous city but, by being built over, also ensured that what remained would be difficult of access for modern researchers. We know about many buildings, especially churches such as Hagia Sophia and the Stoudios monastery of St John, because they are still standing at least in part; or their remains are closer to the surface when excavations begin, such as the church of St Polyeuktos.

Having set our chronicler firmly in his physical and social context at Constantinople we will then be in a position to examine

---

[10] Croke (1981*b*), 112–47.

[11] Marcell. s.a. 480. 1. For the date: see Croke (1995), 103 (in opposition to Stein (1949), 787).

[12] Grattarola (1989), 237–49 (for the 396 quake) and Cameron, Alan (1987), 355 (for that in 400, dated by Marcellinus to 402).

more closely how this influences and shapes the choice of subject matter and viewpoint of the chronicle. In particular, we can detect and explain the author's reaction to the religious controversy of his day and the frequent civil violence of the city. We can also see how his selective picture of individual emperors is conditioned primarily by his attitude to their religious policies. Of special significance is the testimony which the chronicle provides to the texture of public life at Constantinople. Marcellinus offers an important insight into civic ceremonial and the development of the Byzantine liturgical calendar in the fifth and early sixth centuries.

MONUMENTS AND CEREMONIES

To contemporaries early Byzantine Constantinople was known by a variety of titles: it was 'New Rome', 'Second Rome', 'the Royal City', 'the August City', or just simply 'the City'.[13] Perhaps the most common of these epithets is the 'imperial' or 'royal' or 'august' city, thus advertising its character as an imperial capital and residence of the court. Marcellinus refers to Constantinople most frequently as the *urbs augusta* (s.a. 381. 1, 431. 2, 435. 2, 436, 438, 447. 1, 447. 3, 501. 3, 509, 511) and the *urbs/civitas regia* (s.a. 393, 433, 439. 2, 446. 2, 480. 1, 487, 527, 528, 532). Marcellinus had once been part of the court himself and his chronicle is essentially a document of the *urbs augusta*. Embedded in it is a great amount of material relating to the monuments and public life of the city, the monumental stage for the liturgical theatre of the imperial capital.

Although Marcellinus was a *cancellarius* to Justinian in the early 520s and must have had a close familiarity with the sprawling buildings and grounds of the imperial palace itself, he never says as much. In fact he only mentions the palace on a single occasion in passing (532).[14] Likewise, he says relatively little about the hippodrome, that other monumentally grand construction so central to the life of the city where the emperor and his people came together in their common enthusiasm for the charioteer and the ceremony surrounding a day at the races.[15] In the chronicle

[13] In general: Fenster (1968), 20–96.
[14] For the palace: Müller-Wiener (1977), 229–30.
[15] For the hippodrome: Dagron (1974), 320–47; Guilland (1969), 1. 369 ff.; Müller-Wiener (1977), 64–71.

the hippodrome is the scene of frequent riots (s.a. 445. 2, 473, 491. 2, 507. 1, 2) during one of which the northern stairway collapsed just as the emperor was entering the hippodrome (507. 2). The hippodrome also appears in the chronicle as the setting for Justinian's consular games in 521 and the Nika revolt in 532. As for its physical appearance and layout, there is no reference in the chronicle to the *spina* except for the erection of the obelisk whose base displays reliefs of Theodosius presiding at the games (390. 3). However, there is mention of the 'imperial box' (*kathisma*): during the monophysite riots in 512 the populace assembled and called for Anastasius 'in front of his throne' (512. 6); while Marcellinus offers the only extant indication of the fact that in 528 Justinian remodelled and elevated the *kathisma*, presumably making it more conspicuous or prominent, along with restoring the porticoes from which the senators watched the races:[16]

The emperor Justinian the Victor rebuilt the imperial box and its ancient throne designed for viewing and applauding the contests in the hippodrome, making it more elevated and brighter than it had been. With customary generosity he also reconstructed each portico where the Senators sat as spectators. (528)

Furthermore, the hippodrome and palace were integral parts of a ceremonial site which also incorporated the patriarchal church of Constantinople—the 'great church', Hagia Sophia. In the chronicle of Marcellinus the 'great church' appears as 'our church' (s.a. 380, 399. 2, 431. 2) where the Goths sought refuge during the reaction against Gainas in 400. Consequently, the angry Byzantine mob, in time-honoured Roman fashion, stripped off part of the roof and hurled down tiles on the hapless Goths inside (399). The church was soon repaired and in 403 a porphyry column, topped by a silver statue of the empress Eudoxia, was set 'beside the church' (403. 2) according to Marcellinus who says it is 'still standing' (*hactenus sistit*). The statue offended the patriarch John Chrysostom and his comments on the vanity of the empress led to his exile in 404. Not long after, as Marcellinus records, the church was burnt down (404. 1) and, eleven years later, he notes its rebuilding and rededication by the patriarch Atticus (415. 1).

---

[16] Bury (1923*b*), 83 suggests these were 'probably at the lowest row', although senators might be expected to have preferred a view further back from the dust and noise of the track.

Nothing has been recovered of the original Hagia Sophia, but part of the facade of the Theodosian church has been discovered.[17] Hagia Sophia appears in the chronicle on two other occasions which require elucidation. First, a massacre in the church and the firing of the altar in 431:

The barbarians who were being sheltered by the imperial city converged on our church in a threatening manner. When in their hostility they hurled fire into the church in order to burn the altar, they killed each other because God was against them. (431. 2)

A group of barbarian domestics, fleeing ill-treatment at the hand of their aristocratic master sought refuge in the church. The domestics drew their swords and defied all attempts to persuade them to desist until they eventually lost hope and fell on each other's swords 'because God was against them' (431. 2). Second, Marcellinus notes in 446 that a fire destroyed (or at least affected) the 'temple' of Constantinople—'the church of the imperial city was burnt in a fire' (446. 2). Assuming that *templum* does mean the 'church' (and it is difficult to see what else it could mean here), then we have to include in the history of the pre-Justinianic Hagia Sophia the fact that it also caught alight for some reason in 446.[18] Besides Hagia Sophia, there are other churches of the imperial city but Marcellinus' information on them is not of decisive importance for their construction or location: SS Cosmas and Damian where Laurence was healed (516. 3), St Anastasia's where Gregory Nazianzen preached (380), St Theodore's (512. 3), the church of the Macedonians outside the Constantinian walls (429. 1) and that of St Laurence (439. 2), where relics of Stephen gained by Eudocia in 439 were venerated in the time of Marcellinus and which was finally completed by Pulcheria in 453, the year of her death (453. 5).

In the early sixth century the public life of the city, as it always had at Rome, centred around the large and splendid public places where the populace could meet to converse or admire, to protest or transact business. The original forum of Constantinople in the time of Septimius Severus was a porticoed area called the 'tetrastoon', just north-east of the palace and in front of it the senate house was constructed by Constantine.[19] Constantine

---

[17] Müller-Wiener (1977), 84–6.
[18] Schneider (1941), 383 n. 2.
[19] Mango (1959), 42–7; Guilland (1969), 2. 40–54; Müller-Wiener (1977), 248.

named it the Augusteon after he had erected there a column and statue of his mother, Helena Augusta. Throughout the fourth and fifth centuries it served as a forum, being rebuilt and expanded with porticoes in 459. The Augusteon was eventually destroyed in the Nika riots. Indeed, Justinian was repairing and remodelling it when Marcellinus wrote the continuation of his chronicle in 534 but Justinian's Augusteon did not cover the entire area of the former forum. The new Augusteon served less as a public forum and more as an enclosed courtyard for the 'great church'. In the square of the Augusteon stood several statues among which was a silver statue of Theodosius atop a column. Marcellinus describes the column and statue in 518 (and presumably 534) as still visible (390. 3). It is possible that the column survived the Nika conflagration and was in fact still standing in 534, in which case Justinian only took it down at a later date. In either case it was probably on the same site that Justinian erected his famous pillar and bronze equestrian statue in 543.[20]

Moving in a north-westerly direction along Middle Street (*Mese*) lined with double porticoes from which, at frequent intervals, imperial images watched over the passers-by, we come to the Forum of Constantine, shaped in the form of an ellipse. Within this area with its massive gates at each end stood a tribunal to review troops, a senate house, and many statues notably one of Apollo from Troy.[21] From the forum there radiated splendid porticoes to the west (*Forum Tauri*) and north (*Strategion*), the latter of which, so we learn from Marcellinus, were destroyed in a damaging fire 'from the Forum of Constantine as far as the very delicate statue of Perdix' (509. 1). The central monument of the Forum of Constantine was a porphyry column of the emperor, known in its present form as the 'Burnt Column'. On top of it stood a statue of Constantine later replaced by a cross,[22] and in the statue itself were lodged fragments of the 'True Cross' sent to Constantine by his mother Helena (Soc. *HE* 1. 17). Marcellinus refers to the column in locating the *cisterna maxima* constructed in 407—'beside the porphyry column of the emperor Constantine under the street crossing in his forum' (407), that is, near where the Mese led into the sigma-shaped eastern portico of the forum.

[20] Details in Janin (1964), 74; Guilland (1969), 2. 41, and esp. Mango (1993*c*), 1–8.
[21] On the forum and its many statues: Janin (1964), 62–4 and Müller-Wiener (1977), 255–6.   [22] Janin (1964), 79; Mango (1993*b*), 1–6.

By Marcellinus' day the Forum of Constantine was already known simply as 'The Forum', obviously from the time when it was the only forum (as such) in the city and formed a central location in imperial processions.[23] It was during one such procession in 512 that a religious riot broke out and which Marcellinus describes in detail as an eyewitness (s.a. 512. 3–6).[24] According to him, the trouble began on Sunday 4 November in Hagia Sophia when, at the instigation of the emperor, a decree was read by which the monophysite verse 'who was crucified for us' was added to the Trisagion by Marinus, the finance minister of Anastasius, and Plato the city prefect, standing in the pulpit. Thereupon, the orthodox continued to chant the original hymn even louder. Some were forcibly removed from the church and later died in prison, some perished on the spot. On the next day, still following Marcellinus, even more of the orthodox were put to death in the church of St Theodore.[25] By this stage the ranks of the orthodox were mutinous and prepared for nothing less than the replacement of the impious emperor. Consequently, on the following day (Tuesday 6 November) the orthodox arranged to assemble in the Forum of Constantine. Some had marched across town to the Forum putting to death along the way certain monastic supporters of Anastasius; while others had been continuing their chant of the Trisagion day and night; still others brought to the forum keys of the city gates and the military standards so that they turned the forum into a sort of military camp ('where they had measured out a religious camp'). They had chosen to camp in the Forum of Constantine because the emperor was due to appear there, in the liturgical procession marking the anniversary of the eruption of Mt. Vesuvius on 6 November 472 (s.a. 512. 3, cf. 472. 1). Action was taken, however, before the emperor arrived.

Marcellinus notes precisely that the orthodox mob proclaimed Areobindus emperor while Anastasius was actually on his way from Hagia Sophia to the forum—'while Anastasius was passing in procession' (512. 4). He continues his account by describing how the statues and images of Anastasius (presumably in the Forum and the porticoes of the streets leading from it) were torn

[23] Dagron (1974), 98.
[24] For the sources: Stein (1949), 177–8 and Charanis (1974), 77–9.
[25] Vict. Tonn. 513 (II, 195) conflates the events of Sunday and Monday.

down and how, when the generals Celer and Patricius were sent to placate the mob, they were pelted with a barrage of rocks, and that the homes of Marinus and Plato were put to the torch. The rioting and looting continued for three days, according to Marcellinus, while Victor of Tunnuna (513 (ii. 195)) reports that the porticoes along the path of the procession were burnt for a distance of ninety-four columns in the direction of the Forum of Constantine. On the third day of the rioting, Marcellinus continues, the orthodox moved from the Forum of Constantine to the hippodrome brandishing crucifixes and copies of the gospels and chanting the Trisagion in front of the *kathisma*. They also screamed for Marinus and Plato to be thrown to the wild beasts.[26] At this point the emperor appeared without his crown and offered to abdicate. The crowd, however, was struck by the gesture and soon drifted away peaceably, following words of reassurance from the emperor. Yet for some of the orthodox, like Marcellinus himself, these were the monophysite emperor's 'usual lies and empty words' (512. 7).

The porticoed Mese led out from the Forum of Constantine to the Forum of Theodosius, the next public place along the route about 500 metres away.[27] Also known as the Forum Tauri[28] it was built by Theodosius I in imitation of the forum of Trajan at Rome. In 386 Theodosius erected a huge column with his statue upon it in the forum. The forum was inaugurated in 393 and an equestrian statue of the emperor dedicated the following year.[29] The column was also a conscious imitation of that of Trajan and was adorned with spiral reliefs depicting the military triumphs of Theodosius, presumably those commemorated at Constantinople in 386.[30] This forum was graced at either end by a large arch, was decorated with many statues and later contained a palace of Leo I.[31] Such a heavily built forum could be particularly dangerous during an earthquake. Marcellinus reports that in the devastating one of 447 which caused the celebrated rebuilding of the

---

[26] Although *venationes* were outlawed by Anastasius criminals were still thrown to the beasts (Cameron, Alan (1973), 230 n. 6).

[27] In general: Janin (1964), 64–8; Müller-Wiener (1977), 258–65.

[28] The reason is not clear. It has been suggested that it was named after the patrician Taurus who died in 449 (*PLRE* 2. 1056–7), but it was already called the *Forum Tauri* by the time of the *Notitia* of Constantinople (*c*.425).

[29] Theoph. AM 5878 (70. 20–1); *Chron. Pasch.* 563. 6–8.

[30] Marcell. s.a. 386. 1 with Janin (1964), 46 and Mango (1985), 43–4.

[31] Janin (1964), 65–7; Mango (1985), 43–5.

Theodosian walls, many of the statues fell down along with some large blocks (*saxa ingentia*) on top of an unspecified building (*in aedificio posita*). They were probably from the basilica, the only building of suitable size in the area at the time. Nevertheless, so we are told, no one was hurt (s.a. 447. 1). However, the earthquake of 447 did not shake down the column of Theodosius. It continued to stand until the onset of a much more damaging quake in 478 when the statue of Theodosius and its two supports collapsed, although the column itself was unaffected. As Marcellinus notes, 'the statue of Theodosius the Great, which had been placed in the forum of Taurus above the spiral column, collapsed after two of its supports had given way' (480. 1).

The base of the column was where foreign ambassadors were received with ceremony, and where the emperor was welcomed home when returning from the west.[32] It was there, for example, that the city prefect Ursus offered a gold crown to Theodosius II on his return from Heraclea in 416.[33] It was probably at this site in 384 that Persian ambassadors were received, as recorded by Marcellinus (s.a. 384. 1).[34] All these events took place in the forum. The Theodosian column continued to stand without its statue until 506. Then, according to Malalas (16. 13), John the Paphlagonian restored all the bronze statues of Constantine and made a very large statue of Anastasius which he placed on top of a vacant column in the Forum of Theodosius. Marcellinus describes it thus: 'a statue of the emperor Anastasius was set up on top of a lofty column in the Forum of Taurus in the same place where that of Theodosius the Great had once stood' (506). The fate of the statue of Anastasius is not known, although it has been suggested that it was torn down during the 512 riots against Anastasius.[35] Marcellinus does mention 'images and statues' of Anastasius 'hurled to the ground' (512. 5) but seems to be referring more to the area of the Forum of Constantine and the Mese up to the region of the palace. Surely the 'images and statues' of the chronicle were easily accessible ones within the area of the 512 procession where they could be reached and violated by an enraged mob without great effort. If a statue on top of the column

---

[32] *Patria CP* 2. 47 (Preger (1901), 176).
[33] *Chron. Pasch.* 574, cf. Const. Porph. *Caer.* 1. App. (496–7).
[34] Müller-Wiener (1977), 253–4, cf. Soc. *HE* 5. 12.
[35] Guilland (1969), 2. 59.

of Theodosius could survive a violent quake like that of 447 intact, then it hardly seems likely that it was easily overturned during a mere riot. The column itself and its reliefs finally disappeared around 1500, at least it was no longer standing when Pierre Gilles visited the city in 1550.[36] Another monument from the Forum of Theodosius is the triumphal arch of Theodosius which had collapsed in an earthquake in 740. However it is reconstructed, the arch was a monument of unusually large proportions, certainly larger than any known triumphal arch. It supported statues of both Honorius—facing the west, and Arcadius, facing the east, and probably served as a magisterial entrance to the forum.[37]

From the Forum Tauri the Mese leads through the Forum Bovis, about which little is known and little unearthed[38] and thence to the Forum of Theodosius in Region XII, more commonly known as the Forum of Arcadius or Xerolophos after the hill on which it was built. The forum contained a bronze sculptured spiral column of Arcadius erected in 402/3 to commemorate victory over the Goths.[39] That much is certain. The rest is confusing and the information of Marcellinus crucial. Under 421 he reports 'Theodosius dedicated a huge statue on an enormous column to his father Arcadius, in his forum' (421. 2) which indicates that in 421 the forum was called the Forum of Arcadius. Whether the statue had stood on the column, or whether the column had stood without a statue until 421 and was only formally dedicated on 10 July in that year, is not certain although the latter alternative is preferable.[40]

The other major forum in the Constantinople of Marcellinus was located in Region V.[41] It too was called 'the Forum of Theodosius' but was more commonly known as the 'Forum Strategii' since it was the area of the old Strategion or exercise-ground for troops.[42] The forum contained a tripod of Hecate, and

[36] Ibid. It seems that the column was dismantled by Sultan Bayazid and parts incorporated into the building of a nearby bath. Some of these fragments were brought to light in 1928 during the British excavations (Casson and Talbot Rice (1929), 57–60).

[37] Schneider (1936), 19; Mango (1985), 44.

[38] Schneider (1936), 95 n. 16 reports the discovery of a large number of marble columns which may belong to the forum.

[39] Theoph. AM 5895 (77. 24–5) with Müller-Wiener (1977), 250–3.

[40] Janin (1964), 65 confuses this statue with that of Theodosius in the Forum Tauri.

[41] *Notitia CP* in *ND*, 233.

[42] In general: Janin (1964), 431–2.

a large equestrian statue of Constantine. Near this statue stood a pillar upon which was engraved a law designating Constantinople as the New Rome.[43] Lastly there is mention in the chronicle of Marcellinus of a bronze female statue holding a 'horn of plenty' which was damaged in a fire of 510 and immediately repaired by the *statuarii* :

A copper image standing in the forum of Strategius above an arch and holding a horn of Fortune's plenty caught alight in a fire and was burnt. It lost an arm which, however, the sculptors refashioned immediately. (510. 1)[44]

The Theodosian forum in the Strategion played a lesser role in public ceremony than the other fora. However, it was the place where the emperor was received back into the capital when returning from the east. The emperors of the fifth century and early sixth were far more sedentary than their fourth-century counterparts and eastern expeditions were rare. Such ceremonial receptions at the Forum Strategii, like those at the Forum Tauri, were recorded at Constantinople. That explains the significance of Marcellinus' entry in 436 when 'the emperor Theodosius set out with his fleet for the city of Cyzicus and, when he had demonstrated considerable generosity towards that city, he sailed back to the imperial city' (436). There is no other record of this expedition which has been dated to between April and June, 436,[45] but it was perhaps to offer 'considerable generosity' (*multa munificentia*) following some natural disaster such as an earthquake. The entry under 443 is to be explained in the same way—the emperor's ceremonial reception in the forum when 'the emperor Theodosius returned to the city from his Asian expedition' (443. 2). On 27 August Theodosius returned from a trip via Bithynia to Heraclea in the Pontus where he made attempts to restore the fallen city, again like the 436 visit to Cyzicus.[46]

At the seventh milestone from the city was located the region known as the Hebdomon.[47] It was originally a parade-ground for soldiers but later became an important residence of the imperial

---

[43] Soc. *HE* 1. 16, cf. *Patria CP* 2. 43 (Preger (1901), 138).

[44] The statue is often referred to by the patriographers (references in Janin (1964), 438) while its damage in the fire of 510 is also mentioned by Zonaras (3. 141).

[45] Seeck (1919), 365.

[46] Roueché (1986), 130–2.

[47] Janin (1964), 446–9.

court and a useful assembly area. In 394, before setting out against the usurper Eugenius, Theodosius mustered his army there (Soc. 7. 24) and Marcellinus informs us that in 514 the rebel Vitalian encamped there with his 60,000 supporters (s.a. 514. 1). By the later fourth century, it had become an imperial retreat. However, its real importance lay in the fact that it became the place where the new emperor was proclaimed by the army. As mentioned by Marcellinus, Arcadius (383. 2) and then Honorius (393) were proclaimed there. So too the fifth-century emperors Theodosius II, Marcian, Leo I, and Zeno were all proclaimed at the Hebdomon. Among the several monuments at the Hebdomon was a granite column of Theodosius II dedicated by his sisters to celebrate the emperor's peace with Persia and the Huns after 422,[48] an occasion reflected in Marcellinus' simple entries: 'the Huns devastated Thrace' (422. 3) and 'the Persians made peace with the Romans' (422. 4).

These public places and their monuments, the streets and the fora of Constantinople, were places where the populace could congregate at any time but a special significance derived from their function as the stage for the liturgical theatre of the capital in the time of Marcellinus. They provided a location for the increasingly elaborate ceremonial of imperial elevations and annual processions in commemoration of certain anniversaries; or other ceremonies like that held each year on 5 October when the city's fourteen regionarchs would dance in the Augusteon in honour of the reigning emperor.[49]

THE LITURGICAL DIMENSION OF PUBLIC LIFE

Although not explicitly founded as a Christian capital, Constantinople soon became one. Through most of the fourth century the ceremonial of Christian life in Constantinople was limited and grew only slowly. Accordingly, in the martyrology of Jerome there are very few commemorations recorded for Constantinople, considerably less than for Antioch which was a much more important imperial Christian city at the time.[50] There were, however, some

---

[48] Demangel (1945), 33 ff.; Holum (1977), 153 ff.; Croke (1977), 347 ff.

[49] *Patria CP* 2. 15 (Preger (1901), 158).

[50] Constantinopolitan commemorations are noted for: S. Anastasius (25 Dec.); Timothy (9 Mar.); Effucus, Serapio, and others (18 May); Paul, Fortunatus, and others (7 June);

local saints to be honoured[51] and a growing number of local shrines and churches.[52] For a fixed ceremonial to develop there needed to be a mainly resident emperor and a stable court. Between the foundation of the city in 330 and the death of Valens in 378 emperors had only ever spent brief periods (weeks and months) there usually resting and resupplying between military campaigns. The reign of Theodosius I ushered in a period of rapid change. From 379 the emperor began to spend years in the capital, and was rarely in the field, while from 395 emperors hardly ever left the city. It was in this period during the reigns of Theodosius I, his son (Arcadius) and grandson (Theodosius II) that the city's imperial and liturgical calendars and ceremonial took shape, so that by 451 the patriarch was fully involved in the coronation of an emperor (Marcian).[53] The elevation of the patriarch's status at the Council of Constantinople in 381 to equality with the bishop of Rome advanced his role. The ensuing development of the prestige and authority of the patriarch also enhanced his ceremonial function, while the demilitarization of the court and its attendant pageantry were augmented further by the emergence of a local aristocracy of office.

During this period the ever-increasing imperial ceremonial became liturgified, the people became integrated into the ritual, and the monumental shape of the city's layout (particularly the great public places and churches) was established. By the mid-fifth century Constantinople, likewise Antioch and other major Byzantine cities, had become the theatre for public displays in which an institutionalized religious tenor and structure replaced a secular ceremonial.[54] Constantinople became the city where emperors were born, married, elevated to the throne, celebrated their anniversaries and victories, died and were buried. All of these events gave rise to an official public proclamation of a stylized and detailed written announcement, normally by the city prefect in the case of Constantinople.[55] Indeed, it was required that 'whenever any of our auspicious achievements are

Nuus, Migetia, and Mingini (15 June); Olius and Stephen (27 Aug.); bishops Alexander and Vivianus (30 Aug.); bishop John (13 Sept.).

[51] Details in Dagron (1974), 392–406.
[52] Details in Maraval (1985), 400–10.
[53] Treitinger (1956), 16–18; Dagron (1974), 48, 78–93.
[54] Dagron (1974), 405–9, 454–8, 495; Patlagean (1977), 215; MacCormack (1981), 62ff.
[55] McCormick (1986), 190–5.

announced, if wars should cease, if victories should arise, if the honour of the bestowal of royal vestments be added to the calendar, if the announcement of the tranquillity of peace that has been concluded is to be spread abroad, if by chance we display the sacred imperial countenances to the larger multitudes, such occasions shall be announced and received without price' (*CTh* 8. 11. 4: 2 Feb. 383). The city was decorated, the streets were cleared and cleaned, and the participants carefully prepared.

The full variety and range of ceremonial surrounding all these announced occasions is embodied in the tenth-century *Book of Ceremonies* of Constantine Porphyrogenitus and the various *synaxaria* document the occasion and course of specifically religious processions,[56] including the ritualized protocol for all these occasions.[57] A key feature of this process was the adaptation of the stational liturgy of Jerusalem to the much newer urban environment of Constantinople,[58] but equally important was the definition of the city's religious space. These were the areas which played a major role in focusing the energies and interests of the people in the liturgical and theological celebrations of the day. This ritualized use of the city's main public areas reinforced a sense of public religious commitment and doctrinal unity.[59] The tenth-century calendar which documents the liturgical commemorations of the city was basically laid down in the fifth century. In other words, by the time of Marcellinus most of the liturgical processions recorded in later Byzantine calendars were already institutionalized at Constantinople.

Many of these processions marked the arrival of relics in the imperial capital.[60] The earliest was probably when the relics of Timothy (356), followed by those of Luke and Andrew (357), were deposited in the church of the Holy Apostles, then the arrival in Constantinople in 360 of the bodies of Pamphilus, Theodulus, and their companions.[61] In 391 Theodosius solemnly received the head of John the Baptist at his new Hebdomon church, while the reigns of Arcadius and Theodosius II regularly witnessed such

---

[56] Janin (1966), 69–88 for the processions and Cameron, Averil (1987), 106–36 for the context of the *Book of Ceremonies*.

[57] Dagron (1974), 92–102, 409 ff.; Nelson (1976), esp. 101–14.

[58] Baldovin (1987), 239; Smith (1987), 91–5.

[59] Dagron (1977), 1–25; Baldovin (1987), 182 ff., 211–14.

[60] Details in Maraval (1985), 93–6.

[61] Ced. 1. 523.

occasions. Great ceremony surrounded the arrival of relics of Samuel in 406,[62] of Zachariah, and then of Stephen which may be represented on the Trier Ivory,[63] the unearthing of the relics of the forty martyrs of Sebaste and their triumphal entry into the city which was witnessed by Sozomen (*HE* 9. 2), of the discovery of Stephen's relics on 16 September (*SEC* 52. 4–6) followed, on 22 December, by the arrival of the relics of Anastasia from Sirmium in 458 (Theoph. AM 5950 (III. 7–9)). In all these cases it was the commemoration of the arrival of the relics in Constantinople and their deposition, a moment of destiny for the city highlighted by this latest divine blessing, which became important.[64]

By the mid-fifth century many other commonplace functions gave rise to an organized ritual involving stylized language and behaviour: the announcement of victory, for example, or natural disasters such as earthquakes; the reception of ambassadors; all imperial family occasions. In fact, the normal imperial movements in and around the city had become conventionally ritualized in the Roman tradition of *adventus*. The common features of all these processions and liturgical re-enactments was the role of the imperial household and patriarch, integrated with the populace in a common cause of propitiation and celebration. The ceremonial frequently involved repetition of prayers and slogans, often of a directly political nature. Such acclamations were an established feature of late Roman urban life and culture. The rhythmical chanting of slogans had the effect of attracting the uncommitted.[65] Sometimes it also attracted hostility and conflict. At all times, however, acclamations required recording and reporting to the emperor as the reflection of an almost oracular insight.[66] Panegyrics too frequently accompanied the ritual encounter between the people and the emperor or his highest officials. The emperor of the panegyrics came to be portrayed as the 'focal point of a complex courtly ritual'.[67]

The impetus for this major development of Byzantine ceremonial in the fifth century was the imperial court and its almost daily progresses into, out of, and around the city on a range of occasions.[68] In the chronicle of Marcellinus we can discern

[62] Holum (1982), 90ff.   [63] Holum and Vikan (1979), 113–33.
[64] Brown (1980), 92–3.   [65] Gregory (1982), 212, 217.
[66] Roueché (1984), 187–8.   [67] MacCormack (1981), 6.
[68] Dagron (1974), 91–2.

something of the importance of the imperial household in this ceremonial, and the impact of other processions and commemorations. Some of these (the procession of November 512, Theodosius II's returns from Cyzicus in 436 and from Asia in 443) have already been mentioned. Imperial anniversaries were a cause for great rejoicing and ceremony, so too the birth of new princes and princesses and their baptism, to judge from a contemporary account of Theodosius II (Markos Diakonos, *Vita Porphyrii* 47). The chronicle notes a number of imperial occasions (see Table 4.1).

TABLE 4. 1. *Imperial occasions noted in Marcellinus' Chronicle*

Births	Honorius (384); Flaccilla (397); Pulcheria (399); Theodosius II (401); Marina (403); Valentinian III (419); Eudoxia (422).
Deaths	Theodosius I (395); Eudoxia (404); Arcadius (408); Flaccilla (431); Arcadia (444); Marina (449); Pulcheria (453); Valentinian III (455); Ariadne (515).
Marriages	Theodosius II and Eudocia (421); Valentinian III and Eudoxia (437).
Anniversaries	V Arcadius (387); V Theodosius II (406); X Theodosius II (411); XXV Honorius (422); XXX Theodosius II (430); XL Theodosius II (439); XLV Theodosius II (444).

Other specifically imperial events recorded in the chronicle are: the transference to Constantinople of the bodies of both Valentinian I on 21 February 382 (s.a. 382. 1) and Theodosius I on 8 November 395 (s.a. 395. 2) which became the day for annual Byzantine commemoration of Theodosius (*SEC* 205. 24–5); the entry of Galla into Constantinople in 386 (s.a. 386. 2); the expulsion of Honoria to Constantinople in 434, as well as the elevation of both Pulcheria (s.a. 414. 1) and Galla Placidia (s.a. 424. 1) to the rank of *Augusta*. Dedications of monuments, many of them imperial, are also included in the chronicle and these too were occasions for great public celebrations: the *thermae Theodosianae* in 427,[69] the *thermae Arcadianiae* in 394,[70] the Achillean baths in 433,[71] and the cistern of Aetius in 421, named after the city prefect at that time.[72] However, there is one particular dedication of an imperial monument which became notorious, the silver statue of

[69] Janin (1964), 219.   [70] Ibid. 217.   [71] Ibid. 216.
[72] Ibid. 203.

Eudoxia: 'A silver statue of Eudoxia, the wife of Arcadius, was placed on a porphyry column beside the church. It is still standing' (403).

It was dedicated in 403 by the city prefect Simplicius and celebrated with loud acclamations, dancing, games, and other manifestations of public rejoicing usually observed on the erection of statues of emperors.[73] It stood very close to the church of Hagia Sophia, a proximity which the patriarch John Chrysostom found offensive, in the area called Pittakia in front of the senate house. It was John's vociferous objection to this statue which set off the chain of events leading to his expulsion from Constantinople.

Besides the ceremonies on the occasion of the dedication of monuments the population of the capital provided an audience for, as well as participated in, the increasing number of ceremonial processions to and from various parts of the city. Traces of some of these can be found in Marcellinus' chronicle. In 431 he notes that, en route to the public granaries, the emperor Theodosius was stoned by the hungry populace: 'At this time, while the emperor Theodosius was in procession to the public granaries, he was pelted with stones by a hungry populace because of the severe grain shortage among the people' (431. 3).

Every year, probably in summer, the emperor and the City Prefect would travel in full procession to inspect the current levels of grain reserves. This will have occurred during the emperor's annual inspection of the granaries which is described in the *Book of Ceremonies* (*caer.* 2. 51 (699)). Other indications in the chronicle of processions can be found in 507 when the northern stairway of the hippodrome, together with its arch, collapsed in a fire while the emperor was in procession (*in processibus commorante*). Exactly what this procession might be is unclear, perhaps just a ceremonial entry into the hippodrome. We have already explained events surrounding the Vesuvius procession in 512, to which should be added Marcellinus' record of the actual eruption itself and the fact that it is celebrated annually by the Byzantines (*Byzantii*, 472). Likewise, he mentions under 480 an earthquake which is celebrated by the *Byzantii* on 24 September each year (s.a. 480. 1). In fact, the earthquake took place in 478 (not 480) and on 25 September (not 24) but what is interesting about this is that by the early sixth century it was not clear which annual commemoration

---

[73] Soz. *HE* 8. 20.

recalled which earthquake.[74] By the time of Marcellinus there were earthquake processions on 26 January and 25 September. It was during the 26 January procession in 457 that the emperor Marcian was taken ill and died.[75] The great fire of 464 (s.a. 465. 1) was commemorated each year thereafter on 1 September (*SEC* 6. 3–9).

Besides the processions in commemoration of natural disasters, the chronicle records the original occurrence of other events which must have especially interested the chronicler because they were associated in his time with annual liturgies and processions in which he presumably participated: in 428 the memory of John Chrysostom (*SEC* 46. 8–16) and the arrival in Constantinople of his remains on 27 January (*SEC* 425. 23–30); in 453 the discovery of the head of John the Baptist (s.a. 453. 1–4) on 24 February (*SEC* 524. 8–10; *Typ.* 244–6); in 484 the arrival in Constantinople of the victims from the persecution of Huneric in Africa on December 8 (*SEC* 287. 28–289. 36). Although not the subject of processions, there were annual commemorations of various church councils and of individual emperors. The sacralization of time is reflected above all in the ceremonial to commemorate the start of the new indiction on 1 September (*SEC* 1. 25–7) and the new consular year on 1 January (the *Kalends*), as well as the birthday and *dies imperii* of the current emperor. Of course, the central feasts of the Nativity, Epiphany, the Paschal triduum, and Ascension also involved the imperial court and were all in place before the end of the fourth century.

It is incontestable that the late sixth-century, more precisely the reign of Justin II, was a crucial point in the development of devotion to the Virgin and to icons, as well as in the relocation of much ceremonial, including coronations, to an ecclesiastical setting. It was also the time when the ceremonial of an imperial triumph was concentrated within the hippodrome for a more structured and restricted audience.[76] However, the wider claim that this was also the period when the Byzantine processional calendar was 'now probably for the first time being regulated . . . the emperor took possession of the city',[77] or that the 'public life of the emperor took on a liturgical quality'[78] is not so easily justified.

---

[74] For the date: Croke (1995), 103.
[75] Croke (1978*b*), 5–9.
[76] McCormick (1986), 77–9, 94–9.
[77] Cameron, Averil (1979), 5.
[78] Browning (1980), 29.

Rather it would appear that the late fourth and the fifth centuries saw the development of the essential structure and content of the Byzantine liturgical year with ever-present ceremonial and processions through the streets of Constantinople, just as it saw a rapid expansion in the construction of new churches and monasteries.[79] As an indication of this period of development it is instructive to take a conspectus of the tenth-century liturgical processions mentioned in the *synaxarion* of Hagia Sophia. There were more than fifty processions being celebrated annually at Constantinople in the later tenth century. Most of them originated at a specific point in time normally on the anniversary of the natural disaster, the reception of the relics in Constantinople or the promulgation of the feast. The century in which the Byzantine feasts involving processions were first held can be analysed as in Table 4.2.[80]

To summarize, seventeen of the tenth-century liturgical processions were instituted in the fourth century and fourteen in the fifth; four in the sixth century; five in the seventh; three in the eighth; four in the ninth and one in the tenth century. In other words, almost two-thirds of the annual Byzantine tenth-century liturgical processions were already in place by the time Marcellinus arrived in Constantinople around the turn of the sixth century. It is no wonder that this ceremonial looms so large in Marcellinus' record of fifth- and sixth-century Constantinople. This growth in ceremonial is another indication of the city's fundamental development in the period from the mid-fourth to the early-sixth century. That this was a key period in the city's development is also evident from the fact that the overwhelming majority of its great palatial residences, many of which were subsequently turned into churches or monasteries, were constructed before the mid-sixth century.[81] It has been remarked of those whose remains can be identified, the mansions of Lausus and Antiochus for example, that 'we cannot help being struck by their enormous proportions and ceremonial character'.[82] Indeed, there

---

[79] Mango (1986), 125.

[80] The processions are set out sequentially in Janin (1966). The original dates can be determined from the text of the *SEC* entry or the editor's annotation. For some processions, however, the original date is indeterminate: Death of Apostle John (26 Sept.); St Thyrsos and friends (14 Dec.); Prophet Elijah (20 July).

[81] These residences which survive in the toponym *ta Antiochou, ta Areobindou* etc. can be located in Janin (1964), 304ff.

[82] Mango (1986), 128.

was clearly a connection between the city's new ceremonial life and its new architecture, both private and public.

TABLE 4. 2. *Byzantine feasts involving processions by century of commencement*

4th cent.	Sunday after Christmas; S. Polyeuktos (9 Jan.); S. Timothy (22 Jan.); S. Gregory Nazianzen (25 Jan.); Constantine and Helena (21 May); Patriarch Metrophanes (4 June); SS Peter and Paul (29 June); S. Procopius (8 July); S. Panteleemon (27 July); S. Thecla (14 Sept.); S. Thomas (6 Oct.); SS Sergius and Bacchus (7 Oct.); S. Luke (18 Oct.); Archangel Michael (8 Nov.); S. Menas (11 Nov.); Presentation of Virgin (21 Nov.); Christmas Eve (24 Dec.)
5th cent.	Earthquake of 447 (26 Jan.); S. Chrysostom, relics (27 Jan.); Head of John the Baptist (24 Feb.); Forty Martyrs, Sebaste (9 Mar.); S. Stephen, relics (2 Aug.); Assumption of Virgin Mary (15 Aug.); John the Baptist, beheading (29 Aug.); Indiction (1 Sept.); Nativity of Virgin (8 Sept.); Earthquake of 438 (25 Sept.); Vesuvian eruption, 472 (6 Nov.); Exile of John Chrysostom (13 Nov.); S. Stephen (27 Dec.); Virgin Mary, Blachernae (28 Dec.)
6th cent.	Purification of Virgin Mary (2 Feb.); Annunciation Eve (24 Mar.); Annunciation (25 Mar.); Presentation of Virgin (21 Nov.)
7th cent.	Avar attack, 629 (5 June); Saracen attack, 617 (25 June); Virgin's Robe, Blachernae (2 July); Virgin at spring, dedication (9 July); Avar/Persian attack, 626 (7 Aug.)
8th cent.	Earthquake, Constantine VI (16 Mar.); SS Cosmas and Damian (1 July); Saracens siege, 717 (16 Aug.)
9th cent.	Patriarch Photius (6 Feb.); Patriarch Stephen (27 May); Patriarch Nicephorus (2 June); Patriarch Methodius (14 June)

That the liturgical calendar was already largely established by the early sixth century is also reflected in the chronicle of Marcellinus, as well as in seventh-century Syriac *menologia* where the latest emperor commemorated is Theodosius II.[83] All these religious processions, plus other ceremonial occasions like the consulship of Justinian which Marcellinus describes in detail (s.a. 521), reflect the life of the city through the eyes of the chronicler and highlight the chronicle's essentially Byzantine character. In his record of local Byzantine monuments and events Marcellinus provides for his local audience an account which reflects the vibrant and dynamic, but increasingly ritualized, public life of the city and its inhabitants.

[83] There are commemorations in the 7th-cent. menologion (PO 10. 31 ff.) for Theodosius I (18 Jan.); Honorius (10 Nov.); Gratian (14 Nov.) and Theodosius II (30 July).

CIVIL DISCORD IN THE CHRONICLE

As the population of Constantinople increased in the fourth and fifth centuries the city became more and more crowded, more and more cosmopolitan. This factor, coupled with increasing social mobility, led to frequent and serious unrest.[84] The picture of the populace of Constantinople which emerges from the literary remains, especially the Byzantine chronicles such as that of Marcellinus, is that of a restless and undisciplined one.[85] In general, the period of Marcellinus' residence in the imperial city was punctuated by a general air of uneasiness and tension, continually vented in violent civil disturbances, in the streets and particularly in the hippodrome. Indeed, the normal level of tension and trouble was accentuated even further during the reign of Anastasius, as factional rivalry was channelled into the confines of the hippodrome.[86] The chronicle of Marcellinus, especially because it is a contemporary witness, provides an important dossier of material for analysing the phenomenon of factional and religious violence during the reigns of Anastasius, Justin I, and Justinian (to 534).

It is in Marcellinus' chronicle that we find the first indication of hippodrome strife at Constantinople under the year 445 when he writes that 'A popular insurrection arose in the Hippodrome at Byzantium and many slaughtered each other. Many bodies of men and beasts inside the city perished through disease' (445. 2). There is no other record of this riot which has been taken as an instance of Blue/Green violence.[87] This may be so, since the violence originated in the hippodrome. However, since it is linked to a subsequent outbreak of disease, the possibility must also be considered that it was a food riot, occasioned by a severe shortage of grain—a not uncommon occurrence in the city. A food riot in 412, for example, left many corpses in the streets and seriously endangered the life of the prefect (*Chron. Pasch.* 571. 5–11). For the reigns of Marcian, Leo, and Zeno, Marcellinus records no riots at Constantinople except for one in which the hippodrome crowd turned on the Isaurians (s.a. 473. 2). Again, Marcellinus provides the only extant testimony for this.

With the accession of Anastasius the relative calm of the

---

[84] Beck (1973*a*), 17; (1966), 25–6.
[85] Beck (1965*a*), 35.
[86] Cameron, Alan (1973), 232ff.
[87] Ibid. 233; Greatrex (1997), 65.

previous years suddenly disappeared. Under 491 Marcellinus reports that 'Civil strife (*bellum plebeium*) arose among the Byzantines and most of the city and the hippodrome was engulfed in a blaze' (491. 2). At first sight this would appear to be another Blue/Green riot since the hippodrome was burnt. However, it was apparently more complex in that it originated in the disquiet of the populace at the city prefect imposing restrictions on theatrical shows at Constantinople. Marcellinus' account is to be compared with a passage of John of Antioch (fr. 214b (2) (*FHG* 5. 29–30)) who says that during a spectacle at which the emperor was present the Byzantines clamoured against the urban prefect, Julian, whereupon Anastasius ordered the excubitors to intimidate the rioters who in turn fired the hippodrome and violated the emperor's statues.[88] Also entangled in the issue somehow was public opposition to the Isaurians,[89] while the patriarch Euphemius was implicated in the trouble because of his sympathy for the Isaurians.[90] What seems to have happened is that the populace combined in launching their latent ill-feeling on the Isaurians confident that with no Isaurian emperor any more they would receive imperial encouragement. This is precisely what occurred in 473, also in the hippodrome (Marcell. s.a. 473. 2). The consequence of the riot was the expulsion of the Isaurians from Constantinople. In 493 the people revolted against Anastasius and exerted their rage by dragging statues of the emperor and his wife through the streets of the city. As Marcellinus reports, 'Civil strife (*bella civilia*) occurred at Constantinople against the rule of Anastasius. Statues of the emperor and empress were bound with ropes and dragged through the city' (493. 1). The causes and consequences of this direct protest against the emperor are not evident but the incident indicates the ongoing uneasy relationship between the emperor and his people.

The vicious civil strife and consequent tension continued. In 498 some Greens were arrested and, in reply to a request for their freedom, the emperor turned his excubitors on them. In the

[88] Bury (1923a), 432, cf. Stein (1949), 82 and Capizzi (1969), 95. Cameron, Alan (1973), 234 has reservations.

[89] Brooks (1893), 232–3.

[90] Charanis (1974), 55 on Theod. Anag. *HE Epit.* 449 (126), it is difficult to see how the riot started over Anastasius' religious inclinations (Brooks (1893), 232) or (even more so) why the Isaurians would have stirred up the Greens and Blues in order to generate hostility against Anastasius (Capizzi (1969), 95).

ensuing fracas Anastasius narrowly escaped injury. The trouble subsided when the emperor agreed to appoint Plato, patron of the Greens, as City Prefect.[91] Marcellinus does not mention this incident nor the Brytai riots in 499/500 (Jo. Ant. fr. 214c (*FHG* 5. 31)). However, under 501 he records another savage massacre at the Brytai festival in which an illegitimate son of Anastasius was killed. The description of Marcellinus is quite detailed and, assuming that he was in Constantinople by this stage, may even constitute an eye-witness account.

Marcellinus describes how Constantine the city prefect was presiding at the afternoon session of the aquatic festival known as the Brytai while the Greens were laying plans for an assault on the Blues in the theatre. They had secreted swords and stones in earthenware jars and concealed similar weapons among the fruit sold by sympathetic vendors in the portico outside the theatre. Inside there was a great din. While the crowd's customary chanting (of acclamations presumably) grew louder and louder weapons which could be 'heard before being seen' began to hurtle through the air. Willing or not, everybody was caught up in the showers of stones and many were killed by spectators brandishing swords. In the panic the wooden seating began to creak and give way. Many were killed when the seating collapsed and many others were drowned when an artificial lake in the theatre (part of the pantomimes) collapsed and inundated the arena. In all more than three thousand lost their lives that afternoon (s.a. 501. 2). The 'royal city' was shocked and in mourning while the Brytai festival was never held again.[92] The abolition of the *venationes* in 498 and the pantomimes in 502 focused rivalry more exclusively on the hippodrome races. During Anastasius' Persian war (502–5) there is no mention of any factional disturbance. Then in 507 Marcellinus records more trouble when 'a popular uprising (*seditio popularis*) broke out in the hippodrome. The armed soldiery thwarted it' (507. 1). This brief notice summarizes a major confrontation between Anastasius and the Greens.[93] After the disastrous strife in 507 we hear nothing more of circus rivalries in the reign of Anastasius, at least not in Marcellinus who omits the 514 riots recorded by John of Antioch (fr. 214e (12) (*FHG* 5. 33)).

[91] Jo. Mal. 16. 4 (394. 11–395. 5) with *De insid.* fr. 38 (168. 11–25).
[92] Jo. Mal. 16. 2 (392. 11–393. 11) with *De insid.* frs. 36 (167. 21–3) and 39 (168. 26–34).
[93] Details in Croke (1995), 113.

Nonetheless, the Blues and Greens were not the only agents of violence in the time of Anastasius. Equally explosive was the apparent favouritism of the emperor for the monophysites. The Constantinopolitan patriarch Euphemius had objected to the emperor from the earliest and had coerced him into signing a guarantee of orthodoxy, or at least not to interfere with the orthodox. Anastasius resented this extortion and placed little trust in the allegiance of the patriarch. The latent hostility between them burst into the open in 494 when, Marcellinus reports:

The emperor Anastasius began to declare civil war (*intestina proelia*) on the dignity of those of the orthodox faith. With evil scheming he first demonstrated the cruelty of his punishment against Euphemius, the bishop of the city, who was resisting the emperor manfully on behalf of the faith of the orthodox. (494. 1)

This account of Marcellinus captures the ill-feeling the orthodox were displaying towards the emperor, and was probably meant to encapsulate the confrontation in the hippodrome between the supporters and opponents of Euphemius.[94] The next time the emperor's religious policies led to violence was in 512 when he made his dramatic appearance in the hippodrome without his crown. This constitutes one of the most detailed and lengthy of Marcellinus' accounts and is very likely a first-hand record. As we have seen, in the Forum of Constantine the crowd's anger erupted, and statues and images of Anastasius were hurled to the ground; some high imperial officials were subjected to a barrage of stones while the houses of two others were burnt down (s.a. 512. 5).

Despite frequent comment on the futility of the factions,[95] reaction to this sustained violence and bloodshed is rare. Justinian, on his accession, issued a comprehensive decree outlawing violence[96] and later attempted to curb civil unrest by prohibiting the sale of arms and controlling the entrances of the city. Yet Procopius (*Anek.* 7. 1 ff.) took Justinian to task for letting the factions get out of hand; while another contemporary John Malalas commented on the unpopularity of factional strife (18. 151 = *de insid.* fr. 51 175. 29–176.19). As for Marcellinus, it is possible to trace a hint of his opinion on the rioting through which he lived.

---

[94] Refs. in ibid. 108.
[95] Cameron, Alan (1976), 272–3.
[96] Jo. Mal. 17. 18 (422. 9–21); *Chron. Pasch.* 617. 1–6.

In his first-hand account of the Nika riots in 532 Marcellinus singles out the rioters as 'criminal citizens' (*sceleratos cives*), who may be contrasted to the 'good citizens' (*bonis civibus*) who avoid stone-throwing or rabble-rousing of any kind and who rejoice in the public punishment of those who do so indulge (s.a. 523). The occasion for this comment is an incident in 523 when Justin appointed Theodotus to the Urban Prefecture. His task was primarily to root out the malefactors responsible for factional violence but the enthusiastic Theodotus interpreted his mandate more broadly and a general round-up of all sorts of trouble-makers followed. It is for this that Marcellinus provides an approving contemporary account of those burned and strung up: 'Most of the stone throwers, bandits and ravagers of the city, when they were caught, were put to the sword, burnt and hung because of their crimes, thereby providing a grateful sight for the good citizens' (523).

This comment comes from a time when Marcellinus was acting as *cancellarius* to Justinian, so he will have known of these events at first-hand. It is therefore interesting to note that he omits to mention Theodotus the prefect responsible for this crackdown. What had happened is that in his zeal Theodotus had put to death a certain distinguished senator Theodosius for his involvement in urban violence. The resentment aroused by this action had obliged Justinian to dismiss Theodotus and exile him to Palestine. Consequently, Marcellinus (and perhaps by implication his employer Justinian) would appear to be fully supporting Theodotus' vigorous campaign in 523 without mentioning his name.[97] Marcellinus' support for opposition to Anastasius and for Justinian's anti-violence policies prompt enquiry as to his attitudes to the emperors under whom he lived in Constantinople and how his reaction to them conditioned the way they are represented in the chronicle.

MARCELLINUS AND THE EMPERORS

The picture of Anastasius to emerge from the chronicle is almost totally hostile. All that Marcellinus can favourably attribute to Anastasius are the donations to the soldiery in 496 and 500, the latter to the Illyrian soldiery only in the wake of the disastrous

[97] Details in Croke (1995), 123.

defeat by the Bulgars in 499. There is no mention at all in the chronicle of Anastasius' popular financial measures, like the abolition of the *chrysargyron* which gave rise to scenes of delight throughout the eastern provinces.[98] This is a curious oversight. Anastasius, aided by his able minister Marinus, was the most comprehensive and effective economic reformer of late antiquity and the popularity of his actions among all sectors of early Byzantine society is clearly reflected in the literary records. However, Marcellinus does mention Anastasius' reform of the coinage (498. 3). By this measure Anastasius attempted to stabilize the ratio between gold and copper by instigating multiple coin units. This reform was made necessary because of the extremely variable quality of the current copper coinage which was no longer acceptable at its face value.[99] Marcellinus also ignores other successes of Anastasius. Although strongly opposed to the excesses of the factions, and the Brytai festival which led to the theatre riots in 501, Marcellinus does not mention that Anastasius took effective action to curb this violence by abolishing the pantomimes in the first instance, and by attempting to eradicate violence in general after serious incidents in Constantinople and Antioch in 507. This is especially striking when contrasted to the similar measures taken by Justinian in 523 which Marcellinus strongly applauds.

The explanation for the inability of Marcellinus to acknowledge anything good in Anastasius' policies is the emperor's unfavourable attitude to the orthodox. This is an unpardonable shortcoming for the uncompromisingly orthodox Marcellinus writing in the heady days of Justin's restoration of orthodoxy at Constantinople. This was the time of the restoration to the diptychs of the names of the former patriarchs Euphemius and Macedonius, as well as those of the councils of Nicaea, Constantinople, Ephesus, and Chalcedon, along with the condemnation of Severus of Antioch. In 494 Anastasius was opposed for his treatment of the patriarch Euphemius and for stirring up *intestina proelia* in Constantinople (Marcell. s.a. 494. 1) when marches and rallies were held against the emperor. In 495

[98] Capizzi (1969), 143–4.

[99] Hendy (1985), 475 ff.; Metcalf (1969), 1, 13; Melville-Jones (1991), 9–13 proposing *teruncianos* followed by Croke (1995), 110 although a case can be made for retaining Mommsen's *Terentianos* (Gusso (1997), 278).

Euphemius was exiled, 'wrongly accused by Anastasius' in the opinion of Marcellinus (s.a. 495). The chronicler takes exception not only to the exile of Euphemius but to that of his successor, Macedonius, as well—'surrounded by the treachery and lies of the emperor' (511). As far as Marcellinus is concerned, the treachery and lies of Anastasius are notorious: in describing the monophysite riots in 512 he notes how Anastasius quelled the seething crowd with his 'usual lies and empty words' (512. 7) and again in 514 Vitalian was lulled into a false sense of security as a result of Anastasius' 'pretences and lies' (514. 1). But Marcellinus is critical of Anastasius on other occasions as well. It was the emperor's approval ('on the order of Anastasius Caesar') of the addition to the Trisagion of the theologically controversial phrase 'who was crucified for us' which led to the riots of 512 (512. 2). Similarly, a hostile attitude to the emperor's sanction is evident in his descriptions of the installation of the monophysite Severus as bishop of Antioch in place of Flavianus 'in accordance with the will of Anastasius Caesar' (513), the slaying of Dorotheus of Ancyra (513), and the exile of Elias of Jerusalem who had refused to recognize Severus (516. 2).

In addition, Marcellinus relates how the *comes domesticorum*, Romanus, and the *comes scholarum*, Rusticus, won a naval battle in 508 and promptly proceeded to plunder the Italian coast near Tarentum.[100] To this action Marcellinus shows little kindness, regarding it as a 'shameful victory which Romans snatched from Romans with piratical daring' (508). Such veiled criticism of the emperor can be detected too in his information on the admission of the Heruli within the borders of the empire in 512 'by order of Anastasius Caesar' (512. 11). Finally, there is the curious fact that Marcellinus never once calls Anastasius 'Augustus' but always 'Caesar' (511; 512. 2, 4 (bis), 7; 513; 515. 3). The consistency of this incorrect attribution suggests that somehow or other Marcellinus could not bring himself to consider the shifty and heretical Anastasius as a full and legitimate emperor, that is 'Augustus'.

All in all, Marcellinus' treatment of Anastasius is consistently hostile but oversimplified. As a persecutor of the orthodox, the emperor is capable of no worthwhile measures. So all his popular reforms and actions are conveniently omitted while others, such as the raid on Italy in 508, are introduced only to invoke criticism.

---

[100] Capizzi (1969), 170.

Equally straightforward is his treatment of the main opposition to the reign of Anastasius—the *count of the federates*, Vitalian. The background to Vitalian's rebellion is not completely understood but it seems that he mobilized the *foederati* under him because of their discontent and this was fuelled by his personal animosity towards the *magister militum* of Thrace, the emperor's nephew Hypatius. Marcellinus' chronicle provides important information for Vitalian's revolt. He begins by noting that in 514 Vitalian approached Constantinople with 60,000 men and marched up to the 'Golden Gate'. Negotiations proceeded, an agreement was worked out and Vitalian retreated to Odessos on the Black Sea coast (s.a. 514. 2).

Marcellinus' explanation for Vitalian's rebellion is quite simple—it was 'on behalf of the orthodox faith' (514. 1)[101] and on behalf of the exiled patriarch Macedonius. Vitalian certainly did claim to stand as the champion of orthodoxy and did, later, take an active role (in that he sided with the Pope) in the settlement of the Acacian schism. However, in the account of Marcellinus Vitalian is the general of orthodoxy pure and simple. There is no mention of any other motive for his march on Constantinople. The general Hypatius, whom Vitalian opposed, was replaced by Cyril. This general was himself soon done away with by Vitalian, an act of blatant and daring aggression. Marcellinus is able to exonerate the champion of orthodoxy by offering the explanation that Vitalian found Cyril, an unsuitable and improper master of the soldiery, sleeping between two concubines. He managed to extricate Cyril from them and then ran him through. This moralizing excuse on the part of the chronicler is plainly designed to vindicate Vitalian, the orthodox hero combating the heretical emperor who now declared him a public enemy.

Marcellinus then proceeds to describe how Vitalian advanced in 515 with his army to Sycae, opposite Constantinople, and was subsequently bought off with gold and the Thracian generalship. The emperor's nephew, being held hostage, was returned (s.a. 515. 3–4). The following year, Vitalian marched on Constantinople, but suffered a disastrous loss in a naval battle on the Golden Horn and was replaced by Rufinus (Marcell. s.a. 516. 1). Thus his rebellion came to nothing. Marcellinus, consistent with his positive appreciation of the orthodox Vitalian, refers to the

---

[101] A phrase inadvertently omitted from the translation in Croke (1995), 37.

appointment of Rufinus over Vitalian as an upturn of trust and makes no mention whatsoever of the defeat of Vitalian and his subsequent escape (516. 1). This would not have suited his purpose in portraying Vitalian as a successful champion of orthodoxy who challenged the despicable monophysite emperor. So much for Anastasius.

For Marcellinus, the orthodox Justin is a virtual non-entity about whom he has little to say. What he does offer, though, is decidedly positive, in particular the execution of Amantius. On the death of Anastasius (9 July 518) the *praepositus* Amantius arranged for Justin to distribute money to the household troops to secure their support for his candidate, Theocritus. As events transpired, it was Justin himself who was eventually raised to the purple and Theocritus bypassed. The veracity of these events is not doubted but explanations of them vary: Bury considered the whole affair as a highly elaborate plot contrived by Justin;[102] Vasiliev thought that the excubitors were simply taken in by the fact that Justin offered the money and were not concerned with its origin,[103] while Greatrex has argued that Justin's accession was self-evident to him as virtually the only serious Chalcedonian candidate left standing.[104] Marcellinus' brief account of this episode is an interesting contemporary comment: Amantius and his lackeys (Misael, Andreas, and Ardabur) were seized as traitors to Justin. Amantius and Andreas were slain, while Misael and Ardabur were exiled to Serdica. Marcellinus concludes by describing how Theocritus was tied up in prison, stoned to death, and his body thrown into the sea, offering the caustic comment that Theocritus 'forfeited a burial as well as the empire to which he aspired' (519. 2). This is surely the orthodox imperial version of these events which had settled into the tradition by the early 530s. The conspirators were a danger mainly because they were anti-Chalcedonian (so the conventional slur 'Manichees') and Theocritus' hideous death was timely and proper. Marcellinus' account reflects the urging of the congregation in Hagia Sophia on 16 July to 'Throw out all the Manichaeans', to 'throw out the new Tzumas [Amantius] . . . The Trinity has triumphed. From now on do not fear Amantius the Manichaean.'[105] His chronicle may have been written with these words still ringing in his ears.

---

[102] Bury (1923*b*), 17–18.
[103] Vasiliev (1950), 81.
[104] Greatrex (1996), 135–6.
[105] Quoted in Vasiliev (1950), 141–3.

What is especially interesting about Marcellinus' account of Justin's reign is that he views it as part of the reign of Justinian, just as Procopius did (*Anek.* 6. 19, 26; *Aed.* 1. 3. 3). In other words, by the time Marcellinus was writing in 534 the period from 518 to 527 was being represented as an integral part of Justinian's imperial tenure. In the chronicle the only mentions of Justin are his elevation (519. 1) and death (527). Instead, it is Justinian who emerges most prominently from these years and it is quite plain that Justinian was very popular with Marcellinus. First of all, there is Justinian's consular games in 521 which Marcellinus describes at length and judges the 'most famous of all eastern ones' because the consul was 'considerably more generous in his largesses' (521). Details are furnished: 288,000 solidi were distributed to the populace, exceptional games were provided in the amphitheatre with 20 lions and 30 leopards topping the bill. In addition, he donated caparisoned horses and chariots in the hippodrome. So unruly was the hippodrome crowd that the consul was forced to withhold the running of the last race from the 'clamouring populace' (521). All this detail leads one to suspect that Marcellinus was associated with Justinian on this occasion.[106] As explained previously, Marcellinus was quite possibly *cancellarius* to Justinian as early as 520. If so, then he would have certainly been involved in these celebrations. After all, the consulship of the Illyrian general Justinian was peerless and that is how it struck all Byzantines not just his associates, but in Marcellinus we have a first-hand account.[107]

For the next few years when Marcellinus acted as *cancellarius* to Justinian we find nothing special in the chronicle to reflect this closer proximity to events and personalities. Writing to celebrate Justinian's African victory in 534, he left the year 522 absolutely empty (the only blank year in the chronicle), while 523 covers the court's zealous anti-violence measures, 524 an oil shortage, 525 the visit of Pope John and 526 an earthquake at Antioch. The 'most noble' Justinian was crowned emperor by Justin in 527 which the chronicler duly records, linking it specifically to the local time reckoning of Constantinople—'in the 197th year from the foundation of the royal city' (527). In the following year ('in the 198th year from the foundation of the royal city'), Marcellinus

---

[106] As supposed by Mommsen (1894), 42.
[107] Jo. Mal. 18. 3 (426. 21–2); Ced. 1. 642 (referring to 528 cos).

explains Justinian's alteration to the hippodrome: as victor he made more elevated and more brilliant the *kathisma* from which the games were viewed by the imperial family and at the same time he restored the senatorial portico 'with his customary generosity' (528). It is reasonable to assume that Marcellinus was a participant or eyewitness for all these events although he provides no direct indication of that.

The continuation of Marcellinus' chronicle from 519 to 534 struck Cassiodorus as remarkably favourable to the emperor Justinian, the chronicler's former employer (*Inst.* 1. 17). This is self-evident. He reflects the point-of-view of Justinian and the court throughout. We have already seen this in relation to the anti-violence campaign of 523, but it is also evident in the detailed first-hand account of the Nika revolt of January 532. The revolt is not portrayed as an expression of popular opposition to the adminis-tration when Blues and Greens confronted the court in concert, nor as a riot that simply escalated. Instead, it is cast as a con-spiracy hatched by the nephews of Anastasius,[108] a victory over 'tyrants' or usurpers (532). Hypatius and Pompeius, as Theocritus in 518, therefore 'paid the penalty and lost the empire before they could obtain it' (532). In addition, Marcellinus' eyewitness account of the Nika riots is interesting in that it demonstrates the involve-ment of senators in the whole affair, which was the immediate justification for the intensity of the imperial reaction to the rioters and the proclamation of Hypatius as emperor.[109] As someone close to the court, Marcellinus was in a position to know Justinian's assessment of support for Hypatius and the advantage of portray-ing the Nika riot as a threat to his throne.

Another indication of Marcellinus' concealing or distorting facts to enhance the image of Justinian is the death of Vitalian in 520. Certainly Justinian was implicated in the act. As noted above, Marcellinus presents an over-simplified account of Vitalian as a legitimate rebel against the anti-Chalcedonian Anastasius. Likewise, he presents the recall of Vitalian by Justin as due to the emperor's *pietas* (519. 3). Such a pledge of good faith is to be contrasted with the treachery of Anastasius. The circumstances surrounding Vitalian's death in July 520 are not clear but it is impossible to escape the fact that Justinian's jealousy of Vitalian's

---

[108] As recognized by Bury (1897), 92–3.
[109] Bury (1897), 93; Croke (1995), 125–6; Greatrex (1997), 83.

growing influence and power was instrumental.[110] Consequently, the silence of Marcellinus is significant. His laconic entry is devoid of praise or blame and says simply that 'in the seventh month of his consulship, the consul Vitalian died in the palace, along with his attendants Celerianus and Paul, after being stabbed sixteen times' (520).

Marcellinus shared the city's admiration for Vitalian as a self-styled symbol of orthodoxy but he could hardly condemn the jealousy of his own patron nor hint at his guilt. His loyalties were here divided and he chose the course of discretion. On the other hand, it is possible that his very inclusion of this incident in a chronicle designed to praise Justinian indicates that the emperor had been falsely implicated. When it came to describing the recent Roman victory in Africa, however, Marcellinus could be more direct. The victory was Justinian's. It is in no way associated with Belisarius who is never mentioned in the chronicle at all. There were other powerful generals at court besides Belisarius. One of these, Mundo, was highly regarded by Marcellinus for his victory over the Bulgars in 530.[111] Subsequently, Mundo replaced Belisarius as commander of Roman forces against the Persians in the East, and he had also played a key role in turning the course of events during the Nika riot.

Marcellinus was therefore writing the updated version of his chronicle at a turning point in the reign of Justinian. The insecure mood engendered by the Nika riots and their aftermath was now eclipsed by the security of imperial victory and its powerful affirming ritual of triumph. By focusing the credit on Justinian and concealing his blemishes, the chronicle in 534 can be seen as contributing to the process of re-establishing the political reputation of its author's former employer. As Cassiodorus had discovered, Marcellinus 'is said to have acted first as *cancellarius* of the patrician Justinian, but who later, with the Lord's help on the improvement of his employer's civil status, faithfully guided his work from the time of the emperor (Justin) to the beginning of the triumphant rule of the emperor Justinian' (*Inst.* 1. 17. 2).

---

[110] Vasiliev (1950), 113, following Procopius and Victor of Tunnuna, puts it most bluntly: 'The conclusion that Justinian premeditated and participated in Vitalian's murder is inescapable.'

[111] Croke (1982a), 125–35.

LOOKING EAST

From Constantinople the main source of wealth, both material and spiritual, lay to the east—across Asia Minor through the mountains of Isauria to Antioch. Beyond Antioch, the administrative and military headquarters of the Roman east, lay the Syrian desert interspersed with strong and prosperous cities, and then the hostile domain of the Persian king. Marcellinus may himself have traversed this territory if, as proposed earlier (Chapter 1) he undertook a pilgrim's journey to Palestine and across Syria to the frontier fortress of Dara. Unlike Illyricum, there is only a small amount of information in the chronicle which relates to Roman activities in the east, and it is principally concentrated on the Isaurian war of Anastasius and later conflicts with the Persians.

The traditionally hardy and uncouth Isaurians had originally come to prominence at Constantinople in the reign of Theodosius II.[112] We hear little of them in subsequent years until 473 when Marcellinus lists an anti-Isaurian riot in the hippodrome, doubtless generated by the emperor Leo's cultivation of their support. They had certainly become unpopular in the capital but when Leo died his son-in-law the Isaurian Zeno came to the throne. The special treatment and the powerful position acquired by the Isaurians under Zeno both fostered ill-will against them and allowed little scope for opposition. It was during this time that the *magister militum* Illus fled to the east and there supported the usurpation of Leontius instigated, or rather proclaimed officially, by Leo's widow Verina at Antioch.[113] Marcellinus mentions that Illus and Leontius were captured in Isauria and their heads later displayed at Constantinople (488. 1), but that is all.

When Anastasius became emperor in 491 the Isaurian domination was suddenly threatened. A riot in the hippodrome that year led to the expulsion from Constantinople of Longinus, brother of Zeno, the general Longinus of Kardala and other Isaurians. Before long, Isauria itself saw the outbreak of a rebellion. According to Marcellinus (497. 2), the *bellum Isauricum* broke out in 492 and lasted for six years, ending in 497 which is exactly correct.[114] The war began with the Roman defeat of the Isaurian Lilingis at Kottyaion in Phrygia where the Isaurian forces had congregated. Some Isaurians then fled through the mountain

---

[112] Thompson (1946), 18–31.   [113] Stein (1949), 28–31.   [114] Brooks (1893), 237.

fastnesses and escaped but the war dragged on—'This Isaurian war lasted for six years' (492). This war is the only event recorded under 492. The chronicle does not include an annual summary of events in the war but simply when it began and when it ended. It does, however, devote some attention to the aftermath: in 497 Marcellinus reports that the head of the Isaurian chief Athenodorus was fixed on a pike and publicly displayed at Tarsus (497. 2). This observation is reinforced by the chronicler's own statement under the following year that Longinus, another Isaurian general, was captured by Priscus and subsequently sent to Constantinople. In describing Longinus' entry into the hippo-drome, an event he may have witnessed himself, Marcellinus records that 'he was bound and led by an official to the emperor Anastasius and provided a great spectacle for the people' (498. 2).

Just as Marcellinus' chronicle provides an outline but complete guide to the history of Illyricum and orthodoxy from 379 to his own day, it also provides a summary account of Roman wars with Persia. Following the emperor Julian's campaign and the cession of Nisibis in 363 peace more or less prevailed in the east until 420 when, as a consequence of the changing direction of court politics at the accession of Vahram, the Persians launched a persecution against the Christians in their territory.[115] The following year the Roman army was on the march in Mesopotamia and by 6 September 421 a cease-fire was granted and peace terms soon arranged.[116] Marcellinus does not bother with details but simply the bare facts of this conflict (s.a. 420. 3, 421. 4, 422. 4). The next time the empire came into conflict with Persia was in 440, about which we know little given the shortcomings of the extant records. Marcellinus simply tells us that the Persians invaded and that the *magister militum* Anatolius arranged a peace treaty with them.[117] These notices were a reminder to his audience that there had been previous conflicts with the powerful Persian empire but they had been peacefully resolved.

During the second half of the fifth century the Romans were greatly troubled by the Gothic armies and the Bulgars in the Balkans, while the Persians had their hands full with the Hephthalite Huns. Thus, they kept the peace with each other. In

---

[115] Holum (1977), 156.
[116] Ibid. 167–71, and Schrier (1992), 75–86.
[117] Details in Croke (1984*a*), 59–74; Blockley (1992), 61–2 and Greatrex (1993), 2–5.

502, however, matters reached a head. Anastasius refused to provide certain financial support for the Persian king Kavadh which provoked him into invading Mesopotamia.[118] He took Theodosiopolis and Martyropolis and then moved across to Amida where he began a siege. At this point Marcellinus takes up the story:

> In the fifth month after commencing his attack on the very rich city of Amida, Choades, the King of the Persians, broke into it after it had been betrayed with the connivance of its monks, and killed its monastic traitors. (502. 2)

Marcellinus does not describe the outbreak of the war nor recount the march of Kavadh through Mesopotamia. Instead, he simply records the story of the monks' treachery in letting the Persians capture Amida and the consequent Persian slaughter of the monks. Although a later invention,[119] the story of the monks' treachery stemmed from rumours which circulated soon after and this version was obviously well entrenched by the time Marcellinus was writing in 518. The capture took place in January 503 but Marcellinus has it under 502, the year it began. Under 503 and 504 the chronicle is concerned only with the Persian war and this may well be taken as an indication of overriding concern in Constantinople at the time for the successful prosecution of the war. In 503 'Areobindus', Hypatius, and Patricius were sent out to take on the Persian army. Before long Areobindus advanced to Nisibis but was forced to retreat to Edessa where he was besieged by Kavadh. Meanwhile, Hypatius and Patricius had failed in their blockade of Amida and had returned to Samosata. Marcellinus begins his account by providing us with a figure for the Roman troops involved—15,000. Given that the chronicler was a contemporary of the campaign and that he seems to have a propensity to quote precise figures when they are available,[120] he is probably indicating the size of the army sent from Constantinople with the *magistri militum* in May 503.[121]

---

[118] Greatrex (1998), 76–8.

[119] Harvey (1990), 59–61; Greatrex (1998), 91.

[120] Ibid. 154–5. For example, his figure of 2,000 for the troops of Celer is the only evidence we have for the size of this contingent; in 499 Aristus set out against the Bulgars with 15,000 soldiers and 520 armed wagons; in 505 Sabinianus' expedition against Mundo consisted of 10,000 troops and Vitalian mustered more than 60,000 for his march on Constantinople.   [121] Greatrex (1998), 96.

Without offering details, Marcellinus comments that the lack of success on the part of the generals, especially during the battle at the *castellum* called Syficus, was due to their lack of bravery (*sine audacia*). Here Marcellinus seems to be repeating what was the commonly held opinion at Constantinople. John the Lydian tells us that the Persians won because Areobindus was addicted to dancing and playing the flute while Patricius and Hypatius were inexperienced and cowardly. In response to this setback, the emperor sent Celer with another 2,000 troops as Marcellinus notes (s.a. 503). Then he mentions the recovery of Amida by 'our generals' (*nostri ductores*) who were required to pay the Persians a considerable sum to win it back after suffering considerable hardship in laying siege to the city.[122] Under 504 he concludes his brief survey of the Persian war with an account of Celer's plundering and looting of the Mesopotamian countryside.[123] Still, it is impossible to tell whether Marcellinus is being critical of the Romans for this or not.

By now, Patricius had moved to Amida and Areobindus into Armenia but the war ended rather suddenly when the Persians agreed to retreat and keep the peace. This took place in 505/6 although, again for the sake of simplicity, Marcellinus put it under 504 where he relates that Celer was responsible for arranging the treaty and was assisted by the imperial secretary Armonius who had been sent expressly for that purpose (s.a. 504). Possibly his fellow-Illyrian Celer was his source of information, to judge from the concentration of detail on Celer. Following the conclusion of the peace, Anastasius decided to consolidate the Roman defence system in Mesopotamia by constructing a powerful fortress base at the little village of Dara between Amida and Nisibis. In fact Marcellinus provides an important contemporary account of the construction of Dara which may derive from his own journey there.[124]

Skirmishes broke out occasionally in the borderlands between Rome and Persia and tensions mounted. In 529, with Persian resentment at Roman support for the Lazi growing, Justinian appointed Belisarius to gather and lead an army into the region. It is this preparatory step which Marcellinus records before

---

[122] Ibid. 114–15.
[123] Ibid. 113–14.
[124] Croke (1984*b*), 77–88; Croke and Crow (1983), 143–59; Whitby (1986), 737–83.

explaining that the expedition lasted for five years before returning to Constantinople in 533 to be redeployed against the Vandals
in Africa:

Since the Parthians were making war the Roman army made ready its
arms and, renewing the fight, it safeguarded its territories. This expedition of ours lasted almost five years and, when diverted from the East,
made for Africa to fight successfully against the Vandals. (529)

Like Anastasius' Persian war under the year 503, this renewal
of hostilities against Persia is the only entry under 529, a reflection
of its paramount concern for the Byzantines. This is neatly
implied too in Marcellinus' identification with the army—'this
expedition of ours' (*haec expeditio nostrorum*), just as in 503 it was 'our
generals' (*nostri ductores*) who brought back Amida. The expeditionary army in 529 was led by Belisarius whom Marcellinus
never mentions in the chronicle. Again, like the war of Anastasius,
Marcellinus does not bother to trace the development of campaign details over successive years, beginning with the battles at
Dara and Callinicum in 530. Instead he simply records its final
outcome after an arduous struggle. In addition, he notes that it
was the envoys Rufinus and Hermogenes who negotiated the so-
called 'Endless Peace' which was ratified by the Roman emperor
and the Persian king followed by an exchange of gifts (s.a. 532). He
does not mention any of the terms of the treaty.[125] All in all the
chronicle provides a complete survey of Roman wars with Persia
in the period it covers: 420–2, 441, 502–5, 529–32. In each case it
is concerned primarily with the outbreak of the conflict and its
subsequent conclusion. It is a simple summary account. From the
standpoint of the 530s it provides an overview of the crucial
episodes in Roman dealings with the Persian realm.

Looking at the chronicle as a whole, after a detailed analysis of
its main elements, its popularity and superiority (as implied by
Cassiodorus' recommendation) are evident. Designed primarily
for the Latin-speaking communities living in Constantinople,
especially the Illyrians, it provided them with a brief but complete
(and sometimes detailed) summary of the encounters between
Romans and successive tribal groups in Illyricum in the fifth and
early sixth century. At the same time, it served the orthodox and
pro-papal Illyrians with a comprehensive summary of the main

[125] Greatrex (1998), 213–18.

facts of religious history (personalities, councils), stressing the development of the orthodox position. Finally, the chronicle accords considerable attention to the development of the imperial city of Constantinople. It concentrates in particular on the construction of monuments central to the public ceremonial life of the city in the time of the chronicler, as well as listing several events whose significance in a chronicle of this kind derives from their being associated with official and elaborate ceremonies. Increasingly, the chronicle confines itself to the narrow and independent world of the Byzantine capital so that in the continuation of the chronicle from 519 to 534 Marcellinus only once mentions Illyricum (s.a. 530). Instead, his attention is confined to events in Constantinople, except for a brief notice of the Persian war (529, 532). A similar pattern was followed a few years later by John Malalas who concentrated on events at Constantinople in updating his chronicle. By 534 Marcellinus' audience had become more thoroughly 'Byzantine' than it had been in 519.

PART II

THE CHRONICLE AND ITS TRANSMISSION

5

Chronicle Writing in Late Antiquity

No manuscript title for Marcellinus' chronicle survives except those inserted by medieval scribes. In fact the chronicle may not have had its own title, just a statement of transition from Jerome's chronicle which it was continuing.[1] Like so many other such chronicles, Marcellinus' work was merely another brick in a larger edifice thereby requiring no separate titular justification.[2] His coeval Cassiodorus, however, implicitly labels the work *chronica* and recommends it in the course of his discussion of works under that label (*Inst.* 1. 17). Cassiodorus obviously had a clear understanding of what he meant by 'chronicle' since in 519, shortly after Marcellinus, he himself produced a work with precisely that title.[3] Eusebius of Caesarea, Cassiodorus states, wrote *chronica* in Greek which Jerome translated into Latin and continued to the death of the emperor Valens (378). This work was continued by Prosper and by Marcellinus to the early years of the reign of Justinian (534 in fact).[4] Thanks to Cassiodorus' endorsement there are several manuscripts of the chronicle of Marcellinus, as there are for Prosper, whereas other chronicles have not survived at all or only in a single manuscript. This fate applies especially to the continuators of Marcellinus and Prosper, both in Cassiodorus' own lifetime and later. Only one continuation of Marcellinus is extant.

Although failing to describe his work except as an *opus*, Marcellinus himself was consciously continuing that of Jerome, in the same way as Jerome had continued Eusebius, and as both Prosper (430s–440s) and Hydatius (470s) had previously continued Jerome. Indeed, Prosper, Hydatius, and Marcellinus all drew their textual and historiographical authority from Jerome. Prosper, however, had done more than simply continue Jerome;

---

[1] As suggested by Mommsen (1894), 43–4.
[2] Guenée (1984), 5, cf. Burgess (1993*a*), 6.
[3] Ed. Mommsen: *MGH AA* 11. 120–61.
[4] Croke (1982*b*), 225–6.

he had adapted the chronological framework of Jerome by adding annual consuls from the Crucifixion of Christ (dated to AD 28). Otherwise he merely copied entries from Jerome, except that he added a few of his own on different heretics—all taken from Augustine's treatise *On Heretics*—and other imperial matters.[5] In the manuscript tradition Prosper's chronicle is preserved in two main ways: (1) as a separate work from 378, together with the chronicle of Jerome which it continues; and (2) in its complete form.[6] The same situation applies to most of the manuscripts of Marcellinus, that is, they preserve his chronicle together with that of Jerome. In fact either Jerome or Marcellinus might be looked at separately, but within a single manuscript they formed a unity—a conjoint presentation of universal history to the present day (sixth century). In Marcellinus' preface he indicated that in following his model Jerome he was influenced by the importance of defining his chronological framework and by the expected content of such a chronicle. This was an important clue to his readers who had predetermined expectations of a chronicle. In order to understand and appreciate Marcellinus' task it is therefore necessary to examine these expectations by concentrating on (1) how the chronicle developed its late antique format, content and function, and (2) what sort of persons wrote chronicles, for whom, and how these chronicles were subsequently used. These two dimensions are especially significant in the light of the increasing recognition that the historiographical preconceptions which have relegated chronicles to a subordinate role in the development of writing about the past are no longer valid.[7] It is only by defining the common meaning, and the common story, brought by the chronicler and his audience to the text, that we can begin to appreciate the nature and role of late antique chronicles.

EUSEBIUS AND JEROME

The chronicle was a Christian invention designed to demonstrate the unity and universality of human history under God's providence, and to illustrate the nature and pattern of the progress of

[5] Muhlberger (1990), 80; Humphries (1996), 155–75.
[6] Muhlberger (1990), 56ff.
[7] White (1978), 56; (1987), 1–25; La Capra (1985), 11ff.; Iggers (1997), 18–19; Spiegel (1997), 84.

time. It was a novel and integral element of Christian discourse. The first such chronicle was that of Eusebius, originally put together in the early fourth century (*c.*311) and then updated in 325.[8] It was the culmination of a long series of developments in chronological research and presentation going back to Hellenistic times. What Eusebius did, in effect, was to mould together in a single, comprehensive view (tied to a single chronological yard-stick) the whole of recorded history. His achievement was made possible by the researches of previous Christian scholars (and Greek and Jewish scholars before them) who had developed acceptable methods for solving specific chronological problems of contemporary importance.[9] Onto this patchwork of disparate materials Eusebius skilfully and successfully plotted the Christian story.

In archaic and classical times the different Greek states lived by their own local customs for reckoning and recording the passing of time; in Athens, for example, the name of the *archon* defined the year. Although it may not have been a problem for daily life and business, given the limited horizons of the Greek polis, it was inherently difficult to synchronize the recording of past events in different places unless there were some established points of correspondence. A history of a region of Greece, for example, would have to accurately reconcile somehow a variety of different dating systems. In due course some states (generally weaker) adopted the chronological system of other states (generally larger and more powerful). Originally there was not a pressing demand for a uniform dating system across all states. Once the quad-rennial games at Olympia had become well established, however, it grew customary for the increasing number of participating states to date events by Olympiad or the particular year in the four-year Olympic cycle, with each new Olympiad counted in turn from the first one in 776 BC.

Gradually the Olympiad reckoning spread throughout the Greek world, especially following the conquests of Alexander the Great. In the succeeding generations there emerged more strongly the idea of the unity of mankind and therefore a more universal historical vision. It was the single achievement of the

---

[8] Croke (1982*c*), 195–200 and (especially for the dates) Burgess (1997), 471–503.

[9] More detailed accounts in Croke (1983*c*), 116–31; Witakowski (1987), 59–75; Muhl-berger (1990), 10–23 and Adler (1992), 467–81.

Alexandrian scholar Eratosthenes in the third century BC to create a chronology of world history based on an Olympiad scale. He was later followed by Apollodorus whose *chronika* was likewise comprehensive and dated by Olympiads. It contained destruction of cities, migration of races, games, alliances, treaties, deeds of kings, lives of famous men and so on.[10] A similar range of content can be found in the annalistic chronicle preserved on the Parian Marble and in other fragments of chronicles.[11] This was the very pattern subsequently taken up by Eusebius and followed by later chroniclers, including Marcellinus, while the Olympiad reckoning continued to be used in both eastern and western chronicles such as that of Hydatius. For the Greeks, works such as that of Apollodorus were an important point of reference for the synchronization of events across several city-states and they represented a brief conspectus of the past. In addition, these chroniclers were able to utilize the available lists of officials (*pinakes*) and other local annalistic city records (*horographiai*), sometimes in columnar format. These lists could be annotated in the margins and later combined into an elaborated form such as we see in the case of the so-called Atthidographers.[12]

In the Roman world lists of officials were also necessary and frequently compiled. The list of the two chief annual magistrates (consuls) came to be known as *fasti*, deriving from the fact that their names headed the annual calendar which set out the days on which public business was permitted (*dies fasti*) and the dates it was prohibited (*dies nefasti*). Such lists could also form the basis of annalistic narratives as eventually emerged in documents on stone such as the *Fasti Ostienses* which resembles the Parian Marble. By this stage there had also emerged at Rome another annalistic type of document known originally as the *annales maximi*. These *annales* were a published version of the records compiled by the chief priests at Rome—*tabulae pontificum*—in which they recorded events of particular religious or liturgical significance in the life of the city.[13] By the time of Augustus it seems that such records were no longer kept by the priests. There was, however, a comparable

[10] *FGrH* 244 T2.
[11] *FGrH* 239A.
[12] Laqueur (1928), 1885 f.; Fornara (1983), 16 ff.
[13] Most aspects of modern interpretation of the *tabula* and the *annales maximi* are tentative and disputed. For some orientation see Frier (1979); Bucher (1987), 2–61 and Chassignet (1996), xxiii–xlv.

urban record known as the *acta urbis,* for which a local urban
official was responsible. The *acta* were a useful source for documents like the *Fasti Ostienses* and other literary works.[14]

As for chronicles on the Greek model, the Romans did not
really extend the genre. Apollodorus' chronicle was translated by
Nepos but otherwise the term *chronica* does not appear in Latin
again until the fourth century. By then there had developed a
strong tradition of chronicle writing among Christian scholars,
extending the scope of Hellenistic chronographers, in order to
incorporate the whole of known history within a single unified
framework. Even though the connection between Eusebius and
the Greek chronographical writers such as Eratosthenes seems
tenuous and remote, it is discernible and the development of the
tradition can be adequately explained.

The chronicle came to be an integral part of the wider Christian
literary culture which can be defined in its own terms. Chronology, and charting the progress and direction of time (past,
present, and future), were important components of that culture.
These components were developed by a scholarly tradition
anchored in the Christian texts of the Old and New Testaments,
and reinforced in the teaching, preaching, and interpretation of
scripture.[15] Christian chronographic works organized time by the
four kingdoms of the Book of Daniel or the six ages of man
totalling 6,000 years. This chiliastic chronology provided the
foundation of the influential works of Julius Africanus and the
Roman Hippolytus whose extensive lists were later translated into
Latin and enjoyed wide circulation. They are referred to as the
Liber Generationis.[16] As the year 6000 came and went in the late
fifth/early sixth century, exactly when depending upon interpretation of calculations, there emerged a more settled chronology
based on human analogies of growth stages. By this time there
were also tables which provided a projection of dates for cele-
brating Easter in coming years.

Since Easter was (and remains) a moveable feast calculated
on the basis of the lunar calendar, it was necessary for each
Christian community to have an agreed table of future Easter
dates. From the third century onwards different scholars

[14] Details in Croke (1990*d*), 170–7.
[15] Cameron, Averil (1991), 116–17.
[16] Muhlberger (1990), 15–16.

produced increasingly elaborate tables derived from different lunar cycles, but correlated with other dating systems such as consulships and indictions. The most popular tables, for example those of Theophilus of Alexandria, spread throughout the Roman world and, like similar lists of Greek eponyms, Roman consuls, and Hebrew Passovers, the space in their margins could be used to note events of the particular year. Later, one or more such tables could be used in the construction of a more extended annalistic chronicle, perhaps as a continuation of Jerome.[17] The chronicles of Prosper and Victor of Tunnuna seem to reflect traces of such tables. Compilers of Easter tables could also, in turn, make use of chronicles. Certainly Victor of Aquitaine borrowed his list of consuls from Prosper. For the most part, however, writers of Easter tables had no use for the annalistic entries in chronicles. Although there are hardly any interpolations in manuscripts of the *Cyclus Paschalis* of 437,[18] *Liber Paschalis* of 447,[19] the *Cursus* of Victor of Aquitaine,[20] and the sixth-century *Cycle* of Dionysius[21] there are considerably more entries in the *Paschale Campanum*.[22] In fact it has long been assumed (probably erroneously) that early medieval European annals grew out of these interpolations in English Easter tables imported from Britain.[23] Easter tables were not significant in the development of Eusebius' chronicle, however.

Eusebius divided his chronicle into two separate sections, the first being a collection of raw material (such as king lists) derived from ancient historians (such as Diodorus) which provided the basis for constructing the second section. This section called the *canones* was what we traditionally think of as a chronicle since it was the section translated by Jerome. Eusebius' achievement was to elevate the researches of his predecessors to a new plane by constructing an elaborate chronological table in which was noted every year from the birth of Abraham to the time of writing. Every tenth year of Abraham was recorded in the far left margin

---

[17] Details in Jones, C. W. (1943), 3–113 with the useful list in Jones, C. W. (1947), 202–3.
[18] *MGH AA* 9. 507–10.
[19] *MGH AA* 9. 740–3.
[20] *MGH AA* 9. 677–735.
[21] *MGH AA* 9. 753–6.
[22] *MGH AA* 9. 745–50.
[23] Most recently by van Caenegem (1978), 30 ff., Hay (1977), 38 ff., Smalley (1974), 57–8 and O'Croinin (1983a), 74–86. The thesis was originally expounded by Poole (1926) but was effectively challenged by Jones, C. W. (1947), 9 ff. and Newton (1972), 43–59.

(together with Olympiads after 776 BC) and the different ancient kingdoms for as long as they lasted in the columns to the right, so that from 31 BC. there was only the Roman empire to be counted. Events connected to particular years were set out in the middle of the page. Running one's finger across the page could show that Moses' experience on Mt. Sinai took place in the 502nd year from Abraham, the 5th year of Ascatades 16th king of the Assyrians, the 15th year of Marathus 14th king of the Sicyonians, the 38th year of Triopus 7th king of the Argives, the 42nd year of Cecrops the first king of Athens and the 13th year of Chenchres 16th king of the Egyptians.[24] Eusebius had not included the period from Adam to Abraham because he did not believe that the precise chronology of those years could be determined. His successors were soon to fill this gap.[25]

There are traces of possible continuations of Eusebius' chronicle in the fourth century. Certainty begins, however, with Diodorus, bishop of Tarsus in the late fourth century, who evidently produced a chronicle based on a revision of Eusebius' chronology.[26] Then in Alexandria in the early fifth century a monk named Panodorus developed a version of Eusebius' chronicle which was based on dates from Adam rather than Abraham and which provided some coverage of the period between them. Not long after, it seems, another monk named Annianos restructured the chronicle again, this time in order to accommodate a different chronology derived from a different date for Creation (5500). The chronicles of Panodorus and Annianos no longer survive, nor do those of some of the other fifth century Greek chroniclers who would also have adapted and continued Eusebius—writers such as Helikonius, Nestorianos and Domninus. Extant, however, are two isolated and mutilated scraps of papyrus chronicles (*Pap. Berolinensis 13296* (c.5) and *Pap. Golenischev* (c.7/8)) which may be related to one or other of the Alexandrian redactors of Eusebius.[27] Likewise the Greek original of the eighth-century *Barbarus Scaligeri* belongs in this context.

By the turn of the sixth century it was perhaps no longer possible to reconstruct the original chronicle of Eusebius from the

---

[24] Eusebius/Jerome, *Chron.* (Helm, 43a and b).
[25] Adler (1989), 46–50; Mosshammer (1979), 78.
[26] Cited by El. Nis. *Chron.* 6. 15.
[27] Lietzmann (1937), 339–48 for *P. Berol. 13296*, and Bauer and Strzygowski (1906) for *Pap. Golen.*

subsequent redactions and adaptations. The Eusebian chronicle was probably used in the lost works by Eustathius of Epiphaneia, writing in the time of Anastasius, and by Hesychius writing in the early years of Justinian, that is, around the same time as Marcellinus;[28] certainly it was used in the 530s by John Malalas but in a version which was considerably different from the original, yet which still was obviously attached to Eusebius' name.[29] In the Byzantine Greek tradition of chronicle writing Eusebius continued to provide the foundation although later writers built on the more refined versions of Panodorus and Annianos.[30]

Eusebius saw his task of juxtaposing Hebrew and other events as 'useful and necessary'. The aim of the chronicle was to set out 'who ruled in what nation and when, the times divided into each section with each year set out so that we might easily and quite promptly follow who was at what time' and then to record 'the famous deeds' generally recounted for each kingdom.[31] In other words, it was essentially a work of reference, a religious document which helped Christian scholars to relate the chronology of the Bible and the Roman empire to that of the other ancient kingdoms. The sort of material the chronicle included, however, was much in the tradition of Greek chronographical writing as evidenced by Apollodorus and the second-century *Olympiades* of Phlegon of Tralles.[32] Yet in the classical tradition historical time was always local and restricted. For Christians, by contrast, historical time came to mean the whole of time[33] while chronology was essentially a philosophy of history in the modern sense.[34] The chronicle became a basic Christian text and the chronology it advanced became an integral part of the tradition acquired by new Christians on their conversion.

Consequently, when Christianity was adopted by other cultures they also absorbed its chronology, as established in Eusebius' chronicle and its later adaptations. There were, for example, two

---

[28] Eustathius' *chronike historike* (*FHG* 4. 138–42) covered the period from Adam to 503; Hesychius' *chronike historia* (Photius, *Bibliotheca* 69) ranged from Assyrian times to 518.

[29] Jeffreys (1990), 180.

[30] Adler (1989), 72–105, Mango (1988/9), 360–72, Croke (1990*b*), 32–3 and Adler (1992), 482–5.

[31] Eusebius/Jerome, *Chron.* (Helm, 18. 18–19. 6).

[32] *FGrH* 257.

[33] Guenée (1976/7), 25–8.

[34] Momigliano (1963), 83.

separate seventh-century translations of Eusebius into Syriac, or
at least two separate chronicles based on Eusebius or a later
chronicler (such as Panodorus) who had modified Eusebius: one
by Simeon of Beth Garmai and one by Jacob of Edessa. It was
probably Simeon's translation which was used by the so-called
Epitome Syria written in *c.*636 and which is preserved as part of the
chronicle of pseudo-Dionysius of Tel-Mahre, and it was probably
Jacob's version which is preserved in the Maronite Chronicle and
Michael the Syrian.[35] In addition, the earliest fragment of a
Coptic chronicle shows its dependence on Eusebius,[36] while from
the sixth century there was an Armenian translation of Eusebius,
or of a subsequent redactor of Eusebius such as Annianos and
Panodorus. This translation was apparently based on an earlier
Syriac translation, as well as the Greek original, and it provided
the foundation for subsequent chronographical literature in
Armenian. The Syriac, Coptic, and Armenian chronicles, as with
the Greek and Latin, not only translated Eusebius but in doing so
they adapted his format by simplifying it and by incorporating
local chronological structures and entries.

The chronicle reached the Latin world in the early 380s
through the translation by Jerome, although there may have been
an earlier Latin translation in circulation which was later used by
the early Irish chroniclers.[37] A century after the Eusebian original
there was no longer need for the first part of the chronicle because
the argument it contained about the superiority of Christian
chronology had long been settled. So Jerome translated only the
canons but he continued them from 325/6 to the year 378. In his
introduction Jerome confessed that his translation was dictated
very quickly (*velocissime*) and he recognized the problem of following the format of the chronicle and the order in which it should
be read. The first part of the canons from Abraham to the fall of
Troy is 'pure translation' while for the later part he was able to
supplement Eusebius with entries drawn from Suetonius and
others including Eutropius and Aurelius Victor, as well as the
putative 'Imperial History' which they both appear to have used.[38]

---

[35] Details in Witakowski (1987), 77ff.

[36] Gorteman (1956), 385–402.

[37] Proposed by Morris (1972), 80–93. It is possible, however, that the Irish variations
from the version of Jerome are the result of the scribal tradition rather than a separate
translation of Eusebius.

[38] Burgess (1995), 349–69. The proposal (by Ratti (1997), 479–508, esp. 507–8) that

It is also possible that Jerome was able to make use of material contained in the traditional Roman *acta urbis* for a number of entries.[39] His preface concludes with the explanation that the purpose of the chronicle format is to enable the easy discovery of what prophets, kings, and priests there were in the time of the Jews, Greeks, and barbarians, and what false gods were trusted by different nations. Further, the chronicle sets out when and where cities were founded, and the names of famous writers, philosophers, and poets. Jerome's chronicle is preserved in over one hundred manuscripts, versions and fragments—some of which can be dated within a few decades of the original.[40] Yet even the oldest manuscripts are incomplete, as we can see from the Lucca manuscript which preserves genuine entries from Jerome not otherwise preserved in the manuscript tradition.[41]

JEROME'S CONTINUATORS AND IMITATORS

The Eusebian chronicle was a complicated document designed to provide a point of reference for Christians engaged in studying and interpreting their sacred texts of the Old and New Testaments. In the fourth century we can see it being used by both Cyril of Alexandria and Epiphanius in the course of outlining their theological arguments. Likewise, the chronicle of Jerome soon passed into circulation in aristocratic Roman circles. Paulinus of Nola, Sulpicius Severus, Rufinus of Aquileia, Ambrose, and Augustine were all studying scriptural issues which involved using the chronicle of Jerome as a key resource.[42] In fact Sulpicius Severus himself produced a compact narrative chronicle (*chronica*) designed to instruct those who needed to grasp the essentials of Christian chronology.[43] So too, Ausonius compiled a (lost) chronicle *ab initio mundi usque ad tempus suum* which sounds like a version or rival of the chronicle of Jerome.[44] How soon the

Jerome used the *Annales* of Nicomachus Flavianus, or that Nicomachus was the author of the 'Imperial History' seem less likely.

[39] Mommsen (1850*a*) = *GS* 7. 557–9, 632; (1850*b*). A version of the *acta urbis* was also utilised by the 'Chronographer of 354' (9. 141–2, cf. Mommsen (1847) = *GS* 3. 69–70).

[40] Mosshammer (1979), 38.

[41] Mosshammer (1976), 203–40.

[42] Croke (1983*c*), 125–6.

[43] See Prete (1955).

[44] Ausonius' *chronica* is known only from Giovanni Mansionario's 14th-cent. list (Green (1991), 720 with Burgess (1993*b*), 495).

chronicle of Jerome was continued by later chroniclers is not known although there are fragments of fifth-century copies of Jerome which may have been continued beyond 378.[45] In fact, in the Oxford manuscript containing the chronicle of Marcellinus the Jerome section which was written in the fifth century is followed by an updated chronographical summation to 435 (Bodleian MS *Auct*. T. 2. 26, fo. 145). This may well represent the time of writing of the manuscript itself, or it may be a direct copy of an exemplar written in 435.

The earliest extant chronicler of the fifth century seems to have been Prosper of Aquitaine writing in the 430s and 440s.[46] There were in fact three separate editions of Prosper's chronicle. It was first written to 433 and later updated by the author to 445 and then 455. The supposed edition to 444 is based on the fact that over a century later Victor of Tunnuna says that he is continuing Prosper from this point, whereas what he actually means is that he is rewriting Prosper in accord with his theological preferences.[47] Prosper was one of the leading scholars of his day, a champion of Augustine, and wrote extensively in verse as well as prose on a range of theological issues.[48] Why he wrote the chronicle is not stated but it may be that he desired simply to imitate Jerome and at the same time aim some decisive blows against the Pelagians. Like Jerome, Prosper was a ferocious foe of heretics and this is evident enough in his chronicle.[49] Prosper's chronicle formed part of the continuous story which began with Eusebius and was continued by Jerome. As suggested by the title of the work (*epitoma de chronicon*), it is a narrow western summary of the chronicle of Eusebius/Jerome) to which has been added the generations from Adam to Abraham (deliberately ignored by Eusebius) and from the Crucifixion all the consulships (instead of Jerome's imperial years), as well as what occurred between 379 and his own day in 445. After the point at which Jerome ends in 378 Prosper remarks 'we have taken the trouble to add what follows' (1166 (460)) and

---

[45] Notably *CLA* 1075 (8, 17) and *CLA* 1704 (10, 12).

[46] Details can be found in Muhlberger (1990), 48–135 and Humphries (1996), 155–75; more narrowly in Molè (1980), 204–39.

[47] That is, he ignores Prosper's theological entries after 444 although he continues to include other entries up to 455, as demonstrated by Muhlberger (1986), 240–4. cf. Placanica [1997], xiii–v.

[48] Schanz, Hosius, and Krüger (1920), 491–501; Muhlberger (1990), 48–55.

[49] Markus (1986), 39–40.

where Prosper's chronicle originally ends (433) he concludes with a chronological summation from Adam (1318 (474)). The two subsequent editions carry on from this point, to 445 and 455 respectively.

Prosper's chronicle is preserved in a variety of ways. There are manuscripts of only the original part of the chronicle from 379 (as far as both 433 and 455) as well as the complete work from Adam. In the manuscript of the chronicle used shortly after its composition by Victor of Aquitaine it is included as a continuation of the original chronicle of Jerome.[50] This is the pattern in many of the manuscripts. Others, however, preserve not the original form of Eusebius/Jerome but the form in which Prosper himself had reworked it, that is, beginning with Adam. These manuscripts also include his continuation from 379 as part of a new chronicle. In other words those who preferred to have the complete version of Jerome only needed to copy Prosper from 379. Again, however, this version of Prosper is extant in a variety of manuscripts: some to 443, some to 455, some without interpolations, others with world years added. On top of these there are abbreviated versions of the chronicles in some manuscripts, and several manuscripts in which the chronicle is continued anonymously to different points. There are anonymous continuations of both the 445 and 455 versions, in addition to occasional interpolations at various points throughout the chronicle.[51] The chronicle of Prosper is therefore typical of the complex pattern of transmission of a late antique chronicle. There is really no single 'pure' manuscript but rather a range of manuscripts with adaptations, interpolations, and continuations although all bear the name 'Prosper'.

A further complication, again typical of chronicles, is that some later manuscripts are cross-contaminated which means that they include entries from other chronicles.[52] This is a natural process since the format of the chronicles lent them so easily to such additions. For example, the earliest modern editions of Prosper contain entries which are identical to those in the chronicle of Marcellinus and so it used to be thought that Marcellinus had borrowed them from Prosper. In fact they are nothing more than later insertions in the manuscript tradition of Prosper but

---

[50] *Cursus Paschalis* 7 (*MGH AA* 9. 681).
[51] Holder-Egger (1876*a*), 15–50; Mommsen (1892), 345 ff.; Muhlberger (1990), 55–60.
[52] *MGH AA* 9. 497–9.

actually taken directly from the chronicle of Marcellinus.[53] Besides this variety of form in the manuscripts of Prosper, there are manuscripts of another Gallic chronicle which bears the name 'Prosper' but which is not his either. These manuscripts include a continuation of Jerome from 379 which is attributed to Prosper but which is clearly not his work. Since the fullest version of this continuation (contained in British Museum *Add. MSS* 16974) terminates at 452 the author is known as the 'Chronicler of 452'. As with the anonymous sixth-century continuator of Marcellinus (see Chapter 7) and Prosper, the 'Chronicler of 452' presents a coherent and identifiable viewpoint and culture. It appears that he came from Marseilles, was considerably less enthusiastic about Augustine than Prosper had been, and was able to utilize in his chronicle an extensive range of recent ecclesiastical texts.[54] His chronicle continues the regnal chronology of Jerome and is a contemporary record for its latter years.[55] Its gloomy picture of events in Gaul suggests it may have been designed to stress to the governing aristocracy the seriousness of the Hun threat.

An exact contemporary of Prosper was Hydatius, an aristocratic bishop from Gallaecia in north-west Spain. It was around 470, as an old man, that Hydatius wrote his chronicle in continuation of Jerome. He followed Jerome's dating system by Olympiads, years from Abraham, and regnal years, to which he added Spanish era dates and a system of Jubilees.[56] Hydatius had actually seen Jerome in Jerusalem while on a visit there as a boy. Like Prosper, he was a highly educated theologian who became a bishop in 427 but who lived in difficult times for his region, given the settlement of the Vandals and Suevi. He was, like Prosper, known to Pope Leo as a champion of orthodoxy although in Hydatius' case it was Priscillianism that posed the threat. His chronicle concentrates on the occupation of the tribes and of the fortunes of the church in Spain—a valuable provincial record— and also for his own intervention in affairs.[57] At one stage (431) he

---

[53] *MGH AA* 9. 497–9; Holder-Egger (1876a), 31–4.

[54] Muhlberger (1990), 136ff.

[55] The vexed question of which dating systems in the manuscripts were contemporary and which were later interpolations seems to have been settled through recent debates: Muhlberger (1983), 23–33, Jones and Casey (1988), 368–98 and, most decisively, Burgess (1990), 185–95.

[56] This central feature of the chronicle has only recently been uncovered by Burgess (1993a), 31–3. [57] Muhlberger (1990), 193 ff.; Burgess (1993a), 3–10.

was deputed as envoy to the Roman general Aetius. His local emphasis would presumably appeal most to a local audience. Episcopal letters, especially those recounting prodigies, and oral reports of envoys provided much contemporary information while for the earlier period he used Sulpicius Severus and a version of the so-called 'Fasti Hydatiani'.[58]

In terms of its transmission Hydatius' chronicle did not have the benefit of Cassiodorus' recommendation, as had those of Prosper and Marcellinus. So it is not so abundantly extant. It survives essentially in a single Berlin manuscript (B) copied at Trier in the ninth century, although this manuscript is lacunose and incomplete (because summaries of Hydatius include entries not to be found in B) and its years from Abraham were only added by a later hand.[59] These summaries consist of several Spanish ones, that contained in the chronicle of Fredegar and one at Montpellier. All of these are interpolated to some extent and some of them have adapted or modified the dating framework of Hydatius.[60] Yet again we have no pure or complete version of the chronicle. Each time it was copied it became a new chronicle either by virtue of being summarized or else by being interpolated. Also making extensive use of Hydatius, as well as Orosius and the now anonymous Gallic chronicle which terminated in 452, was another chronicler writing in Gaul in 511, hence the modern title 'Gallic chronicler of 511'. This writer whose work is extant in a single thirteenth-century Madrid manuscript provided, or more likely copied, a condensed summary of Jerome's chronicle and continued it preserving Jerome's system of regnal years of emperors.[61]

Hydatius seems not to have been aware of Prosper's work and, unlike Prosper, his own chronicle does not seem to have been continued by later writers. It was not among those specifically recommended by Cassiodorus who perhaps was not aware of it at all. On the other hand, Cassiodorus was very familiar with Prosper's chronicle when he produced his own in 519 to celebrate the consulship of the Gothic prince Eutharic. At the time of writing his chronicle Cassiodorus was utilizing his erudition and

---

[58] Muhlberger (1990), 207–11; Burgess (1993a), 199–202.
[59] Muhlberger (1990), 281; Burgess (1993a), 11–26.
[60] Burgess (1988), 357; (1993a), 47–58.
[61] Mommsen (1892), 626–8; 632–66 with Muhlberger (1990), 142–4.

literary talent on behalf of the Ostrogothic king of Italy. His work runs from Creation but, except for a brief survey of the period of the Assyrian kings, is mainly concerned with the Roman world from the foundation of the city. It is based on the full chronicle of Prosper for the most part, but on a version which had subsequently been used by Victor of Aquitaine. For the period beyond the end of Prosper and closer to his own lifetime Cassiodorus uses Italian documents, some of which may have been previous chronicles. Despite Cassiodorus' subsequent literary influence his chronicle was not much used by later writers.[62]

After Cassiodorus there is no extant annalistic chronicle in the west for more than another half-century until that of Marius of Avenches (530–592/3).[63] Marius' chronicle was composed as a direct continuation of that of Prosper. Like both Prosper and Hydatius, Marius was evidently a man of theological learning described in his epitaph as *pervigil in studiis*.[64] In fact he was bishop of Avenches for some twenty years from 574. Marius' chronicle bears no title but as a continuation of Prosper from 455 it is organized by consulships from 455 until 523. Thereafter, it follows the pattern of Marcellinus by using both indictions and consulships from 523 to its end in 581. The chronicle concentrates on local Gallic events but also includes several eastern entries and has many years left blank. Although various suggestions have been made about Marius' sources the most likely seem to be some previous Italian chronicle and Burgundian annals, perhaps others too.[65]

The chronicle of Jerome was popular not only in the west but also in Constantinople with its large community of Latin speakers. There is evidence for the chronicle being copied there in the early sixth century for the sons of the Syrian praetorian prefect Marinus,[66] and it was continued by Marcellinus in his chronicle to 518. Also available in Constantinople was the chronicle of Prosper. Whether Marcellinus knew Prosper's chronicle is not

[62] Mommsen (1861), 547–696 with O'Donnell (1979), 38ff.

[63] There was, höwever, the now lost chronicle of Maximian bishop of Ravenna which was quite a detailed work, to judge from the notices in Agnellus, a later bishop of Ravenna, who used it (78, 82 (*MGH AA* 9. 257)).

[64] Quoted in *MGH AA* 11. 228.

[65] Santschi (1968), 17–34 and Morton (1982), 107–15. There are various problems with the reliability of Marius' consular list (*CLRE* 50–1, cf. Favrod (1990), 1–20).

[66] Contained in a poem and letter in a Leiden MS of Jerome's chronicle (*MS Scaliger* 14, 187ᵛ–190ʳ), on which see Croke (forthcoming *c*).

clear although he does include an entry on him, and it has been
thought traditionally that Marcellinus' date for Prosper's death
(463) must therefore be accurate;[67] assuming that he knew
Prosper's chronicle, then his own work may have been designed
to complement that of Prosper by concentrating on events in the
east. Marcellinus, like Prosper, updated his own chronicle (in 534)
and was continued (in the 550s) by another, now anonymous,
writer.

Prosper certainly was used at Constantinople in the 560s by
Victor of Tunnuna, the exiled African bishop, in composing a
new world chronicle. The period to 444 was apparently a supplemented abbreviation of Prosper and has not survived, just as
Prosper's chronicle to 378 had been a supplemented abbreviation
of Jerome.[68] Victor then continued Prosper as far as 563 organis-
ing his entries by consulships, although he left some years blank,
and then resorted to using the imperial year of Justinian for the
last four years.[69] Victor too was a bishop but fell foul of the
emperor Justinian over the question of the 'Three Chapters' and
ended up in exile in Constantinople where he wrote his chronicle.
The chronicle, which depends heavily on the *Ecclesiastical History*
of Theodore Lector, concentrates on ecclesiastical developments
involving the major patriarchates, with a strong division into those
for and against Chalcedon, and was apparently designed to provide a clear record to support the case of those in Constantinople
and Africa who opposed recent developments.[70] The audience at
which Victor aimed his chronicle was evidently the ecclesiastical
literati of Constantinople. Certainly, as for Marcellinus too, it has
a local emphasis in its selection of events and betrays the influence
of Greek as well as Latin culture in the capital.[71]

Thirty years later Victor's chronicle was being used in Spain
where it was continued by John of Biclaro to the year 591. John
was a Goth who had been educated at Constantinople in Greek
and Latin and on his return to Spain had been active in founding
a monastery at Biclaro where he wrote the chronicle and a great
many other works which have not survived. Later he became

---

[67] Holder-Egger (1876a), 58–9—this is not necessarily so, however (Muhlberger (1990),
54, cf. Pintus (1984), 807).

[68] *MGH AA* 11. 180.

[69] *MGH AA* 11. 180–1; Placanica (1997), xxvii–viii, 131.

[70] Cf. Isidore's description (*De uir ill.*, 49 and *Chron. praef.* (*MGH AA* 11. 424)).

[71] Croke (1983b), 81–91; Placanica (1997), xviii ff.

bishop of Gerona. The seven or seventeen (a textual problem) years John had spent in the capital had obviously influenced the way he would describe events in his chronicle although the only trace of his presence in the city is his personal witness to the plague in 573.[72] Still he may have planned and begun the chronicle there. As with Victor's chronicle, John's was meant to champion the cause of orthodoxy against the Arian kings of Visigothic Spain. In his chronicle John dates by both imperial (Roman) and regnal (Visigothic) years which makes the chronology look disorganized, except that he appears normally to begin each year on 1 January.[73] The chronicles of Victor and John were transmitted in manuscripts, mostly now lost, in which, following Jerome and Prosper, they form a continuous chronicle from Abraham to 591.[74]

In the margin of those sections of the sixteenth-century Escorial manuscript covering the chronicle of Victor and John there are several annotations derived from some other chronicle and transmitted in earlier manuscripts now lost. If this particular manuscript were itself to be copied it is likely that these annotations would eventually be incorporated in the text of Victor and John which would then make it difficult to detect them as interpolations. We know this happened all the time with chronicle manuscripts and we can often identify the interpolations, as in the case of the Copenhagen Continuator of Prosper for example, from Gregory of Tours.[75] In the Oxford manuscript of Marcellinus too there are marginal comments in the Jerome section which were clearly written by the scribe himself in the fifth century. However, in later manuscripts derived from the Oxford manuscript many of these marginal comments have passed unobtrusively into the text of Jerome's chronicle. In the case of the Escorial manuscript of Victor and John the marginal entries have been plausibly identified as deriving originally from the chronicle of Maximus of Saragossa whose work is otherwise lost, although, given the difficult manuscript tradition involved here, it is impossible to be certain.[76] Like Prosper and John of Biclaro at least, Maximus was an experienced author. He was bishop of Saragossa in the late sixth

---

[72] John of Biclaro, *Chron.* 573.4 (ii. 213).

[73] On John see Hillgarth (1970), 261–352 and (1966), 483–508; Teillet (1984), 428–55; Herrin (1987), 81–2 and Wolf (1990), 1–11.

[74] Mommsen (1894), 165–6; Placanica (1997), xxxii ff.

[75] Wynn (1998), 100–6.

[76] *MGH AA* ii. 221–3.

and early seventh centuries. Although it is not possible to reconstruct the aim and span of his chronicle, the marginal additions
to Victor and John run from 450 to 568; perhaps Maximus'
chronicle too had been a continuation of Prosper.

Victor, John, and Maximus were all known to Isidore of Seville
as eminent ecclesiastical writers whose literary oeuvre included
chronicles. Soon afterwards (615) Isidore himself produced a new
world chronicle. This work, like all the other chronicles, was
essentially dependent on his predecessors. Isidore tells us that he
set out to provide a brief outline of world history from Creation to
the time of Heraclius and king Sisebut.[77] To achieve this he
simply excerpted from the chronicles of Jerome, Prosper, Victor,
and John as far as the year 591 (occasionally inserting an entry
from other sources, as Prosper and Victor had done) and then
added his own continuation to 615. Like that of Jerome, Isidore's
chronicle was organized as a series of events under individual
reigns rather than on a strictly annalistic basis, but it included
dates from Creation at the beginning of each new reign. In
addition, the whole chronicle was encased in a framework of the
six eras of mankind with the remainder of time beyond human
investigation.[78] Isidore's chronicle was popular in the Middle Ages
and it survives in many manuscripts. Some manuscripts contain a
continuation to 624[79] while several others include a range of
entries interpolated from other sources.[80] In all these respects it is
simply characteristic of all late antique chronicles.[81]

Quite soon after its completion Isidore's chronicle was being
utilized not only in Italy by the Continuator of Prosper but also in
Ireland. As elsewhere, Jerome's chronicle had become the basis
for local chronicles in Ireland. Although the details remain
obscure, the earliest Irish chronicle was probably composed at
Iona in the early seventh century and the existence of this chronicle is inferred from entries in the extant Irish annals of later times.
This original chronicle was constructed as a continuation of
Jerome. In fact it used the chronicle of Marcellinus as the immediate successor of Jerome. Further, as we shall see (Chapter 8), it
was probably this Irish chronicle which was used directly and
verbatim by Bede in his own chronicle written as part of a larger

[77] *Praef. MGH AA* 11. 425.
[79] *MGH AA* 11. 489–490.
[81] Reydellet (1970), 363–400.

[78] *Chron.* 418 (*MGH AA* 11. 481).
[80] *MGH AA* 11. 491–4.

work *de temporum ratione* in 725. As a separate extract with a separate manuscript tradition, the chronicle of Bede became one of the most popular books of the Middle Ages. Bede's chronicle imitated that of Isidore in that it was organized by years from Creation and grouped events under imperial reigns. From the time of Heraclius the chronicle of Bede provides a more detailed account of events in Britain. It survives in numerous manuscripts and versions, replete with interpolations and omissions, and was continued anonymously in several manuscripts.[82]

Not long after the development of the Iona chronicle, and before the time of Bede, another composite chronicle began to circulate in the Frankish realm. It goes by the modern name of 'Fredegar' but was the work of a single author writing in the late 650s. Essentially, like most chronicle manuscripts, this is a composite chronicle consisting of the Hippolytan *Liber Generationis* from Creation, followed by various lists, then extracts from Jerome, extracts from Hydatius' continuation of Jerome, and a version of Books 2–6 of Gregory of Tours' *History* which leads into an original chronicle for the period 584–642. As with all chronicles, manuscripts of Fredegar include continuations to 734, 751, and 768. Certainly, there are difficult problems to be encountered in determining the extent of Fredegar's own contribution to the work which passes under his name.[83] Nonetheless, the chronicle is a good example of a medieval chronicle text and a good example of how the work of earlier chroniclers was so easily cannibalized and corrupted in the course of being reworked for other purposes. Unfortunately, for the student of the late antique chronicles, it is often these later versions which must form the basis of analysing the original chronicle and its author. The best-known medieval chronicle manuscripts thought to preserve intact genuine late antique chronicles are the ninth-century Cod. Berol. Phillipps 1829 (*Fasti Hydatiani* or *Consularia Constantinopolitana*), the eighth-century Cod. Sangall. 878 (*Excerpta Sangallensia*), the ninth-century Cod. Berol. Phillipps *1885* (*Excerpta Valesiana*), the eleventh-century Cod. Mers. Dom. 202 (*Fasti Ravennates / Annals of Ravenna*), the twelfth/thirteenth century Cod. Havniensis 454 (*Prosperi Continuatio*

---

[82] Edited by Mommsen (*MGH AA* 13. 247–327) which was virtually reprinted by Jones, C. W. (*CCL* 123B), and discussed in Jones, C. W. (1947), 16–27 and van den Brincken (1957), 108–113. The various interpolations and continuations are set out by Mommsen in *MGH AA* 13. 334–54.

[83] Wallace-Hadrill (1962), 71–94; Goffart (1963), 206–41.

Havniensis) and the fifteenth-century Cod. Vindob. 3416 (*Fasti Vindobonenses*). The contention that the chronicles preserved in these manuscripts are related to each other and belong to a separate genre called 'consular annals' is highly questionable.[84]

Yet such versions and manuscripts essentially reflect (and form part of) the unfolding of the Christian story canonized by Eusebius and Jerome. They also demonstrate how the influence and authority of the Christian chronicle genre derived from its format, its content, and its links with preceding chronicles right back to Eusebius and Jerome. The textual authority of the late antique chronicle was originally reinforced by continuing the authoritative Jerome, then transmitted to subsequent chronicles which were themselves linked to Jerome.

CHRONICLERS AND THEIR AUDIENCE

Nowadays, with a well-established historical profession, we can speak of 'historians' in a strict sense and can make a pejorative contrast with 'chroniclers'. We rely for this on an ancient Roman distinction. But the distinction was only ever an academic one and is not soundly based in historiographical practice. Moreover, the distinction applied only to the literary products, not their authors. Sempronius Asellio and Verrius Flaccus distinguished 'history' and 'annals', not 'historians' and 'annalists'. In late antiquity Isidore made formal claims about the nature and boundaries of literary genres distinguishing 'chronicle' and 'history', but not 'chroniclers' and 'historians'. This was because the production of a chronicle or a history was a specific writing task, not a permanent intellectual or occupational predilection.

In late antiquity and throughout the ensuing centuries the production of any historical work, including an annalistic chronicle, required access to a good library.[85] So the writer of a chronicle was a bishop (Hydatius, Marius, Victor, John of Biclaro, Isidore), or at least theologically educated (Jerome, Prosper), or an imperial official (Marcellinus, Cassiodorus, John Malalas) because such people formed an important part of the literate community of the empire. In the Roman world the best educated were traditionally the senatorial and provincial aristocracy but many scions of aristocratic families, men such as Prosper and Hydatius, now

[84] Croke (forthcoming *a*).   [85] Guenée (1980), 100, cf. 45, 156.

became God's men rather than the emperor's. Their chronicles were not therefore the products of those capable of nothing better. The best educated were frequently the best travelled too. Among the chroniclers Jerome, Hydatius, Victor, and John of Biclaro were well travelled. As a widely travelled imperial official himself, Marcellinus was therefore not unusual for the writer of a chronicle.

Marcellinus was probably not a cleric yet he obviously possessed a reasonable knowledge of ecclesiastical literature and church affairs. Further, his chronicle was one of several major literary works of the same author. Chroniclers were patently not ill-educated and incompetent; rather they were highly educated and literate. Likewise, chronicles do not represent the best efforts of popular historical writing in an age of decline to be compared to the rhetorical histories written for an elite in an earlier age of high culture. Rather they belong to the broader field of Christian discourse designed to appeal to all social groups and levels.[86]

As a literary activity, writing a chronicle involved the processes of compilation and copying, and to some extent research and note taking. As such it was no different from any other kind of literary activity and those who wrote chronicles also wrote other works such as histories (Eusebius, Cassiodorus, Isidore, Bede), theological treatises (Prosper), topographical books (Eusebius, Jerome), scripture commentaries and saints' lives (Jerome, Bede), as well as monastic rules (John of Biclaro). So in writing other works on topography and chronology Marcellinus was not an unusual chronicler either. The term 'chronicler', however, can be misleading for producing a chronicle was merely a single literary activity, not a permanent calling.[87] Jerome and Bede, for instance, were at one and the same time chronographer, exegete, and hagiographer. In this sense Marcellinus was chronographer and topographer, as well as chronicler.

Style, originality, and faultless research may be the hallmarks of modern historical writing, but they were never those of antiquity and the Middle Ages. Instead, writers such as the late antique chroniclers sought to be derivative and conservative. They drew their value and impact, as well as their historiographical

---

[86] Whitby (1992), 59–66, cf. Cameron, Averil (1991), 200–3, and Croke and Emmett (1983*a*), 3–4.
[87] Guenée (1977), 5.

authority, from the way their works hung together, the way they progressively simplified their format. That is what the chronicler's audience expected, namely, to see a new chronicle as a continuation of a familiar but ongoing Christian story which was plotted within a single coherent framework. The chroniclers wrote for the literate of society, that is predominantly the ecclesiastics and the educated laity. Hydatius, for example, specifically addressed his chronicle 'to all the faithful in Our Lord Jesus Christ who serve him in truth',[88] while the chronicle of Jerome was discussed and passed around among the Christian aristocracy in late fourth-century Rome.[89] Cassiodorus wrote his chronicle explicitly at the request of the consul Eutharic in order to highlight his consulship in 519 and hoped that its comprehensive scope might prove instructive to the Gothic consul.[90] The chronicle's publicity value would have been for the senatorial aristocracy of Ostrogothic Italy, not the army or the peasantry.

For the most part, however, the chronicle writers provide no direct indication of their audience and purpose. Rather these are taken for granted. Jerome's chronicle was utilized by the educated aristocracy, as we have seen, and he saw the aim of the work as being the provision of 'easy discovery' (*facilis inventio*)—discovery of who ruled when, who invented what, the dates of famous writers and philosophers, prodigies and martyrdoms. Marcellinus (*Chron. praef.*) followed Jerome in these aims. In a similar vein Isidore saw his task as providing a clear chronological layout so that the reader might become acquainted briefly with the complete history of the world and the cumulative number of years.[91] As a chronicler himself, he therefore found the chronicle of John of Biclaro 'extremely useful'.[92] John had set out to continue what Eusebius, Jerome, Prosper, and Victor had skilfully woven together 'for our understanding' (*ad agnitionem nostram*) by providing a concise record of his own time for the benefit of posterity (*studuimus ad posteros notescenda brevi stilo transmittere*).[93] How the late antique chronicles were introduced to their audience is not known either. It is possible that they were recited aloud as ancient histories had been although their format suggests that there were more suited to reference than recitation. Jerome, for

---

[88] Hyd. *Chron. Praef.* (71).

[89] References in Croke (1983c), 125–6.

[90] *MGH AA* II. 120.

[91] *Praef.* 2 (425).

[92] *De vir.ill.*, 62 (63).

[93] John of Biclaro, *Chron. praef.* (II. 211).

example, was fearful of his work sounding tedious.[94] The few glimpses we catch of their use is as a reference and ancillary tool, a sort of handbook for historians, theologians, and others.

As a genre, the late antique chronicles have not traditionally been accorded high historiographical status. This situation has arisen primarily because they have usually been evaluated by modern criteria of reliability as an historical 'source'. They have been judged on the basis of an historiographical paradigm which describes the history of writing about the past as a progressive development in method and scope from classical times with such rudimentary forms as the chronicle to the present.[95] In this model writing about the past finally reached its ideal positivist form in the nineteenth century with the creation of a sense of historical objectivity based on canons of evidence, research and truth. More recently, discussions on the nature of historical narrative have reinforced the traditional devaluation of the chronicle. In particular, it is argued that chronicles are defective as narrative and as history because they are merely factual, disconnected from other events and devoid of interpretation.[96] Indeed, it has been suggested that 'only chronicles are structured with absolutely no reference to a general theory of historical change'[97] and that a chronicler is 'totally unconcerned with any question of the meaning of the whole'.[98]

Such a view is based on a failure to appreciate a chronicle's narrative conceptualization. That is, the chronicle tells a coherent story which has a beginning, middle, and end (even if the end is only implied). There is therefore a sense of pattern and meaning, as well as a narrative closure in a chronicle such as that of Marcellinus when it is set in its fuller context as a continuation of Jerome who tells the story up to 378. A good example of this historiographical pattern and meaning is to be found in the chronicle of John of Biclaro. In the thirteenth-century Madrid manuscript containing the chronicle of John is also found the chronicle of Jerome, continued then by Prosper, then by Victor, then by John culminating in John's chronological summary of

---

[94] *Praef.* (Helm, 18. 14–15).
[95] Typical examples are Barnes (1962), 64–8, and Breisach (1983), 82, 126 ff.
[96] E.g. White (1987), 42; Kellner (1989), 331–2; Berkhofer (1995), 117.
[97] McCullagh (1998), 300.
[98] Stanford (1998), 219.

years from Adam to the time of writing in 592.[99] Likewise, Victor had continued Prosper, who had continued Jerome,[100] and concluded with a chronological summary from Adam to his time of writing (567), just as both Jerome and Prosper had done in concluding their chronicles.

The late antique chronicles can now be more fully appreciated in the light of recent approaches to analysing writing about the past, whereby due attention is paid to both the limitations of larger-scale narrative history and the configurational role of all writers of history.[101] The notion of the past contained in the chronicles, and the pattern of time and change it implies, was part of the shared world-view of the late antique chronicler and his audience. The story told by successive chroniclers, and the way it was constructed and presented, was shaped by this shared world-view and the expectations to which it gave rise. The chronicle became the central mode of presenting and interpreting the past in late antiquity.

The late antique chronicles grew out of traditional literary forms (Hellenistic chronography, Roman consular lists) but they are based on a Christian perspective of time as well as a Christian interpretation of the course, direction and meaning of history. Their importance derived from the fact that they provided a summary and comprehensive guide to God's time and the totality of the human past, and to where the present belongs in the grand scheme of things. Further, because the chronicles were designed to be universal they fitted together in manuscripts in which one chronicle continued another. Some of the continuations of Jerome were more celebrated than others and survive, some do not. There are fragments too—perhaps from known chronicles, perhaps not.

In textual terms we possess an exceptional advantage in the case of Marcellinus in that there is a manuscript dating to within a generation or two of the autograph original, namely *Auct.* T. 2. 26 (late sixth century) in the Bodleian Library at Oxford. Even so, it is clear that this manuscript contains omissions and interpolations, which is a salutary reminder of how early this textual

---

[99] John of Biclaro, *Chron* (ii. 220). For the Madrid manuscript: Mommsen (1894), 167–72; Placanica (1997), xxxii–iii.

[100] Vict. Tonn. *Chron.* 567 (ii. 206); Placanica (1997), 61.

[101] Details in Jenkins (1995), 15 ff. and Iggers (1997), 1–31.

process commences. This manuscript is a typical chronicle manuscript, that is, it includes Jerome to 378, followed by a chronological summary to 435 and a brief list of persecutions against Christians—all by the same fifth-century scribe; then in a later sixth-century hand is the chronicle of Marcellinus to 534 followed by a continuation of Marcellinus to 548 where the manuscript breaks off. How much further it continued is not clear. So this manuscript constituted, in effect, a world chronicle from Abraham to the 550s or later and Marcellinus was simply an integral component of that chronicle. The chronicle of Marcellinus is, like all the late antique chronicles, a serious work written by an educated writer for a specific audience. As we have seen in this chapter, the nature of his chronicle and its subsequent fate need to be understood in the context of chronicle writing in late antiquity and the way chronicle manuscripts were copied and utilized. The main themes of this chapter are pursued further when attention is devoted to the chronicle's composition (Chapter 6) and transmission (Chapters 7 and 8).

6

Constructing the Chronicle

The chronicle of Marcellinus, like any similar work, represents its author's attempt to constitute a picture of the past which is meaningful for his contemporaries. In producing his chronicle Marcellinus read earlier historiographical texts such as Orosius' *History* from his present perspective and purpose. Out of the documents which he chose to use, and guided by both the dictates of the genre and the expectations of the audience at which he was aiming, Marcellinus configured and formatted his story. For the most part, he does not so much engage directly with the past as indirectly through the records to which he had access. The chronicle is a textually mediated outline account of events from 379 to 534, as they were commonly understood at the time of writing, and his picture of the previous 140 years is captured in the language of his day. Consequently, to view, utilize or judge the chronicle as merely a mine of facts for modern researchers is to misconstrue it seriously.

The chronicle is essentially a literary text, constructed for a particular purpose and for a particular audience so it lends itself to all the different ways a text can be analysed; that is to say, one can investigate its language and style as well as its method of construction and its sources of information. This chapter addresses the formal textual aspects of the chronicle as another means of illuminating the nature of the document, its author and its audience. The discussion proceeds from identifying the sources of information used by Marcellinus in the chronicle to analysing how the chronicle was assembled from those sources. In addition, it attempts to clarify the nature and development of the putative (and controversial) 'City Chronicle' of Constantinople, long acknowledged as one of the chronicle's main sources of information.

A late antique chronicler did not set out to engage in detailed critical research with the goal of preparing an absolutely accurate and detailed historical account. Rather, he was primarily concerned with showing the pattern of events and their nature, especially how they indicate the hand of providence in ongoing human history. Constructing such a work did not compel the writer to gather and critically compare vast numbers of historical records with a view to ensuring there was a detailed record for every listed year. The process was necessarily different. In the writing of Marcellinus' chronicle, as for any late antique chronicle, there were three distinct stages:

1. *Establishing and laying out the chronographical framework:* a choice of Years from Creation or Abraham, indictions, regnal years, Olympiads, and consulships. Marcellinus chose the potentially conflicting arrangement of using both indictions (beginning 1 September) and consuls (beginning 1 January).

2. *Identifying potential sources of information for the chronicle's entries.* Since a chronicle required entries to be dated to at least a year (reckoning by consuls, indictions, etc.) it was natural for a chronicler to rely heavily on annalistic documents, especially previous chronicles. Nonetheless, other sources of information could also provide material for entries. As both Hydatius and John of Biclaro specified, these sources could be both written and oral, as well as the chronicler's own experience and observation.[1]

3. *From these sources, the chronicler configured his plot by extracting the required information and putting it in his own words or copying it verbatim.* He was primarily concerned with finding information to stitch together to form the sequence of the story, not to engage in critical verification of data or to synthesize conflicting and complementary accounts. Every chronicle, no matter how derivative, is worth studying in terms of where an author finds his information, and what he includes and omits, for it tells us something about his perspective and his methods of composition.[2] So too, the chronicler's specific purpose and the shape of his story require elucidation.

---

[1] Hydatius: *Chron. praef.* 5 (74)—*partim ex studio scriptorum, partim ex certo aliquantorum relatu, partim ex cognitione . . .*—with Muhlberger (1990), 204 ff.; John: *Chron. praef.* (11. 211)—*ex parte quod oculata fide pervidimus et ex parte quae ex relatu fidelium didicimus.*
[2] Cf. Guenée (1980), 214.

ANNALISTIC RECORDS

For the chronicle of Marcellinus, as for any chronicle structured on the basis of an annual chronology, an annalistic record was ideal because it enabled events to be recorded in their correct years. That is why such records are so predominantly used in extant chronicles. Prosper used Jerome, Cassiodorus used Prosper, and so on. In these particular chronicles the previous annalistic record, a prior chronicle, can be identified but this is not normally the case. Instead, hypothesis and speculation predominate, with the most commonly deduced annalistic record being a chronicle record local to the writer. Moreover, it has been suggested, at least in the case of the Byzantine chroniclers, that their main source of information usually reflects the locale of its particular writer.[3] This explains, for example, why Antioch stands at the centre of the chronicle of the Antiochene John Malalas who derives a good deal of material from an official or semi-official record of local events. This record has been labelled the Antiochene 'City Chronicle' (Stadtchronik).[4] Similarly, behind the Chronicle of Edessa there lie local Edessan records,[5] and a local Alexandrian city record can be traced in the chronicle of Theophanes.[6] This model holds true for the west as well where the regionalization of continuations of Eusebius and Jerome was based on local records. For instance, behind the chronicles of Hydatius and John of Biclaro, directly or indirectly, there lie Spanish records; behind the chronicles from which, eventually, descended the *Fasti Vindobonenses* (fifteenth century) and the *Auctarium Havniense* (twelfth century) of Prosper are local records of Rome and Ravenna; behind the so-called Gallic chroniclers of 452 and 511 are local records of southern Gaul, predominantly Arles and Marseilles.[7] Such records are visible not only in the bias of information they contain but also in the use of local dates. The 'Spanish era' is to be found in Hydatius and Isidore, while Malalas dates according to the local system of Antioch and the Chronicle of Edessa according to the local era of that city. The early Irish annals which used the chronicle of Marcellinus, as we

---

[3] Krumbacher (1896), 321.
[4] Explained by Freund (1882), cf. Croke (1990a), 203–5.
[5] Witakowski (1987), 77.
[6] Mango/Scott (1997), lxxviii–lxxx.
[7] Holder-Egger (1875).

shall see (Chapter 8), employed a complicated local dating system based in identifying years by the day of the week when the Kalends of January fell ('K.i'; 'K.ii', 'K.iii' etc).

For medieval western Europe, including Britain and Ireland, we are familiar with the scope of continuous annalistic chronicles (as opposed to world chronicles): they centre around particular courts and monasteries so that a change of outlook, content, and style may follow with a change of author.[8] Such institutional localization was not so extensive in the period from the fourth to the seventh centuries. Instead, at this time annalistic records still centred around a basic administrative unit of antique society—the city. The origins and history of individual cities, especially one's native city, was a frequent topic of historical research and rhetorical presentation, a task made easier by the existence of local chronicles/annals preserving a record of important events in the public life of the city. Such records had long been a traditional part of urban life and record-keeping. To the Greeks they had been known as *horographiai*. When the annalistic chronicle became a common form of historical writing from the fourth century the traditional annalistic records became especially useful sources of information. So, in many of the chronicles of late antiquity can be located the local urban records of Rome, Ravenna, Alexandria, Antioch, and Constantinople, their 'City Chronicles' (to use a controversial but helpful term).[9] It is likely that Marcellinus made extensive use of such a record, either directly or indirectly.

MARCELLINUS' USE OF AN EASTERN CHRONICLE

Since Marcellinus' self-professed aim is to concentrate on the eastern empire (*Orientale tantum imperium* (*praef.*)) it would only be natural to expect him to be utilizing predominantly eastern records or documents. The most obvious indication of Marcellinus' eastern perspective is his use of indictions and the list of consuls he employs. As for indictions, by the time of Marcellinus the indiction had come to represent the normal Byzantine calendar year commencing on 1 September and concluding on 31 August. The indictional year commenced with a solemn liturgical celebration at Constantinople.[10] It was a natural chronological

[8] Taylor (1965).
[9] Croke (1990*d*), 165–203 with the critique of Burgess (1993*a*), 182–6.
[10] *SEC* 1. 4–2. 5 with Janin (1966), 73.

system for anyone writing an annalistic chronicle in the imperial capital in 518 or in 534. Not long after, on 31 August 537, Justinian decreed that from the year commencing the next day the indiction should be recorded in all official documents (*Nov. Just.* 47. 1). Public and official records and documents should include first the year of the emperor's reign, followed by the indiction with the exact day and month, and then the consulship. The indiction was not normally used in the west at this time and is therefore not to be found in western chronicles such as those of Prosper, Hydatius, or Cassiodorus.

Where two consuls are named in the chronicle for a particular year Marcellinus names the eastern one first. This occurs throughout the chronicle.[11] More significant, however, is the fact that Marcellinus' consular list reflects the status of the annual consuls from the viewpoint of the eastern imperial court, except that he omits Venantius (cos. 507) who seems to have been added only later in the year.[12] Therefore the list omits western consulships not recognized by the eastern court. Further, where there is some confusion in the surviving records because of problems of mutual recognition of consuls between the eastern and western courts Marcellinus' list usually corresponds to that contained in the *Chronicon Paschale* even though it sometimes includes unrecognized western consuls.[13] In the case of the year 477 which Marcellinus heads 'without consuls' it may be that he failed to understand the arrangements for the designation of such a year as being 'post-consular', that is, the consuls designated for practical purposes were those of the previous year namely the usurper Basiliscus and his nephew Armatus.[14] On the other hand, 'without consuls' may simply denote his refusal to adorn the year with the names of two already deposed and discredited individuals. Except for the inexplicable inclusion of a 'Felix' in 463, the only two problems with Marcellinus' consuls are at 399 where he appears to have insisted on keeping in the list the disgraced Eutropius, and at 446 where he creates a new consulship for the emperor Valentinian

---

[11] For the overall reliability of Marcellinus' consular list and its eastern orientation see Holder-Egger (1877), 80–82 and *CLRE* 56.

[12] *CLRE* 549.

[13] The following years fit this pattern: 424 (*CLRE* 383), 451 (436), 452 (439), 458 (451), 459 (452), 475 (484), 484 (503), 485 (505), 487 (508), 488 (511), 489 (513), 490 (515), 493 (521), 494 (523), 515 (565), 517 (569).

[14] Marcellinus' designation is paralleled by the *Fasti Heracliani* (*CLRE* 57 and 489).

III instead of Symmachus.[15] In the case of both Felix and Valentinian one cannot be certain that the error is to be imputed to Marcellinus himself rather than a copyist.

In maintaining two separate annalistic dating systems there were bound to be problems, as noted by a thirteenth-century French scribe who used the manuscript of Marcellinus' chronicle now in the Bodleian library.[16] The primary dating framework of the chronicle is that of indictions running from 1 September to 31 August each year, the secondary one being that of consulships running from 1 January to 31 December each year. What Marcellinus does is to list for each consulship the indiction ending in that consulship. For example the very first year of the chronicle is headed 'Seventh Indiction. Consulship of Ausonius and Olybrius' (so that the chronicle actually begins on 1 September 378). The seventh indiction ended on 31 August in that year (379) and the eighth indiction commenced on 1 September 379 although it is not listed until the following consular year (380). Occasionally, therefore, an event is placed in the correct indiction but the wrong consulship (s.a. 429. 2; 445. 1; 465. 1, 469, 480. 1), or the correct consulship but the wrong indiction (s.a. 380, 382. 2, 394. 3, 439. 1, 472. 1, 512. 3). Presumably in the former instances Marcellinus had only an indictional date for the event in his source document, while in the latter he had only a consular date.

In addition to the consular lists, Marcellinus' use of imperial titulature clearly reflects the eastern origin of his viewpoint and information.[17] For the emperors of the west, Gratian is *Augustus* (379. 1) and Valentinian II *imperator* (388. 1, 391. 1; 392. 1). Maximus, however, is a *tyrannus* (388. 1), so too Eugenius (394), except that he is also referred to as *Caesar* (392. 1). In 424 Valentinian III is correctly styled *Caesar*. After his death in 455 there is the usurper Maximus (Avitus is ignored altogether) and then Majorian consistently designated *Caesar* by Marcellinus (457. 2, 461. 2) since that is how he seems to have been acknowledged by the eastern court. Following the death of Majorian there is Severus (461. 2, 465. 2), never recognized in the East, and after that Anthemius *Augustus*, again an indication of the sanction given by the eastern emperor

---

[15] *CLRE* 333 (Eutropius), 427 (Symmachus), 461 (Felix), cf. Mommsen (1894), 44 n. 1 and 57.

[16] At fo. 146 quoted in Fotheringham (1905), 47.

[17] Details of nomenclature are set out in Gusso (1991), 149–51 with the tables in Gusso (1996), 125, 127.

in his legitimacy (467). Olybrius succeeded on the death of Anthemius and after him Glycerius, consistently entitled *Caesar* (473, 474. 2), that is, not an usurper but an emperor subordinate to the eastern one, then Nepos who was a candidate of Zeno and is recognized as *imperator* (475. 2). Finally, there is the boy-emperor Romulus (475. 2) who was not recognized by the time he was deposed in 476 but who had come to be reckoned as the last Roman emperor in the west (476. 2) by the time Marcellinus was writing his *Chronicle*.

From this list it is clear that Marcellinus, although not always strictly consistent and legally accurate (e.g. Eugenius *Caesar*, Valens *Caesar (praef.)*), for the most part employs the conventional titles of *Caesar* and *Augustus* in their proper manner to illustrate the relationship between the eastern and western emperors but from the point of view of the east. The eastern emperors are similarly cast. Theodosius is *Augustus* (383. 2) but Arcadius only *Caesar* in 387 and Honorius *Caesar* in 392 and 394. This seems to mean that Marcellinus could envisage only one *Augustus* at a time so that before the death of Theodosius I his sons were only *Caesar*. Likewise Theodosius II becomes *Caesar* in 402. 2 but after the death of Arcadius is entitled *Augustus* (431). Marcian is *Augustus* (452), so too Zeno (483, 485, 487, 491) and Justinian (532). On the other hand Leo II is crowned *Caesar* by his father in 474, just as the son of Aspar, Patricius had been made *Caesar* earlier (471) and Marcus the son of Basiliscus soon after (476).

The ambiguous case for Basiliscus' legitimacy is reflected in Marcellinus. He is described as an usurper (*tyrannus*) but at the same time his consulship in 476 is recognized, although the post-consulate of 477 is ignored. In the reign of Zeno both Illus and Leontius are lumped together as *tyranni* although only Leontius was raised to the purple by Verina in 484. Marcellinus' description of Leontius as *interrex* (488. 1) is a novel usage.[18] The most interesting case of all, however, is Anastasius: never once does Marcellinus call him *Augustus* (except in the consular list at 492, 497, 507) but always *Caesar*. The mere consistency of this title (507; 508; 511 (bis); 512. 2, 4 (bis), 7; 513 (bis); 515. 3) suggests not so much carelessness or ignorance by Marcellinus of the status of a contemporary emperor. Rather, it probably suggests a deliberate

---

[18] Ibid. 142–3.

attempt to play down the legitimacy of an emperor who was detestable because of his harassment of the orthodox. All in all, the framework of Marcellinus' chronicle, its indictions, consuls, and imperial terminology, reflects the standpoint of the east and clearly suggests that the western empire is only considered in so far as it comes into contact with the east. In this respect it is to be compared to the *Romana* of Jordanes.[19]

It has been long-established that Marcellinus used a local Constantinopolitan record as a basic source for the whole of the chronicle from 379 to 518, and this record has long been identified as the so-called 'City Chronicle'; furthermore, it has been presumed that he used a Latin version of this particular record.[20] By comparing side by side Marcellinus, the *Chronicon Paschale* and the *Consularia Constantinopolitana* for the period from 379 to 395 it can be observed that there is a direct relationship between these three accounts, in particular that the original source of Marcellinus closely resembled the document which ultimately lies behind the ninth-century *Consularia Constantinopolitana*. For the period beyond 395 it is equally obvious that Marcellinus is still using the Constantinopolitan chronicle source as his basic repository of information. Mommsen considered this relationship so close and necessary to grasp that he printed the *Chronicon Paschale* text alongside the relevant portions of Marcellinus for the period 395–469, as well as alongside the *Consularia Constantinopolitana* in his edition of that work (*MGH AA* 9. 205–45). Unfortunately, some scholars have been mislead into believing that the Greek of the *Chronicon Paschale* is part of Marcellinus' chronicle.[21] Again a direct comparison, which can so easily be done in the pages of Mommsen's edition, makes obvious the dependence of Marcellinus and the *Chronicon Paschale* on a common source of information.

After 470 the degree of correspondence between Marcellinus and the *Chronicon Paschale* diminishes abruptly. Although Mommsen thought this rupture indicated the terminal point of their common source,[22] it rather reflects the movement of the

---

[19] Bartonková (1967), 185–94.

[20] Mommsen (1894), 44–5; Holder-Egger (1877), 62–3.

[21] This may, for example, explain why Grant (1976), 329 included Marcellinus in a list of Greek writers.

[22] This assumption involves the problem of identifying a likely source which terminated around 470. Mommsen considered but rejected Nestorian because the evidence is too slight (1894, 45 n. 2). Nestorian is cited only by Malalas (Jeffreys [1990], 187).

Chronicon Paschale to a closer dependence on the chronicle of John Malalas at precisely this juncture.[23] It does not mark the end of Marcellinus' use of the Constantinopolitan chronicle, however. Unlike the *Chronicon Paschale*, Marcellinus' chronicle shows no evident change of character or style in the period after 470. His attention is still firmly riveted on the eastern empire and Constantinople in particular. Furthermore, his account of events after 470 continues to resemble Malalas, the *Chronicon Paschale* and Theophanes. That Marcellinus continued to depend on his Constantinopolitan chronicle document is plain.[24] Moreover, a comparison of Marcellinus and Jordanes for the period beyond 470 shows how they both depend on a common Latin record which is clearly of Constantinopolitan character and emphatically eastern,[25] rather than the lost *Roman History* of Symmachus.[26]

Besides specifically Constantinopolitan events, Marcellinus is preoccupied closer to his lifetime with the movements of Theodoric the Amal and Theodoric Strabo in Thrace and Illyricum (s.a. 479. 2, 481. 1, 482. 2, 483), and with the manoeuvrings of Illus and Leontius at the court of Zeno (s.a. 484. 1, 485, 488. 1). For the reign of Anastasius it remains true that Marcellinus is still relying on Constantinopolitan records even when he describes events in his own lifetime. Although there is now less verbal similarity between Marcellinus and (say) Malalas and the *Chronicon Paschale*, the common origin of much of their information is plain. For many Constantinopolitan events Marcellinus is our only extant testimony (s.a. 472. 3; 493. 2; 494. 2; 496. 1, 2; 497. 1; 499. 2; 500. 2; 506; 507. 2; 508; 509. 1, 2; 510. 1; 512. 1; 512. 10), while he occasionally expanded something which interested or concerned him (s.a. 479. 1, 479. 2, 484. 2, 499. 1, 503, 504, 505, 512. 11, 517, 518. 1). That he continued to use local sources of information, even into the second edition of the chronicle, is suggested by the two entries which he dates in the year from the foundation of Constantinople (527, 528)—*anno regiae urbis conditae*. This is perhaps an indication that his source was an official document which dated events from the foundation of the city, as had traditionally been the case at Rome. In any event, happenings at Constantinople (as for other eastern cities) were recorded in public documents by their date from the foundation of the city (*annus civitatis*)

---

[23] Jeffreys (1990), 253.
[25] Ibid. 54–5; Krautschick (1986), 360.

[24] Mommsen (1894), 46.
[26] Croke (1983a), 89–119.

and this practice was reinforced by Justinian in 537 (*Nov. Just.* 47. 1).

So far we have explained why scholars have always recognized that behind Marcellinus there lies an eastern annalistic chronicle used in his chronicle, as well as by the authors of both the *Consularia Constantinopolitana* and the *Chronicon Paschale*. Taking this analysis a step further, it is worth looking more closely at the totality of the common material as a pointer to the scope and nature of the common source. One way of achieving this is to categorize the entries common to Marcellinus, the *Chronicon Paschale* and the *Consularia Constantinopolitana* (see Table 6. 1).

TABLE 6. 1. *Entries common to Marcellinus,* Consularia Constantinopolitana, *and/or* Chronicon Paschale

Entry content	Marcellinus	Cons. Const.	Chron. Pasch.
Adventus (imperial and relic arrivals)	381. 2	381. 3 (241)	—
	382. 1	382. 1 (241)	—
	384. 1	384. 1 (241)	563. 9
	389. 1	389. 1 (242)	564. 7–10
	395. 2		566. 1–2
	401. 1		567. 18–19
	414. 1		571. 14–16
	453. 1		591. 7–12
Victories/battles	379. 1	379. 3 (241)	—
	382. 2	382 (241)	—
	388. 1	388 (241)	—
	400		576. 15
	421. 4		579. 19–20
	439. 3		583. 5–7
	441. 3		583. 14–15
	469		598. 3–8
Imperial accessions and anniversaries	379. 1	379. 1 (241)	561. 1–4
	383. 2	383. 1 (241)	562. 19–563. 2
	387. 1	387. 1 (242)	—
	402. 2		568. 5–8
	450. 2		590. 8–10
	467. 1		597. 16–18
Imperial deaths	404. 2		569. 3–6
	408. 3		570. 13–17
	449. 1		586. 18–20
	450. 1		589. 17–590. 5
	453. 2		591. 6
	457. 1		592. 17–19

Imperial births	384. 2	384. 2 (242)	563. 9–11
	397		567. 1–2
	399. 2		567. 5–6
	403. 1		568. 10–11
Imperial marriages	421. 1		578. 13–17
	437		582. 13–18
Prodigies (earthquakes,	401. 2		568. 1–2
eclipses, etc.)	404. 1		568. 14–19
	417. 2		574. 7–10
	418. 2		574. 13–15
	433		582. 4–6
	447. 1		586. 6–14
	465. 1		595. 1–3
Imperial building/	415. 1		572. 13–573. 2
restoration	421. 2		579. 15–18
	427. 2		580. 19–581. 3
	443. 2		583. 18–584. 2
Church councils	391. 1		562. 9–16
	449. 2		587. 3–6
	451		591. 1–4

What the breakdown of entries in Table 6. 1 shows is how much of their common material had to do with episodes related to the court at Constantinople, as well as the ceremonial and ritual of the city itself. The common facet of all these categories of information is imperial ceremonial. In other words, Marcellinus' chronicle gives rise to the hypothesis that his Constantinopolitan source was a record which reflected the ceremonial urban life of the imperial capital. It would appear to have included the main ceremonial occasions which formed part of the liturgified ritual of the court and city. When entries from it were copied or recorded elsewhere, especially in brief chronicle form such as in Marcellinus, the original ceremonial nexus was often lost or obscured and this has always made it difficult to ascertain the common nature of so much of this chronicle material. At Constantinople, as previously at Rome, the arrival of ambassadors and the reporting of earthquakes and the overthrow of usurpers in distant lands were as much occasions for ceremonial as an imperial birth, death, accession, or anniversary. This would have been well understood by the readers of Marcellinus' chronicle who continued to share and experience this pattern of public life. Indeed many of them may have been intimately involved in it, as was Marcellinus himself at one stage.

Clearly the pattern of content in the source common to Marcellinus, the *Consularia Constantinopolitana* and the *Chronicon Paschale* suggests an eastern, probably Constantinopolitan, chronicle source. Whether, or not, this source may be identified with the so-called 'City Chronicle' of Constantinople, postulated by earlier scholars, is an important question requiring closer attention.

The 'City Chronicle' of Constantinople

By the time the late antique chronicles were first subjected to close critical scrutiny in the mid-nineteenth century they were already encased in a paradigm which relegated them to a status of inferior historiography. Further, the prevailing scholarly approach was now to focus on the accuracy and reliability of documents, and to trace the origin of the historian's every statement. This preoccupation with 'Quellenkritik' did not easily lend itself to chronicles, given their format and the peculiar manuscript tradition occasioned by that format. Scholars laboured long and minutely in the cause of unravelling the sources behind the chronicles and the connections between them. While much of this effort was misguided and inappropriate it did highlight the fact that the chronicles relied heavily on earlier annalistic records. Since these records no longer survive modern scholars gave them imposing names. So we find, variously, terms based on the concept of 'annals' ('Consultafelannalen', 'Constantinopolitanische Consultafelannalen', 'Consularannalen', 'Constantinopolitanischen Annalen') or of *fasti* ('Fasten', 'Consulfasten', 'Constantinopolitanischen Fasten', 'oströmischen Fasten'). Whatever they were called, these putative documents were usually considered to be a brief chronicle of events with precise dates and in passive impersonal language. Moreover, such documents (so it was argued) were copied more or less verbatim by later chroniclers so that the original text could be reconstructed on the basis of a comparison of the later chroniclers.[27]

The annalistic sources which scholars proposed to underlie chronicles such as that of Marcellinus, with a focus on Constantinople, were originally thought to be imperial annals (Pallman,

---

[27] e.g. Holder-Egger (1876*b*), 238 ff., 344 ff.; (1877), 82–8.

1864), then local annals something like the traditional Roman *acta diurna* or *acta urbis* (Kaufmann, 1876). Certainly, this was the view of Holder-Egger (1877) in his major work on the sources of Marcellinus, although he did not elaborate on the nature of the Constantinopolitan annals. In his study of Malalas and the *Chronicon Paschale*, Freund (1882) discussed the Constantinopolitan 'City Chronicle' as a source of information, following the claim of Holder-Egger (1876a and 1987b). His study further proposed that the 'City Chronicle' is reflected in the works of a variety of writers of later date (George the Monk, Theophanes and Nicephorus Callistus). In fact, so Freund argued, some quite late works contain genuine information on the fifth century which is not recorded earlier and which may derive ultimately from the 'City Chronicle'.[28]

Mommsen's long and intimate acquaintance with the chronicle manuscripts culminated in his editions of them in the 1890s. In the course of explaining the conclusions already reached on the relationship of Marcellinus, the *Consularia Constantinopolitana* and the *Chronicon Paschale* Mommsen declined to discuss the Greek witnesses to the 'City Chronicle' since it would not be proper in a collection of records for German history (i.e. the *MGH*), and he dismissed the debate about whether the chronicle was official or not as an 'inane controversy'.[29] However, he did insist that Marcellinus in fact used a Latin version of the 'City Chronicle' for the period up to 470 and probably after. He did not attempt to describe the nature of the 'City Chronicle', its extent, or the form in which it was used by the chroniclers, except to assume that there were Greek and Latin summaries of the chronicle.[30]

Tracing the development of the scholarly argument about the nature and definition of the material common to the chronicles, and how this might be used to identify the sources behind them, is important. It shows how assumptions have been compounded, as well as how fragile and uncertain the resulting hypotheses are, even when strongly held. In the final analysis, the labours of Mommsen and his pupils (Holder-Egger, Seeck) and contemporaries pointed to a close similarity and a continuity between the urban records of the Roman republic and early empire and those appearing to lie behind the late antique chronicles. As we have seen (Chapter 5), at Rome, from the early days of the Republic,

[28] Freund (1882), 36.   [29] Mommsen (1892), 200, 251.   [30] Mommsen (1894), 45.

the chief priest (*pontifex maximus*) would note on a white wax tablet (*tabula dealbata*) the names of consuls and other magistrates followed by the main events of the year, especially those with pontifical significance: wars, earthquakes, famines, triumphs, dedication of temples and other monuments. In other words these *tabulae pontificum* were essentially a record of religious ceremonial compiled progressively day by day, year by year, and later published as the *annales maximi*.[31] From these priestly annals it was possible to make summaries on a yearly or monthly basis, or to make extracts covering particular periods. Eventually the *tabulae* were replaced by what are called the *acta urbis* which was similar in content, and these kinds of documents were maintained throughout the imperial period.[32] What has been postulated, then, is that the 'City Chronicles' such as that of Constantinople were the continuation of civic records kept in Rome since republican times, centuries before Marcellinus.

This hypothesis of a Constantinopolitan 'City Chronicle' similar to the Roman *acta urbis* lying behind the chronicles of Marcellinus and the Chronicon Paschale has been discounted, however, on the basis of an argument that there is no evidence for a city chronicle nor any need to expect such a document ever existed. Instead, commonality of material shared by Marcellinus and the *Chronicon Paschale* is to be explained by their separate use of *consularia* or annalistic sources which were 'practical guides or antiquarian handbooks . . . of miscellaneous local and urban information, peppered most liberally with references to the emperor and his activities, not only because there was a natural interest in the emperor and his deeds, especially in the imperial capitals, but also because these formed a great part of the cere- monial and religious life of any major city'.[33] As such they were compiled privately by (in this case) Constantinopolitan booksellers for a customized market. These *consularia* (such as the *Consularia Constantinopolitana*) were, on this reconstruction, fundamentally different from chronicles (such as that of Marcellinus) in terms of content and style; moreover, 'those who compiled consularia were fundamentally different from those who compiled chronicles'.[34]

---

[31] Wiseman (1979), 3–26; Frier (1979); Bucher (1987), 2–61; Chassignet (1996), xxiii–xlv.
[32] Croke (1990*d*), 174–77 and works there cited.
[33] Burgess (1993*a*), 179–81.
[34] Ibid. 179–81.

Although this critique recognizes the urban and ceremonial focus of the material common to Marcellinus and the *Chronicon Paschale*, as well as the origin of much of that information in the official publication of imperial notices, it has certain limitations. First, it depends on a modern (not ancient) distinction between chronicles and annotated annalistic documents given the generic label of *consularia*. This distinction in terms of style, content, and authorship is purely artificial and cannot be sustained by the extant chronicle fragments used to justify it.[35] Second, this hypothesis revives that put forward by Seeck (1889*b*) who suggested that the so-called *consularia* originated as the customized work of Constantinopolitan booksellers who were prepared to include entries on local officials as a means of glorifying the official concerned.[36] Among other things, Seeck ignored the fundamental question of how a bookseller went about creating such a chronicle; that is, where the private compiler or bookseller found the relevant information in the first place, and what was the process of getting the information of the imperial announcements into the annalistic document prepared by the bookseller. Likewise, Seeck's attempt to identify when the 'City Chronicle' began to be compiled by contemporaries failed to distinguish between both the manuscripts and their immediate and remote sources.[37] In the final analysis, it would appear that the argument for attributing common material to *consularia* only succeeds in replacing one hypothetical source ('City Chronicle') with another (*consularia*), no less hypothetical. It does not eliminate the existence of the city chronicle as such, nor does it deny Marcellinus' use of such a source or of other documents deriving originally from a record which provided a summary account of public notices announced in the city.

Notwithstanding the complexity of the issues involved and the tenuousness of the documentation, the fact remains that behind the chronicle of Marcellinus, the *Chronicon Paschale*, and the *Consularia Constantinopolitana* there lies a similar written record. Their common entries reflect the fact that their common source contained notices of imperial births, deaths, marriages, accessions, and anniversaries as well as a range of prodigy reports and

---

[35] As explained in Croke (forthcoming *a*).

[36] Seeck (1889*b*), 619ff.

[37] Ibid. 623–4.

other civic occasions such as the opening of churches and the arrival of ambassadors. There is an identifiable and explicable pattern to this range of content. It was essentially a record of public civic and imperial ceremonial and ritual. Whether or not this record was officially maintained at Constantinople by a responsible office, say the city prefect, cannot be determined. Nonetheless, it is more likely that we are dealing here with a single original record or set of records rather than three independent records of the same events which just happen to include mainly common material, or a series of *consularia* prepared periodically and sold by local booksellers but subsequently collected and welded together into a single continuous chronicle record. That single record, or set of records, whether or not it is conceptualized as a 'City Chronicle' of Constantinople on the model of the *acta urbis* of earlier generations at Rome, reflected the public life of the city. Ceremonial occasions provide its unifying element including the reception of ambassadors, the arrival of relics and the appointment of officials, many such occasions resulting in the publication of official notices which a later writer could use.[38] While this local record concentrated on local events it also included those publicly reported from elsewhere, which explains how many western events for example turn up in eastern chronicles, and vice versa. It was only natural too that in the imperial capital where the emperor and his court dominated the life of the city it was imperial events which loomed in subsequent written accounts.

We can therefore proceed on the hypothesis that Marcellinus had access in Constantinople to a local record of events in the life of the city. It may be speculated further that this record was either maintained currently or compiled retrospectively on an annual basis, listing under each year the main events of that year. Perhaps a summary version, monthly or yearly or both, was publicly proclaimed on stone (on the model of the *Fasti Ostienses*) or some other hard medium such as bronze (on the model of the *tabulae pontificum* of the Roman Republic) so that it could be copied by anyone who wished. That too is no more than speculation, based on previous Roman practice.

Given Marcellinus' location and position, assuming some sort

---

[38] Croke (1990*d*), 182–5. For the publication of imperial notices: Scott (1981), 17–20; (1985), 100–4.

of civil service appointment at the time the chronicle was written in 518, it is possible that he could have consulted a local 'City Chronicle' directly. Alternatively, he may have relied on a previous annalistic chronicle or some other version of events at Constantinople from 379. The potential variety of such versions was enormous. Any annalistic document could easily be incorporated into some other dated record such as a chronicle to form a more elaborate or detailed account. This was the habit of chronicle writers. Subsequently material was copied from one chronicle to another and in the process was abbreviated or expanded, copied carelessly or incorrectly, and combined with other information either deliberately or inadvertently. Chronicles and versions of chronicles were recopied and summarized, extracted, and continued. It is therefore difficult to make precise determinations about the original record used in a fifth-century chronicle, let alone to attempt to reconstruct that record from much later manuscripts and versions of chronicles.

What is likely is that in 518, and perhaps in 534 too, Marcellinus made direct use of the 'City Chronicle' of Constantinople. If not, then he probably used an annalistic chronicle (never cited and no longer extant) which had itself used the 'City Chronicle' or extracts/summaries of it. In that event it may have been the same chronicle document used by Jordanes in his *Romana*.

Western Events in the Chronicle

Although Marcellinus set himself the task of recording events only in the eastern empire he does include some information on western events. This information is, generally speaking, confined to imperial deaths and accessions, the sort of information to be known in all parts of the empire and to be found in the Constantinopolitan source common to the *Consularia Constantinopolitana* and the *Chronicon Paschale* for instance. Marcellinus did not necessarily need to resort to a western source of information since so many of these events were formally announced and recorded at Constantinople. In the *Chronicon Paschale* we read of the death of Honorius' wife Thermantia, in 415 because it was reported at Constantinople on 30 July (*Chron. Pasch.* 572. 5–7). In the same year is recorded the death of the Visigothic chief Athaulf, again mentioned in association with its announcement in the eastern capital (*Chron. Pasch.* 572. 8–11). Under the following year (416) is recorded the death of the usurper Attalus—announced in Constantinople on 28 June and celebrated with games in the theatre (presided over by the city prefect Ursus) and later in the hippodrome (*Chron. Pasch.* 573. 15–19), while the accession of Anthemius at Rome in 467 was announced and his laureate image received at Constantinople (*Chron. Pasch.* 597). Philostorgius reports the arrival in Constantinople of messengers announcing the accession of Constantius III and bearing his image which Theodosius refused (*HE* 12. 12). So too, in 423 the death of Honorius was reported in Constantinople and the city went into mourning.[39] All these examples point to the fact that the deaths and accessions of western emperors and members of their family as well as usurpers, were reported, recorded, and well known in Constantinople so that a local chronicler, like Marcellinus, did not need to resort to an exclusively western document for such basic information.[40]

We have already seen how Marcellinus' view of the legitimacy of western emperors, along with his use of indictions and a consular list, reflects a distinctly Byzantine origin. Both Marcellinus and Jordanes describe the successive western emperors from an eastern point of view except that Marcellinus ignores Avitus altogether, while Jordanes (*Rom.* 338) ignores Olybrius and makes Glycerius the successor of Anthemius. Moreover, this is precisely the sort of mistake to be found frequently, almost invariably, in all the Byzantine chronicles. John Malalas, for example, who was writing at much the same time as Marcellinus has Gratian killed at Constantinople (Jo. Mal. 13. 36 (344. 5–8)), instead of Lyon, and Constantius III defeating Alaric to win back Galla Placidia (Jo. Mal. 13. 49 (350. 2–4)). Furthermore, Malalas makes no mention of Avitus, Glycerius and Severus, places Majorian between Olybrius and Nepos (Jo. Mal. 14. 45 (375. 7–8)) and has Theodoric defeating Odoacer at Rome (Jo. Mal. 15. 9 (383. 13–19)). He apparently was not in a position to check the precise chronology of events in the west for he has Gaiseric abducting Eudoxia in the reign of Theodosius II, then reports that Theodosius was thoroughly aggrieved on learning of this (Jo. Mal. 14. 26 (365. 16 ff.)). Evagrius (*HE* 2. 8) later in the sixth century

---

[39] Theoph. AM 5915 (84. 14–16)).
[40] Kaufmann (1884), 486; Seeck (1889*b*), 604–5; Croke (1990*d*), 188 ff.

had no clear concept of western chronology either for he thought that Marcian had died not in January 457 but during the reign of the western emperor Severus (461–5).

Most of Malalas' mistakes passed into Theophanes who had another document for the last western emperors from Maximus to Severus, although his calculation (Maximus: 1 year; Majorian: 2 years; Avitus: 3; Severus: 3 years) and ordering of emperors (note Avitus succeeding Majorian) are, for the most part, inaccurate. Finally, the *Chronicon Paschale* which has almost nothing to say about the west places Valentinian's death in 378 (*Chron. Pasch.* 560. 15–16) and calls the usurper Eugenius 'Diogenes' (565. 9–10) perhaps an intelligent recollection of an emperor who represented himself on his coins in a philosopher's beard. All in all, western events were ill-remembered in Constantinople and with the passing of time their precise order, especially in relation to the east, became quite confused and mistaken. In addition, the Byzantine chroniclers made no special effort to gather accurate information on the fifth-century west, least of all did they resort to chronicles of Rome and Ravenna. Marcellinus, the closest Byzantine chronicler to the period in question, was little interested in the west. He provides (except where he copies Orosius) only the most basic information on imperial accessions and deaths.

Failure to appreciate that Marcellinus' western information was largely eastern in origin has led to much misguided interpretation of the chronicle. Although it has always been argued that all Marcellinus' western information must derive from a western (probably Ravennan) chronicle,[41] it has long been observed too that the western events he records could just as easily have been noted in an eastern source.[42] Certainly the main events recorded in Marcellinus' chronicle would be known and recorded there.[43] There was a level of general knowledge which one might expect to be recorded in several places.[44] Mommsen, in his introduction to the edition of Marcellinus (1894), was still inclined to attribute certain entries (indicated in the margin) to a western origin although he noted the reporting of western events at Constantinople and was sceptical about the extent of the

---

[41] Holder-Egger (1876*b*), 251–2.
[42] Pallmann (1864), 200–3; Kaufmann (1884), 486–7; Seeck (1889*b*).
[43] Ibid. 285–7.
[44] Kaufmann (1876), 268.

Ravenna chronicle.[45] In any event he preferred to speak of Italian rather than Ravennan.

To explicate further why Marcellinus' western entries (such as that on the significance of Romulus' demise) need not derive from a local western document or documents, it will be helpful to focus on the passages of Marcellinus attributed by Mommsen (and others before him) to an Italian chronicle. These are the entries which have been used to argue for the western origin of Marcellinus' information: 383. 3 death of Gratian; 389. 1 Theodosius I in Rome; 390. 1 comet; 393 eclipse at Honorius' elevation; 408. 2 tremors at Rome; 418. 2 eclipse; 430. 2 Felix killed in Ravenna; 438. 3 Valentinian III enters Ravenna; 452. 3 Aquileia besieged; 461. 2 Majorian killed; 464 Beorgor killed; 465. 2 Severus killed; 467 earthquake at Ravenna; 468 Marcellinus in Dalmatia; 472. 2 Anthemius killed; 473. 1 Glycerius raised; 474. 2 Glycerius killed; 475. 2 Nepos raised; 476. 2 Odoacer in Italy; 477 Brachila killed at Ravenna; 480. 2 Nepos killed. Despite his claim to be focused on only the eastern empire, it is possible that Marcellinus found some or all of these entries in an Italian chronicle. While not denying this, it is just as likely, however, that all or most of his notices of events in the west were based on local eastern sources of information.

Marcellinus could easily have discovered the information on imperial accessions and deaths in a Constantinopolitan record: the accessions of Glycerius (473. 1), Nepos (475. 2) and Odoacer (476. 2); deaths of Gratian (383. 3), Majorian (461. 2), Severus (465. 2), Anthemius (472. 2), Glycerius (474. 2) and Nepos (480. 2). Likewise, since the eclipses of 393 and 418 were visible at Constantinople as well as in Italy they do not require an exclusively Italian source.[46] Further, Theodosius' visit to Rome in 389,[47] the tremors at Rome in 408,[48] the death of Felix at Ravenna (430) and Marcellinus in Dalmatia (468) are also recorded in Byzantine chronicles independent of Italian sources of information. We are now left with a small number of entries which could have derived from a western document: 390. 1 comet; 438. 3 Valentinian III enters Ravenna; 452. 3 siege of Aquileia; 464

---

[45] Mommsen (1894), 46, cf. (1892), 298 n. 3 and 300 n. 3.

[46] Seeck (1889*b*), 606; Newton (1972), 452–3, 538–9; Schove (1984), 62–4, 72–3.

[47] *Chron. Pasch.*, 564. 8–10; Theoph. AM 5881 (70. 31–3).

[48] Theoph. AM 5900 (80. 5).

death of Beorgor; 467. 3 earthquake at Ravenna; 477 death of Brachila at Ravenna, to which might be added another not marked by Mommsen, namely the deaths of the philosophers Philip and Sallust (423. 4). Unfortunately, nothing else is known about these evidently significant men but their deaths are also noted in the eleventh-century Merseburg fragment of an illustrated chronicle.[49] Although it is possible to presume (with Seeck) that the siege of Aquileia (452. 3), the deaths of Philip and Sallust (423. 4) and Valentinian's entry into Ravenna (438) were announced and recorded in Constantinople, Marcellinus may have relied on a western source for all this information. If so, they would be among the few entries he bothered to take from a western source.

Since Mommsen, the origin of Marcellinus' entries on western events has not been seriously investigated. Indeed it was taken for granted by Ensslin,[50] and then Ensslin was taken for granted by Wes in his elaborate attempt to trace one of Marcellinus' western entries, namely the deposition of Romulus Augustus in 476, to an exclusively western source, the lost *Roman History* of Symmachus (cos. 485).[51] This is what Marcellinus actually says (476. 2):

Odoacer condemned Augustulus, the son of Orestes, with the punishment of exile in Lucullanum, a fort in Campania. With this Augustulus perished the Western empire of the Roman people (*Hesperium Romanae gentis imperium*), which the first Augustus, Octavian, began to rule in the seven hundred and ninth year from the foundation of the city. This occurred in the five hundred and twenty-second year of the kingdom of the departed emperors, with Gothic kings thereafter holding Rome (*Gothorum dehinc regibus Romam tenentibus*).

A great deal of ink and angst have been expended on making sense of these few lines, giving rise to ever more novel and subtle hypotheses. In the final analysis, given the nature of Marcellinus' chronicle and its author's working methods, certain key considerations are unavoidable.

1. A late antique chronicle normally concluded with the most recent event because bringing the story up to the present was the very point of the genre. Since there is no reason to think that Marcellinus was any different in this respect, he wrote in 518 probably not long after the death of Anastasius on 9 July 518. Wes

---

[49] Bischoff/Koehler (1939), 127.   [50] Ensslin (1948).   [51] Wes (1967).

argued that Marcellinus took his entry on 476 from the *Roman History* of Symmachus. If Symmachus wrote before 518, and he possibly did, then his history could have been used by Marcellinus. However, a critical part of Wes's argument for Symmachus requires that he wrote in 519 exactly, that is after (not before) Marcellinus.[52] More recently, it has been proposed that Marcellinus could have written later, in 519/20 in fact, and could therefore have had virtually immediate access to Symmachus' pro-Anician history because Symmachus was in Constantinople in 519/20.[53] Apart from the facts that the date of Symmachus' sojourn in Constantinople was not necessarily as late as 519/20, and that Marcellinus cannot be easily linked with the Anician family in Constantinople (Chapter 3 above), he most likely completed his chronicle before the end of 518.

2. Chronicles which were later updated by their author were normally just extended rather than completely reworked, because the point was keeping the story up to date. Accordingly, it is most unlikely that the entry on 476 was only inserted in the 534 edition and was therefore absent from the 518 edition,[54] or that it was inserted later still by the Continuator in the course of extending the chronicle of Marcellinus beyond 534,[55] or that its inclusion in the 534 edition meant it was derived from Cassiodorus' *Gothic History* written in the 520s.[56] All these options have been proposed in recent times. Instead, the 476 entry belonged in the original edition and represents a contemporary perspective in 518.

3. Writers of chronicles normally just copied or summarized their few sources because the point was to show continuity of events, not to provide a detailed and elaborate product based on careful and extensive research. Where Marcellinus' entry can be compared to its source, as in the case of material taken from Orosius and Gennadius as will be seen below, it is clear that the chronicler's method is simply to cut and paste appropriate information with little or no alteration. It is therefore reasonable to assume that such was his method in the remainder of the chronicle for which we lack his original source of information. In other words, for his few entries on the fifth-century western emperors Marcellinus is not likely to have sifted and scrutinized a multi-

[52] Ibid. 169–75.   [53] Zecchini (1993), 86.   [54] Gusso (1995), 594–5.
[55] As proposed by both Zecchini (1983), 91 and Gusso (1995), 598–9, 607.
[56] Gusso (1995), 610–11, 617.

plicity of sources, but to have simply copied and summarized from a single document.

4. Marcellinus deliberately designed his chronicle to focus on the east (*Orientale tantum secutus imperium (praef.)*) so his attention to events in the west was subsidiary rather than central and viewed from his eastern vantage point. He has been interpreted, however, as having been able to derive western information only from western sources.[57] Since his western entries reflect a distinctly eastern perspective his single source for these events is most likely to have been eastern, rather than exclusively and necessarily western.[58]

5. Marcellinus' 518 perspective on the year 476 was reinforced by his judgement of Aetius, *magna Occidentalis rei publicae salus*. In recording the death of Aetius in 454 he observed that this marked the virtual end of Roman imperial authority in the west (*Hesperium regnum*) and that it has not subsequently been able to be reinstated (*nec hactenus valuit relevari*). This positive evaluation of Aetius, first noted here by Marcellinus in 518, was shared by other sixth-century eastern authors especially Procopius. In a real sense the death of Aetius both coincided with and contributed to the final occupation of Roman provinces by the Goths, Vandals, and Burgundians, as was plain by the sixth century.[59] It has been argued, however, that because Aetius was attached to the Anicii, Marcellinus' positive view on Aetius could only derive from an Anician source and the obvious such source was the *Roman History* of Symmachus. On this hypothesis, Procopius too (despite writing in the 540s) must have been influenced by Symmachus in his view of Aetius.[60] The reality is that the various positive estimations of Aetius to be found in eastern historical accounts (from Priscus onwards) reflect local opinion and local perspective, not the traces of western influence and propaganda.

6. Marcellinus' interpretation of 476 is pragmatic and perspectival, not contemporary and constitutional. There is therefore no need to reconstrue his calculation to align his statement with the death of Nepos in 480, rather than with the deposition of Romulus in 476.[61] The significance of the deposition of Romulus,

---

[57] Zecchini (1993), 76. [58] Croke (1983a), 87–9, 101–3.
[59] Cf. Heather (1995), 29 ff. [60] Zecchini (1983), 52; (1993), 72, 76–7, 79.
[61] As proposed by Zecchini (1993), 77 but erroneously counting the '522 years' of Roman imperial rule from 45 BC rather than 43/42 BC (cf. Gusso (1995), 600).

as interpreted by Marcellinus, only makes sense with considerable hindsight. It was not obvious in 476 that there would never be another emperor holding authority in Italy, nor in the 480s when Odoacer enjoyed strong senatorial support. Nor was it a foregone conclusion before 498 when Theodoric and Anastasius finally agreed on the continued Gothic administration of Italy, following previous negotiations with Zeno in 491 and Anastasius in 492.[62] Towards the end of Anastasius' reign, however, forty years after the deposition of Romulus, reuniting the eastern and western realms was a more open question. Indeed, it gathered momentum with the settlement in 518/19 of the Acacian schism.[63] It was just at this time that Marcellinus was writing his chronicle. His comments on Aetius (454) and the significance of 476 could not have been formulated by anyone much before the early sixth century. They may well constitute his own considered view in 518, or he may have taken them over from some earlier document such as the history of Eustathius of Epiphaneia.[64]

7. Since Marcellinus' sources for western events in the fifth century were eastern in origin and since 476. 2 derives from an eastern perspective it is therefore reflected in the Byzantine tradition. Marcellinus' entries on both Aetius and on 476 are Byzantine perspectives. The equation of the end of the western empire with Romulus' deposition is found in successive generations of Byzantine chroniclers and depends on a local tradition which underpins them.[65] On the other hand, all eastern citations have been traced to Symmachus' lost *Roman History* on the mere assumption that it influenced both Theodor Lector (taken up by Evagrius and Theophanes) and Procopius.[66] To say the least, this assumption is highly dubious.[67] No less dubious are the key presumptions of Wes and others that Symmachus necessarily lamented the loss of a separate emperor in the West, that he was necessarily hostile to Theodoric and his regime, and that these themes must have dominated his *History*.[68]

---

[62] Cf. Thompson (1982), 61–76.

[63] Amory (1997), 216–17.

[64] Varady (1976), 478 and Croke (1983a), 117. Zecchini (1993), 77–8 also allows for this possibility, except that he unnecessarily contends that Eustathius had 480 for the fall of Rome but that Marcellinus somehow linked the Eustathian date with information from Symmachus to get 476.

[65] Details in Croke (1983a), 116–18.

[66] Zecchini (1993), 79.   [67] Cf. Placanica (1997), 81.   [68] Heather (1993), 333–5.

8. Marcellinus' statement on 476 does not preclude similar sentiments being expressed in the west, however. Sidonius Apollinaris, for instance, saw the eventual submission of his see of Clermont to the Gothic king Euric in 476 as marking a transition from emperor to king (at least in Gaul),[69] while by 511 Eugippius (*Vita Severini* 20. 1) could feel that the empire had slipped away (at least in Noricum) without citing a particular concluding point, let alone 476.[70] It is just that Marcellinus' statement is both precise and comprehensive, and does not necessitate a western viewpoint and/or a western source for that precision.

9. Other statements in the west linking the rupture of imperial authority to the deposition of Romulus in 476 are harder to identify.[71] Certainly the twelfth/thirteenth-century Copenhagen continuation of Prosper contains two versions of some earlier document which link upheaval to the year 476 precisely.[72] These entries derive from a seventh-century compiler and probably were his original invention, thereby reflecting a perspective well-entrenched by the seventh century, rather than having been necessarily copied at second or third hand from an exactly contemporary fifth-century document,[73] let alone being from 'an official chronicle edited year by year by the imperial court'.[74] In other words, we cannot be certain that the entries in the twelfth/thirteenth-century Copenhagen continuation predate Marcellinus. In any event, rather than specifically marking the end of the line of western emperors they only describe general loss of territory and authority (*provincias et dominationem amiserunt*) in noting the simultaneous capitulation of Italy to Odoacer and part of Gaul to Euric.[75]

Modern scholars have tended to invest the deposition of Romulus in 476 with political and constitutional significance

[69] Harries (1994), 241–2.

[70] Thompson (1982), 117–18; Markus (1982), 1–6, cf. Krautschick (1986), 356.

[71] The attempt (cf. Zecchini (1993), 87) to derive meaning from the list of emperors inserted between the years 387 and 388 in a seventh century manuscript (*Cod. Vat. Reg.* 2077) of Prosper can be discounted because it fails to provide any significant detail, is not necessarily contemporary and cannot be used to distinguish numbered 'real' emperors (to Romulus) from the unnumbered Zeno and Anastasius.

[72] Details in Muhlberger (1984), 79 and 82.

[73] As postulated by Muhlberger (1984), 57.

[74] Proposed by Zecchini (1993), 66.

[75] *Auct. Havn. Ordo prior.* 476.4 (9. 311) with 476.1 (9. 309); even less precisely in *Ordo post.* (*margo.*). 476.1 (9. 309).

because this event has (since the Renaissance) been so firmly embedded in the European historiographical tradition and imagination. Marcellinus' comment on the passing of the imperial government in the western empire in 476 merely reflects, however, the pragmatic perspective of the eastern capital on the accession of Justin I as evident in several other extant documents.[76] Marking a precise point (i.e. 476) when the political establishment of the west could no longer be seen as part of the Roman empire, and was not yet (*nec hactenus*) reattached to it, presupposes an ideology which promoted unity and reunification of east and west, as well as a quest for reattachment.[77] Moreover, reunification was predominantly an eastern concern and eastern perspective. Marcellinus therefore in 518 remains the earliest extant indication of the narrower imperial view that the western Roman empire had come to an end with the deposition of Romulus in 476.

A LIST OF POPES

One aspect of continuing the chronicle of Jerome was to continue his list of bishops of Rome, which Marcellinus does. Moreover, as an Illyrian Marcellinus naturally shared the traditional Illyrian allegiance to the bishop of Rome, whose hold over the Illyrian provinces provoked constant annoyance in Constantinople. This explains, therefore, why he incorporated a list of popes into his chronicle by recording the accessions and deaths of each, together with the length of their reign. The first papal lists were produced in the second century and these were followed by others subsequently. Eusebius had used a papal list in his chronicle which Jerome continued. Also available by this time was the so-called 'Liberian Catalogue' of popes which is contained in the list included by the 'Chronographer of 354'.[78] Marcellinus' papal list which cannot be connected with any other, eastern or western, was used only in the first edition of the chronicle written in 518. Consequently, in the updated section (519–34) he makes no mention of the accession of Popes John (13 August 523), Felix IV (12 July 526), Boniface II (22 September 530), and John II (2

---

[76] Croke (1983*a*), 89–119.
[77] Cf. Krautschick (1986), 368–71.
[78] Details of these early lists can be found in Davis (1989), ii–iii and Salzman (1990), 47–50.

January 533), although he does note the length of the reign of Pope Hormisdas (515: *vixit novem annos*) who died on 6 August 523.

Although Marcellinus claims to be excepting in his list (382. 3) Liberius, who was banished by the emperor Constantius II for refusing to enter into union with Arian bishops, and Felix who was appointed in his place, they are included in practice since Damasus would not then be the 35th pope.[79] Perhaps, on the other hand, Marcellinus intended to say that he did not count separately the period when Liberius and Felix were counted as co-pontiffs (357–65). In reckoning the sequence of popes and in counting 525 as the 485th year of the papacy he is, as in other respects, following Jerome's computation which dates its origin in AD 41.[80] Marcellinus normally includes notices from the papal list under a given year as the first entry (s.a. 383, 398, 402, 420, 423, 432, 461, 482, 498, 500, 515) or, by a reverse process, the last entry (s.a. 382, 417, 440, 494). In terms of compilation this suggests that Marcellinus turned to his papal list first at the appropriate years, recorded the information he wanted, then moved onto the material for the other entries, though sometimes the process of compilation was reversed. On one occasion (467) he copied the papal list as the second entry, placing it between two Constantino-politan notices. The lengths of each reign and the numerical sequence of the popes are written out fully except for two occa-sions when they are abbreviated (417, 498. 1).

The full list of Marcellinus' entries on the popes is set out in Table 6. 2, with the years of accession and reign lengths recorded in the chronicle, while the dates and lengths in brackets represent the exact dates and periods.

The list makes plain that Marcellinus' source for the popes was a list which contained nothing more than the pope's name and the length of his reign in whole years with the result that some accession dates are too late and some are too early. Occasionally his dates are accurate (s.a. 417, 432, 461) but that is more by coincidence than design. He begins with Damasus and his eighteen-year reign which he counts from 366 (Jerome's date for his accession (*Chron.* 366 (244e)). Thereafter, he normally just adds the number of years of the papal reign to the previous date of accession (e.g. Siricius fifteen years from 383 to 398, Innocent four

[79] Duchesne (1886), xxiv and Mommsen (1896/7), 167–79 (= *GS* 6 (1910), 570–81).
[80] Duchesne (1886), xxiv and Mommsen (1894), 46.

years from 398 to 404 and so on). The exact dates of accession and reign lengths were apparently not known to Marcellinus; at least they were not contained in his list. Nor was he able to ascertain that Felix's reign was eight, not twelve, years. Presumably his list was a local Constantinopolitan one for it pays no attention to the schism between the supporters of the rival claimants, Laurence and Symmachus, which threw the papacy into confusion in 498, and which lasted for a number of years. Instead it simply records Symmachus. By the same token, Marcellinus' count of years for Pope Zosimus (three years) would appear to include the period of Eulalius who was elected to succeed him but whose election was contested. Boniface was also elected and eventually prevailed with Eulalius being relegated to the Campanian countryside.

TABLE 6. 2. *Marcellinus' list of papal reigns*

Pope	Accession	Reign Length
35th Damasus	d. 382 (11 Dec. 384)	18 y. (18 y. 3 m. 11 d.)
36th Siricius	383 (Dec. 384)	15 y. (14 y. 3 m.)
37th Anastasius	398 (27 Nov. 399)	4 y. (3 y. 10 d.)
38th Innocent	402 (21 Dec. 401)	15 y. (15 y. 2 m. 21 d.)
39th Zosimus	417 (18 Mar. 417)	3 y. (1 y. 3 m. 11 d.)
40th Boniface	420 (28 Dec. 418)	3 y. (3 y. 8 m. 6 d.)
41st Celestine	423 (10 Sept. 422)	9 y. (8 y. 10 m. 17 d.)
42nd Sixtus	432 (31 July 432)	8 y. (8 y. 19 d.)
43rd Leo	440 (Aug./Sept. 440)	21 y. (21 y. 1 m. 13 d.)
44th Hilarus	461 (19 Nov. 461)	6 y. (6 y. 3 m. 10 d.)
45th Simplicius	467 (3 Mar. 468)	15 y. (15 y. 1 m. 7 d.)
46th Felix	482 (13 Mar. 483)	12 y. (8 y. 11 m. 17 d.)
47th Gelasius	494 (1 Mar. 492)	4 y. (4 y. 8 m. 18 d.)
48th Anastasius II	498 (24 Nov. 496)	2 y. (1 y. 11 m. 24 d.)
49th Symmachus	500 (22 Nov. 498)	15 y. (15 y. 7 m. 27 d.)
50th Hormisda	515 (20 July 514)	9 y. (9 y. 17 d.)

NARRATIVE ACCOUNTS

Orosius

Under the year 416 Marcellinus records *Orosius presbyter Hispani generis septem libros historiarum descripsit* (416. 1). Although this is copied from Gennadius' *De viris illustribus*, and although the recording of a work in the chronicle does not mean the chronicler had actually read it, there can be no doubt that he did use Orosius' *Historia adversus paganos*. Orosius wrote his historical apology for Christianity at Carthage at the behest of his master Augustine, and it became one of the most popular books in medieval Europe, especially Britain. The work was essentially an attempt to place the Roman empire in the context of world history and to catalogue the disasters of pre-Christian times.[81] The history of Orosius must have been well known in Constantinople for it was also used by Jordanes in his *Romana* (composed in 551). Both Marcellinus and Jordanes used Orosius extensively for the period to 416 where his history ends.

For a chronicler or epitomator such as Marcellinus, Orosius' history was ideal. It presented its material in a fairly compendious, abbreviated form which could be easily fused with a date given in an annalistic source.[82] To characterize Marcellinus' use of Orosius as a whole, it seems that he chose to summarize his history but often simply excerpted verbatim. In addition, he preferred to include a whole Orosian episode (covering events over several years) under one particular year rather than break it up (see Table 6. 3).

TABLE 6. 3. *Marcellinus' entries derived from Orosius*

Marcellin.	Oros.	Marcellin.	Oros.
379. 2	7. 34. 5	398	7. 36. 2–4
381. 2	7. 34. 6	406. 2	7. 37. 4–5
382. 2	7. 34. 7	406. 3	7. 37. 12–16
384. 1	7. 34. 8	408. 1	7. 38. 1–6
385	7. 34. 8	410	7. 39. 1–15; 40. 2
386. 1	7. 34. 9	411. 2	7. 40. 4, 7
387. 2	7. 35. 2	411. 3	7. 42. 3–4
388. 2	7. 35. 5	412. 1	7. 42. 6
391. 2	7. 35. 10	412. 2	7. 42. 9
392. 1	7. 34. 11–12	413	7. 42. 16–24
394. 2	7. 35. 19	414. 2	7. 43. 12

Of the eighty-two entries the chronicle contains between the years 379 and 414, twenty-one of these come from just nine chapters of Book 7 of Orosius, proof that Orosius was used extensively for the period for which he was available. Furthermore,

---

[81] Lacroix (1965), 31–50.   [82] Holder-Egger (1877), 56.

except for the earthquake at Rome (408. 2), no western event is recorded for the period to 414 which does not actually come from Orosius; that is to say, Orosius was Marcellinus' sole guide to western events so that after 414 such notices became rarer and are mainly confined to imperial accessions and deaths.

Marcellinus uses Orosius in several ways. Firstly, he sometimes copies his source word for word (388. 2 = 7. 35. 5; 394. 2 = 7. 35. 19; 412. 2 = 7. 42. 9); or he combines it with information originating in his Constantinopolitan chronicle source (379. 2 = 7. 34. 5 + *Cons. Const.* 379 (241); 381. 2 = 7. 34. 6–7 + *Cons. Const.* 381 (241)). Another method of Marcellinus in using Orosius is to summarize an episode, drawn out over a number of years under one particular year. Under 398, the year of Gildo's death, Marcellinus has a relatively full entry describing in outline the whole Gildo episode, taken entirely from Orosius 5. 36. 2–12. There is nothing in Marcellinus that is not also in Orosius. He even takes over Orosius' personal judgement that Mascezel deserved victory (7. 36. 5). A similar method is evident in Marcellinus' account of Uldin and Sarus (406. 3 = 7. 37. 12–16), on Stilicho placed under the year of his death (408. 2 = 7. 38. 1–6) and on Alaric under the year of the sack of Rome (410 = 7. 39. 1–15, 40. 2). Marcellinus was quite capable of summarizing Orosius himself and there is no need to assume that he must only have had access to Orosius through some intermediate source such as the lost *Roman History* of Symmachus, as has been argued.[83]

As noted above, Marcellinus normally combines Orosius with the date given for the particular event in his Constantinopolitan source. What must be emphasized here is that the alterations made to Orosius which appear in the chronicle are Marcellinus' own. For example: *Eodem anno universa gens Gothorum, Athanarico rege defuncto, Romano sese imperio dedit* (382. 2). We have here two simple facts: the death of Athanaric and the Gothic surrender. Both are found in Orosius 7. 34. 7 (*universae Gothorum gentes rege defuncto . . . Romanae sese imperio dediderunt*). Two alterations are apparent— Marcellinus adds the name of Athanaric and changes the plural (*universae gentes . . . dediderunt*) to the singular (*universa gens . . . dedit*). Both alterations are immaterial in a work of this kind. Also the entry under 384. 1 (*legati Persarum Constantinopolim advenerunt*

[83] By Ensslin (1948) and Wes (1967), but as detailed in Croke (1983*a*), 103 ff.

pacem Theodosii principis postulantes). There are two facts: Persian embassy, and the demand for peace. This is from Orosius 7. 34. 8 (*Persae . . . ultro Constantinopolim ad Theodosium misere legatos pacemque supplices poposcerunt*). Once more the difference in exact wording is immaterial. Certainly it does not imply the existence of an intermediary between Marcellinus and Orosius. The general method of reducing Orosius' narrative to a brief sentence or two placed under the year suggested by the Constantinopolitan source is to be seen in Marcellinus' notices of the usurpations of Constantine (411. 2, 3 = 7. 40. 4, 7; 42. 3, 4), Jovinus and Sebastian (412. 1 = 7. 42. 5) and Heraclian (413 = 7. 42. 10–14). In all these cases Marcellinus omits information included by Orosius but never adds anything to Orosius. That would be unnecessary in such a chronicle.

GENNADIUS

The compilation of Gennadius, a priest from Marseilles, continued Jerome's *de viris illustribus* and was a collection of brief biographies put together in the later fifth century (467/78).[84] Recommended by Cassiodorus (*Inst.* 1. 17), it was always a popular work as the enormous number of manuscripts testify. Marcellinus relies on it quite heavily for the period after 414, just as he relied on Orosius for the prior period. The chronicle contains eleven entries derived from Gennadius, covering the period 415 to 486 where Gennadius' work terminates (see Table 6. 4).

Why does Marcellinus include these eleven only, at the expense of others? What is it about them that makes them worth recording in a chronicle of this nature? Do they have anything in common which might betray a consistent interest? The search for a common denominator is not productive. There may be something in the fact that of the eight for whom Marcellinus actually records the name of their works, in the case of four (Isaac, Prosper, Theodoret, John) he chooses their writings against Eutyches, especially when he selects from among a wider range of works found in Gennadius' account. He was possibly interested in them for their anti-Eutychian viewpoint although it must be pointed out that he ignores other anti-Eutychian writers included in Gennadius (e.g. Mocimus, *De vir.ill.* 71; and Samuel of Edessa,

[84] Ed. Bernoulli (Freiburg, 1895). On Gennadius: Pricoco (1980), 241–73.

De vir ill. 82). Furthermore, Marcellinus includes four pre-Eutychian writers with no apparent common purpose: Lucianus, Orosius, Atticus, and Evagrius. In short, beyond being examples of pious men of letters, there does not appear to be a common factor or identifiable purpose uniting those whom Marcellinus copied details from Gennadius.

TABLE 6.4. *Marcellinus' entries derived from Gennadius*

Gennad.	Marcellin.
Lucianus 46	415. 2
Orosius 39	416. 1
Atticus 52	416. 2
Evagrius 50	423. 2
Eucherius 63	456. 2
Isaac 66	459
Prosper 84	463
Theodoret 88	466
Gennadius 89	470
Theodolus 90	478
John 91	486

Less obtrusive, but perhaps more instructive, is the fact that of the eleven entries eight are, for the precise year under which they are placed, the *only* entry. This could imply that Marcellinus considered their importance to override all else for that year; on the other hand a more realistic explanation might be that the chronicler could find little worth reporting (from his point of view) in these years and so drew upon Gennadius to fill the gap. Holder-Egger first queried the integrity of Marcellinus' use of Gennadius but did not explain his misgivings at length.[85] There can be no doubt that Gennadius' entries for Lucianus and Orosius are under the correct year because they could be cross-checked with an annalistic source. The same may also be true of Atticus (416). However, the remaining entries, so far as is known, could not be tied to a particular year.[86] Gennadius certainly does not ascribe them to particular years. It is probably indicative of such that Theodoret is placed in 466, eight years after his death!

In general it would appear that Marcellinus merely used Gennadius' biographies to avoid gaps in his chronicle so that the

[85] (1877), 58.   [86] Cf. Pintus (1984), 795–812.

only blank year in the chronicle occurs in 522, that is, well after the last of Gennadius' lives. Furthermore, Marcellinus' method in abbreviating the lives betrays the same arbitrary technique: where the Gennadian entry is a short one (Lucianus, Atticus, Evagrius, Isaac) Marcellinus merely copies it in full; where it is longer he does not summarize it but reduces its length by excerpting parts of it. Marcellinus used Gennadius' brief lives in an arbitrary way and his reference to particular writers and their works must not be taken as an indication that he had read them himself, although this remains likely enough.

PALLADIUS

For an orthodox Byzantine like Marcellinus, John Chrysostom was a revered figure. Possibly every year he participated in the annual liturgies at Constantinople in memory of Chrysostom. Writing a chronicle covering the period of John's patriarchate gave Marcellinus the opportunity to provide an outline of his deeds for which he turned to the *Dialogus de vita Johannis Chrysostomi* written soon after John's death in 407 by Palladius, bishop of Helenopolis. Marcellinus used this work for his entries on Chrysostom under the years 398, 403 and 404.[87] However, Mommsen did not think that Marcellinus used Palladius directly; rather he used another source similar to Palladius but much later, and which included the entries for 428 and 438. Perhaps such a life might have been contained in a homily for the feast day of John; on the other hand, since the entries for 428 (the first commemoration of John's memory) and 438 (the return of his relics to Constantinople) were probably both recorded in the Constantinopolitan source, Marcellinus may have taken them from there.[88]

Since the chronicle's information on John is accurate and reliable he probably made direct use of Palladius in the original Greek.[89] His technique was the same as that employed on Orosius, that is, he used the life to provide detailed information for an entry which he put under the year indicated by his annalistic source. Under 398 Marcellinus provides a brief survey of John's career: born in Antioch, lector there under the patriarch

---

[87] Holder-Egger (1877), 91–2.
[88] 428: Ced. 592; 438: Soc., *HE* 7. 45. 2; Theod. *HE* 5. 36.
[89] Baur (1958), xliii and (1907), 78.

Meletius, deacon for five years, priest for twelve, then patriarch of Constantinople where he wrote many agreeable books and had certain bishops (whom Marcellinus names) as antagonists. The chronology of John's career before becoming patriarch is derived from Palladius, *Dialogus* 5. 18. Marcellinus must have read Palladius carefully to cull out this information[90] and especially the names of the bishops opposed to John (from *Dialogus* 5. 19, 5. 21, 9. 31), although he (or possibly a scribe) mistakenly calls Cyrinus the bishop of Chalcedon (cf. Soc. *HE* 6. 15; Soz. *HE* 7. 16) by the name of 'Severus'.

The banishment of Chrysostom and his subsequent misfortune are recorded under 403; and the entry is fitted together from various sections of Palladius' life: the extra thirty bishops (8. 28), the opposition of Arcadius (inferred from 10. 34), the exile (11. 36–8) and the appearance of Basiliscus (11. 38). Under the following year Marcellinus describes the fire which engulfed the 'Great Church' after John's exile and this comes from *Dialogus* 10. 35. In addition, the information was also available to Marcellinus in local Constantinopolitan sources since it occurs in other Byzantine chronicles.[91]

Finally, there is a point of interest in Marcellinus' statement that the feast of Chrysostom which was celebrated in 428 was held each year on 26 September. As it happens there were two Byzantine feast days of Chrysostom: 13 November and 27 January. Marcellinus' '26 September' has proved a mystery.[92] It may be possible to explain it, however. We learn from the *Synaxarium Ecclesiae Constantinopolitanae* that the 13 November feast was not always celebrated on that day. It used to be held on 14 September but since that was the feast of the Exaltation of the Holy Cross, 'the holy fathers changed it making it 13 November'.[93] Now 14 September is not 26 September, but XXVI (as in Marcellinus) is a quite intelligible corruption of XIV. It is probable, then, that the commemoration of John's exile was still celebrated on 14 September in the time of Marcellinus. At some later stage, probably connected with Heraclius' recovery of Jerusalem and the Cross, when the feast of the Exaltation of the

[90] Holder-Egger (1877), 92.
[91] Jo. Mal. 13. 46 (Tusculan Fragment), *Chron. Pasch.* 568. 14–19; Zos. 5. 25; Soc. *HE* 7. 18 and Soz. *HE* 7. 22.
[92] Baur (1958), 9.
[93] *SEC* 46. 8–16.

Holy Cross became more important it was decided to switch the commemoration of Chrysostom to 13 November, the anniversary of the arrival in Constantinople of the news of his death.[94]

Anonymus, *Inventio Capitis S. Johannis Baptistae*

The longest single entry in the chronicle occurs under 453. It is a detailed description of the discovery and subsequent fortune of the head of John the Baptist. What made the event important was that like the earthquakes and other events, the discovery was commemorated each year at Constantinople on the exact day Marcellinus mentions—24 February. A procession would lead from Hagia Sophia to the *prophetion* of John in the district known as *ta Sphorakiou*.[95] Consequently, the original occasion of this procession probably appeared in Marcellinus' Constantinopolitan chronicle source.[96]

His detailed information, however, was borrowed by the chronicler from an anonymous treatise known as the *Inventio capitis S. Johannis Baptistae*.[97] This document, which falls into two parts, was obviously a popular one in Marcellinus' day and it was translated into Latin by Dionysius Exiguus at that time. Since Marcellinus' translation is clearly different from that of Dionysius it is likely that Marcellinus employed the original Greek version in compiling his entry, as he had done with Palladius' work on John Chrysostom.

The detailed account of Marcellinus begins with the discovery, by two eastern monks who had recently come to Jerusalem, of the head of John the Baptist in the place where Herod once lived. On their way home the monks encountered a potter from Emesa and gave him the saddle-bag containing the head. Oblivious of its contents the potter was advised of his burden in a dream by John the Baptist himself. The potter continued to venerate the head until his death, before which he entrusted its protection to his sister who had not known of it. She kept it stored and sealed and left it to some heir. Eventually it came into the possession of the Arian Eustochius of Emesa who was in turn expelled from the city. At some stage the urn containing the head had been buried and over the site a monastery was built. Then John appeared to

[94] Van Ommeslaege (1978), 338.
[95] *Typ.* I. 238. 10–13, *SEC* 487. 8–10.
[96] Cf. Ced. 562, *Chron. Pasch.* 591. 7–12.
[97] *PL* 67. 420C–430D.

the monk Marcellus and showed him where the head was buried. So it is agreed, concludes Marcellinus, that it was Marcellus who discovered the head in 453 while Uranius was bishop of Emesa.[98]

A comparison of the account of Marcellinus and the *Inventio* shows that he simply translated and abbreviated it as he went, and concluded by copying the precise date. Marcellinus certainly did use this anonymous treatise for the details of his entry but it is worth pointing out, yet again, that the main outline of the story would not be unfamiliar to his audience. Each year on 24 February, the occasion of Marcellus' discovery of the head was celebrated at Constantinople. So perhaps some version of the story was given during the liturgy and procession held on that day. In the tenth-century *Synaxarion*, for example, a summary version of the story can be found but it is not as detailed as that of Marcellinus.[99]

MISCELLANEOUS DOCUMENTS

Besides the works discussed above, Marcellinus will have used other sources of information in compiling his chronicle. Exactly what these sources were, and how he used them, is unknown. However, to judge from how he used Orosius, Gennadius, Palladius, and the *inventio* of John the Baptist these sources will simply have been copied, truncated, and summarized. Some of these unknown sources may have been chronicles, others histories, yet others particular documents of relevance and accessibility. His series of entries on the Huns and Goths in the Balkans (s.a. 422. 3, 434, 441. 1–3, 442. 2, 445. 1, 447. 2, 447. 4–5, 454. 1, 481. 1, 483, 487, 488. 2, 489) may derive from a history or histories such as that of Priscus and possibly Eustathius of Epiphaneia, while his special knowledge of Illyricum and Thrace (s.a. 479. 1–2, 481. 2, 493. 2, 499, 500, 502, 505, 517) including the rebellion of Vitalian (s.a. 514. 1–3, 515. 2–4, 516. 1, 519. 3, 520) would have been based on both direct knowledge and written records. Other entries such as Huneric's persecution of catholics (484. 2) may derive from a separate report, as the earthquake in Dardania (518. 1) may have been taken from the *relatio* of the local

---

[98] There is some uncertainty over the exact date (details in Croke [1995], 91–2 with Whitby [1996]).

[99] *SEC* 485. 29–487. 7.

governor reported and filed at Constantinople. The entries on Anastasius' wars in Isauria (492, 497. 2–3, 498. 2) and Persia (503–4, 529, 533) may be dependent on a more extensive account, something similar to that of Joshua the Stylite.

Under the year 430 Marcellinus reports a letter of Pope Celestine to Nestorius. Holder-Egger believed that this is an indication that Marcellinus did actually read Celestine's letter[100] and he may well be correct. Whether Marcellinus discovered the letter in a dossier relating to the first Council of Ephesus where it now resides[101] is more questionable. It may have been independently available. It is uncommon enough for a late antique chronicler to make use of a single letter as a source for a brief entry in a chronicle, even more unusual that Marcellinus should use this letter on more than one occasion for under 426 he describes Sisinnius, patriarch of Constantinople, in a phrase (*vir sanctae simplicitatis et simplicis sanctitatis*) borrowed from the letter of Celestine (*simplex sanctitas et sancta simplicitas*).

Holder-Egger also concluded that Marcellinus used the acts of the Councils of Ephesus and Chalcedon as well as unspecified church history documents of similar content.[102] This is highly unlikely, given the facts that he does not elaborate on the councils but merely records their occurrence, that this basic information appears in the other Byzantine chronicles, and that the councils were commemorated annually in the liturgical calendar. The same can be said for the suggestion that he did use the *Church History* of Socrates produced in the 440s. The events Marcellinus and Socrates have in common are also found in the *Chronicon Paschale* and the *Consularia Constantinopolitana* which, as explained above, reflect the local orientation of the events described.[103]

Finally, it needs to be pointed out that Marcellinus did not use the late fourth-century *Epitome de Caesaribus*, nor Zosimus and Eustathius of Epiphaneia either, as is sometimes presumed. First, the *Epitome*: now Theodosius was remembered in Constantinople

---

[100] 1877, 90.

[101] *ACO* i. 2 (1925), 7–12.

[102] (1877), 97.

[103] Marcellin. s.a. 380 (Gregory and the Arians) ~ Soc. *HE* 5. 7; 381.1 (Council of Constantinople) ~ Soc. *HE* 5. 8; 403. 2 (statue of Eudoxia) ~ Soc. *HE* 6. 18; 428. 1 (election of Nestorius) ~ Soc. *HE* 7. 29; 429. 1 (church of Macedonius) ~ Soc. *HE* 7. 31; 438. 2 (relics of Chrysostom) ~ Soc. *HE* 7. 45. A more complete tabulation can be found in Geppert (1898).

as a Spaniard and in the ninth century there still stood statues in the Chalke of 'Theodosius the Spaniard'.[104] Marcellinus states that Theodosius, like Trajan, came from Italica in Spain which is actually incorrect. He came from Cauca in Galicia.[105] Marcellinus could discover from Jerome that Trajan was from Italica, but why also take Theodosius as a native of Italica? Holder-Egger[106] supposed that Marcellinus was misled by the *Epitome*'s statement *Theodosius genitus patre Honorio, matre Thermantia, genere Hispanus, originem a Traiano trahens* (*Epit.* 48), and suggested that his notice on the removal of Theodosius' body to Constantinople in 395 likewise derived from the *Epitome*. Given the common association of Trajan and Theodosius, especially in the east, a written source is not required to explain Marcellinus' error in ascribing Theodosius and Trajan the same birthplace. In addition, his entry describing the arrival of Theodosius' body in Constantinople (395) probably derives from his Constantinopolitan chronicle document since it is also described in similar terms in the *Chronicon Paschale* (566. 1–2) and Sozomen (*HE* 6. 43).

As for Zosimus, the same limitations apply. Holder-Egger drew attention to several apparent correspondences between Marcellinus and Zosimus, notably the death of Rufinus (395. 5) and the exile of his wife and daughter (396. 1), the revolt of Gaïnas at Constantinople (399. 3, 400), the Isaurian invasion (405) and the death of Stilicho (408. 1). In each case the events were recorded by a variety of Constantinopolitan writers (Eunapius, Olympiodorus, Socrates, Sozomen and Philostorgius) which probably derive ultimately from the same source or complex of sources. Indeed Holder-Egger did not himself go so far as to believe that Marcellinus did use Zosimus directly. He did, however, consider Eustathius of Epiphaneia a likely source.[107] Eustathius is certainly a possible source for Marcellinus but his use can be neither proved nor disproved since Eustathius' chronicle does not survive. It was probably a work similar to that of John Malalas.[108]

Personal Recollection

It is only natural to assume that as Marcellinus began to record events in his own lifetime his personal interests become more

---

[104] Preger (1901), 70. [105] Hyd. *Chron.* 379. 1 (74). [106] (1877), 103.
[107] Holder-Egger (1877), 105–6. [108] Jeffreys (1990), 180.

prominent and his entries fuller. This is shown more clearly by a few rudimentary calculations. If we take 491 as a ready dividing line between the lifetime of Marcellinus and what preceded him we can see the contrast. Of the 238 entries from 379 to 490, thirty-two (13 per cent) represent sole extant testimony; of the seventy-seven entries between 491 and 534, thirty-three (45 per cent) are unique extant testimony. In other words, although numbers are not required to make this point obvious, how is it to be explained?

To begin with, in the latter part of the chronicle, Marcellinus is recording events he himself witnessed in Constantinople—the monophysite riots in 512, the visit of the Illyrian bishops in 516, Justinian's consulship (521) and imperial inauguration (527), the Nika revolt (532) and the African triumph (534), as well as events in his native Illyricum (500, 502, 505, 517) including the rebellion of Vitalian (514. 1–3, 515. 2–4, 516. 1, 519. 3, 520). Naturally enough, his personal account of events is more valuable and less derivative than his record of (say) the early fifth century. Nonetheless, it is during exactly that period when Marcellinus was closest to the centre of power, as Justinian's *cancellarius*, that we find the only blank year in the whole chronicle (522). Likewise, it is within only recent memory that we find a major dating error— 531 rather than 529 for the promulgation of Justinian's *Code*. Marcellinus would probably not have misplaced such a momentous event in legal history, were he operating from a written record. So it probably means that, at least for the second edition of the chronicle, Marcellinus was in a hurry to update his work in order to capitalize on Justinian's celebration of victory in Africa. Consequently, he relied very much on his memory and had no spare time to verify his facts, and to seek out material to fill in the gaps, nor to include the papal deaths and accessions which had occurred since 518. Human memory can be very deceptive, even over the most recent past.

Quite apart from eyewitness accounts, the latter part of the chronicle covers a more localized span—chiefly Constantinople itself—and therefore tends to provide more detail because his audience would naturally be more interested in local history. Yet this does not mean that he relied entirely or even exclusively on oral information. A chronicler clearly needed an annalistic source to guide him even for events in his own lifetime.

TELLING THE STORY

The selection and organization of material in a late antique chronicle was governed by the expectations of the audience and the tradition of the genre as much as by the author's own knowledge and predilections. The modern historical audience has precise and rigorous expectations of form and content but in the time of Marcellinus expectations were quite different.[109] The expectations and understanding of an audience are linked to contemporary life and culture, as well as to the nature of the literary genre. In the case of the late antique chronicler the well-defined tradition of the genre (based mainly on Eusebius and Jerome) required a writer to include entries on renowned rulers and events, on the foundation of cities, and on famous writers, philosophers, and poets. Especially important too were the numerous prodigies (earthquakes, famines, floods, eclipses, etc.) experienced in all parts of the world, because these events demonstrated the hand of God at work in human affairs. The author of the chronicle understood that and took it for granted; so did his audience. No explanation or elaboration was required and that is the reason why chroniclers, Marcellinus included, generally desist from such reflections.[110]

A chronicle provides little scope for elaboration on the causes and meaning of events and the larger pattern of history. Historical causation was considered a relatively simple matter. In the Christian world-view, reflected in the chronicle of Marcellinus, the role played by fate in the historical explanation of earlier times has been replaced by God. Divine punishment and favour now provide the causal mechanism for human history. God provides victory such as that over the Vandals (534), and punishes rebels and traitors such as Eugenius (394. 2), Arbogast (394. 3), Rufinus (395. 5) and others (e.g. 418. 1, 420. 2, 422. 2, 425. 1, 438. 1). Human mortality forever looms (480) and the western empire can disappear in God's time (454. 2, 476. 2). Within this historical scheme discerning the mind of God in human events is very important. Prophecy and portents fulfil this function in Christian discourse, especially in chronicles such as that of Marcellinus who finds the invasion of the Slavs in 517 foreshadowed in Jeremiah. Portents, in particular, provide signs of God's wrath, warnings of

---

[109] Partner (1977), 184.   [110] Guenée (1980), 6.

things to come or they sometimes ratify the significance of events. Marcellinus' chronicle contains many examples of events which were interpreted as portents in his day: earthquakes at Constantinople (402. 3, 447. 1, 480. 1) and elsewhere (394. 3, 396. 3, 408. 2, 417. 2, 419. 2, 424. 3, 460, 467. 3, 472. 3, 494. 2, 499. 2, 518. 1, 526), auroras and comets (389. 3, 390. 1, 418. 3, 423. 5, 442. 1, 512. 1), eclipses (393, 417. 1, 418. 2, 497. 1, 512. 10), fires (404. 1, 433, 465. 1), unusual tracts of ice (401. 2, 443. 1), floods (444. 3) meteorites (452. 2), plagues (456. 1), and the eruption of Mt. Vesuvius when ash fell on Constantinople (472. 1). Miracles and divine epiphanies are evidence of God's power and therefore need to appear in such historical records as chronicles. Equally straightforward too, as we have seen, is the chronicler's judgement of individuals: Theodosius I (379. 1, 380) and Marcian (457. 1) are 'good' emperors because they upheld the orthodox cause, Anastasius is a bad emperor for not doing so (494. 1, 495, 511, 512. 2–7, 514. 1, 516. 3). This, like the whole chronicle, simply reflects the interests and attitudes of the author and his audience. Moreover, it highlights the fact that Marcellinus was deliberately continuing and imitating the style and pattern of content of Jerome's chronicle, and drew his own historiographical authority from his model.

Writing a chronicle such as that of Marcellinus was not meant to be a time-consuming process nor was it designed to produce a work of impeccable research or accuracy by modern standards. It may be safely speculated that a late antique chronicle took its author days or weeks rather than months or years. Cassiodorus' chronicle, given the occasion, was possibly produced in a hurry for the consulship of Eutharic in 519; so too the updated version of Marcellinus' own chronicle in 534 (Chapter 1). Certainly the process required a deal of preparation and research: identifying and collecting materials, establishing the chronological pattern to be followed, selecting entries. The actual process of compilation and composition was probably the quickest part of producing a chronicle. In the case of Marcellinus it is possible to delineate his technique of composition, at least to a certain extent. He began with a local consular list (correlated with indictions) as his framework. As an administrative official in the imperial government, if that were his role when the chronicle was first written, he will have had easy access to a consular list or lists needed to cover the period from 379 to 518. Then he selected his sources, beginning with a previous annalistic chronicle which provided a detailed year by year account of events in the life of the city of Constantinople in particular, and events of the wider world in so far as they were 'announced' and recorded at Constantinople.

In addition, he selected other helpful texts which he used quite arbitrarily. For the period to 416 he seems to have used Orosius quite heavily, and when Orosius was no longer available, the ecclesiastical biographies of Gennadius. In the case of both these authors the chronicler took his material from them in an arbitrary rather than a systematic way. In addition to these, he otherwise employed few sources: a papal list, an anonymous treatise on the discovery of the head of John the Baptist (453), as well as Palladius' life of Chrysostom—both in Greek—and possibly an official damage report (*relatio*) for the Dardanian earthquake in 518. The point of the exercise was continuity and pattern, not accuracy and depth. Moreover, in some cases (Orosius, Palladius, Gennadius, the *Inventio* of John Baptist) we have Marcellinus' original source of information to compare to the chronicle. On that basis we can see how he treated his sources of information, that is, simply and dependently. This comparison, in turn, suggests how he probably utilized the other (now lost) sources of information for the chronicle. Furthermore, by making assumptions about how Marcellinus will have treated these lost documents we can begin to visualize the nature and scope of the documents themselves.

The fundamental aim of the chronicler was to present his information in the most compact form possible. Consequently events occurring over a period of years are compounded together under a single given year (respectively: 398. 3 (Chrysostom), 398. 4 (Gildo), and 408. 1 (Stilicho)). Equally important for Marcellinus, so it seems, is the need to be comprehensive. The chronicle provides a complete but outline summary of the invasions of Illyricum and Rome's relations with Persia are similarly treated. In the case of two (the Isaurian war and the conflict with Persia from 529) a simple statement of duration is given. Marcellinus' method of composition is relatively straightforward. At times he can be seen merely copying or abbreviating entries in Orosius or Gennadius; sometimes he inserts an entry from his papal list at the beginning or end of the particular year. That part of his work was fairly simple. At the same time, he retained a sense of control of his text. For instance, the occasional back references to earlier parts of the chronicle (403. 3, 425. 1, 495) indicate the author's sense of coherence in producing his text.

Marcellinus has been accused of having little sense of historical significance or judgement when he ignores the march of Attila and his Huns into Gaul in 452 but includes instead an entry on three meteorites falling to ground in Thrace.[111] It is a jibe typical of much modern scholarship which presupposes that the late antique chronicles were designed for the ill-educated masses and crammed with information assumed to be most palatable to such people. In fact the analogy is often made between the modern tabloid newspaper or illustrated magazine and the late antique chronicle, on the grounds that both display a predilection for the sensational and unusual, the trivial and banal. Further, since the tabloid is designed for a 'low brow' audience the same is assumed for the chronicles.[112] Again, such analogies betray a modern rather than an ancient perspective. The newspaper analogy is quite mis-leading not least because it is a mass-produced and widely-circulated document, the daily product of several minds and authors. The chronicle, by contrast, always had a restricted circu-lation and was the one-off product of a single author. A slightly better modern analogy would be those retrospective media reviews of years and decades which often actually go by the name of 'chronicle' (e.g. 'The Chronicle of 1997', 'The Chronicle of the 20th Century', 'The Chronicle of Australian History' or the *Encyclopaedia Britannica Yearbook*). This analogy is more effective because a media review is selective; it highlights the most memorable and newsworthy events of the year or decade in just a few lines of print or a few moments of film. Almost invariably, the events selected for brief encapsulation tend to be wars and coups, natural and man-made disasters, royal births, deaths, marriages, journeys and enthronements, installation of new religious leaders, great sporting feats (including the winners of the local football league), sensational scientific and medical dis-coveries or explorations, deaths of celebrities, inventions, the most popular books and movies. In other words, there is a striking parallel with the content of the late antique chronicles but the

---

[111] Holder-Egger (1877), 107.
[112] e.g. Baynes (1925), 35–6; Bury (1923*b*), 435. Similar assumptions in Thompson (1948), 20 and Cameron, Alan (1976), 128.

explanation lies not in a common preoccupation with the limited and sensational taste of the masses; rather it is to be found in their common requirement to be brief and selective, and to concentrate on events of interest to everyone. It is the dictate of the genre.

The process of producing a chronicle was one of selection and compilation, with the overriding aim of covering an expanse of time in a succinct way. Chroniclers did not therefore seek to provide a continuous event-filled record but were content to leave years empty, sometimes over long periods. The reason for this is that what mattered to contemporaries was identifying the overall trajectory of God's time and purpose, not filling every annual space which is the modern expectation of such historical records. Where chroniclers explain their work they tend to emphasize brevity and compilation as their mode of operation. Such a process was simply what the genre required; it was not that writers of chronicles were capable of nothing more. One has only to compare Jerome's or Prosper's chronicle with their exegetical or theological works to see that; or to compare Bede's chronicle chapters in his *De temporum ratione* with the remainder of that work, or with his biblical commentaries.

Likewise, the style of chronicles reflects the expectations of the audience. The language was simple and unadorned. It was designed for direct communication of facts, not a striving after rhetorical effect. Once more the chronicle's style does not by itself reflect the limits of the author's capability, as can be illustrated by comparing the style of Cassiodorus' chronicle with his *Variae*. Nor should a chronicle's style be taken to reflect a different, less educated kind of audience. As with the Byzantine chronicles, style was a function of literary purpose and genre rather than education and intellect.[113] This simplicity of style remained a standard feature of chronicles and annals throughout the Middle Ages.[114]

Marcellinus was an Illyrian and his Latin shows traces of his local origin;[115] he may also possibly have known a local Illyrian language. Although Latin was still the language of the army when he was *cancellarius* to the general Justinian, he would have also needed Greek for that position. He clearly used Greek sources

---

[113] Beck (1965*b*), 197.   [114] Guenée (1980), 215–16.   [115] Mihaescu (1978), 9–10.

directly and there are traces of Greek orthography in the language of the chronicle.[116] Marcellinus' *opus rusticum* was a conventional claim not an indication of culture or audience.

Writers of chronicles evidently regarded their works as practical and useful. Eusebius saw his chronicle that way, as did his translator and continuator Jerome. Isidore of Seville used these same criteria in evaluating chronicles so that he found Victor of Tunnuna 'a most noble history of military and ecclesiastical events' (*De uir. ill.* 25) and John of Biclaro 'extremely useful' (*De uir. ill.* 31). Marcellinus' chronicle stood in this tradition. Its view and its presentation of the past was that found in Jerome. The chronicle began in fact with a preface in which the author set out his indebtedness to Jerome and how he followed the chronology of Eusebius and Jerome in which the date of Creation was calculated as 5579 BC. This was an important statement for Marcellinus because it heralded his preference for an unfashionable chronology. The Byzantines had come to refine and overturn the Eusebian chronology by constructing more elaborate methods of computation, thereby giving rise to what became the standard Byzantine era of 'Years from Creation' or 'Years of the World' which in modern terminology puts Creation in 5508 BC.[117] By following Jerome in this respect Marcellinus is probably signifying his active adherence to the Eusebian date or perhaps his disregard for the subsequent Byzantine calculations.

Throughout the chronicle Marcellinus consciously continued Jerome's work, as did other late antique writers of chronicles. Marcellinus' chronicle was designed to carry forward a single unified story, to exemplify continuity of historical development and to illustrate the ways of God to man. This preoccupation explains both the frequent mention of natural disasters (and other divine signs), and the inclusion of the major stepping stones in the development of the prevalent orthodoxy of early sixth-century Constantinople. It also explains the ceremoniousness or liturgical dimension which lies behind so many of the chronicle's entries, an illustration of the continuity of Byzantine ceremonial life which represented a bonding of heaven and earth in the historical record. In other words, the chronicle of Marcellinus as an historio-

---

[116] e.g. *Cherronesum* (400), *Gizericus* (455. 3), *Eutychetem* (451), cf. *Eutychen* (463) and *Eutychem* (466), *Calchedonam* (451, 511, cf. 458), and *Denzicis* (469).

[117] Croke (1995), 54.

graphical text possesses the structure, purpose, plot, coherence, and understanding of historical change which scholars continue to deny to chronicles and chroniclers.[118]

[118] Most recently, Stanford (1998), 219 and McCullagh (1998), 300.

7

The Continuator of Marcellinus

Marcellinus wrote his chronicle as a continuation of that of Jerome from 379 to 518 and later updated it to 534. Just as Marcellinus continued Jerome, Marcellinus was himself continued by an unknown author, at least to 548 and probably into the 550s. This author is usually called the 'Continuator' of Marcellinus and his work the *Additamentum*. The *Additamentum* is preserved in the archetypal manuscript T (= *Auct*. T. 2. 26, Bodleian Library, Oxford) and the fourteenth-century manuscript descended from it called R (= *Cod. Par. Lat*. 4870, Paris) which breaks off slightly before the end of T which itself breaks off in 548. As was the pattern with chronicle manuscripts, the manuscript sequence of Jerome–Marcellinus–Continuator constituted a continuous universal chronicle, created in the late sixth century, covering the totality of human history right up to the 550s. Earlier editions of Marcellinus also contain a continuation of the *Additamentum* itself to 558, but this was attributed in error to Marcellinus by Onophrio Panvinio in his edition (1558). It is actually part of the twelfth-century chronicle of Hermann of Reichenau.[1]

The *Additamentum* is a significant document in so far as it provides a representation of recent history to be set beside other contemporary representations, most notably those of Procopius and Jordanes. Indeed, the scholarly attention it has so far attracted has been mainly because of its evident correspondence to the *Romana* of Jordanes which was written in Constantinople in 551. The relation to the texts of Jordanes has brought the *Additamentum* into the centre of research on the Vivarian manuscripts of Cassiodorus, as well as on the political stance of the Italian emigres in Constantinople in 550–1.[2] Yet, it has never really been examined in its own right.

---

[1] Mommsen (1894), 42–3 (first demonstrated by Waitz (1857), 38–40).
[2] Originally by Momigliano (1956), and more recently by Barnish (1984).

The Bodleian Manuscript

On 18 March 1889 Theodor Mommsen was working in the Bodleian Library, Oxford collating manuscripts for his *Variae* of Cassiodorus and *Chronica Minora* volumes of the *MGH* when the librarian handed him a manuscript (*Auct.* T. 2. 26) which the Bodleian had been keeping especially for Mommsen. Although it had been in the library since 1824 the manuscript had somehow eluded notice and had only recently been drawn to the librarian's attention. It had therefore not been available to Mommsen on his previous stint in the Bodleian in September 1885.[3] It would appear that the significance of the manuscript and its contents were first noticed in September 1887 by the German scholar Heinrich Schenkl who was then gathering material for his *Bibliotheca patrum latinorum Britannica*, published in 1891. In December 1888 the Bodleian's librarian E. B. Nicholson had the manuscript (or part of it) photographed and sought the opinion of E. M. Thompson, the eminent palaeographer at the British Museum, on its date. Mommsen was well known to both Thompson and Nicholson and they would have been aware that it would be of major interest to the Berlin professor.

The manuscript brought to Mommsen's desk on 18 March 1889 contained Jerome's translation of Eusebius' chronicle beginning with the year of Abraham 555 (the earlier section is missing), his own continuation to 378, a brief chronological summary to 435 appended to Jerome's own summation (although that final page is also missing), then the chronicle of Marcellinus to 534 as well as a continuation of Marcellinus to 548 where the manuscript breaks off.[4] As reported in *The Times* the following week:

Professor Thomas [*sic*] Mommsen paid last week a visit to Oxford, where he examined the MSS. of Cassiodorus' 'Epistolae' [*Variae*]. His attention was drawn by the librarian to an early MS. (at the latest, of the end of the sixth century) which contains St. Jerome's translation of Eusebius' chronicle, followed by that of Marcellinus. This seems to be the earliest MS. known of this work. Neither the Latin Professor nor the Latin reader in the University knew of its existence. The MS belongs to a collection which has never been catalogued: the hand-list gives barely the name, without dates or any other description. (Sat. 30 Mar. 1889, 6).

---

[3] Hardy (1890), 277.
[4] Descriptions of the MS can be found in Mommsen (1889*a*), 393–401 (= *GS* 7. 597–605) and Fotheringham (1905), 1–2, 25–9 with catalogue details in Madan (1897), 441.

Mommsen worked on the manuscript in the Radcliffe Camera and ended the day by being collected and taken back to Exeter College for dinner and conversation until late into the night.[5] Mommsen had recently acquired many friends and admirers in Oxford who were always keen to help him out in his scholarly enterprises. On this occasion he evidently leaned on others to copy or check parts of the manuscript for him, including the two scholars cited by *The Times*, namely Henry Nettleship (22 March), the Latin Professor, and Robinson Ellis (1 April), the Latin Reader, as well as E. R. Hardy (2 April).[6] Hardy evidently did the main collation for Mommsen, and later checked the manuscript against the proofs of Mommsen's edition of Marcellinus.[7] Within six months he was able to forward his published article (1889*a*) on the manuscript to Nicholson, the Bodleian Librarian, and explain to him that not only was he using the manuscript for his edition of Marcellinus, but that it had already been collated by Hardy for a new edition of Jerome's chronicle being prepared by Alfred Schoene. Mommsen commented aptly to Nicholson: 'So you see the seed you have sown is growing.'[8]

The manuscript had been bought for the Bodleian (at a cost, incidentally, of 131 guilders—noted on the inside cover) in 1824 by Thomas Gaisford at a sale of Meerman's library in The Hague, after being previously purchased from the sale of the Jesuit library at Clermont in 1764.[9] The Jerome section with later summary (fos. 33^r–145^v) is dated to the fifth century, that of Marcellinus and his continuator (fos. 146^r–179^v) to the late sixth century and in an Italian hand.[10] In other words, somewhere in Italy in the late sixth century this fifth-century manuscript of Jerome's chronicle was

---

[5] Details in Croke (1991), 50–7, cf. Rebenich (1993), 131ff.

[6] *Bodleian Library Records* b.593, unfoliated.

[7] Mommsen (1894), 50; Fotheringham (1905), 2, cf. Hardy (1890), 277.

[8] Mommsen to Nicholson (letter, 8 Sept. 1889) in *Bodleian Library Records* d.360, fo. 236^r with Nicholson's reply to Mommsen of 10 Sept. 1889 (*Mommsen Nachlass*, Staatsbibliothek zu Berlin).

[9] Details in Fotheringham (1905), 25.

[10] *CLA* 223a and 223b (p. 32). The Marcellinus section of the MS had originally been dated to the late sixth century by E. M. Thompson at the British Library (Mommsen (1889*a*), 598; Hardy (1890), 277). Thompson's assessment, dated 17 Dec. 1888, is filed with the MS itself (cf. Madan (1897), 441). When Thompson actually inspected the MS directly (Feb. 1890) he was more inclined to think it was 7th cent., so Nicholson reported to Mommsen by letter on 16 March 1890 (*Mommsen Nachlass*, Staatsbibliothek zu Berlin). This uncertainty may explain Mommsen's own ambiguity, listing it as '7th cent.' in the *libri adhibiti* (1894, 38) but elsewhere as 'late 6th cent.' (1894, 48–9).

augmented by copying its continuation by Marcellinus followed by a further continuation from the end of Marcellinus in 534. In the millennium between its composition in Italy and its appearance in the possession of Jean du Tillet (Tilianus—hence the Bodleian's 'T'), bishop of Meaux (1564–70), no trace can be found of the manuscript although its marginalia in a fourteenth-century French hand suggest its location at some French monastery at that stage.[11] It was acquired in the 1540s by the industrious and learned du Tillet, commissioned by Francis I to seek out manuscripts throughout the realm.[12]

The interest and importance of this manuscript are obvious. It is of exceptional antiquity—in fact the oldest Latin manuscript the Bodleian possesses, and the oldest non-biblical Latin manuscript in Britain. Thus it provides a great advantage to the editors of the chronicles of Jerome and Marcellinus.[13] Since Marcellinus' chronicle, in its updated form, first appeared at Constantinople in 534, we have here an Italian copy only one or two generations from the autograph original. The Italian provenance of this manuscript, especially its relationship to the monastic community founded and fostered by Cassiodorus on his Vivarium estate near Squillace, remains an object of some dispute. Significant arguments have been based on the palaeographical character of folios 146^r–179^v of *Auct.* T. 2. 26 without the manuscript itself ever being properly examined.

While researching into the Vivarium monastery and attempting to identify manuscripts which may have been originally produced there, Courcelle discovered what he considered to be a new component in this process.[14] He noted that Cassiodorus (*Inst.* I. 17) recommended the following corpus of chroniclers: Jerome–Marcellinus–Continuators of Marcellinus; and suggested that the Bodleian manuscript, because of the age difference between the Jerome (fifth century) and Marcellinus (sixth century) sections, may have represented the original fusion of these chronicles into a single corpus. That is to say, it was put together within the 'entourage immédiat' of Cassiodorus himself.[15] Now, in assisting with his work on the Bodleian manuscript of Marcellinus,

---

[11] The conjecture of Turner (1905), 63.
[12] Fotheringham (1905), 25.
[13] Mommsen (1894), 48; Mosshammer (1979), 49ff.
[14] Courcelle (1954), 425–8.
[15] Ibid. 428.

Mommsen had arranged for the librarian (E. B. Nicholson) to have the first folio of Marcellinus and the last of the *Additamentum* photographed.[16] He later included these photographs of the manuscript in his edition. It was an examination of these photographs, not the original manuscript, which led Courcelle to perceive a distinction between the hands of the copyist of Marcellinus and his continuator thus suggesting the possibility that this represented the original addition of the *Additamentum* to Marcellinus. Both Momigliano[17] and Markus,[18] however, examined the manuscript subsequently and were convinced that the two sections are not palaeographically distinct, as Courcelle had stated; but neither Momigliano nor Markus analysed the manuscript systematically. The implications are clearly significant. If the hands are distinct then Courcelle's case for regarding *Auct*. T. 2. 26 as possibly a Vivarian original is considerably fortified, and if identical then the manuscript is removed a step further from Cassiodorus' 'entourage immédiat' and the consequences have to be worked out.

First of all, the overt characteristics of both the Marcellinus and the continuation parts of the manuscript are the same, not different. The rulings are the same; so too the ink and the number of lines per page (30) but, most importantly, the *Additamentum* is contained in the same quire as the last folios of Marcellinus. This means that if it were added separately and later it must have been on folios left blank in the last quire, a possibility which experienced palaeographers consider unlikely. It remains to consider, then, whether or not the hands are identical. The least cumbersome way of approaching this analysis is to take in turn the aspects of letter formation which Courcelle claimed were formed differently in Marcellinus and his continuation.[19] Examples have been chosen deliberately from the more legible folios so they can be easily verified.

   1. According to Courcelle, a difference in the formation of the letter 'x' could be observed between Marcellinus and the

---

[16] Nicholson to Mommsen, letter 30 May 1889 (*Mommsen Nachlass*, Staatsbibliothek zu Berlin) with Mommsen's belated reply of 8 Sept. 1889: 'The photographs are so as I wished them, the first is extremely fine and that of the last page as good as the damaged parchment could give it' (*Bodleian Library Records*, d.360, fo. 236^r).

[17] Momigliano (1956), 271.

[18] Markus (unpublished).

[19] Courcelle (1954), 428 n. 3.

Additamentum, although he does not specify the nature of this difference. There is a regular uncial 'x' and this is most common and consistent in the Marcellinus section; e.g. fo. 146ʳ line 25 (*sex*.) It is also consistently formed in identical manner in the *Additamentum*, e.g. fo. 177ᵛ line 16 (*ex*); fo. 176ʳ line 27 (*exercitu*). However, within the *Additamentum* there are some instances of an 'x' not identically formed, e.g. fo. 175ᵛ line 28 (*expugnato*), where the downstroke drops more vertically; fo. 178ʳ line 17 (*iudex*) where the tail of the downstroke takes an uncharacteristic loop. Similar inconsistencies in the formation of 'x' can also be found in the Marcellinus section, e.g. fo. 147ʳ line 23 (*sextus*) where there is a thick downstroke; fo. 148ʳ line 7 (*Alexandria*) has a longer than normal downstroke terminating in a narrow loop. From this it becomes apparent that they must be interpreted as simply unavoidable variations which occur frequently even in such a stylised script.

2. Courcelle considered the letter 'p' showed a different thickness and length of the vertical bar of the downstroke. Again a considerable variation can be observed between different instances of the letter in both parts of the manuscript. To take a convenient example where more than one 'p' occurs in a single line: fo. 146ʳ line 14: *secutus imperium per indictiones perque consul[es]* each is different; the third (*perque*) is fractionally longer and lighter than the other two. The second (*per*) curves off centre. Similar variations can also be observed in the *Additamentum*, e.g. fo. 170ʳ line 23 [*impera*]*torem per episcopum civitatis Asisina* [*tium*]. Here each 'p' in *episcopum* is at a slight slant whereas the first 'p' (*per*) is directly vertical. To the naked eye they are of the same length. Examples of unequal length can, however, be found, e.g. fo. 169ᵛ: [*pa*]*tricius atque praefectus praetorio*. The 'p' of *praetorio* is definitely longer than the 'p' of *prefectus*. Likewise there are internal variations in the *Additamentum*, e.g. fo. 177ʳ line 5: *Parthiis persistentibus inimicis Belisar*[*ius*] where the 'p' of *Parthiis* has a pronounced loop lacking in the 'p' of *persistentibus*.

3. The curve of the 'g' is regarded by Courcelle as differing in degree in the two sections. Yet again, the variations observed from Marcellinus and the *Additamentum*, are no more than normal variations within each part, e.g. fo. 156ʳ line 2 (*egressi*) where the 'g' has a distinct curve, whereas that of *magistri* in line 6 is straight. In an identical manner this difference can also be perceived in

Additamentum, e.g. fo. 176^r line 21 (*Ingreditur*) has a straight down-stroke compared to line 2 (*Vitigis*) with a vertical downstroke terminating in a loop, or line 29 (*Genuam*) with a very pronounced curve.

4. In the *Additamentum* the word *imperator*, written fully in Marcellinus, is abbreviated *imp*. at fo. 179^v which is possibly explained by the scribe being in a hurry and trying to fit in the whole of the *Additamentum* realizing that this was his last quire. What is more likely, though, is that he simply copied his source faithfully and accurately (assuming, therefore, that the *Additamentum* was not composed originally by the scribe himself) which had itself included the abbreviation. Such abbreviations are common elsewhere in the Marcellinus folios: e.g. 'DNI NI' fo. 172^r line 11; 'SCI' fo. 167^v line 25; 'SCA' fo. 167^v line 7; 'XRO' fo. 160^r line 23; 'AVG' fo. 160^r line 18; and in the *Additamentum* folios as well, e.g. 'DNO' fo. 174^v line 29. Furthermore, *imperator* occurs in its full form on other occasions in the *Additamentum* (e.g. fo. 174^v lines 4, 9; fo. 175^v line 6; fo. 176^v line 17; fo. 178^r lines 4, 12). Certainly *imp*. cannot be taken by itself as a distinguishing and characteristic feature of the *Additamentum*. It is best explained as a unique example, accurately copied.

This systematic analysis of the letter formations of T, although only confined to the aspects cited by Courcelle, is sufficient to show that his observations have no foundation in fact. An exhaustive analysis would only reinforce this conclusion. The chronicle of Marcellinus and the continuation were copied by the same scribe in the same hand. In other words they constitute a single stage of copying, not a process of addition undertaken at Vivarium. To be fair to Courcelle, however, it would appear that he was led astray not so much by his powers of observation as by Mommsen's choice of folios to reproduce. The variations in letter formation which Courcelle noticed between the first and final folios can be seen to exist. They do not, however, represent an abrupt change in hands but conceal a consistent variation in the letter formation throughout the manuscript indicating a perceptible decline in the careful attention of the scribe to his work. A similar variation is also evident throughout the folios containing Jerome's chronicle and the chronological summation added to it.[20]

[20] Fotheringham (1905), 26–7.

The Bodleian manuscript is thus removed from the Vivarium community by at least one step. Furthermore, it is not absolutely certain from Cassiodorus' statement *forte inveniatis alios subsequentes* (*Inst.* 1. 17) that this particular continuation of Marcellinus existed at Vivarium in the first place, nor that a fixed corpus of chroniclers (Jerome–Marcellinus–Continuator) should be ascribed to Cassiodorus' design. This comment, in the section on Christian historians in his *Institutiones,* applies as much to continuations of Prosper's chronicle as to a continuation of Marcellinus. There were many continuations of Prosper, several of which survive.[21] The most we can say is that T may be copied from an exemplar which itself added the continuation to Marcellinus (either copying the *Additamentum* or being its author) and that this exemplar may have been produced in response to Cassiodorus' instructions in the *Institutiones.* There is no profit in further speculation. What is more important is the content and context of the *Additamentum.*

THE CONTINUATOR'S CULTURE AND PERSPECTIVE

The continuation of Marcellinus' chronicle ceases in 548 when the final folio of T breaks off. How far beyond 548 it continued is not known although it was probably a period of several years. At least one folio is missing but there may have been even more.[22] This fact alone implies a completion date no earlier than the mid to late 550s, but possibly as late as the 560s or 570s, that is after (possibly well after) the final defeat of the Goths and the re-establishment of Roman government in Italy as reflected in the so-called 'Pragmatic Sanction' (554). If Cassiodorus took the completed work of the Continuator back to Italy with him in the early to mid-550s then that would provide a *terminus ante quem* for the *Additamentum,* but any such claim would be no more than conjectural.

In the extant part of the *Additamentum* there is no sense of immediacy or passion, nor of current political engagement or connection. The events reported (i.e. from 534/5) could have occurred twenty or more years ago at the time of writing. In that

---

[21] *MGH AA* 9. 487 ff.

[22] Cf. Mommsen (1894), 49. This leaf, or leaves, must have been lost early since the manuscripts derived from T do not continue any further than T in its present form (cf. Fotheringham (1905), 27).

case what we are considering is a manuscript which contained a chronicle record of world history to the 550s. This chronicle was adding the chronicle of Marcellinus to an already existing manuscript of Jerome's chronicle, then (using the simple link *quo tempore,* 534) carrying the story down to the present day in the same way that both Jerome (continuing Eusebius) and Marcellinus (continuing Jerome) had done earlier. For the Continuator, as for the chronicle he was continuing, the important consideration was not the thoroughness or verifiable accuracy of the information recorded so much as the continuity and shape of the story.

The *Additamentum* is anonymous and there is no real information to link it to any contemporary figure. The only possible candidate for authorship would be Maximian who was bishop of Ravenna in the mid-550s, having previously spent time in Constantinople, and who did indeed write a chronicle.[23] If the *Additamentum* were an extract from the chronicle of Maximian we would probably expect to see more information on Ravenna, possibly including the dedication of the Justinianic churches with which he was associated. We might also have expected more detail on ecclesiastical matters and on the war in Italy particularly around Ravenna. Maximian does not appear a strong contender for identification with the Continuator.

Although it is not known who the Continuator was and where he wrote, some cogent inferences can be assembled. In 543 the Continuator records the bare fact of the ongoing struggle with Persia but in doing so identifies himself with the Roman side— 'while the conflict between the Persians and our army continued' (543. 3). 'Our army' (*nostri*) are the Romans, the subjects and supporters of Justinian. It is the same designation used by Marcellinus, that is to distinguish himself as 'Roman' from the empire's adversaries such as Huns and Persians.[24] More interesting is the content of the *Additamentum*. The author is clearly well informed about and interested in Italy, although not necessarily an Italian himself, and his entries contain a predominance of Italian events and the citation of precise locations in Italy: Rome (536, 537, etc.), Naples (536, 546), Ravenna (536, 540), Rimini (538), Milan (538), Verona (542), Firmum (545), Asculum (545),

---

[23] It was fairly detailed to judge from the later references to it by Agnellus (details in Mommsen (1892), 257–8).

[24] For 'Romani' in Marcellinus: Gusso (1996), 141.

Auximum (545), Assisi (545), Clusium (545), Mucelli (542), Urbino (538, 542), Placentia (540), Orvieto (538), Genoa (539), Petrapertusa (542), Aeternum (538) and the *campi barbarici* (536). This list, covering the various theatres of the war in Italy, does not suggest any particular geographical concentration or local knowledge. On the other hand, the Continuator's greater attention to Italy is best appreciated by comparing his treatment of Italy to entries for Africa where Carthage (535. 1) is the only place ever named, and to the eastern entries where we find reference only to Dara (537) and Antioch (540. 2).

The Italian coverage of the *Additamentum* does not mean, however, that the Continuator was necessarily an Italian himself, nor that he had lived through the events described. In any event, it is Constantinople which emerges as the convergent centre of action, or pivot, for the chronicle. The great military figures of the period 535–48 are constantly under review journeying back and forth to Constantinople. Narses leaves from Constantinople one year (538. 5) and returns the next (539. 1). Belisarius sets out from Constantinople in 535 and returns there from Italy in 540. He leaves Constantinople for the East soon after (541. 1) and later returns to the imperial capital (545. 3), whereupon he once again departs from there for Rome. Upon Belisarius' arrival in Italy John, the nephew of Vitalian, is sent back to Constantinople (535. 3) and the next year the eastern army returns there (536. 4). The thread of events in Africa reflects the same focus. Germanus succeeds Solomon who is sent back to Constantinople (536. 2) and they later swap positions once again with Germanus returning to the capital (539. 5). The next year he leaves for the east (540. 1) and, when replaced by Belisarius, returns to Constantinople once more (541. 1). In the same year Solomon is killed and Sergius sent from Constantinople to replace him (541. 3). Sergius remains in Africa until 546 when he is recalled to the capital and replaced by Areobindus (546. 3): through all this movement of commanders and armies back and forth across the Mediterranean Constantinople is the pivotal point from which they are viewed. Then there are popes—Agapetus (535. 2, 536. 10) and Vigilius (547. 4)—likewise entering and leaving Constantinople, and the (otherwise unrecorded) embassy of the bishop of Assisi, Aventius, to the imperial capital on behalf of the regime of the Gothic king Totila (547. 1).

The common designation of Constantinople as the 'royal city' (used regularly by Marcellinus) is also employed by the Continuator of Marcellinus (s.a. 535. 4, 541. 1), although he also refers to it simply as 'Constantinople' (s.a. 536. 5, 10; 537. 5, 538. 5, 539. 1, 546. 4, 547. 4). The Continuator of Marcellinus therefore wrote in Constantinople although, unlike Marcellinus, he pays almost no attention to the cultural and civic life of the capital itself with the exception of the inauguration of Hagia Sophia (537. 5). The fact that two of the events recorded are linked to exact dates—Hagia Sophia (537. 5) and Pope Vigilius' arrival (547. 4)—suggests a local Byzantine record for this information.

The viewpoint of the Continuator can be defined even more precisely. He was, for example, strongly orthodox as he makes quite plain that Pope Agapetus was correct to depose the patriarch Anthimus and elect Menas in his place. Anthimus, previously bishop of Trebizond, had usurped (*invadit*) the episcopate of the patriarch Epiphanius in contravention of church law (535. 4). Conversely, his successor Menas is praised as an obedient servant of Justinian—'he contemplated nothing contrary to the faith just as he was adjoined by the emperor' (536. 10). The Continuator's attitude is close to the eastern court in another way too, for he accepts the idea that the Gothic war was Justinian's just revenge for a cruel misdeed (534 *Additamentum*).[25]

For the Continuator, Belisarius is a hero. When he acts it is strictly 'for the good of the empire' (535. 1), and with the Almighty favourably disposed (*favente domino*, 536. 8). This uncompromising view is interesting in so far as Belisarius had always enjoyed a mixed reputation at Constantinople, particularly in the aftermath of the drawn-out war in Italy. Moreover, Belisarius was still alive at the time the Continuator was writing (assuming mid to late 550s). It was Narses and his all-out approach which prevailed in the end, but the Continuator's attitude to Narses and his campaign is unknown because the crucial pages covering the years after 551 have not survived. Another hero is Germanus who is kept before the reader's mind (s.a. 536. 2, 536. 9, 537. 3, 539. 5, 540. 1, 541. 1). Indeed, the comment at 536.9 'Germanus administered Africa successfully' suggests a pro-government eastern perspective.

The obverse of this pro-Roman attitude is that it is partly anti-

---

[25] Cf. Proc. *Wars* 5. 4. 30 with Amory (1997), 141–2.

Gothic. The Gothic king Vitigis is simply an usurper (537. 1) and his marriage to Matasuentha a show of compulsion (*plus vi quam amore*, 536. 7). In reality, Vitigis had been justifiably proclaimed as king by his army and then sought legitimation from Justinian who did not immediately reject his claim. The marriage to Matasuentha was designed to connect the new Gothic king to the Amal family of Theodoric.[26] In the end, however, Vitigis' authority derived from his military experience and reputation, and Justinian responded by resuming hostilities. The author's strong reaction to king Totila who successfully regrouped the Goths and reignited resistance throughout the 540s begins with Totila's crossing of the river Po, *malo Italiae* (542. 2). This critical view of Totila is sustained throughout the *Additamentum* (s.a. 544. 1, 545. 1, 4; 546. 1; 547. 5; 548. 1). Totila had a certain degree of support in Italy and there was strong sentiment in favour of negotiating a settlement with him. Justinian and the imperial court preferred, however, to keep on the offensive against him. The Continuator reflects the determination of the imperial regime to confront and defeat Totila, and presumably vindicates too the wisdom of that policy in hindsight.

The Continuator's loyalty to Belisarius is reinforced by his hostile attitude to both John the Cappadocian whose house Belisarius acquired when the former was exiled (544. 3), and the empress Theodora whose jealousy and victimization of Belisarius is alluded to without her being directly blamed (545. 3). The Continuator is writing well after the death of Theodora in 548 and never mentions her at all. By the time of writing John had long been recalled to Constantinople and speculation about Theodora's interventions against Belisarius were more widespread.[27] The tenor of imperial propaganda emerges too in the Continuator's representation of the abduction of Pope Vigilius from Rome as an invitation from the emperor (546. 1). Vigilius had refused to accept Justinian's condemnation of three eastern theologians in a document which became known as the 'three chapters' and had effectively been abducted and brought to the court by imperial agents. While the Continuator evidently reiterates aspects of the imperial position on contested events, such as the summoning of Vigilius to Constantinople, the *Addita-*

---

[26] Wolfram (1988), 343; Heather (1996), 263–4, and Amory (1997), 261–2.
[27] Cf. Cameron, Averil (1985), 70 ff.

mentum contains nothing specifically eulogistic or laudatory of Justinian. The emperor is not a central figure in the *Additamentum*; indeed, he is scarcely mentioned by name.[28]

The picture of the Continuator of Marcellinus which emerges from the extant part of his work is that of an orthodox Latin-speaking resident of Constantinople, anti-Gothic and certainly not averse to the idea of Italy's reconquest. He was possibly, but not necessarily, an Italian. There is certainly no evidence to link him closely with aristocratic refugees from the Gothic war living in Constantinople in the 550s—men like Cethegus, Pope Vigilius, and Cassiodorus.[29] Nonetheless, it has come to be assumed that the Continuator, Cassiodorus, and Jordanes, as well as Cethegus and Vigilius, were part of the same circle of Italians seeking around 551 to influence Justinian or other senatorial colleagues to accept a rapprochement between Romans and Goths in Italy, rather than a continued prosecution of the war.

By 551, the Gothic war had been dragging on for over fifteen years. The capture of the Gothic king and his triumphal parade in Constantinople in 540 appeared to mark the end of the war. However, the Goths fought on and under Totila found themselves in a position to win back many key towns. The Italians were tired of war and the devastation and disruption it was causing although they did not necessarily advocate or actively support a victory for either side. Constantinople was becoming home to an increasing number of captured Gothic soldiers as well as to Italian senators and aristocrats who had fled the insecurity of Italy for the security of Constantinople. Many of them, including by now Pope Vigilius, were urging Justinian to mount a decisive offensive against Totila and to restore peace and stability to Italy. Justinian was eventually persuaded. The underlying ideology was one of reconquest and reclamation. The Goths were now seen to have forfeited their mandate (dating to the time of Zeno and Anastasius) to exercise authority and power in Italy. The only option now considered viable, and the one being actively pursued, was military victory. Compromise arrangements for power sharing and reconciliation had lapsed. The ambivalence of many Italian

---

[28] Justinian is referred to but twice by name (534, 537. 5), otherwise simply as *imperator*. s.a. 535. 1, 537. 4, 538. 1, 540. 3, 546. 1, 546. 3, 547. 1, 547. 6, 548. 2.

[29] Proc., *Wars* 7. 35. 9–10. Cethegus is associated with Cassiodorus' alleged quest for reconciliation by Momigliano (1955, 207–45).

aristocrats, men such as Cassiodorus, had long eroded. As far as Justinian and the imperial court were concerned the Gothic interlude in Italy was over. By the time the Continuator was writing, however, in the mid to late 550s these events were well past and their outcome resolved.

In this context it is not unreasonable to assume that someone writing in Constantinople in the 550s with a close interest in the continuing war in Italy should be seen as an Italian and a refugee from that war. In the case of the Continuator, an Italian connection may be surmised from the frequent geographical locations mentioned (cited above). Perhaps too a note of local affiliation is detectable in his comment on Totila's treatment of the inhabitants of Firmum and Asculum (545. 1), and his reaction at the sack of Rome in 547 (547. 5), or in his reference to the bishop of Assisi's mission to Justinian (547. 1). Furthermore, his criticism of the soldiers of Justinian's army at Verona (542. 1) shows some feeling for the effects of the war on the Italians themselves. On the other hand, this could be taken as an example of the indiscipline of the Byzantine army, a common contemporary criticism and, as such, not the exclusive preserve of Italians.

The argument that the Continuator is to be associated with the interests of the aristocratic Italian refugees in Constantinople is based on a series of cumulative and interlocking assumptions, beginning with the notion that the Continuator is to be connected with Cassiodorus and Jordanes by ascribing to him a specific south Italian origin.[30] Cassiodorus' ancestral estates were located at Squillace but in 551 he was in Constantinople, and it is argued that the Jordanes who wrote the Roman and Gothic histories was the same person as the bishop of Crotone, not far from Squillace, who was also in Constantinople in the early 550s. Indeed, on this interpretation, the Continuator is endowed with the same political ideals and social milieu as the Italians in Constantinople, especially Cassiodorus and Jordanes.[31]

In Constantinople Cassiodorus was mainly preoccupied with theological pursuits, writing his *Commentary on the Psalms* in particular and at least gathering material for the *Historia Tripartita*. At

---

[30] Momigliano (1956), 272. Courcelle (1954), 428 had claimed a special interest in Calabria for the Continuator.

[31] Momigliano (1956), 273 ('con animo non diverso da quello di Cassiodoro e di Iordanes . . . formato non lontano da Iordanes e Cassiodoro').

the same time he was keeping in touch with his growing monastic community back in Squillace.[32] He was moving in a different world from those he occupied in the 520s and 530s as a distinguished official and mouthpiece of the Gothic regime in Italy. While in the service of the Goths, at least by 533, he produced a *Gothic History* in which he somehow integrated the story of the Goths into that of the Romans and traced back seventeen generations of the noble house of the Amali.[33] Cassiodorus' history has not survived but it has been proposed that in 551, when Cassiodorus was in Constantinople, he undertook a revised and updated version of the *History* explicitly designed to promote a policy of reconciliation between Goths and Romans. Such a process of reconciliation would lead to a lasting settlement in Italy. This hypothesis was founded on attributing to Cassiodorus the culmination of Jordanes' *Getica* in which he describes the offspring of the marriage of Germanus and Matasuentha in 551 as giving hope for both peoples (*Get.* 314). In other words, so it is claimed, when Jordanes says he utilized the *Gothic History* of Cassiodorus he means that he merely copied a revised and just recently completed edition of the history, not the original edition written about two decades earlier.[34]

There are several reasons why this reconstruction is untenable for the Continuator of Marcellinus. First, the interest of the Continuator is neither confined to, nor specially concentrated on, southern Italy but rather on Italy as a whole, north as well as south. As noted above, his coverage of Italian affairs derives from describing a theatre of war but there is not enough detail to suggest any local affiliation or provenance. In addition, it is very unlikely that Jordanes (the author of the *Romana*) was the bishop of Crotone. Yet other objections have been raised to the hypothesis in recent years which make it unsustainable.[35] However, quite apart from the case for discounting the relationship between Jordanes and Cassiodorus in 551 there remains the relation of both to the Continuator.

Here too the notion that the Continuator is necessarily linked

[32] Barnish (1989), 159 ff.

[33] Goffart (1988), 32 ff.; Heather (1989), 103–28, (1993), 317–53; Croke (forthcoming *b*).

[34] Originally argued by Momigliano (1955), 207–45 and (1956), 249–76, and more recently by Barnish (1984), 347–61 and Wolfram (1988), 15.

[35] Details in Varady (1976), 441–87; O'Donnell (1982), 223–40; Croke (1987), 117–34; Goffart (1988), 20–111; Heather (1991), 3–67; Amory (1997), 291–307; Croke (forthcoming *b*).

to Jordanes and Cassiodorus is difficult to sustain. Besides the fact that it is weakened by subtracting from the Continuator a south Italian provenance, and by questioning the relationship between Cassiodorus and Jordanes, it is undermined by more substantial matters. For instance, both the *Additamentum* and Jordanes contain the same negative comment on the marriage of Vitigis and Matasuentha (536. 7~*Rom.* 373) and both pass the same judgement on Totila *malo Italiae* (542. 2~*Rom.* 379). In each instance the *Additamentum* and Jordanes reproduce the official government view in circulation at Constantinople at the time they were writing. The contemporary attitude to the marriage of Vitigis and Matasuentha is reflected clearly in Procopius, for example.[36] Finally, there is a major chronological difficulty for the idea that the Continuator is closely linked to Jordanes and the putative revision of Cassiodorus' history in 551 if (as is quite likely) the Continuator was writing in the mid to late 550s with the subjugation of Italy behind him. Although the Continuator occasionally passes adverse judgement on events in Italy there is, as noted above, no sense of immediacy, advocacy, or engagement in his description. He is compiling a matter of fact record of events whose outcome was clearly settled.

Indeed, that the Continuator was not close to the events being described is suggested by the many inaccuracies traceable in his record.[37] His chronology of events in Africa, for example, is poorly informed so that most of his entries are misplaced. The revolt against Solomon which broke out in March 536 (cf. 535. 1) is dated to 535, the disputes with the Moors which lead to the death of Solomon and his replacement by his nephew Sergius in 544 are dated (for no apparent reason) to 541 (541. 3), while the events of 544 in Byzacium are confused with those of 543 in Tripolitania (543. 3). Then the recall of Sergius to Constantinople and his replacement by Areobindus in 545 is dated to 546 (546. 3), and the events leading to the arrival of John Troglita in 546 are placed in 547 (547. 6). There are similar problems with the chronology of the Gothic war. Belisarius returned to Italy in the summer of 544, not 545 (545. 3). John's advance to Italy in 545 is dated to 547 (547. 2), while the Goths captured and entered Rome in December 546

---

[36] *Wars* 7. 39. 14–15.
[37] *Contra* Mommsen (1894), 42. Further details in commentary on individual entries in Croke (1995), 127–39.

not 547 (547. 5) although this event is dated to the correct indiction (beginning September 546). Even Constantinopolitan events can be misdated: the fall of John the Cappodocian in 541 is put in 544 (544. 3), and the embassy of the bishop of Assisi, Aventius, took place early in 546 not 547.[38]

Taken together, these blemishes in the *Additamentum* would appear to imply a writer who was not intimately involved as a contemporary in the events described. They certainly do not suggest someone who formed part of a cabal of Romans in exile in Constantinople with close access to the imperial court and who were seeking to persuade the emperor to conclude the war in 551 with a permanent reconciliation between the court and the Gothic regime in Italy. Rather, they suggest someone writing after the events were decided. That is, after the decisive military victories of Narses over Totila at Busta Gallorum and then over Teias at Mons Lactarius in 552, after the formal specifications for the reassertion of imperial power in Italy through the 'Pragmatic Sanction' (554), and after the return of many of the aristocrats to Italy, including Cassiodorus. It seems most likely that when the Continuator was writing Cassiodorus was already engaged fully in the building up of his new community of Christian learning at Vivarium.

The most that can be said is that the Continuator adopts or reflects a set of pro-Justinianic attitudes shared by others in Constantinople in the 550s. The *Additamentum* cannot be linked to Cassiodorus, nor the political ideology of the Anicii at Constantinople, although it is necessarily linked to Jordanes. Moreover, Jordanes and his historical work belong in the same context as Marcellinus, that is, as part of the Illyrian Latin culture of Constantinople.[39]

THE *ADDITAMENTUM* AND JORDANES' *ROMANA*

Irrespective of the precise date of the Continuator, and the nature of any personal relationship to Jordanes, there are some textual correspondences between their works which require explanation: a brief comparison will suffice to illustrate their points of correspondence (see Table 7. 1).

---

[38] Stein (1949), 582 with n. 1.
[39] Croke (1987), 117–34; Goffart (1988), 20 ff.; Amory (1997), 291 ff.

TABLE 7.1. *Comparison of* Additamentum *with* Romana

Additamentum	Jordanes, Romana
536.7 Ravennamque ingressus Matesuentham nepotem Theodorici <u>sibi</u> sociam in regno <u>plus vi copulat quam amore</u>	373 privata coniuge repudiata regiam puellam Maathesuentam Theodorici regis nepotem <u>sibi plus vi copolat quam amori.</u>
542.2 Gothi Erario rege occiso Totilam in regnum manciparunt. qui <u>malo Italiae</u> mox Padum transit et ad Faventiam Aemiliae civitatem <u>Romanum exercitum superat</u>, duces effugat.	379 . . . Erarius qui et ipse vix anno expleto peremptus est et in regno. <u>malo Italiae</u> Baduila iuvenis nepus asciscitur Heldebadi. qui mox et sine mora Faventino in oppido Emiliae soli proelio commisso <u>Romanum superant exercitum.</u>

The use of identical phraseology—*malo Italiae* (applied by the Continuator to Totila's campaign across the Po, and by Jordanes to his elevation alone) and *plus vi quam amore* suggest a clear connection, at least for these two expressions of opinion. It is possible that the Continuator (writing in the mid to late 550s) was simply copying Jordanes (writing in 551) at this point and that he had access to other texts besides Jordanes for further information. On the other hand, Jordanes' account (*Rom.* 368–9) of the rebellion in Africa under Solomon contains details not in the *Additamentum* (535. 1); so too does his description of Evremud's switch of allegiance (*Rom.* 370–3 ~ *Additamentum* 536. 1). Likewise, the *Additamentum* has information on Belisarius' reinforcements (537. 2) not in Jordanes, as well as information relating to the war in Italy (538. 1–7, 539. 2–4) not in the *Romana*.

If the Continuator was not simply using Jordanes as one text among several on which to draw relevant information for his work, then the correspondences are best explained by their use of a common document.[40] Such a common document behind the *Romana* and the *Additamentum* can only be inferred, however. From this brief comparison it is evident that both Jordanes and the Continuator drew on their common text closely and sometimes copied it/them literally.[41]

What more can be said about the Continuator's sources of

[40] Krautschick (1986), 363.

[41] I suggest this tentatively from the fact that the Continator has two different spellings for the successor of Athalaric: *Theodahadus* (534 *Add.* 536. 4, 5) and *Theodatus* (535. 2, 536. 1, 6) which may reflect two different sources.

information? If both the Continuator and Jordanes used the same document or documents for these years then they are covered by the indefinite statement of Jordanes at the conclusion of the *Romana*, namely that further details may be found in the *annales consulumque seriem* (*Rom.* 388) by which Jordanes means historical works generally but perhaps particularly those such as the chronicle of Marcellinus.[42] Mommsen was inclined to think the common source was the same body of material which Marcellinus and Jordanes had drawn on independently for the period to 534.[43] It is only such a source which would provide precisely dated entries like the dedication of Hagia Sophia (537. 5) and the arrival of Pope Vigilius in Constantinople (547. 4).

More broadly, the very structure of the *Romana* and the *Additamentum* may reflect that of a common document. If so, then it was an extensive record of events compartmentalized into the three different parts of the known world (Europe, Africa, and Asia) so that under each year of the *Additamentum* are recorded events in each of Italy, Africa, and the East except for two occasions (538, 542) where only events in Italy are recorded. Generally speaking, however, the three zones of interest appear in the order: Italy–Africa–East and this is probably a reflection of the structure of the common source (e.g. 536, 537, 544, 545, 546). This tripartite structure can also be seen in the *Romana* which is organized according to the reigns of successive emperors, Justinian's being the longest (*Rom.* 363–87). Sections 363–6 cover events in Constantinople, the Persian frontier and Africa up to 534, an indication that Jordanes was following the chronicle of Marcellinus which ended in that year. After 534 the structure of the *Romana* changes into a tripartite one—Europe, Africa, and Asia. Hence, without interpolation *Rom.* 367–75 treats of events in Italy; 376–7 in the east, 378–83 Italy once again, 384–5 in Africa and 386–7 in Italy. Jordanes' source or sources of information listed the events of each year under these geographical divisions so that in the self-styled 'summary of the chronicles' (*Get.* 1) Jordanes grouped the events of different years together under their geographical region to give a coherence to the narrative. In addition, he made an attempt to link the different sections with his usual connective (*Rom.* 378, 380) and in one instance by explaining the connection

---

[42] Explained in more detail in Croke (forthcoming *a*).
[43] Mommsen (1894), 54–5, cf. (1882), xxix.

between the Persian invasion of 540 and the preoccupation of the army in Italy (*Rom.* 376). This simple technique of grouping chronicles into a narrative is precisely what Jordanes claims to be doing, and what he can be shown to have done, throughout the *Romana*.[44]

If, behind the *Additamentum* and the *Romana* lies a chronicle text common to both Jordanes and Marcellinus then both writers excerpted and arranged it, according to the design and interests of each. Jordanes' use of it, generally speaking, was more balanced than that of the Continuator; his information on Africa and the east is more detailed and extensive, for example.[45] The Continuator, on the other hand, is clearly more concerned with Italy than elsewhere, but was consciously creating a coherent work as indicated by his connection of two separate entries on Pope Agapetus (535. 2 ~ 536. 10, *ut diximus*).

In sum we must seek to loosen the close connections of provenance and political viewpoint alleged for the Continuator of Marcellinus, Cassiodorus, and Jordanes. This leaves us with a far more untidy and less engaging picture of the relative status and viewpoint of each of these writers living and writing in Constantinople in the 550s. The most we can claim is a literary relationship between the *Romana* and the *Additamentum*, both written in Constantinople. Indeed, this relationship is best explained by their use of a common record rather than the Continuator having simply copied Jordanes. The Continuator may, or may not, have known Jordanes and his writings. Even so, both Jordanes and the Continuator share the same attitudes of their common source of information, or at least some of them: they are orthodox, pro-Justinianic, and opponents of the reign of Totila. As such they reproduce in the subsequent generation the attitudes of Marcellinus whose chronicle they both knew and used.

Although Cassiodorus too learnt of Marcellinus' chronicle in Constantinople, and doubtless took a copy back to Italy with him, his remarks in the *Institutiones* indicate that not only was he not an intimate of the Continuator, but that he did not even know of the existence of the *Additamentum* in particular. That is unsurprising since it was probably written after he left Constantinople in 554. Yet the *Additamentum* soon made its way to Italy where it was

---

[44] Goffart (1988), 47 ff.   [45] Cf. Momigliano (1956), 274.

copied, and recopied, in the late sixth century and included in a manuscript now in the Bodleian Library. It belongs in the same context as Jordanes but that context is the wider world of Byzantine politics in the mid-sixth century. Jordanes was as much the contemporary of John the Lydian, John Malalas, and Procopius as he was of Cassiodorus.

8

The Chronicle's Afterlife

How quickly after 518, and then after 534, the chronicle of
Marcellinus gained popularity and in what circles cannot be
determined. It may have attracted the attention of the chronicler
and former Ostrogothic courtier Cassiodorus in the 530s although
he may only have come across it for the first time in the late
540s/early 550s when he was himself in Constantinople, seeking
safety from the continuing war in his native Italy. It was at precisely this time that the chronicle was also being used by Jordanes
in his brief history of the world, and especially of the Roman
empire, to his own day. Jordanes wrote his *Romana*, together with
a history of the Goths based on that of Cassiodorus, at Constantinople in 550–1.[1] It is possible that Jordanes was in Constantinople as early as the 530s when Marcellinus was still alive, and
he may even have met him. Certainly their works have some
essential features in common. In the *Romana* Jordanes made considerable use of the chronicle of Marcellinus although he never
cites it by name.[2] A few years later another writer took
Marcellinus' chronicle as his starting point (just as Marcellinus
had taken Jerome) and continued it to the early 550s. Jordanes
may have known this Continuator of Marcellinus too. At any rate,
he appears to have used one of the Continuator's main sources of
information. As we have seen (Chapter 7), the work of the Continuator only survives in an incomplete form so it is not possible
to tell precisely where it ended. Cassiodorus may also have known
this Continuator, although he gives the impression that there were
many such chronicles being compiled at the time without identifying any particular one (*Inst.* 1. 17).

---

[1] Croke (1987), 117–34; Goffart (1988), 20 ff.; Heather (1991), 34 ff.
[2] Details in Mommsen (1894), 53–5 with Croke (1983a), 81–119.

THE CASSIODORAN TRADITION

On returning to Italy from Constantinople Cassiodorus presumably took a copy of Marcellinus' chronicle with him.
Certainly he soon had a copy in his Vivarium library at Squillace
and was recommending it as vital reading for monks.[3] Although
not Cassiodorus' original copy, as once argued, it is possible that
the most important surviving manuscript of the chronicle, the
Bodleian Library's *Auct.* T. 2. 26 (= T), was copied from Cassiodorus' own copy. This manuscript is of fundamental importance
because it contains the Continuator of Marcellinus to some
terminal point probably in the 550s. It appears, therefore, that
from very early on there were copies of the chronicle emanating
from the monastery of Cassiodorus which contained the addition
from 535 and it is only to be expected that monastic libraries keen
to follow Cassiodorus' recommendation and acquire a copy of
Marcellinus would apply to Vivarium or, later, to a foundation
whose copy would most likely have descended from Cassiodorus'
original.

The bulk of the extant manuscripts of Marcellinus stand in
what might be described as the 'Cassiodoran tradition'. Two of
the other three significant manuscripts, those from Udine (U,
eleventh century) and Paris (R, fourteenth century), both descend
from the Bodleian manuscript (T). In fact R is the only other
manuscript to contain any of the continuation of the chronicle. In
addition to these there are a number of later (fifteenth-century)
manuscripts which are copies of T or manuscripts in the tradition
of T, although these are of no independent value for establishing
a critical text of the chronicle. All of these manuscripts follow the
Cassiodoran exhortation and include the chronicle of Jerome
before that of Marcellinus, while some fill Cassiodorus' recommendation even more completely by adding the chronicle of
Prosper between Jerome and Marcellinus.[4] Palaeographically the
Jerome section (folios 33^r–144^v) of the Bodleian manuscript
belongs to the fifth century, probably to around 435 (15th cos. of
Theodosius) to judge from the chronological summary at the end
of Jerome's chronicle contained in folio 145 but which is in the
same hand as the Jerome section.[5] Sometime in the late sixth

---

[3] For the wider context: Barnish (1989), 157–87.

[4] Mommsen (1894), 47–53.

[5] Fotheringham (1905), 25–7 (*contra* Mommsen (1894), 48–9).

century were added the folios (146–78) covering Marcellinus and his continuation.

The manuscript T first comes to light in the sixteenth century in the possession of Jean du Tillet who presumably lent it to the Augustinian monk Onophrio Panvinio (1529–68), an indefatigable and pioneering scholar responsible for collecting so many of the records of early church history. In his volume on the Roman consular lists he utilized the manuscript to produce in 1558 the first published edition containing both Marcellinus and his continuation. Subsequently, Joseph Scaliger utilized Panvinio's edition in adding the chronicle of Marcellinus to his monumental *Thesaurus Temporum* (1606) but he made some errors in transcription.[6] Scaliger's errors were corrected by the Jesuit Jacques Sirmond (1559–1651) who next used T for his original edition of 1619, collating it with a twelfth-century Bruges manuscript now in Brussels (*Cod. Brux.* n. 6439–6451) and that of St Victor in Paris which Mommsen was unable to locate for his edition.[7] The first scholar to include a publication of the chronicle, however, was the statesman and poet Iohannes Cuspinian (1473–1529) who lived and worked in Vienna. He used another descendent of the Bodleian manuscript, namely the local *Cod. Vindob.* 138. His work on Marcellinus was contained in his critical edition of the Roman consular lists, although it was not published until 1553, long after his death.

THE ST OMER TRADITION

The other chief manuscript for the chronicle, besides T, is to be found at St Omer and in textual terms represents a different tradition. The Bodleian manuscript passed from its composition within the orbit of Cassiodorus in southern Italy to southern France where it is to be found in the fourteenth century. On the other hand, the eleventh-century manuscript at St Omer (*Codex Sanctomerensis* 697, or S) would appear to derive from a line which began originally in Ireland in the sixth or seventh century, and moved thence to the Northumbria of Bede in the eighth. As Mommsen perceived, Bede must have used an ancestor of the St Omer Manuscript.[8] If so, it is likely that S was copied from an

---

[6] Grafton (1993), 531–3.

[7] Mommsen (1894), 52.

[8] Mommsen (1894), 54. In support of Mommsen's observation, two further instances

exemplar which originated in Ireland or Britain and which reached the continent through one of its many insular monastic foundations in the period from the sixth to the ninth centuries. Antonius Sconhovius who produced the first published edition of the chronicle of Marcellinus in 1546 in Paris used S as well as the Brussels manuscript (*Cod. Brux.* n. 6439–51).

IRISH ANNALS

It is over a century after the time of Cassiodorus and Jordanes that we next see the chronicle of Marcellinus in use, this time in Irish monastic culture at the other end of the civilized world from Constantinople. What can be established with some certainty is that in the early to mid-seventh century an Irish chronicle which formed the foundation for all subsequent Irish chronicles and annals used the chronicle of Marcellinus as a source of information for events outside Ireland during the period from 379 to 534. This original Irish chronicler did not apparently know of the continuation of Marcellinus preserved in the 'Cassiodoran Tradition'.

As with most chronicles, there are extremely complex textual and literary problems involved in the study of the Irish chronicles and annalistic tradition which need not concern us in detail here. Essentially, however, there exist a number of later manuscripts and versions of chronicles from a variety of places in Ireland, and their entries for the fifth and sixth centuries clearly derive ultimately from a common document, or documents. In particular we have a group of three Bodleian manuscripts: (1) *MS Rawl. B.* 503 of the eleventh century which reaches to the year 1092 and which contains what is known as the *Annals of Innisfallen* (hereafter *AI*); (2) *MS Rawl. B.* 502 of the twelfth century containing two chunks of chronicle to AD 360; and (3) *MS Rawl. B.* 488 which contains two separate chronicle sections from 487 to 766 and from 974 to 1178. Both these latter manuscripts represent parts of a common work known as the *Annals of Tigernach* (*AT*). As well as these Oxford manuscripts there is a fifteenth-century chronicle manuscript in Trinity College Dublin (H.1.8) known as the *Annals of Ulster* (*AU*) and a seventeenth-century one known as the *Chronicon Scotorum* (*CS*) which is more or less an abbreviated

can be cited: For *Emetzena* (Marcellin. s.a. 453. 1) S reads *Emisene* (*Emisen, Emisenam*) hence Bede's *Emissa* and for *Hunericus* (s.a. 484) S reads *Honoricus* (cf. Bede, *DTR* 503).

summary. Finally there is another seventeenth-century work, surviving in several copies, known as the *Annals of Clonmacnoise* (*AClon.*). This situation is similar to the so-called Anglo-Saxon chronicle where there are various later manuscripts of chronicles which show a common dependence on an earlier chronicle for the period to the 890s. In addition, it appears that the manuscripts of medieval Welsh annals, known as the *Annales Cambriae*, also derived originally from the Irish annalistic tradition.[9]

Despite the differences of time, locale, and format between all these manuscripts of Irish annals there is a demonstrable commonality of material for the late Roman period. From analysis of this common material it has been argued that the earliest Irish chronicle was in fact from Iona, where the abbot Adomnán wrote his treatise on the 'Holy Land' sites in the late seventh century, and probably commenced at the time of Iona's founder, Columba (560s).[10] Subsequently, a version of the Iona chronicle to the year 740 was continued in Ulster thereby forming the basis of the *Annals of Ulster*.[11] Another copy of the original chronicle went to Clonmacnoise and established the tradition found in the *Annals of Tigernach*, while another version of the chronicle passed to Munster and from it the *Annals of Innisfallen* eventually derived. Since these later annals provide, for the earlier period, a record of world history into which the history of the Irish has been woven it is very likely that the Iona chronicle was actually a continuation of the chronicle of Jerome; or else it incorporated such a continuation.[12] In fact, an earlier continuation of Jerome may have terminated at 607 because (1) *AT*, *AU*, and *AClon.* record *finis chron. Eusebii* at the year 607, and (2) the Irish chronicle mentions Popes down to the death of Sabinianus in 606 but not his successor Boniface III (consecrated February 607).[13]

It is not really possible to define in detail the nature and authorship of this earliest Irish chronicle, let alone resolve the even more complex question of when individual notices became con-

---

[9] Hughes (1980), 67–100.
[10] Hughes (1972), 99–159.
[11] Smyth (1972), 1–48.
[12] This reconstruction is challenged by O'Croinin (1983a), 75–7 but without offering an alternative explanation for the direct use and citation of Marcellinus in the extant versions of the Irish Annals.
[13] Morris (1972), 83.

temporarily recorded, but it is clear that Marcellinus was used extensively by the chronicler, for he is specifically named. The *Annals of Tigernach*, for instance, twice make explicit reference to Marcellinus thus implying that Marcellinus formed part of the original Irish chronicle: *ut Marcellinus monstrat*, s.a. 511 (127); *huc usque perduxit Marcellinus Cronicon suum*, s.a. 535 (135). Marcellinus is also cited in the *Annals of Ulster*[14] and the *Annals of Clonmacnoise*,[15] and used without citation by the *Annals of Innisfallen* and the *Chronicon Scotorum*.

How the chronicle of Marcellinus came to be known in Ireland (more particularly, Iona) in the early seventh century is not clear, although it was probably in one of two ways: either from the Continent, or direct from Constantinople. Manuscripts are known to have reached the west country of England and southern Ireland from the east.[16] More indirectly (but more commonly) eastern manuscripts would reach Ireland by way of southern Gaul or Spain. Indeed the close connections between Ireland and the newly Catholic kingdom of Visigothic Spain also explain the rapid appearance in Ireland of the works of Isidore of Seville,[17] while most of the extensive computistical literature in Ireland and Britain originated not so much in Italy as in Africa and Spain.[18] Since there is no trace of Marcellinus' chronicle ever being known to any Spanish writer, perhaps the direct route Constantinople–Ireland (Iona) is preferable. The work of Marcellinus' contemporary in Constantinople, the grammarian Priscian, also reached Ireland at an early stage.[19] Since Adomnán at Iona clearly possessed other eastern manuscripts (including possibly Marcellinus' books on Jerusalem, as suggested in Chapter 1) he could easily have had a copy of Marcellinus' chronicle at Iona so that Marcellinus could have formed part of the original Iona chronicle—whether compiled in the time of Adomnán or earlier.

[14] *AU* 432 (38): *sicut enumerat . . . Marcellinus*; 449 (42): *sicut adfirmat Marcellinus*; 456 (44): *ueluti Marcellinus docet*; and 536. 1 (70): *huc usque Marcellinus perduxit cronicon suum*. Marcellinus is also used at *AU* 432 (38), 440. 1 (40), 448 (42), 449 (42), 456 (44), 457. 1 (44), 460 (46), 461. 1 (46), 465. 1 (48), 466. 1 (48), 473. 1 (50), 481. 2 (52), 491. 1 (54), 492. 2 (54), 493. 2 (56), 497. 1 (58), 498. 3 (58), 499. 1 (58), 515 (62), 518 (64), 525 (66), 527. 3 (66), 536. 1 (70).

[15] *AClon.* 535 (78): 'Marcellinus hath brought his chronicles thereunto.'

[16] Hillgarth (1961), 444–5.

[17] Hillgarth (1962), 167–94 and (1984), 1–16 (strengthening his earlier case, and answering critics, by advancing further evidence of the use of Isidore in Ireland before anywhere else). [18] O'Croinin (1983*b*), 230.

[19] Bieler (1963), 43, 94, 124.

Adomnán's main activity was as a biblical scholar and exegete so that works of topography and chronology were fundamental to his own scholarly life. Moreover, Iona's significance also lay in the influence it provided for the establishment of literary culture in Northumbria. So, it is possible that it was Adomnán who introduced the chronicle of Marcellinus into Northumbria although other avenues cannot be discounted.

A century after its use in the early Irish chronicle, the chronicle of Marcellinus is to be found at Jarrow in Northumbria where it was cited by Bede in his commentaries on the Gospel of Mark (*c.*718) and on the Epistle of James (*c.*715); it was also copied (either directly or indirectly) on two occasions in his *Ecclesiastical History* (1. 13, 21), written in the 730s. The chronicle of Marcellinus could have come into Bede's possession as a result of one of Benedict Biscop's trips to Rome, gathering up manuscripts for his monastery. It could also have come from Canterbury where its bishop Theodore of Tarsus had been responsible for establishing an extensive and sophisticated library from the 670s including many eastern works, in Greek and Syriac as well as Latin. Theodore himself could well have become familiar with a chronicle such as that of Marcellinus during his time in Constantinople, or even later in Rome.[20] Another possibility is that it came from the monastic library at Aldhelm's Malmesbury. On the other hand, it is not likely that Bede would have been directly prompted by Cassiodorus to seek out the chronicle of Marcellinus since the *Institutiones* were not known in England in his time.[21] A more likely origin for Bede's copy of Marcellinus, however, is Ireland where the *Institutiones* were known. Moreover, it is now clear that Bede made extensive use of manuscripts and works from Ireland, particularly biblical commentaries and the various *computi* used in calculating the date of Easter and that these may have reached him through the library at Malmesbury.[22]

Bede set about writing his *De temporum ratione*, usually known as his 'Chronicle', in 725.[23] Whether Bede knew and could utilize in

[20] Lapidge (1995), 1–29.

[21] Meyvaert (1996), 827ff.

[22] Exegesis: Kelly (1986), 65–75; *Computi*: Hillgarth (1984), 1–16; O'Croinin (1983*b*), 229–47.

[23] Ed. Mommsen (*MGH AA* 13. 247–327) which was virtually reprinted by C. W. Jones (Bede, *DTR*), and discussed in Jones (1947), 16–27; cf. van den Brincken (1957), 108–13. The various interpolations and continuations are set out by Mommsen in *MGH AA* 13. 334–54.

his own chronicle the Irish one, which had itself made use of Marcellinus, is not clear. Certainly, an annalistic chronicle such as that of Marcellinus was an ideal source of information for Bede. There are many entries in Bede's chronicle which can be traced to Marcellinus and it has always been assumed that he used Marcellinus' chronicle directly, despite never citing it.[24] Since many of Marcellinus' entries which are reflected in Bede's chronicle are also to be found in the Irish chronicle the relationship between all three texts needs to be closely examined. In particular, it is worth asking whether Bede merely copied Marcellinus' entries from an Irish chronicle, or whether the correspondences between the three of them can be explained by simply inverting the order of priority, that is, by concluding that the Irish annals derive from an original later than 725 (from Iona or elsewhere) and which therefore merely copied Bede. Or did Bede simply rely on the Irish compilation as his basic guide while having access to his own copies of the very sources of the Irish chronicle, including Marcellinus?

Bede's chronicle was evidently used by Irish annalists subsequently but this involves one curious problem. Much of the information for which Bede is specifically cited (*sicut enumerat Beda*, etc.) is a mistaken attribution since the information is not to be found anywhere in Bede.[25] This would appear to imply that a manuscript was in circulation in Ireland which was compiled partly from Bede and partly from the 'Irish Chronicle' but which was ascribed entirely to Bede. This situation was fairly common among the chronicles of late antiquity because their format was so amenable to interpolation. We have previously noted, for example, how entries from Marcellinus' chronicle came to be incorporated into later manuscripts of the chronicle of Prosper (Chapter 5).

Resolving the question of the relationship between Marcellinus, the Irish chronicle, and Bede's *De temporum ratione* requires a textual comparison, in the light of the traditional assumption that Bede copied his entries directly from Marcellinus.[26] Taking the Irish chronicle as reflected in the *Annals of Innisfallen*, its informa-

---

[24] Marcellin. s.a. 379/80 (= Bede, *DTR* 452); 381 = 454; 383 = 457; 392 = 462; 410 = 469; 416 = 472; 425 = 478; 439 = 486; 442 = 487; 453 = 490; 458 = 495; 476 = 500; 481/2 = 502; 484 = 503; 534 = 516; 531 = 519.

[25] e.g. *AClon.* 543 (78); *AU* 432 (38), 440 (40), 460 (46).

[26] Mommsen, *MGH AA* 13. 227, cf. II. 55.

tion may be compared with Marcellinus and with Bede as shown in Table 8. 1.

TABLE 8. 1. *Comparison of Marcellinus, Bede, and the* Annals of Innisfallen

Marcellinus (*MGH AA* XI)	Bede (CCL 123B)	*Annals of Innisfallen* (ed. S. MacAirt, 1951)
410 Halaricus trepidam urbem Romam invasit partemque eius cremavit incendio, sextoque die quam ingressus fuerat depraedata urbe egressus est.	469 Halaricus <u>rex Gothorum</u> Romam inuasit partemque eius cremauit incendio <u>VIII kal.Sept. anno conditionis eius millesimo centesimo sexagesimo quarto</u>, ac sexto die quam ingressus fuerat depredata urbe egressus est.	Alaricus <u>rex Gothorum</u> Romam invasit partemque eius cremavit incendio <u>in viii Kal. Septembris anno millesimo clxiiii conditionis eius</u>.
415. 2 Lucianus presbyter vir sanctus, cui revelavit deus his consulibus locum sepulchri et reliquiarum corporis sancti Stephani primi martyris scripsit ipsam relationem Graeco sermone ad omnium ecclesiarum personam.	470 Lucianus presbyter, cui reuelauit Deus <u>VII Honori principis anno</u> locum sepulchri et reliquiarum beati protomartyris Stephani <u>et Gamalihelis ac Nicodemi, qui in Euangelio et in Actis Apostolorum leguntur</u>, <u>scripsit</u> ipsam reuelationem Greco sermone ad omnium ecclesiarum personam.	Lucianus presbiter cui revelavit Deus <u>in septimo Honorii anno</u> locum sepulchri reliquiarum beati protomartyris Stefani<u>, Gamahelis, Necomedi qui in evangelio et in actis apostolorum leguntur scripsit</u> ipsam relationem Greco sermone ad omnium eclesiarum personam.

The comparison in Table 8. 1 of the two entries of Marcellinus preserved in the *Annals of Innisfallen*, the oldest of the extant Irish annals manuscripts,[27] suggests that there is a dependent relationship between Bede and the Irish chronicle; in other words one is borrowing from the other. The changes made from the original text of Marcellinus, upon which these entries are based, are identical in both Bede and the *Annals of Innisfallen*, although the

[27] For Marcellinus' use in the *AI*: Grabowski (1984), 10–14, 26–7.

one difference (s.a. 415: *relationem* not Bede's *revelationem*) shows that the Irish chronicle is closer to the original Marcellinus (*relationem*). But, who is copying whom? The relationship between these three annalistic documents becomes even more explicit when we look at how the later part of Marcellinus' chronicle is used in Bede and the *Annals of Tigernach*.

An analytical comparison of the period from 490 (the beginning of *AT*, fragment 3) to 534 (the end of the chronicle of Marcellinus) illustrates the correspondences between the *AT* and the four entries from Marcellinus in Bede for these years (505, 508, 516, 518) in relation to their respective use of Marcellinus. The entries across all three documents may be grouped in two categories, as shown in Table 8. 2a and 8. 2b.

TABLE 8. 2a. *Entries in Marcellinus,* AT, *and Bede*

	Marcellin.	*AT*	Bede, *DTR*
Anastasius as emperor	518	492. 1 (121)	505
Anastasius' death	518	518. 3 (128)	508
Capture of Carthage	534	528. 1 (131)	516
Code of Justinian published	531	531. 2 (131)	519

TABLE 8. 2b. *Entries in Marcellinus and* AT, *but not Bede*

	Marcellin.	AT
Death of Zeno	491	491 (121) ~ *AU* 491 (54)
Gelasius as pope	494	493. 1 (122)
Solar eclipse	497	496. 2 (122) ~ *CS* 493 (33)
Anastasius as pope	498	497. 1 (122); 498. 2 (123)
Pontic earthquake	499	498. 1 (123) ~ *CS* 495 (34); AU 497 (58)
Symmachus as pope	500	499. 1 (123)
Hormisdas as pope	515	512. 3 (127) ~*AClon.* 515 (73)
Dardanian earthquake	518	518. 2 (128) ~ *AClon.* 518 (74)
Justinian as emperor	527	525. 2 (130) ~*AU* 527 (66)

From the textual comparison in Table 8. 2a and 8. 2b it can be noted that: (1) in Bede, for the period from 490 to 534, there is no entry taken from Marcellinus which is not also in the *AT*; (2) on the other hand there are several entries from Marcellinus in this section of the *AT* which are not contained in Bede: two (491, 527) refer to imperial accessions, two (500, 515) refer to papal accessions, and three (497, 499, 518) describe natural phenomena; (3) the order of entries in Bede is identical with that of the Irish annals. Further, comparing the texts directly shows that there is no entry in Bede that is not also virtually verbatim in *AT*, as illustrated in Table 8. 3.

TABLE 8. 3. *Direct comparison of texts of Marcellinus, Bede, and* AT

Marcellin. (*MGH AA* XI)	Bede, *DTR* (CCL 123B)	*AT* (ed. Stokes, 1897)
518. 2 Anastasius imperator subita morte praeventus maior octogenario periit	508 Anastasius qui heresi favens Euticetis catholicos insecutus est, diuino fulmine periit	518 (128) Anastasius imperator subita morte praeuentus maior quia scilicet haeresi Eutichetis fauens catolicos insecutus est divino fulmine percussus periit (~*AU* 518 [64])

Two possible conclusions emerge from the comparison in Table 8. 3: either (1) the Irish chronicle (lying behind the *AI* and the *AT*, as well as *AU*) postdates Bede and used Bede's chronicle as a basis, supplementing it with extra entries direct from Marcellinus;[28] or (2) Bede copied the original Irish chronicle verbatim omitting as he saw fit. On the basis of this analysis it may be concluded (at least provisionally, given the uncertainties surrounding the textual history of the Irish annals) that the latter is the more likely, that is to say, Bede copied the original Irish chronicle verbatim, at least for this part of his work, thereby confirming the suspicion aired by John Morris when comparing earlier sections of Bede with the Irish annals.[29] Consequently, if we had a fuller version of the Irish chronicle for earlier events then we would expect it to closely resemble the earlier sections of Bede, especially where there are correspondences with Marcellinus, and if we had the original Irish chronicle for the period from 534 (end

[28] The only entry in the *AT*, for the period to 534, whose source cannot be traced in Marcellinus, Isidore or the Liber Pontificalis is that of Dionysius (*AT* 531. 2 (131) ~ AU 531 (130); *AClon.* 525 (77)) but there is every possibility that, given the persistent Irish involvement in the paschal question it was independently inserted in the Irish annals at an early date. Certainly Dionysius' works were known in Ireland in the 7th cent.

[29] Morris (1972), 80–93.

of Marcellinus) to its termination then what is extant in Bede would closely resemble it also. Certainly for the period from 534 (end of Marcellinus) to the time of Heraclius (Bede, *DTR* 522–38) there is nothing in Bede which is not also in the *AT*.

In this context it is significant that several of Marcellinus' entries for the period prior to 490 which are preserved in the Irish annals other than *AT*, whose manuscript only begins at 490, are not to be found in Bede either. Marcellinus s.a. 472, for instance, can be found in the preface to the *Annales Cambriae* (p. xxxvi), while *AI* has s.a. 442 (56) and 453 (57); *AU* has Marcellin., s.a. 432 = *AU* 432 (38), 440 = 440. 1 (40); 441 = 441. 1 (40); 448 = 448 (42); 449 = 449 (42); 456 = 456. 1 (44); 457 = 457. 1 (44); 460 = 460 (46); 461 = 461. 1 (46); 465 = 465. 1 (48); 466 = 466. 1 (48); 473 = 473. 1 (50); 481 = 481. 2 (52); 488 = 488. 2 (52). Again, the inference is that the more complete text (i.e. the Irish annals) is the original, the less complete (i.e. Bede) the copy. Since none of these entries are to be found in Bede's *De temporum ratione*, it appears as if he used a chronicle originally constructed as an Irish continuation of Jerome and which he may have obtained from Iona.[30] If so, then the Irish chronicle he used was probably written in the mid- to late seventh century for it to have used Isidore's chronicle completed in 615.

This hypothesis concerning Bede's direct use of the Irish chronicle seems preferable to that of the later Irish annalists themselves supplementing Bede's chronicle with entries from Marcellinus, as well as Isidore and the Liber Pontificalis. In short, as with Bede's computistical work generally, his *De temporum ratione* was derived from previous Irish works. This situation is not surprising since the remainder of Bede's work is so heavily influenced by Irish *computi*.[31] Likewise, Bede's use of AD dating may well come from the Irish chronicle too,[32] especially since there is now some evidence that Dionysius Exiguus' dating system was known in Ireland and possibly used by the early annalists.[33] Further research on the origin and development of the Irish annals will need to take account of the fact that (1) the various extant annals incorporate material from a previous Irish chronicle (probably

---

[30] The strong possibility of this is reinforced by Duncan (1981), 1–42.
[31] O'Croinin (1983*b*), 229–47, cf. Stevenson (1995), 26–7.
[32] Proposed by Morris (1972), 43.
[33] Harrison (1979), 65–75.

linked to the chronicle of Jerome) which used the chronicle of Marcellinus and was compiled (possibly at Iona) in the first half of the seventh century; and (2) Bede appears to have simply copied the basic content of this Irish chronicle in preparing his own Chronicle in 725 rather than use Marcellinus independently.

BEDE

Demonstration of Bede's lack of direct use of Marcellinus in the *De temporum ratione* prompts more careful attention to the other instances of his use of Marcellinus. In his sermon on the beheading of John the Baptist (*In decollatione sancti Iohannis Baptistae*), Bede makes use of material to be found in the chronicle of Marcellinus. Citing unspecified 'ecclesiastical histories' Bede explains that they tell us about the separation of John's body and head, the former being found in Sebaste with the latter being revealed to two monks at Jerusalem who carried it to Emesa where it was concealed but later revealed once more.[34] Although Marcellinus does record this latter discovery he took his information from an earlier popular account, as we have seen (Chapter 6). Bede may intend to include Marcellinus under the 'ecclesiastical histories' but he could also have derived his information from elsewhere at this point. More definite is his commentary on the Gospel of Mark where Bede quotes Marcellinus on the discovery of John's head. Bede points out that the date 'IV Kal. Sept.' celebrates not the date of John's decapitation but the date on which the severed head was revealed at Emesa, the story of which is filled in from the entry of Marcellinus:

Since indeed, as the chronicle of Marcellinus shows, in the time of the emperor Marcian two eastern monks came to worship in Jerusalem . . . from that time in the same city [Emesa] began to be celebrated the beheading of the blessed forerunner [John] on the very day, so we believe, on which his head was found or disinterred. You will find these things written about more extensively in the aforesaid chronicle book.[35]

---

[34] *Hom.* 2. 23, lines 224 ff. (*CCL* 122. 355–6): *in quibus uidelicet historiis hoc quoque reperimus quod caput eius sanctissimum longo post decollationem tempore ab ipso reuelationem sit duobus monchis orientalibus . . .*

[35] *In Marci Evangelium Expositio* 2. 6. 37 (*CCL* 120. 512–13): *Siquidem ut chronica Marcellini comitis testantur tempore Marciani principis duo monachi orientales uenerant adorare in Hierosolimis et loca sancta uidere quibus per reuelationem assistens idem praecursor domini praecepit ut ad Herodis quondam regis habitaculum . . . Ex quo tempore coepit in eadem civitate beati praecursoris decollatio ipso*

Marcellinus' chronicle would here appear to be available to Bede for direct consultation.[36] Bede also draws on Marcellinus in his commentary on the Epistle of James. Commenting on James 3: 7, which points out that although wild beasts have been tamed by man no one has tamed the human tongue which is uncontrollable and full of evil, Bede cites a passage of Pliny (*Nat. Hist.* 8. 25) and from Marcellinus he takes the entry for 496 which runs thus:

India sent as a gift to the emperor Anastasius an elephant, which our poet Plautus calls a Lucanian cow, and two giraffes. (496. 1)

In his need to cite an instance of a tamed wild animal, Bede actually gets Marcellinus wrong here. He says that India sent to the emperor a domesticated tiger, and not an elephant and two giraffes which would have lent less weight to his point:

We read further that count Marcellinus has written that a domesticated tiger (*tigridem mansuefactam*) was sent by India to the emperor Anastasius.[37]

How is this mistake to be explained? It has been suggested that Bede may have confused Marcellinus' entry with other information of Pliny the Elder (*Nat. Hist.* 8. 65) that at the dedication of the theatre of Marcellus a tame tiger was involved. This is an unnecessary association. There is a far simpler solution. Bede has simply confused this with another entry from Marcellinus (s.a. 448.1) which mentions that India did in fact send a domesticated tiger, but to the emperor Theodosius II, not Anastasius.[38] He simply neglected (or was unable) to verify his information.

Taken together these two notices, both mistaken, indicate only a very slight and imperfect knowledge of Marcellinus on the part of Bede and they may cause one to doubt whether, at the time of writing the commentaries, he knew Marcellinus' chronicle at first hand or only through hearsay. If there was a copy in the library

ut arbitramur die quo caput inuentum siue eleuatum est celebrari. De quibus latius in praefato chronicorum libro scriptum repperies.

[36] This passage was misconstrued by Ogilvy (1967, 198) who read *praefatio* for *praefato* (aforesaid) which lead him to the conclusion that 'possibly Bede's text of Marcellinus contained material not found in Migne's'.

[37] *In Epistolas Septem Catholicas. In Iac.* 3. 7 (*CCL* 121. 206): *Legimus item scribente Marcellino comite mansuefactam tigridem ab India Anastasio principi missam.*

[38] s.a. 448. 1: 'The province of India sent a domesticated tiger (*tigrim domitam*) as a gift to the emperor Theodosius.' An alternative possibility is that Bede (or perhaps even his manuscript of Marcellinus) read *pardus* (panther) [or *pardulus*] for *camelopardalas* which would at least represent a greater degree of fierceness in the Indian gift.

at Jarrow he did not utilize it to check his information. Although Bede's biblical commentaries were a significant and integral part of his scholarly work they have been little studied, especially in the context of his other historical treatises. What is becoming clearer, however, is that the commentaries (including those on Mark) were considerably influenced by the Irish exegetical tradition.[39] So it is possible that Bede's citation of Marcellinus in his commentaries on Mark and James came originally from earlier Irish commentaries on Mark and James used by Bede, just as his chronicle (at least to the early seventh century) seems to have been derived from the original 'Irish chronicle'.

It remains then to consider the *Ecclesiastical History* where we find a close correspondence in two places between Bede and Marcellinus, enough to suggest that Marcellinus may have been copied as a source although this must not be automatically assumed (see Table 8. 4). It is clear that in these notices Bede's information derives ultimately from Marcellinus but they must not necessarily be taken to suggest that Bede actually copied Marcellinus himself at first hand. If Bede did in fact have a copy of the chronicle of Marcellinus (if not while he was writing the commentaries then by the time of the *Historia Ecclesiastica*), which there is no good reason to doubt, then he will probably have acquired it from Ireland or perhaps borrowed it from some other English monastery, possibly Canterbury. Overall Bede's use of Marcellinus cannot be said to be either extensive or careful; in fact it may be that he was entirely dependent on Irish documents (commentaries and annals) for his knowledge of the chronicle. If not, then it is very likely that he obtained a copy of the chronicle from Iona where it was obviously well known and used, or at least a copy of a separate extract covering the beheading of John the Baptist which he cites on two separate occasions. Such an extract is preserved in an eleventh-century manuscript in the cathedral Library at Verona under the title *Inventio capitis sancti Iohannis Baptistae ex cronica Marcellini comitis.*[40]

---

[39] Ray (1982), 5–20; Kelly (1986), 65–75 (esp. 67–9).
[40] Mommsen (1894), 56.

TABLE 8. 4. *Showing correspondences between Marcellinus and Bede*

Marcellinus	Bede
445. 1 Bleda rex Hunnorum Attilae fratris sui insidiis interimitur	*HE* 1. 13 eo tempore bellis cum <u>Blaedla et Attila regibus Hunnorum</u>
447.2 ingens bellum et priore maius per Attilam regem nostris inflictum paene totam Europam excisis invasisque civitatibus atque castellis conrasit,	erat occupatus et, quamvis anno ante hunc proximo <u>Blaedla Attilae fratris</u> sui sit <u>interemptus insidiis</u>. Attila tamen ipse adeo intolerabilis reipublicae remansit hostis, ut <u>totam paene</u>
446. 1 His consulibus magna fames Constaninopolim invasit pestisque ilico subsecuta.	<u>Europam excisis invasisque civitatibus et castellis</u> conroderet. Quin et hisdem temporibus <u>fames Constantinopolim</u>
447. 1 ingenti terrae motu per loca varia inminente plurimi urbis augustae muri . . . quinquaginta septem turribus conruerunt . . . plurimis nihilominus civitatibus conlapsis: fames et aerum pestifer odor multa milia hominum iumentorumque delevit.	<u>invasit nec more, pestis secuta est, sed et plurimi eiusdem urbis muri cum LVII turribus conruerunt multis quoque civitatibus conlapsis fames et aerum pestifer odor plura hominum milia iumentorumque delevit.</u>
455. 1 Valentinianus princeps dolo Maximi patricii, cuius etiam fraude Aetius perierat in campo Martio per Optilam et Thraustilam Aetii satellites iam percusso Heraclio spadone truncatus est.	*HE* 1. 21 Nec multo post Valentinianus ab Aetii patricii quem occiderat <u>satellitibus</u> interimitur anno imperii Marciani sexto cum quo simul <u>hesperium concidit regnum.</u>
454. 2 Aetius . . . in palatio trucidatur atque cum ipso Hesperium cecidit regnum nec hactenus valuit relevari.	

ANGLO-SAXON DOCUMENTS

In the period after Bede there are traces of the chronicle of Marcellinus in Anglo-Saxon documents. In the first place there is an Old English martyrology which is only partially complete but its entry covering the death of John the Baptist appears to have depended on Marcellinus' account (s.a. 453). Evidently this was an especially popular section of Marcellinus in Anglo-Saxon Britain for, as noted above, it was used by Bede on more than one occasion. It may be that the Old English martyrology took its information from Bede rather than directly from Marcellinus, or possibly even from the Irish tradition since Irish exegesis influenced the Old English Martyrology just as it had influenced Bede.[41] It has been argued, however, that Marcellinus was used directly by the writer of the martyrology which would be further evidence for the use and circulation of the chronicle in Anglo-Saxon England.[42]

Similarly, in one of the manuscripts of Anglo-Saxon chronicles (*BM Cotton MS. Domitian* A viii) the same section of Marcellinus (s.a. 453) seems to be the ultimate source for an entry on the discovery of the head of John the Baptist. The shape of the *Anglo Saxon Chronicle* has many affinities to the Irish annals. It too is not a single chronicle but a series of different manuscripts, some with continuations of their own. Like the Irish annals, the *Anglo-Saxon Chronicle* has most of its entries in the vernacular but has non-native entries (mainly for the period from the fourth to the sixth century) in Latin and taken from an earlier chronicle or chronicles. So too, for all the manuscripts of both the *Anglo-Saxon Chronicle* and the Irish annals there is a common source for the early part (the Irish annals to *c*.607, the *Anglo-Saxon Chronicle* to 891). In both there is also not always an entry under each year in the early period but only significant dates, and in some manuscripts there are later additions inserted between the lines and in blank spaces. The original West Saxon chronicle used by the later chronicler may have utilized Bede for its entry on the discovery of the head of John the Baptist or, since the entry is not to be found in any of the other Anglo-Saxon chronicle manuscripts covering this period, it may have been added by a later hand.[43] Otherwise there is no indication that Marcellinus was used in the Anglo-Saxon chronicle although it now appears that Isidore, rather than Orosius, was the main source of the chronicle's information for the period before the fifth century.[44] Despite all this uncertainty there are enough traces to indicate that the chronicle of Marcellinus was known in Anglo-Saxon Britain; if not the whole chronicle then at least the account of the discovery of John's head, an account which may have circulated separately.

Connected to the Anglo-Saxon literary tradition is another

---

[41] Cross (1981), 173–92.

[42] Cross (1975), 159.

[43] It appears that at least part of Bede's *HE* (the chronological epitome at 5. 24) was used in the Anglo-Saxon Chronicle (Bately (1986), 233–54).

[44] Bately (1979), 177–94.

work which used the chronicle of Marcellinus, the so-called *Liber Monstrorum* which may itself have been a source of information for *Beowulf*. The *Liber* is a curious and curious work but it is increasingly likely that it was written in Britain sometime in the period from 650 to 750. It is essentially a collection of unlikely and amazing creatures, derived from a wide range of literary sources and catalogued under the headings of monsters, beasts and serpents. It would appear, then, that the writer of the *Liber* had access to a good library such as that at Aldhelm's Malmesbury. Indeed it is possible that Aldhelm himself is the author of the *Liber Monstrorum*.[45] In the second part of the work, that on monsters, the writer utilizes the chronicle of Marcellinus by taking the entry (s.a. 496. 1) which Bede had confused. This author also confuses or misremembers what Marcellinus wrote because he, or his manu-script of Marcellinus, has turned the two giraffes (*duas camelo-pardalas*) and an elephant into a little leopard (*pardulus*) riding on a camel (*in camelo*) and another on an elephant:

And on one occasion the king of India, since they are especially to be found there, sent two little leopards to King Anastasius of Rome on a camel and an elephant which the poet Plautus jokingly named a Lucanian cow.[46]

So the writer of the *Liber Monstrorum*, whoever he was, knew the chronicle at first hand and certainly independently of Bede.[47] It would not be surprising either to discover that his copy of Marcellinus derived from Ireland, directly or indirectly.

OTHER MEDIEVAL TEXTS

The anonymous writer of the *Laterculus Imperatorum* (seventh century) to the time of Justin I may also have used Marcellinus although Mommsen thought it more likely that the *Laterculus* shared a common source with Marcellinus,[48] or perhaps the

---

[45] Details in Lapidge (1982), 162 ff. (suggesting Aldhelm) and Orchard (1995), 86–115. The author of the *Liber Monstrorum* cannot be Virgil of Salzburg (as assumed in Croke (1995), 109).

[46] [Anonymus], *Liber monstrorum de diversis generibus*, 2. 6 (ed. and tr. Orchard (1995), 292–3): *Et Indorum rex, quodam tempore (quia ibi maxime nascuntur) ad regem Romae Anastasium duos pardulos misit in camelo et elephanto, quem Plautus poeta ludens 'Lucam bovem' nominavit.*

[47] The identification of Marcellinus as the source of this section of the *Liber Monstrorum* is not made in the list of sources for individual passages in Orchard (1995), 319.

[48] *MGH AA* 13. 418–19 (introd.) and 419–23 (text).

Laterculus used a source which had itself used Marcellinus or his source. Not long after Bede the chronicle of Marcellinus was used by the writer of the *Gesta Episcoporum Neapolitanarum*. Whether the Neapolitan writer had a complete copy of the chronicle is unknown. At least only a portion of the chronicle was utilized in the *Gesta* and nothing after 453 (discovery of the head of John the Baptist).[49] In later sections where Marcellinus might have been used the author preferred the more recent works of Isidore and Bede. The *Gesta* attests to the availability of the chronicle of Marcellinus in eighth century Italy and this is confirmed by the *Historia Romana* of Paul the Deacon. For the fifth century Paul's narrative account is based on a variety of sources, not all of which can be identified.[50] One of them appears to have been Marcellinus' chronicle. There are just a few correspondences between the chronicle and the *Historia Romana*.[51] Besides Marcellinus, Paul made use of Jordanes' *Romana* (an obviously suitable source) and it is possible that many of the passages indicated as deriving from Marcellinus may actually come from Jordanes who in turn had used Marcellinus, or a source common to both Marcellinus and Jordanes.

The same situation applies with the Chronicle of Freculph, bishop of Fulda (823–51); that is, while he appears to record information from Marcellinus it is just as likely that it comes from Jordanes who is specifically cited.[52] In the case of Hermann of Reichenau (1013–54), lame from birth and so known as 'Hermannus Contractus', his Chronicle from Christ to 1054 also made use of Marcellinus but not, as once thought, from a manuscript which involved the continuation of Marcellinus.[53] Finally, during the later Middle Ages, the chronicle is only referred to very rarely. Lambert, a *canonicus* from St Omer copied it in his *Liber floridus*, written in 1120 and an attempt to match the prophecies of Daniel with the six ages of Augustine. It is plain that he was using the local St Omer manuscript (S) which indicates its presence at the monastery of St Bertin in the early twelfth century. Lastly Marcellinus' chronicle is used in the compilation entitled *De terrae*

[49] *MGH Scriptores Rerum Langobardorum* (ed. G. Waitz), 402–36: *Gesta*, ch. 7 (p. 406) ⟨Marcellin. s.a. 380, 381, 382.2⟩; ch. 8 ⟨Marcellin. s.a. 398, 403⟩; ch. 9 ⟨Marcellin. s.a. 453⟩.

[50] Goffart (1988), 352ff.

[51] *Hist. Rom.* 15. 1 (Marcellin. s.a. 465); 15. 18 (s.a. 491).

[52] 2. 5. 14–21 (*PL* 106. 1245–52).

[53] Mommsen (1894), 43 following Waitz (1857), 38–40.

motu signisque diversis excerpta Marcellino de gestis Francorum, now in Paris.[54]

The use of Marcellinus by later writers, especially by the early Irish chronicles and Bede, throws much light on the manuscript tradition of the chronicle and provides a concrete example of the process of cultural transmission from Antiquity to the Middle Ages. More specifically, it highlights the instrumental role of Irish scholars and copyists in that process. In addition, Bede's citation of information from the chronicle of Marcellinus provides a means of establishing that for the period up to Heraclius (610–41) Bede's chronicle (*De temporum ratione*) relied almost exclusively on an earlier Irish one. The remainder, after the period of Heraclius, is more likely to be his original construction.

Marcellinus' chronicle was a relatively popular work in the Middle Ages because it was recommended by Cassiodorus. Although written in Constantinople the chronicle was soon absorbed into western cultural life because, together with Jerome's chronicle, it told the story of human history up to the sixth century. From Constantinople the chronicle spread and came to be used by later writers in Italy, Britain, and Ireland. Tracing the use of Marcellinus in the Irish annals and in Anglo-Saxon England helps illuminate the interaction between their respective Latin and native literary cultures. Further, and more fundamental, research on the Irish annals and Bede will be required, however, before the issue of the precise relationship between them can be securely resolved. Meanwhile, judging by the way they used Marcellinus, it appears that Bede was more dependent on earlier Irish annals than has usually been conceded.

---

[54] Mommsen (1894), 56.

9
Conclusion: Chronicles and Christian Culture

Like all late antique chronicles, that of Marcellinus was written within a particular social and intellectual context. This study has attempted to define and explicate the different elements which constitute that context: the author's own background and position in life, his native territory of Illyricum, the city and community of Constantinople in which he lived and worked, the nature of his chronicle as typical of its literary genre, the expectations of author and audience, and the way it has been transmitted to the present. Rather than the traditional understanding of the chronicle as being a product of western Latin aristocratic circles in Constantinople,[1] it has emerged that Marcellinus' work is really a Byzantine chronicle — in Latin. As a continuation of Jerome, the format of Marcellinus' chronicle is more akin to Latin chronicles such as that of Prosper. Yet its content, identity, and emphasis have closer affinities with eastern works such as the chronicle of John Malalas. That is, the city whose inhabitants Marcellinus calls the 'Byzantii'[2] (and of whom he was one himself) forms a pivotal focus of the chronicle. The world beyond the city of the Byzantines is described and interpreted from the reference point of the imperial capital. The chronicles of Marcellinus and John Malalas are contemporary and complementary, not mutually exclusive. Both authors were at some time part of the imperial administration, both used official records and public notices, and both subsequently updated their chronicles. There are certainly contrasts between them, not least Malalas' more extensive narrative, but they possess an identifiable common format and model in the chronicle of Eusebius. Many at Constantinople could, and presumably did, read both chronicles. Indeed, Marcellinus and Malalas could read each other's works and perhaps did so.

Instead of the usual depiction of the chronicle of Marcellinus as

---

[1] Represented typically by Momigliano (1955), 249–76, Wes (1967), *passim* and Zecchini (1983), 48–52, 90–1; (1993), 65–90.

[2] Marcellin. s.a. 472. 1, 480. 1, 491. 2, 512. 3.

the product of a man of limited culture and literary ability, a case has been mounted for seeing it as being penned by a literary-minded official of Justinian in the course of a more comprehensive output which included books on topography and chronology. Marcellinus was only typical of his place and time. A native of the Latin-speaking region of the Balkans, he arrived in Constantinople at the turn of the sixth century in the same generation as his fellow-Illyrians Justin, Justinian, and Belisarius. They shared with Marcellinus, and other Illyrian generals and officials in imperial service, a common outlook deriving from the military culture of the Balkan provinces, that is, a preference for strong defences and effective military force, as well as firm doctrinal convictions. Broadly speaking, the Illyrian view of empire involved a commitment to civil order, the rule of law, and orthodoxy of religious doctrine and practice. Like Justinian at least, Marcellinus also brought from Illyricum an education in Latin, and possibly Greek, and he went on to produce a number of Latin works which would have found a ready audience among the Illyrian community at Constantinople (Chapters 1, 2, and 3). In the aftermath of the death of Anastasius in July 518 Marcellinus produced a chronicle continuing that of Jerome down to the present. The chronicle was very much pro-Illyrian, but anti-Anastasian. Evidently, the work won some popularity which probably explains why it was worth updating fifteen years later in order to make it culminate in the recent imperial victory in North Africa. As with all such works, Marcellinus' task was essentially one of selection and copying, but within the overall conceptual approach to the period he intended to cover. He had to set up a chronological framework, using indictions and a consular list; then, operating from a minimum number of documents and his own recollections, he proceeded to fill in entries for each year with the process of selection being guided by his background, the interests and expectations of his audience, and by the nature of his sources of information (Chapters 5 and 6). Accordingly, much of the chronicle has to do with Illyricum and Constantinople.

Marcellinus' chronicle provides a valuable perspective on the invasions of the Balkans in the fifth and early sixth centuries by elucidating the poignant reaction of a local at the destruction and instability generated in his homeland (Chapters 2 and 3). The other significant feature of contemporary culture highlighted by the chronicle is the established ceremonial pattern of public life in Constantinople (Chapter 4). The increasingly codified rhythms and routines of civic life in the imperial capital emerge from the entries in the chronicle where all sorts of contemporary commemorations are recorded. The liturgical year of the 520s, as reflected in the chronicle, is essentially the Byzantine liturgical year canonized in the *synaxarion* and *typicon* of Hagia Sophia in the tenth century, and which set the pattern for the rest of the Byzantine world. Marcellinus enables us to see how much of the Byzantine liturgical calendar and civic ceremonial was already in place by the early sixth century. In actual fact, this liturgical dimension is a significant unifying element in the chronicle. Many of the apparently miscellaneous events recorded by Marcellinus derive their meaning from the fact that they were events which were commemorated in the liturgical calendar of Constantinople in the time of Justinian (Chapter 4). They were familiar to Marcellinus' audience, as part of a shared religious culture and social practice, and it would have been interesting and instructive for them to see precisely when such familiar events originally took place. Other events were significant because they provided a guide to successive imperial reigns, others because of their recent prominence, yet others because of their regional importance. Marcellinus' immediate audience in the 520s and 530s could see from the chronicle that before they were born, or could remember, there occurred a range of events which shaped their present political, religious and social worlds.

Although written in Constantinople for a local audience, the chronicle of Marcellinus was soon circulating in the west, not only in Italy but also in Ireland before too long. Since Marcellinus' chronicle was written in Latin its posterity was to be in the west and, because of its link to Jerome, the chronicle was absorbed into the Irish annals and the chronicle of Bede (Chapter 8). It formed part of the historical framework which was by now an integral element of Christian culture. More importantly, manuscripts of the chronicle were copied and used by the readers of Cassiodorus who had recommended it as an essential part of a monastic library. Much has been made of the Cassiodoran connection. Yet, an emphasis on linking Marcellinus and his perspective to the Italian circles of Cassiodorus has only hindered the understanding of the chronicle as a Byzantine document (Chapter 7). His immediate audience was primarily the Illyrian Byzantines, the community of Illyrian military and imperial officials and refugees living in Constantinople and environs. The chronicle appealed essentially to the two key elements of their identity, namely their region and their religion.

As a distinct mode of Christian discourse, the late antique chronicle is illustrative of wider cultural and literary developments in late antiquity. Traditionally, chronicles have tended to be regarded as an inferior and limited means of presenting the past, but as characteristic of their educationally and culturally debased times. 'We can excuse the brevity of the annalists, but it is much harder to excuse their occasional prolixity,' wrote the Newcastle banker Thomas Hodgkin before singling out Marcellinus: 'When we find one of the best of them devoting only four lines to the capture of Rome by Alaric, and fifty-four to an idle legend about the discovery at Emesa of the head of John the Baptist, it is difficult not to grumble at the want of appreciation of the relative importance of things which must have existed in the mind of the writer, though he was no monkish recluse but a layman and a governor of a province [*sic*!].'[3] Marcellinus can be chided not only for what he reports but also for what he does not report: 'his silence is sometimes interesting, as showing of what slight account transactions which we perceive to have been of incalculable importance to Europe appeared to a Byzantine official',[4] although it may be conceded that on occasion Marcellinus 'rises above his usual level as a mere chronicler' who produced 'a faded chronicle'.[5] Holder-Egger too stressed Marcellinus' lack of any sense of historical significance since he failed in 452 to report Attila's march into Gaul but rather recorded the fall of three meteorites in Thrace, while from this perspective of nineteenth-century German scholarship his entry on the famous physician Jacob in 462 'is unbecoming a continuation of the Chronicle of Jerome'.[6]

Such an approach, and the judgements which arise from it, merely reflect the preconceptions and prejudices of modern writers who are no less imprisoned in their own perspectives than Marcellinus was in his. Further, the history of writing about the past has itself been embedded in an explanatory paradigm in which 'elite' culture is opposed to 'popular' culture, and artificial

---

[3] Hodgkin (1892*b*), 301.   [4] Hodgkin (1892*a*), 708–9.
[5] Hodgkin (1892*b*), 196.   [6] Holder-Egger (1877), 107.

contrasts are drawn between 'classical' and 'Christian' texts. When applied to Christian history writing, the chronicle—an original Christian genre—is taken to be the preserve of the small-minded popular piety of the Christian lower classes, 'Trivial-literatur' in fact.[7] Christianity can no longer be described in such a manner, however. Casting the chronicle in historiographical and cultural terms as a genre of decline is simply misguided. Rather, the chronicle is an integral component of the Christian world-view and Christian scholarship, developed over a long period and ultimately defined by Cassiodorus and Isidore.[8] In late antique culture describing aspects or periods of the past was no longer merely a rhetorical exercise disconnected from present reality. By now the very meaning of one's own life and destiny, not to mention that of the state and society, was bound up with a particular interpretation of the past and the link between past, present, and future. The Christian world chronicle, of which that of Marcellinus formed a part, had become the textual vehicle for laying out the course and meaning of history for all Christians irrespective of social rank, education, and literary culture.

The chronicle should therefore not be judged by what *we* think important, nor devalued because it fails to correspond with *our* received version of the story it tells. Such depreciation has tended to be the fate of chronicle writing in histories of historiography. In the context of late antique life chronicles recorded the most important events in people's experience. They were considered important by the educated Romans (or in Marcellinus' case, 'Byzantines') who read them and found them useful. Moreover, they were the sorts of notices one expected to find in a chronicle. They reflected a style and shape in the past, a function more important to their audience than the imputed modern one of pre-serving knowledge of specifically definable events from previous decades or centuries. So too, since modern students expect dates always to denote events they are apt to be troubled by a chronicle's mere listing of years, sometimes for extensive periods, with no events attached. Such tracts of 'empty' years were no problem for the chronicle's original audience because by themselves these years marked the extent and continuity of God's time.

The late antique chronicle represents a pattern of content

---

[7] Hunger (1978), 237ff.   [8] Cf. Markus (1991), 87–135.

defined originally by Eusebius and continued by Jerome, then followed explicitly by Marcellinus. By the sixth century it had come to be what was expected of a chronicle and the pattern was therefore carried on in turn by the Continuator (Chapter 7). In other words, the chronicle is not a miscellaneous collection of data but a stylized and coherent document. The chronicle of Marcellinus was not designed as a free-standing separate entity. Instead it formed an inseparable part of universal history being linked to Jerome's chronicle as a continuation. That is how it was preserved in the Oxford manuscript, for example, where we find Eusebius/Jerome–Marcellinus–Continuator all bound into a single entity, telling a single continuous story.

The literary and cultural function of a chronicle such as that of Marcellinus was to exemplify historical continuity, to demonstrate how history unfolds the plan of Divine Providence, and to identify the divine epiphany or judgement in each natural and human disaster: the punishment of usurpers and heretics, the triumph of the orthodox, the growth of the theological canon. Some chronicles continued to fill an important chronological function as well, in the way that the chronicle of Eusebius had done originally. Marcellinus' chronicle, however, does not provide any indication of millennial concerns, in contrast with those of John Malalas and later Byzantine and Latin chroniclers such as Isidore and Bede.

Each chronicle is first and foremost a narrative with a clear and recognizable plot. The late antique chronicle carries the story of universal history from creation down to the present, thereby establishing the link which ties together the present, past, and future (under God's providence). Moreover, the chronicle demonstrates where the Roman empire belongs in universal history and how the non-Roman nations were integrated into this political entity. Standing at the centre, symbolizing this very continuity, was the church whose doctrinal integrity and unity had to be guarded and promoted. Marcellinus' chronicle achieves this by its explicit support for the orthodox emperors Theodosius II and Marcian and by his notices on Gregory Nazianzen, Jerome, John Chrysostom, and the church councils. When set against the background of his contemporaries in Constantinople (Procopius, Jordanes, John Malalas) it can be seen how chronicles such as that of Marcellinus merely reflect the way the traditionally classical elements of the legendary and mythical have been brought into the mainstream of culture.[9]

Recording and understanding the past were important for the Christian, since Christianity was essentially an historical religion. Central to its interpretation and practice were the formation and transmission of historical texts, as well as pilgrimage to the historical location of Christ's life. The Bible was the cornerstone of Christian rhetoric and history and, as a Christian genre, the chronicle functioned as an ancillary to the Bible and as the chronological key to it. Christians learned their history from the Bible, from sermons, and from the liturgy, as well as from the artistic representations of past people and events which surrounded them in their churches and on their streets. In particular, the liturgy created and reinforced a view of how history was made and its course to the present. Much liturgy was historical re-enactment which means that the present rhythms of Christian life reflect a continuing interactive dialogue between past and present.[10]

Absolute chronology was a major concern of Christians, in their texts and in their lives. Time was God's to dispense. Time had a direction and overall structure so that chronology became important in itself, especially the organization, pattern, and meaning of time in God's salvific plan. In copying a Christian chronicle text one learnt about the past and in the act of composing a chronicle one made historical sense of the fragmented present. Marcellinus' chronicle would therefore have made sense of much of his audience's public life. Its entries would evoke seeing the procession, hearing and mouthing the words of the liturgy; or being present in a building of traditional importance and meaning. This is the context and the perspective in which chronicles need to be approached and understood, rather than being subjected to an analysis of style and substance according to modern positivist criteria.[11]

The chronicle of Marcellinus, on the few occasions where it has attracted scholarly opinion, has been commended as a 'very well-informed source',[12] whose statements for the reigns of Anastasius,

---

[9] Cameron, Averil (1991), 203 and (1993), 137.
[10] Cameron, Averil (1991), 79, 109 ff.
[11] Cf. Spiegel (1997), 98 and 177.
[12] Vasiliev (1950), 19.

Justin, and Justinian 'always provokingly brief—have a very high value',[13] and as 'executed with care'.[14] Such opinions are themselves the product of an approach to chronicles which evaluates them primarily as sources of 'evidence'. On this view, to cite only recent examples, Marcellinus ranks highly because he is judged to be generally accurate and the chronicle's worth then becomes attributable to the vagaries of posterity. That is to say, it preserves 'data not known from other sources',[15] or that it 'can on occasion help to compensate for the failure of other sources to date events explicitly',[16] or that Marcellinus 'was Justinian's man and uncritical, but he transmits some valuable information'.[17] Although partly concerned with the historical value and validity of the chronicle, this study has attempted to approach it more as an historiographical text deriving from a specific milieu, conditioned by the expectations of its audience as well as the culture and identity of its author, and shaped by a coherent view of the past deriving from the author's Christian culture and outlook. To put it in someone else's words, this study was designed 'to trace the connecting lines between the historian and his book and the world he watched and cared about'.[18]

This approach to late antique literature opens up the broader question of the language and culture of the chroniclers and suggests that the traditional definition of chronicles as being 'low style', as opposed to the 'high style' of more classical and rhetorical historians, is quite inadequate. Instead, the language of the chronicle should be seen as a reflection of the chronicle's purpose and nature, rather than the literary culture of its audience and its author. The essentially religious, rather than rhetorical, purpose of the chronicle dictated its simple, straightforward style. Indeed, a chronicle did not require its own special mode of discourse, rather it involved the same paratactic style of other contemporary genres. Nor is the content of the chronicle to be taken as a determinant of culture or audience; instead it is dictated by the mixed constraints of genre, tradition, and expectation.

For the authors concerned, a chronicle was one of many different kinds of work: Eusebius and Jerome, Prosper and Cassiodorus, Isidore and Bede all produced chronicles as part of a

---

[13] Bury (1898), 524.
[14] Schanz, Hosius, and Krüger (1920), 111.
[15] Moorhead (1994), 3.
[16] Greatrex (1998), 67.
[17] Evans, J. A. S. (1996), 7.
[18] Partner (1977), 6, cf. Spiegel (1997), 110.

comprehensive and sophisticated literary output. The same applies to Marcellinus who wrote other volumes on times and places and on Constantinople and Jerusalem, works now lost but whose character and contents may be inferred (Chapter 1). Who read chronicles such as that of Marcellinus and had them copied is a more difficult question. Jerome was being copied in late fourth-century Rome and Gaul, as well as at Constantinople in the early sixth century for the sons of a high imperial official. Perhaps the sons of imperial officials in the reign of Justin and Justinian were being introduced to the chronicle of Marcellinus as the local Byzantine continuation of Jerome.

That we are still able to read the chronicle, and in a manuscript written just a generation or two after its composition, is attributable to Cassiodorus. His positive endorsement ensured the chronicle's multiplication throughout the monastic libraries of western Europe. Marcellinus' chronicle remains an enlightening relic of the historiographical culture of Justinian's era, at least from its inception in 518 to its consolidation in 534.

BIBLIOGRAPHY

ADLER, W. (1989). *Time Immemorial: Archaic history and its sources in Christian Chronography from Julius Africanus to George Syncellus* (Washington, DC).
——(1992). 'Eusebius' *Chronicle* and its Legacy', in H. Attridge and G. Hata (eds.), *Eusebius, Christianity and Judaism* (Leiden), 467–91.
AFINOGENOV, A. (1992). 'Some Observations on Genres of Byzantine History', *Byzantion* 62: 13–33.
AMORY, P. (1997). *People and Identity in Ostrogothic Italy, 489–554* (Cambridge).
ANTONOPOULOS, P. (1985). 'Petrus Patricius. Some Aspects in his Life and Career', in V. Vavrinek (ed.), *From Late Antiquity to Early Byzantium* (Prague), 49–53.
ARMSTRONG, G. (1969). 'Fifth and Sixth Century Church Buildings in the Holy Land', *Greek Orthodox Theological Review* 14: 17–30.
——(1976). 'Imperial Church Building and Church–State Relations, AD 313–363', *Church History* 36: 17–30.
AVIGAD, N. (1977). 'A Building Inscription of the Emperor Justinian and the Nea in Jerusalem', *Israel Exploration Journal* 27: 145–51.
BALDOVIN, J. (1987). *The Urban Character of Christian Worship* (Rome).
BALDWIN, B. (1991). 'Marcellinus Comes', in *Oxford Dictionary of Byzantium*, 2: 1296.
BARNES, H. E. (1962). *A History of Historical Writing* (New York).
BARNISH, S. J. B. (1984). 'The Genesis and Completion of Cassiodorus' *Gothic History*', *Latomus* 43: 336–61.
——(1989). 'The Work of Cassiodorus after His Conversion', *Latomus* 48: 157–87.
BARTONKOVÁ, D. (1967). 'Marcellinus Comes and Jordanes's Romana', *Sbornik Praci Filos.Fak. Brnenske University* E 12: 185–94.
BATELY, J. M. (1979). 'World History in the Anglo-Saxon Chronicle', *Anglo-Saxon England* 8: 177–94.
——(1986). 'Bede and the Anglo-Saxon Chronicle', in Szarmach (1986), 233–54.
BAUER, A., and STRZYGOWSKI, J. (1906). *Eine Alexandrinische Weltchronik* (Denkschrift der Kaiserlichen Akad. der. Wiss. zu Wien, Phil-Hist.Kl.51).
BAUR, C. (1907). *St Jean Chrysostome et ses oeuvres dans l'histoire littéraire* (Paris).
——(1958). *John Chrysostom and His Times* (London).
BAYNES, N. H. (1925). *The Byzantine Empire* (London).
BECK, H.-G. (1965a). 'Konstantinopel. Zur Sozialgeschichte einer früh-

mittelalterlichen Hauptstadt', *Byzantinische Zeitschrift* 58: 11–45 (repr. in
H.-G. Beck, *Ideen und Realitäten in Byzanz* [London 1972]).

——(1965*b*). 'Zur byzantinischen "Mönchschronik"', *Speculum Historiale*,
ed. C. Bauer *et al.* (Freiburg), 188–97.

——(1966). *Senat und Volk von Konstantinopel: Probleme der byzantinischen
Verfassungsgeschichte* (Bayer Akad.der Wiss., Phil.-hist.Kl. Sitzungsberichte, 6; Munich).

——(1973*a*). 'Grossstadt-Probleme: Konstantinopel vom 4–6 Jahr-
hundert', in Beck (1973*b*), 3–19.

——(1973*b*). *Studien zur Frühgeschichte Konstantinopels* (Munich).

BERKHOFER, R. (1995). *Beyond the Great Story* (Cambridge, Mass.).

BIELER, L. (1963). *Ireland, Harbinger of the Middle Ages* (London).

BIERNACKA-LUBANSKA, M. (1982). *The Roman and Early Byzantine Fortifica-
tions of Lower Moesia and Northern Thrace* (Oxford).

BISCHOFF, B., and KOEHLER, W. (1939). 'Eine illustrierte Ausgabe der
spätantiken Ravennater Annalen', *Medieval Studies in Memory of A.
Kingsley Porter*, ed. W. Koehler (Cambridge), 125–38.

BLOCKLEY, R. (1992). *East Roman Foreign Policy* (Leeds).

BREISACH, E. (1983). *Historiography Ancient, Medieval and Modern* (Chicago).

——(1985) (ed.), *Classical Rhetoric and Medieval Historiography* (Kalamazoo).

BROOKS, E. W. (1893). 'The Emperor Zenon and the Isaurians', *English
Historical Review* 8: 209–38.

BROWN, P. (1980). *The Cult of the Saints* (Chicago).

BROWNING, R. (1974). *Byzantium and Bulgaria* (London).

——(1980). *The Byzantine Empire* (New York).

BUCHER, G. S. (1987). 'The Annales Maximi in the light of Roman
methods of keeping records', *American Journal of Ancient History* 12: 2–61.

BURGESS, R. (1988). 'A New Reading for Hydatius *Chronicle* 177 and the
Defeat of the Huns in Italy', *Phoenix* 42: 357–63.

——(1990*a*). 'The Dark Ages Return to Fifth-Century Britain: the
"Restored" Gallic Chronicle Exploded', *Britannia* 21: 185–95.

——(1990*b*). 'History vs. Historiography in Late Antiquity', *Ancient
History Bulletin* 4: 116–24.

——(1993*a*). *The* Chronicle *of Hydatius and the* Consularia Constantinopolitana (Oxford).

——(1993*b*). '*Principes cum tyrannis*: Two Studies on the *Kaisergeschichte* and
its Tradition', *Classical Quarterly* 43: 491–500.

——(1995). 'Jerome and the *Kaisergeschichte*', *Historia* 44: 349–69.

——(1997). 'The Dates and Editions of Eusebius' *Chronici Canones* and
Historia Ecclesiastica', *Journal of Theological Studies* 48: 471–504.

BURNS, T. S. (1984). *A History of the Ostrogoths* (Bloomington, Ind.).

——(1994). *Barbarians at the Gates of Rome* (Bloomington, Ind.).

BURY, J. B. (1897). 'The Nika Riot', *Journal of Hellenic Studies* 17: 92–119.

Bury, J. B. (1898). 'Appendix' to E. Gibbon, *A History of the Decline and Fall of the Roman Empire*, vol. 4 (London).

——(1923a). *A History of the Later Roman Empire*, 1 (London).

——(1923b). *A History of the Later Roman Empire*, 2 (London).

Callinicos, A. (1995). *Theories and Narratives* (Cambridge).

Cameron, Alan (1970). *Claudian* (Oxford).

——(1973). *Porphyrius the Charioteer* (Oxford).

——(1976). *Circus Factions* (Oxford).

——(1978). 'The House of Anastasius', *Greek, Roman and Byzantine Studies*, 19: 259–76.

——(1982). 'The Empress and the Poet: Paganism and Politics at the court of Theodosius II', *Yale Classical Studies* 27: 212–91.

——(1987). 'Earthquake 400', *Chiron* 17: 343–60.

Cameron, Averil (1976). *Corippus: In laudem Iustini Augusti minoris* (London).

——(1979). 'Images of Authority: Elites and Icons in Late Sixth Century Byzantium', *Past and Present* 84: 3–35 (repr. in Cameron, Averil, *Continuity and Change in Sixth-Century Byzantium* (London 1981)).

——(1985). *Procopius* (Berkeley and Los Angeles).

——(1987). 'The construction of court ritual: the Byzantine *Book of Ceremonies*', in D. Cannadine and S. Price (eds.), *Rituals of Royalty Power and Ceremonial in Traditional Societies* (Cambridge), 106–36.

——(1989). *History as Text. The Writing of Ancient History* (London).

——(1991). *Christianity and the Rhetoric of Empire* (Berkeley).

——(1993). *The Mediterranean World in Late Antiquity AD 395–600* (London).

——(1998). 'The Perception of Crisis', in *Morphologie sociali e culturali in Europa fra tarda antichità e alto medioevo (Settimane di Studio del Centro italiano di studi sull'alto Medioevo, 45)* (Spoleto), 9–31.

—— and Herrin, J. (1984). *Constantinople in the Early Eighth Century:* The Parastaseis Syntomoi Chronikai (Leiden).

——and Conrad, L. I. (1992). *The Byzantine and Early Islamic Near East, I: Problems in the Literary Source Material* (Princeton).

Capizzi, C. (1969). *L'imperatore Anastasio* (Rome).

Carr, D. (1986). *Time, Narrative, and History* (Bloomington, Ind.).

Casson, S., and Talbot Rice, D. (1929). *Second Report upon the excavations carried out in and near the hippodrome of Constantinople in 1928* (London).

Charanis, P. (1966). 'Observations on the Demography of the Byzantine Empire', *Proceedings of the 13th International Congress of Byzantine Studies* (Oxford), 445–63.

——(1974). *Church and State in the Later Roman Empire: The Religious Policy of Anastasius the First 491–518*, 2nd edn. (Thessalonike).

Bibliography

CHASSIGNET, M. (1996). *L'annalistique romaine: les Annales des Pontifes et l'annalistique* (Paris).

CHITTY, D. (1966). *The Desert a City* (London).

CLARKE, G., CROKE, B., MORTLEY, R., and NOBBS, A. (1990). *Reading the Past in Late Antiquity* (Canberra).

CLAUSS, M. (1980). *Der magister officiorum in der Spätantike* (Munich).

COLLINGWOOD, R. G. (1939). *The Idea of History* (Oxford).

CONRAD, L. I. (1990). 'Theophanes and the Arabic Historical Tradition: Some Indications of Intercultural Transmission', *Byzantinische Forschungen* 15: 1–44.

——(1992). 'The Conquest of Arwad: A source-Critical Study in the Historiography of the Early Medieval Near East', in Cameron, Averil and Conrad (1992), 317–401.

COOK, A. (1988). *History and Writing* (Cambridge).

COURCELLE, P. (1954). 'De la "Regula Magistri" au corpus vivarien des chroniques', *Revue des études anciennes* 56: 425–8.

——(1969). *Late Latin Writers and their Greek Sources* (Cambridge, Mass. 1969).

COURTOIS, C. (1955). *Les Vandales et l'Afrique* (Paris).

CROCE, B. (1921). *History. Its Theory and Practice* (New York).

CROKE, B. (1977). 'Evidence for the Hun Invasion of Thrace in A.D. 422', *Greek, Roman and Byzantine Studies* 18: 347–67 (repr. in Croke 1992).

——(1978a). 'Hormisdas and the Late Roman Walls of Thessalonika', *Greek, Roman and Byzantine Studies* 19: 251–8 (repr. in Croke 1992).

——(1978b). 'The Date and Circumstances of Marcian's Decease', *Byzantion* 48: 5–9 (repr. in Croke 1992).

——(1980). 'Justinian's Bulgar Victory Celebration', *Byzantinoslavica* 41: 188–95 (repr. in Croke 1992).

——(1981a). 'Anatolius and Nomus: Envoys to Attila', *Byzantinoslavica* 42: 159–70 (repr. in Croke 1992).

——(1981b). 'Two Early Byzantine Earthquakes and their Liturgical Commemoration', *Byzantion* 51, 112–47 (repr. in Croke 1992).

——(1981c). 'Thessalonika's Early Byzantine Palaces', *Byzantion* 51: 475–83 (repr. in Croke 1992).

——(1982a). 'Mundo the Gepid. From Freebooter to Roman General', *Chiron* 12: 125–35 (repr. in Croke 1992).

——(1982b). 'The Misunderstanding of Cassiodorus *Institutiones* I.17.2', *Classical Quarterly* 32: 225–6.

——(1982c). 'The Originality of Eusebius' Chronicle', *American Journal of Philology* 103: 195–200 (repr. in Croke 1992).

——(1982d). 'The Date of the Anastasian Long Wall in Thrace', *Greek, Roman and Byzantine Studies* 20: 59–78 (repr. in Croke 1992).

——(1983a). 'A.D. 476 the Manufacture of a Turning Point', *Chiron* 13: 81–119 (repr. in Croke 1992).

CROKE, B. (1983*b*). 'Basiliscus the Boy-Emperor', *Greek, Roman and Byzantine Studies* 24: 81–91 (repr. in Croke 1992).

——(1983*c*). 'The Origins and Development of the Christian World Chronicle', in Croke and Emmett (1993*b*), 116–31 (repr. in Croke 1992).

——(1983*d*). 'The Context and Date of Priscus Fragment 6', *Classical Philology* 78: 297–308 (repr. in Croke 1992).

——(1984*a*). 'Dating Theodoret's *Church History* and *Commentary on the Psalms*', *Byzantion* 54: 59–74 (repr. in Croke 1992).

——(1984*b*). 'Marcellinus on Dara: A fragment of his lost *de temporum qualitatibus et positionibus locorum*', *Phoenix* 38: 77–88.

——(1987). 'Cassiodorus and the *Getica* of Jordanes', *Classical Philology* 82: 117–34 (repr. in Croke 1992).

——(1990*a*). Sections in Jeffreys (1990), 203–5.

——(1990*b*). 'Byzantine Chronicle Writing 1: The Early Development of Byzantine chronicles', in Jeffreys (1990), 27–38.

——(1990*c*). 'Theodor Mommsen and the Later Roman Empire', *Chiron* 20: 159–89.

——(1990*d*). 'City Chronicles of Late Antiquity', in Clarke *et al.* (1990), 165–203 (repr. in Croke 1992).

——(1990*e*). 'Malalas, The Man and his Work', in Jeffreys (1990), 1–25.

——(1991). 'Mommsen in Oxford', *Liverpool Classical Monthly* 16: 50–7.

——(1992). *Christian Chronicles and Byzantine History, 5th–6th Centuries* (London).

——(1995). *The Chronicle of Marcellinus: Translation and Commentary* (Sydney).

——(forthcoming *a*). 'Chronicles and Annals in Late Antiquity'.

——(forthcoming *b*). 'Latin Historiography and the Barbarian Kingdoms: Excerpta Valesiana, Cassiodorus, Jordanes, Gildas and Gregory of Tours', in G. Marasco (ed.), *The Later Greek and Roman Historiography: Fourth to Sixth Century AD* (Leiden).

——(forthcoming *c*). 'Marinus the Syrian's family: A rediscovered poem and letter'.

——and EMMETT, A. (1983*a*). 'Historiography in Late Antiquity: An Overview', in Croke and Emmett (1983*b*): 1–12.

——and EMMETT, A. (eds.) (1983*b*). *History and Historians in Late Antiquity* (Sydney and Oxford).

——and CROW, J. (1983). 'Procopius and Dara', *Journal of Roman Studies* 73: 143–59 (repr. in Croke 1992).

CROSS, J. E. (1975). 'Blickling Homily XIV and the Old English Martyrology on John the Baptist', *Anglia* 93: 145–160.

——(1981). 'The Influence of Irish Texts and Traditions on the OE Martyrology', *Proceedings of the Royal Irish Academy* 81 C: 173–92.

CROW, J. (1995). 'The Long Walls of Thrace', in Mango and Dagron (1995), 109–24.

CROW, J., and RICCI, A. (1997). 'Investigating the Hinterland of Constantinople: Interim Report on the Anastasian Long Wall', *Journal of Roman Archaeology* 10: 235–62.

DAGRON, G. (1969). 'Aux origines de la civilisation byzantine: langue de culture et langue d'état', *Revue Historique* 489: 29–76.

—— (1974). *Naissance d'une capitale* (Paris).

—— (1977). 'Le Christianisme dans la ville byzantine', *Dumbarton Oaks Papers* 31: 1–25.

DANTO, A. (1965). *Analytical Philosophy of History* (Cambridge).

DAVIS, R. (1989). *The Book of Pontiffs (Liber Pontificalis)* (Liverpool).

DEKKERS, E. (1961). *Clavis Patrorum Latinorum*, 2nd edn. (Louvain).

DEMANGEL, R. (1945). *Contribution à la topographie de l'Hebdomon* (Paris).

DIHLE, A. (1994). *Greek and Latin Literature of the Roman Empire* (London).

DILL, S. (1899). *Roman Society in the Last Century of the Western Empire* (London).

DOWNEY, G. (1955). 'Earthquakes at Constantinople and Vicinity, A.D. 324–1454', *Speculum* 30: 596–600.

DUCHESNE, L. (1886). *Le Liber Pontificalis, Texte, introduction et commentaire*, 1 (Paris).

DUNCAN, A. A. M. (1981). 'Bede, Iona and the Picts', in R. H. C. Davis, and J. M. Wallace-Hadrill (eds.), *The Writing of History in the Middle Ages* (Oxford), 1–42.

EBERT, A. (1889). *Allgemeine Geschichte des Literatur des Mittelalters im Abendlande* (Leipzig).

ENSSLIN, W. (1948). *Des Symmachus Historia Romana als Quelle für Jordanes*, Sitzungsberichte der Bayer. Akad. der Wiss., Phil-Hist., Abteilung, 3 (Munich).

EVANS, J. A. S. (1996). *The Age of Justinian* (London).

EVANS, R. J. (1997). *In Defence of History* (London).

FAVROD, J. (1990). 'Les Sources et la chronologie de Marius d'Avenches', *Francia* 17: 1–20.

—— (1993). *La Chronique de Marius d'Avenches (455–581)* (Lausanne).

FENSTER, E. (1968). *Laudes Constantinopolitanae* (Munich).

FORNARA, C. W. (1983). *The Nature of History in Ancient Greece and Rome* (Berkeley, Los Angeles, and London).

FOTHERINGHAM, J. K. (1905). *The Bodleian Manuscript of Jerome's version of the Chronicle of Eusebius* (Oxford).

FREUND, A. (1882). *Beiträge zur antiochenischen und zur constantinopolitanischen Stadtchronik* (Diss: Jena).

FRIER, B. (1979). *Libri Annales Pontificum Maximorum: The Origins of the Annalistic Tradition* (Rome).

FRITZ, W. (1968). 'Theodor Mommsen, Ludwig Traube und Karl Strecker als Mitarbeiter der Monumenta Germaniae Historica', *Das Altertum* 14: 242.

GEPPERT, F. (1898). *Die Quellen des Kirchenhistorikers Socrates Scholasticus* (Leipzig).

GOFFART, W. (1963). 'The Fredegar Problem Reconsidered', *Speculum* 38: 206–41 (repr. in Goffart 1989, 319–54).

—— (1988). *The Narrators of Barbarian History* (Princeton).

—— (1989). *Rome's Fall and After* (London).

GOLD, R. (1958). 'The Mosaic Map of Madeba', *Biblical Archaeologist* 21: 50–71.

GORCE, D. (1962). *Vie de Sainte Mélanie* (Paris).

GORTEMAN, C. (1956). 'Un fragment de Chronique Mondiale (P.Copte Bala'izah 55)', *Chronique d'Egypte* 62: 385–402.

GRABOWSKI, K. (1984). 'The Annals of Innisfallen, A.D. 431–1092: Sources, Structure and History', in K. Grabowski, and D. Dumville, *Chronicles and Annals of Medieval Ireland and Wales* (Woodbridge), 10–27.

GRAFTON, A. (1993). *Joseph Scaliger: A Study in the History of Classical Scholarship*, 2 (Oxford).

GRANSDEN, A. (1974). *Historical Writing in England c.550–1307* (London).

GRANT, M. (1976). *The Fall of the Roman Empire. A Reappraisal* (Badnor, repr. London).

GRATTAROLA, P. (1989). 'Il terremoto del 396 e il popolo cristiano di Constantinopoli', in M. Sordi (ed.), *Fenomeni naturali e avvenimenti storici nell'antichità* (Contributi dell'Istituto di storia antica 15; Milan), 237–49.

GREATREX, G. (1993). 'The Two Fifth-Century Wars Between Rome and Persia', *Florilegium* 12: 1–14.

—— (1996). 'Flavius Hypatius, *quem vidit validum Parthus sensitque timendum*. An Investigation of his Career', *Byzantion* 66: 120–42.

—— (1997). 'The Nika riot: a reassessment', *Journal of Hellenic Studies* 117: 60–86.

—— (1998). *Rome and Persia at War, 502–532* (Leeds).

GREEN, R. P. H. (1991). *The Works of Ausonius* (Oxford).

GREENSLADE, S. L. (1945). 'The Illyrian Church and the Vicariate of Thessalonika 378–95', *Journal of Theological Studies* 46: 17–24.

GREGORY, T. E. (1982). *Vox Populi* (Columbus).

GUENÉE, B. (1973). 'Histoires, Annales, Chroniques. Essai sur les genres historiques au Moyen Age', *Annales ESC* 28: 997–1016.

—— (1976/7). 'Temps de l'histoire et temps de la mémoire au moyen-âge', *Annuaire-Bulletin de la Société de l'Histoire de France 1976/7*: 25–8.

—— (1977). 'L'Historien par les mots', in *Le métier d'historien au moyen-âge* (Paris), 1–17 (= *Politique et histoire au moyen-âge* (Paris 1981), 221–38).

—— (1980). *Histoire et Culture historique dans l'Occident médiéval* (Paris).

—— (1984). 'Histoire et Chronique. Nouvelles réflexions sur les genres historiques au moyen âge', in D. Poirion (ed.), *La Chronique et l'histoire au moyen-âge* (Paris 1984), 3–12.

GUILLAND, R. (1969). *Études de topographie de Constantinople byzantine*, 2 vols. (Berlin and Amsterdam).

GUSSO, M. (1991). 'A proposito dell'uso di *interrex* nel *Chronicon* di Marcellinus comes', *Critica Storica* 28: 133–52.

—— (1995). 'Contributi allo studio della composizione e delle fonti del Chronicon di Marcellinus Comes', *Studia et Documenta Historiae et Iuris* 61: 557–622.

—— (1996). *Index Marcellinianus: An index to the* Chronicon *of Marcellinus Comes* (Hildesheim and New York).

—— (1997). 'Il Chronicon di Marcellinus Comes: a proposito di un libro recente', *Cassiodorus* 3: 273–89.

HAMMOND, N. G. L. (1967). *Epirus* (Oxford).

—— (1972). *A History of Macedonia* (Oxford).

HARDY, E. R. (1890). 'The Bodleian MS of Jerome's Eusebian Chronicle', *Journal of Philology* 18: 277–87.

HARRIES, J. (1994). *Sidonius Apollinaris and the Fall of Rome* (Oxford).

HARRISON, K. (1979). 'Luni-Solar Cycles: Their Accuracy and some types of usage', in King, and Stevens (1979), 65–75.

HARVEY, S. A. (1990). *Asceticism and Society in Crisis. John of Ephesus and the Lives of the Eastern Saints* (Berkeley and Los Angeles).

HAY, D. (1977). *Annalists and Historians* (London).

HEATHER, P. J. (1989). 'Cassiodorus and the Rise of the Amals: Genealogy and the Goths under Hun Domination', *Journal of Roman Studies* 79: 103–28.

—— (1991). *Goths and Romans. 332–489* (Oxford).

—— (1993). 'The Historical Culture of Ostrogothic Italy', in *Atti del XIII Congresso internazionale di studi sull'Alto Medioevo* (Spoleto), 317–53.

—— (1995). 'The Huns and the End of the Roman Empire in Western Europe', *English Historical Review* 110: 4–41.

—— (1996). *The Goths* (Oxford).

HENDY, M. F. (1985). *Studies in the Byzantine Monetary Economy c.300–1450* (Cambridge).

HERRIN, J. (1987). *The Formation of Christendom* (Princeton).

HILLGARTH, J. (1961). 'The East, Visigothic Spain and the Irish', *Studia Patristica* 4: 444–5.

—— (1962). 'Visigothic Spain and Early Christian Ireland', *Proceedings of the Royal Irish Academy* 62: 167–94.

—— (1966). 'Coins and Chronicles: Propaganda in Sixth-Century Spain and the Byzantine Background', *Historia* 15: 483–508.

HILLGARTH, J. (1970). 'Historiography in Visigothic Spain', in *La storiografia altomedievale* (Settimane di Studio; Spoleto), 261–352.

—— (1984). 'Ireland and Spain in the Seventh Century', *Peritia* 3: 1–16.

HODDINOTT, R. F. (1975). Bulgaria in Antiquity (New York).

HODGKIN, T. (1892*a*). *Italy and her Invaders*, 1, 2nd edn. (Oxford).

—— (1892*b*). *Italy and her Invaders*, 2, 2nd edn. (Oxford).

—— (1896). *Italy and her Invaders*, 4, 2nd edn. (Oxford).

HOLDER-EGGER, O. (1875). *Über die Weltchronik des sogennanten Severus Sulpitius und die südgallische Annalen des fünften Jahrhunderts* (Diss: Göttingen).

—— (1876*a*). 'Untersuchungen über einige annalistische Quellen zur Geschichte des fünften und sechsten Jahrhunderts: I. Die Chronik Prospers von Aquitanien', *Neues Archiv* 1: 15–50.

—— (1876*b*). 'Untersuchungen über einige annalistische Quellen zur Geschichte des fünften und sechsten Jahrhunderts: III. Die Ravennater Annalen', *Neues Archiv* 1: 215–368.

—— (1877). 'Die Chronik des Marcellinus Comes und die oströmischen fasten', *Neues Archiv* 2: 59–109.

HOLDSWORTH, C., and WISEMAN, T. P. (1986) (eds.), *The Inheritance of Historiography 350–900* (Exeter).

HOLUM, K. (1977). 'Pulcheria's Crusade and the Ideology of Imperial Victory', *Greek, Roman and Byzantine Studies* 18: 153–72.

—— (1982). *Theodosian Empresses* (Berkeley, Los Angeles, and London).

—— (1990). 'Hadrian and St. Helena: Imperial Travel and the Origins of Christian Holy Land Pilgrimage', in Ousterhout (1990), 66–81.

—— and VIKAN, G. (1979). 'The Trier Ivory, Adventus Ceremonial and the relics of St Stephen', *Dumbarton Oaks Papers* 33: 113–33.

HONIGMANN, E. (1939). *Le Synekdemos d'Hiérocles et l'opusculum géographique de Georges de Chypre* (Brussels).

HUGHES, K. (1972). *Early Christian Ireland: Introduction to The Sources* (London).

—— (1980). *Celtic Britain in the Early Middle Ages. Studies in Scottish and Welsh Sources* (Woodbridge).

HUMPHRIES, M. (1996). 'Chronicle and Chronology: Prosper of Aquitaine, his methods and the development of early medieval chronography', *Early Medieval Europe* 5: 155–75.

HUNGER, H. (1978). *Die hochsprachliche profane Literatur der Byzantiner*, 1 (Munich).

HUNT, E. D. (1982). *Holy Land Pilgrimage in the Later Roman Empire* (Oxford).

IGGERS, G. G. (1997). *Historiography in the Twentieth Century* (Hanover).

IRMSCHER, J. (1964). 'Geschichtsschreiber der Justinianischen Zeit', *Wiss. Zeit. der Univ. Rostock* 18: 469–74.

JACOBY, D. (1961). 'La Population de Constantinople à l'époque byzantin: une problème de démographie urbaine', *Byzantion* 31: 81–109.
JANIN, R. (1964). *Constantinople byzantine* (Paris).
—— (1966). 'Les processions réligieuses à Byzance', *Revue des études byzantines* 24: 69–88.
JEFFREYS, E. M. (1990) (ed.), with B. Croke, and R. Scott, *Studies in John Malalas* (Sydney).
—— and JEFFREYS, M. J., and SCOTT, R. (1986) (eds. and trs.), *John Malalas: A Translation* (Melbourne).
JENKINS, K. (1995). *On "What is History?"* (London).
JONES, A. H. M. (1964). *The Later Roman Empire* (Oxford).
—— (1966). *The Decline of the Ancient World* (London).
—— (1971). *Cities of the Eastern Roman Provinces*, 2nd edn. (Oxford).
JONES, C. W. (1943). *Bedae Opera de Temporibus* (Cambridge, Mass.).
—— (1947). *Saints Lives and Chronicles in Early England* (Ithaca, NY).
JONES, L. W. (1946). *An Introduction to Divine and Human Readings by Cassiodorus Senator* (New York).
JONES, M. E., and CASEY, P. (1988). 'The Gallic Chronicle Restored: A Chronology for the Anglo-Saxon Invasions and the End of Roman Britain', *Britannia* 19: 368–98.
KARAYANNOPULOS, J., and WEISS, G. (1982). *Quellenkunde zur Geschichte von Byzanz (324–1453)*, 2. 4 (Wiesbaden).
KASTER, R. A. (1988). *Guardians of Language: The Grammarian and Society in Late Antiquity* (Berkeley, Los Angeles and London).
KAUFMANN, G. (1876). 'Die fasten der späteren kaiserzeit als ein mittel zur kritik der weströmischen chroniken', *Philologus* 34: 235–95.
—— (1884). 'Die fasten von Constantinopel und die fasten von Ravenna', *Philologus* 42: 471–510.
KELLEY, D. R. (1998). *Faces of History: Historical Inquiry from Herodotus to Herder* (New Haven and London).
KELLNER, H. (1989). *Language and Historical Representation* (Madison, Wis., and London).
KELLY, J. F. T. (1986). 'The Venerable Bede and Hiberno-Latin Exegesis', in Szarmach (1986), 65–75.
KING, M. H., and STEVENS, W. M. (1979) (eds.), *Saints, Scholars and Heroes*, 2. (Collegeville, Minn.).
KRAUTSCHICK, S. (1986). 'Zwei Aspekte des Jahres 476', *Historia* 35: 344–71.
KRUMBACHER, K. (1896). *Geschichte der byzantinischen Literatur* (Munich).
LA CAPRA, D. (1985). *History and Criticism* (Ithaca, NY).
LACKNER, W. (1970). 'Westliche Heilige des 5 und 6 Jahrhunderts in Synaxarium Ecclesiae Constantinopolitanae', *Jahrbuch der Oesterreichischen Byzantinistik* 19: 182–202.

LACROIX, B. (1965). *Orose et ses idées* (Paris).

LAPIDGE, M. (1982). ' "Beowulf", Aldhelm, the "Liber Monstrorum" and Wessex', *Studi Medievali* 23: 151–92.

—— (1995). 'The Career of Archbishop Theodore', in M. Lapidge (ed.), *Archbishop Theodore: Commemorative Studies on his Life and Influence* (Cambridge), 1–29.

LAQUEUR, R. (1928). 'Lokalchronik', *RE* 14: 1885–6.

LEMERLE, P. (1945). *Philippes et la Macédoine orientale* (Paris).

LEOPOLD, J. W. (1986). 'Consolando per edicta: Cassiodorus *Variae* 4.50 and Imperial Consolations for natural catastrophes', *Latomus* 45: 816–36.

LIETZMANN, H. (1937). 'Ein Blatt aus einer antiken Weltchronik', *Quantulacumque: Studies Presented to Kirsopp Lake*, ed. R. Casey, S. Lake, and A. Lake (London), 339–48 (repr. in *Texte und Untersuchungen* 67 (1958), 419–29).

LOT, F. (1961). *The End of the Ancient World and the Beginning of the Middle Ages* (New York).

LOWE, E. A. (1972). *Codices Latini Antiquiores*, 2nd edn. (Oxford).

LUBARSKIJ, J. N. (1993). 'New Trends in the Study of Byzantine Historiography', *Dumbarton Oaks Papers* 47: 131–8.

MAAS, M. (1992). *John Lydus and the Roman Past* (London 1992).

MACCORMACK, S. (1981). *Art and Ceremony in Late Antiquity* (Berkeley-Los Angeles-London).

—— (1990). 'Loca Sancta: The Organization of Sacred Topography in Late Antiquity', in Ousterhout (1990), 7–40.

McCORMICK, M. (1986). *Eternal Victory* (Cambridge).

McCULLAGH, C. B. (1998). *The Truth of History* (London).

MADAN, F. (1897). *Summary Catalogue of Western Manuscripts in the Bodleian Library*, 4 (Oxford).

MAENCHEN-HELFEN, O. J. (1973). *The World of the Huns* (Berkeley, Los Angeles, and London).

MANGO, C. (1959). *The Brazen House* (Copenhagen).

—— (1985). *Le développment urbain de Constantinople* (Paris).

—— (1986). 'The Development of Constantinople as an Urban Centre', in *The 17th International Byzantine Congress. Main Papers* (New Rochelle, NY), 117–36 (repr. in Mango 1993*a*).

—— (1988/9). 'The Tradition of Byzantine Chronography', *Harvard Ukrainian Studies* 22 and 3: 360–72.

—— (1993*a*). *Studies on Constantinople* (London).

—— (1993*b*). 'Constantine's Column', in Mango (1993*a*), 1–6.

—— (1993*c*). 'The Columns of Justinian and his Successors', in Mango (1993*a*), 1–20.

Bibliography

—— and DAGRON, G. (1996). *Constantinople and its Hinterland* (London).

—— and SCOTT, R. (1997). *The Chronicle of Theophanes Confessor* (Oxford).

MARAVAL, P. (1985). *Lieux saints et pèlerinages d'Orient. Histoire et géographie des origines à la conquête arabe* (Paris).

MARKUS, R. A. (1982). 'The End of the Roman Empire: A Note on Eugippius, *Vita Sancti Severini*, 20', *Nottingham Medieval Studies* 26: 1–6.

—— (1986). 'Chronicle and Theology: Prosper of Aquitaine', in Holdsworth, and Wiseman (1986), 39–40.

—— (1991). *The End of Ancient Christianity* (Cambridge).

—— (unpublished). 'The Chronicle of Marcellinus *comes* and its Continuation in the light of Recent Work'.

MATTHEWS, J. F. (1975). *Western Aristocracies and Imperial Court* (Oxford).

MELVILLE-JONES, J. R. (1991). 'Nummi Terunciani', *Proceedings of 11th International Numismatic Congress* (Brussels), 3: 9–13.

METCALF, D. (1969). *The Origins of the Anastasian Currency Reform* (Amsterdam).

MEYVAERT, P. (1996). 'Bede, Cassiodorus and the Codex Amiatinus', *Speculum* 71: 827–83.

MIHAESCU, H. (1978). *La langue latine dans le sud-est de l'Europe* (Bucharest and Paris).

MILLER, D. (1969). *Imperial Constantinople* (New York).

MOLÈ, C. (1980). 'Prospettive universale e prospettive locali nella storiografia latina del V secolo', in *La Storiografia Ecclesiastica nella Tarda Antichità* (Messina), 195–239.

MOMIGLIANO, A. (1955). 'Cassiodorus and Italian Culture of His Time', *Proceedings of the British Academy* 41: 207–45 (repr. in Momigliano (1966), 181–210).

—— (1956). 'Gli Anicii e la storiografia latina del VI secolo d.C.', *Entretiens Fondation Hardt* (Geneva), 249–90.

—— (1963). 'Pagan and Christian Historiography in the Fourth Century A.D.', in A. Momigliano (ed.), *The Conflict between Paganism and Christianity in the Fourth Century* (London), 79–99.

—— (1966). *Studies in Historiography* (London).

—— (1969). 'L'età del trapasso fra storiografia antica e storiografia medievale (320–550) d.C.', *Rivista Storica Italiana* 81: 286–303.

MOMMSEN, TH. (1847). 'Über eine milde Stiftung Nerva's', *Zeitschrift für geschichtliche Rechts* 14 (repr. in *GS* 3. 69–70).

—— (1850a). 'Über den Chronographen vom J. 354', *Abhandlungen der königlichen Sächsischen Gesellschaft der Wissenschaft* 2: 547–655 (repr. in *GS* 7. 549–79).

—— (1850b). 'Über die Quellen der Chronik des Hieronymus', *Abhandlungen der königlichen Sächsischen Gesellschaft der Wissenschaft* 2: 669–693 (repr. in *GS* 7. 606–632).

MOMMSEN, TH. (1857). 'Zur byzantinischen Chronographie', *Rheinisches Museum für Philologie* 11: 626 (repr. in *GS* 7. 754).

——(1861). 'Die Chronik des Cassiodorus Senator', *Abhandlungen der königlichen Sächsischen Gesellschaft der Wissenschaft* 3: 547–696 (partly repr. in *GS* 7. 668–90).

——(1882). *Jordanis Romana et Getica, MGH AA* 5. 1 (Berlin).

——(1889*a*). 'Die älteste Handschrift der Chronik des Hieronymus', *Hermes* 24: 393–401 (repr. in *GS* 7. 597–605).

——(1889*b*). 'Ostgothische Studien', *Neues Archiv* 14: 225–49, 453–544; continued in 15 (1890): 181–6 (repr. in *GS* 3. 362–484).

——(1891). 'Das römisch-germanische Herrscherjahr', *Neues Archiv* 16: 49–65 (repr. in *GS* 6. 343–358).

——(1892). Introductions to *Cons. Const.* and *Cons. Ital.* in *MGH AA* IX: 199–204, 251–73.

——(1893). 'Die Bewirthschaftung der Kirchengüter unter Papst Gregor I', *Zeitschrift fur Sozial und Wirtschaftsgeschichte* 1: 43–59 (repr. in *GS* 3. 177–91).

——(1894). Introduction to Marcellinus, *Chronicon* in *MGH AA* XI: 39–59.

——(1896/7). 'Die römischen Bischöfe Liberius und Felix II', *Deutsche Zeitschrift für Geschichtswissenschaft* 7 (= *N.F.* 1): 167–79 (repr. in *GS* 6. 570–81).

——(1898). 'Schlussbericht über die Herausgabe der Auctores Antiquissimi', *Sitz. Berl. Akad.* 1: 288–9 (repr. in *GS* 7. 693–94).

——(1996). *A History of Rome Under the Emperors*, ed. A. and B. Demandt, tr. Th. Wiedemann (London).

MOORHEAD, J. (1994). *Justinian* (London).

MORICCA, U. (1943). *Storia della letteratura latina cristiana*, 3.2 (Turin).

MOROSI, R. (1978). 'Cancellarii in Cassiodoro e Giovanni Lido', *Romano-barbarica* 3: 127–58.

MORRIS, J. (1972). 'The Chronicle of Eusebius: Irish Fragments', *Bulletin of the Institute for Classical Studies* 19: 80–93.

MORTON, C. (1982). 'Marius of Avenches, the "Excerpta Valesiana" and the Death of Boethius', *Traditio* 38: 107–36.

MOSSHAMMER, A. A. (1976). 'Lucca Bibl. Capit. 490 and the Manuscript Tradition of Hieronymus' (Eusebius') Chronicle', *California Studies in Classical Antiquity* 8: 203–40.

——(1979). *The Chronicle of Eusebius and Greek Chronographic Tradition* (Lewisburg and London).

MÜLLER-WIENER, W. (1977). *Bildlexicon zur Topographie Istanbuls* (Tübingen).

MUHLBERGER, S. (1983). 'The Gallic Chronicle of 452 and its Authority for British Events', *Britannia* 14: 23–33.

——(1984). 'Heroic Kings and Unruly Generals: The "Copenhagen"

Continuation of Prosper Reconsidered', *Florilegium* 6: 50–70 (with translation, 71–95).

——(1986). 'Prosper's Epitoma Chronicon: Was there an Edition of 443?', *Classical Quarterly* 81: 240–4.

——(1990). *The Fifth Century Chroniclers* (Leeds).

MURPHY-O'CONNOR, J. (1980). *The Holy Land: An Archaeological Guide* (Oxford).

NELSON, J. L. (1976). 'Symbols in Context', *Studies in Church History* 13: 101–14.

NEWTON, R. R. (1972). *Medieval Chronicles and the Rotation of the Earth* (Baltimore).

OBOLENSKY, D. (1971). *The Byzantine Commonwealth* (London).

O'CROININ, D. (1983a). 'Early Irish Annals from Easter Tables: A Case Restated', *Peritia* 2: 74–86.

——(1983b). 'The Irish Provenance of Bede's Computus', *Peritia* 2: 229–47.

O'DONNELL, J. J. (1979). *Cassiodorus* (Berkeley, Los Angeles, and London).

——(1982). 'The Aims of Jordanes', *Historia* 31: 223–40.

OGILVY, J. D. A. (1967). *Books known to the English, 597–1066* (Cambridge, Mass.).

ORCHARD, A. (1995). *Pride and Prodigies: Studies in the Monsters of the Beowulf-Manuscript* (Cambridge).

OUSTERHOUT, R. (1990). (ed.), *The Blessings of Pilgrimage* (Urbana, Ill., and Chicago).

PALLMANN, R. (1864). *Die Geschichte der Völkerwanderung*, 2 (Weimar).

PALMER, A. (1993) with S. Brock and R. Hoyland), *The Seventh Century in the West Syrian Chronicles* (Liverpool).

PARTNER, N. F. (1977). *Serious Entertainments. The Writing of History in Twelfth-Century England* (Chicago and London).

PATLAGEAN, E. (1977). *Pauvreté économique et pauvreté sociale à Byzance, 4ᵉ–7ᵉ siècles* (Paris).

PEDERSEN, P. S. (1976). *Late Roman Public Professionalism* (Odense).

PINTUS, G. (1984). 'Eucherio di Lione nella cronologia di Gennadio e Marcellino', *Studi medievali* 25: 795–812.

PLACANICA, A. (1997). *Vittore da Tunnuna, Chronica. Chiesa e impero nell'età di Giustiniano* (Florence).

POOLE, R. L. (1926). *Chronicles and Annals* (Oxford).

POULTER, A. (1983a). 'Town and Country in Moesia Inferior', in Poulter (1983b), 74–118.

——(1983b) (ed.), *Ancient Bulgaria: Papers Presented to the International Symposium on the Ancient History and Archaeology of Bulgaria* (Nottingham).

——(1992). 'The Use and Abuse of Urbanism in the Danubian Provinces during the Later Roman Empire', in J. Rich (ed.), *The City in Late Antiquity* (London), 99–135.

PREGER, T. (1901). *Scriptores Originum Constantinopolitanarum*, 2 vols. (Leipzig).

PRESS, G. (1982). *The Development of the Idea of History in Antiquity* (Kingston and Montreal).

PRETE, S. (1955). *I Chronica di Sulpicio Severo* (Rome).

PRICOCO, S. (1980). 'Storia ecclesiastica e storia letteraria: il de viris illustribus di Gennadio di Marsiglia', in *La storia ecclesiastica nella tarda antichità* (Messina), 241–73.

RATTI, S. (1997). 'Jérome et Nicomaque Flavien: sur les sources de la chronique par les années 357–64', *Historia* 46: 479–508.

RAY, R. (1982). 'What Do we Know about Bede's Commentaries?', *Recherches de Theologie Ancienne et Medievale* 49: 5–20.

REBENICH, S. (1993). 'Theodor Mommsen und die Verhältnis von Alter Geschichte und Patristik', in *Patristique et antiquité tardive en Allemagne et en France de 1870 à 1930* (Paris), 131–54.

REDLICH, O. (1916). 'Mommsen und die Monumenta Germaniae', *Zeitschrift für die Österreichischen Gymnasien* 12: 865–73.

REYDELLET, M. (1970). 'Les intentions idéologiques et politiques dans la Chronique d'Isidore de Seville', *Mélanges d'école française de Rome* 82: 363–400.

RIESE, A. (1878). *Geographi Latini Minores* (Berlin, repr. Hildesheim 1964).

ROUECHÉ, C. (1984). 'Acclamations in the Later Roman Empire: New Evidence from Aphrodisias', *Journal of Roman Studies* 74: 181–99.

——(1986). 'Theodosius II, the Cities and the Date of the "Church History" of Sozomen', *Journal of Theological Studies* 27: 130–2.

SALAMON, M. (1981). 'The Nickname "Great" in Latin Historiography in Late Antiquity' (in Polish, with English summary), *Zeszyty Naukowe Uniwersytetu Jagiellonskiego. Prace Historyczne* z.70: 107–22.

SALZMAN, M. (1990). *On Roman Time: the Codex Calendar of 354 and the Rhythms of Urban Life in Late Antiquity* (Berkeley, Los Angeles, and London).

SANTSCHI, C. (1968). 'La chronique de l'évêque Marius', *Revue Historique Vaudoise* 76: 17–34.

SCHANZ, M., HOSIUS, C., and KRÜGER, G. (1920). *Geschichte der römischen Literatur*, 4.2 (Munich).

SCHNEIDER, A. M. (1936). *Byzanz* (Berlin).

——(1941). 'Brände in Konstantinopel', *Byzantinische Zeitschrift* 41: 382–403.

SCHNITH, K. (1983). 'Chronik', *Lexicon des Mittelalters*, 2: 1957.

SCHOVE, D. (1984). *Chronology of Eclipses and Comets AD 1–1000* (Woodbridge).

SCHRIER, O. J. (1992). 'Syriac Evidence for the Roman-Persian War of 421–422', *Greek, Roman and Byzantine Studies* 33: 75–86.

SCOTT, R. (1981). 'Malalas and Justinian's Codification', in E. Jeffreys, M. Jeffreys, and A. Moffatt (eds.), *Byzantine Papers* (Canberra), 12–31.

——(1985). 'Malalas, the *Secret History*, and Justinian's Propaganda', *Dumbarton Oaks Papers* 39: 99–109.

SEECK, O. (1889*a*). 'Cancellarius', *RE* 3: 1456–9.

——(1889*b*). 'Studien zur Geschichte Diocletians und Constantius II. Idacius und die Chronik von Constantinopel', *Neues Jahrbucher für Philologie und Pädagogik* 35: 601–635.

——(1899). 'Chronica Constantinopolitana', *RE* 3: 2454–60.

——(1919). *Regesten der Kaiser und Päpste* (Stuttgart).

——(1920). *Geschichte des Untergangs der antiken Welt*, 6 (Stuttgart).

SIVAN, H. S. (1990). 'Pilgrimage, Monasticism and the Emergence of Christian Palestine in the 4th Century', in Ousterhout (1990), 54–65.

SMALLEY, B. (1974). *Historians of the Middle Ages* (London).

SMITH, J. Z. (1987). *To Take Place: Towards Theory in Ritual* (Chicago and London).

SMYTH, A. P. (1972). 'The Earliest Irish Annals: Their First Contemporary Entries and the Earliest Centres of Recording', *Proceedings of the Royal Irish Academy* 72 C: 1–48.

——(1984). *Warlords and Holy Men. Scotland AD 80–1000* (London).

SPECK, P. (1973). 'Die Mauerbau in 60 Tagen', in Beck (1973*a*), 135–78.

SPIEGEL, G. (1997). *The Past as Text: The Theory and Practice of Medieval Historiography* (Baltimore).

SPIESER, J.-M. (1984). *Thessalonique et ses monuments du IVe au VIe siècle* (Paris).

STANFORD, W. (1998). *An Introduction to the Philosophy of History* (Oxford).

STEIN, E. (1949). *Histoire du Bas Empire*, 2 (Brussels).

——(1959). *Histoire du Bas Empire*, 1 (Brussels).

STEVENSON, J. (1995). *The 'Laterculus Malalianus' and the School of Archbishop Theodore* (Cambridge).

STRUBE, C. (1973). 'Der Begriff Domus in der Notitia Urbis Constantinopolitanae', in Beck (1973*b*), 121–34.

SUNDWALL, J. (1915). *Weströmische Studien* (Berlin).

SZARMACH, P. E. (1986) (ed.), *Sources of Anglo-Saxon Culture* (Kalamazoo).

TAYLOR, J. (1965). *The Use of Medieval Chronicles* (London).

TEILLET, S. (1984). *Des goths à la nation gothique: les origines de l'idée de nation en occident du Ve siècle* (Paris).

THOMPSON, E. A. (1946). 'The Isaurians under Theodosius II', *Hermathena* 68: 18–31.

——(1948). *A History of Attila and the Huns* (London).

——(1982). *Romans and Barbarians: the Decline of the Western Empire* (Madison, Wis.).

TOYNBEE, J. M. (1944). *Roman Medallions* (New York).

Bibliography

TREADGOLD, W. (1997). *A History of the Byzantine State and Society* (Stanford).

TREITINGER, O. (1956). *Die Oströmische Kaiser- und Reichsidee*, 2nd edn. (Darmstadt).

TSAFRIR, Y. (1986). 'The maps used by Theodosius: On the Pilgrim Maps of the Holy Land and Jerusalem in the Sixth Century C.E.', *Dumbarton Oaks Papers* 40: 129–45.

TURNER, C. H. (1905), in Fotheringham (1905), 63.

VACCARI, A. (1953). 'Le antiche vite di S. Girolamo: I. La cronaca di Marcellino', in A. Vaccari, *Scritti di erudizione e di filologia*, 2 (Rome), 32–4.

VAN CAENEGEM, R. C. (1978). *Guide to the Sources of Medieval History* (Amsterdam).

VAN DEN BRINCKEN, A.-D. (1957). *Studien zur lateinischen Weltchronistik bis in der Zeitalter Ottos von Freising* (Düsseldorf).

VAN OMMESLAEGE, F. (1978). 'La Fête de S. Jean Chrysostome', *Analecta Bollandiana* 96: 338.

VARADY, L. (1976). 'Jordanes-Studien. Jordanes und das Chronicon des Marcellinus Comes—Die Selbständigkeit des Jordanes', *Chiron* 6: 441–87.

VASILIEV, A. (1950). *Justin the First* (Washington, DC).

VELKOV, V. (1966). 'Ratiaria. Eine römische Stadt in Bulgarien', *Eirene* 5: 155–75.

—— (1977). *Cities in Thrace and Dacia in Late Antiquity* (Amsterdam).

VEYNE, P. (1984). *Writing History* (Middletown, Conn.).

WAITZ, G. (1857). 'Die angebliche Fortsetzung des Marcellin von 551–558', *Nachrichten von der Göttinger Universität*: 38–40.

WALLACE-HADRILL, J. M. (1962). 'Fredegar and the History of France', in *The Long-Haired Kings* (London), 71–94.

WALKER, P. (1989). *Holy City. Holy Places: Christian Attitudes to Jerusalem and the Holy Land in the Fourth Century* (Oxford).

WES, M. (1967). *Das Ende des Kaisertums im Westen des römischen Reiches* (The Hague).

WHITBY, MICHAEL (1985). 'The Long Walls of Constantinople', *Byzantion* 55: 560–83.

—— (1986). 'Procopius' Description of Dara', in P. Freeman, and D. Kennedy (eds.), *The Defence of the Roman Empire in the East* (Oxford), 737–83.

—— (1988). *The Emperor Maurice and his Historian* (Oxford).

—— (1992). 'Greek Historical Writing After Procopius: Variety and Vitality', in Cameron, Averil, and Conrad (1992), 25–80.

—— (1996). Review of Croke (1995), in *Early Medieval Europe* 5: 222–5.

—— and WHITBY, MARY (1989) (trs.) *Chronicon Paschale 284–628 AD* (Liverpool).

WHITE, H. (1973). *Metahistory* (Baltimore).

——(1978). *Tropics of Discourse* (Baltimore).

——(1987). *The Content of the Form* (Baltimore).

WILKINSON, J. (1971). *Egeria's Travels* (London).

——(1976). 'Christian Pilgrims in Jerusalem during the Byzantine Period', *Palestine Exploration Quarterly* 108: 95–7.

——(1977). *Jerusalem Pilgrims before the Crusades* (Warminster).

WISEMAN, T. P. (1979). *Clio's Cosmetics* (Leicester).

WITAKOWSKI, W. (1987). *The Syriac Chronicle of Pseudo-Dionysius of Tel-Mahre* (Uppsala).

WOLF, K. B. (1990). *Conquerors and Chroniclers of Medieval Spain* (Liverpool).

WOLFRAM, H. (1988). *A History of the Goths* (Berkeley, Los Angeles, and London).

WOOD, I. N. (1992). 'Continuity or Calamity? The Construction of Literary Models', in J. Drinkwater, and H. Elton (eds.), *Fifth Century Gaul: A Crisis of Identity?* (Cambridge).

WOZNIAK, F. E. (1981). 'East Rome, Ravenna and Western Illyricum: 454–536 A.D.', *Historia* 30: 351–82.

WYNN, P. (1998). 'Frigeridus, the British Tyrants and the Early Fifth Century Barbarian Invasions of Gaul and Spain', *Athenaeum* 86: 69–117.

ZECCHINI, G. (1983). *Aezio: L'ultima difesa dell'occidente romano* (Rome).

——(1993). *Ricerche di storiografia latina tardoantica* (Rome).

INDEX